Politics for
Human Beings

Robert A. Isaak
Columbia University

Ralph P. Hummel
John Jay College of Criminal Justice

POLITICS FOR HUMAN BEINGS

Duxbury Press   North Scituate, Massachusetts

Duxbury Press
A DIVISION OF WADSWORTH PUBLISHING COMPANY, INC.

Politics for Human Beings was edited and prepared for composition
by Beatrice Gormley. Interior and cover design by Walter Williams.

L.C. Cat. Card No.: 74−81168
ISBN 0−87872−072−3

PRINTED IN THE UNITED STATES OF AMERICA

2 3 4 5 6 7 8 9 10 — 79 78 77 76 75

to

Gudrun

    & Frank and Leah Allen

Gael

    & Rose and Karl Hummel

Table of Contents

Preface

This book began when the authors asked themselves, How did politics get its bad name?

Americans traditionally have called politics a "dirty" business. Only dirty people could be expected to engage in it—a truism seemingly once more confirmed by Watergate. On the international scene, a psychiatrist recently pointed out, politics has led to the slaughter of a hundred million people in the last fifty years.[1] Apparently in international politics only killers excelled.

Political science itself seemed to endorse this state of affairs as normal by defining politics as essentially and naturally involving conflict. Politics, the dean of American political science told us, is the struggle over who gets what when how.[2] In America specifically, most political scientists saw politics as a struggle over a slice of the pie of goods.

Yet we also remembered that at one time politics was considered the highest form of human activity and political science was considered the master science. In those days the student of politics concerned himself with discovering the purposes of human life and with designing methods to achieve them. And the citizen was expected to work together with other citizens in the design and maintenance of ways of living together—economic, social, and religious ways.

Of course, that was more than 2,500 years ago and in another country. The Greece of that time had long since died, and so, it seemed, had the memory of Aristotle, who defined politics as the attempt to make real the ethics that could be derived from the nature of the ultimate good.

Then we had an idea.

What would happen if we redefined politics? What if we disagreed that politics was mere conflict? What if, in analyzing the nature of politics, we sought to determine what the fundamental assumptions of all types of politics were?

This analysis led us to recognize *politics as a social act through which human beings attempt to resolve the tension between human needs and social facts.*

With this definition we tried to restore the concern of politics for ethics, while recognizing politics as *the* fundamental cooperative activity by which human beings attempt to resolve the tension between their needs and social facts. Conflicts erupt from the inevitable tensions of social relations, but their solution is constructed through cooperation.

The redefinition did something that frightened us. If politics necessarily involved a concern for human needs, then most of what

[1]R. D. Laing, *The Politics of Experience* (New York: Ballantine Books, 1968), p. 28.
[2]Harold D. Lasswell, *Politics: Who Gets What When How* (New York: McGraw-Hill, 1936).

had been called politics by politicians was mere pseudopolitics. For what most politicians were engaging in was the repetition of routines of political problem solving set up in America 200 years ago to resolve the tensions between the needs of people long since dead and their by-gone social facts.

Not only that, but most of our fellow political scientists had been studying not politics in its essential form, but merely the social routines into which what once was truly political activity had descended. They were studying the politics of society maintenance—not the politics of human needs. And they were calling that kind of pseudopolitics "normal."

There was something else implicit in the definition of politics as the attempt to resolve the tensions between human needs and social facts.

If most of what had been called politics was not politics at all, but an aberration that had given this fundamental human activity a bad name, it might be possible to salvage true politics for the purpose of interesting our disillusioned citizenry in it.

In a time of societal decay, the concern for norms—for what should be—was growing rapidly. Further, the monolith of conflict politics was beginning to crumble, with the creation of alternative cooperative lifestyles by such diverse groups as political reformers, "hippies," "Jesus people," and universalistic gurus.

We judged it might be worth some personal risks—and so did our publisher—to praise politics in its essential form as the most creative activity of which men and women are capable.

True politics—a politics for human beings—is at its high point when two human beings somewhere become conscious of the tension between social facts and human needs in which we all live, and when they act with will and courage to translate their solution into practice. Admittedly, as soon as this act of creation is committed, the descent of politics into social routines has already begun. But the moment of creation can be understood under this definition as the infinitely repeatable moment of man's highest triumph.

This is man's damnation: that like Sisyphus he must roll ever upward the stone of his fate, only to watch it roll down again. But the moment of triumph is also not denied us. When we see our human condition, when we determine to improve it, when we first act on that resolve—then we are at our most human and most political. We are momentary but indisputable victors over fate.

TEACHING/LEARNING DESIGN

In this spirit, here is how the book works.

Teachers must begin with what the student is ready to learn. Fellow teachers may have noticed that the day is past when it was possible to force learning down students' throats. Teachers and departments that insist on force-feeding find themselves with dwindling numbers of their key resource: students. Students themselves have political experiences every day—often without knowing it. A book beginning with experiences—real or vicarious—enables a teacher to begin with student interest. Begin with demand to provide supply.

With this in mind, we created experiences for the student, beginning with the first chapter. Here and in other chapters, concrete illustrations provide a common background to which students can apply the analytical tools of political science. These experiences have been reduced to their essence. Such reduction may be appreciated by the teacher who has tried to teach students supposedly difficult concepts, ranging from constitutionalism to behavioralism, structural-functionalism to survey research, balance of power to game theory, systems theory to phenomenology. Such standard tools of political science are more easily grasped when applied to everyday political life.

A second assumption of the learning design is that simple language communicates best. We saw no reason to adopt a third-person detachment, to fill the book with scientific jargon to impress our peers, or to footnote heavily for all the subtleties that engulf analysis and political action. This was to be an introduction, a clearing of heads, a raising of the spirit that says "Yes" to politics. The level of discourse, we hope, will reflect that.

The third teaching/learning design is made up of *invitations*.

In these invitations, the student can apply scientific tools to practical problems. When the invitations are games including more than one player or a whole group, they have been tested in our own classrooms—often with the added benefit of video-tape recordings for later analysis. The purpose of the invitations is gut learning instead of head jamming. Accepting the invitations can be a voluntary act that adds another dimension of learning. In other words, you know something more intensely and remember it longer when you put your imagination and your actions into the learning process.

For both content and learning process, here is how the book works: **CONTENT**

Chapter I opens the book with an allegory in which the basic ideas and activities of politics emerge out of the experience of two human beings constructing their own political system. Concepts introduced range from the political act to the nation-state. The basis of this chapter is to suggest that all politics can be understood by reducing its activities to interaction between human beings. By ending the mystique of politics, we free the mind to take up tools of analysis.

Chapter II suggests to the reader that he follow his own intuitions in recognizing that politics surrounds him everywhere. In suggesting a new definition, we have attempted to reduce politics in all its forms to its basic elements and to reconstruct our understanding from there.

Chapter III presents specific tools for unmasking politics in everyday life, for taking a critical stance on social and political problems, and for organizing and doing politics.

Chapter IV provides an example of how these tools can be used. The student is asked to follow an analysis of the 1972 primary campaign of George McGovern and of the Watergate affair—and to speculate how he might organize to do better.

In Chapter V, a number of different approaches lead to an understanding of different components of American political life. The approaches include constitutionalism, institutionalism, and behavioralism. Behavioralism is represented through group theory, personality studies, and socio-political survey research. The American political scene itself is divided into three arenas: a shrinking arena of official public politics; a rapidly growing arena of corporate politics, in which elites pre-empt decisions while leading citizens into an apolitical life; and an arena of private politics, into which Americans vainly seek to escape from public and corporate pressures.

Chapters VI and VII—comparative politics—emphasize the utility and difficulty of looking to other countries for problem-solving techniques. The use of comparative analytical tools, including structural-functionalism and Weberian sociology, is demonstrated in scenarios and analyses of contemporary tensions. Psycho-history, anomie, and charisma are introduced as concepts for understanding other cultures in change or decay.

International politics is introduced in Chapters VIII and IX through the lives of diplomats located at strategic international points of contact in dramatic historical periods: Bismarck, Hammarskjöld, and Kissinger. Out of this experience, the ambitious reader can learn how to play games of balance of power, of collective security, and of revolution. He is presented with the necessity and possibility of cooperative interaction through phenomenological understanding as a key to global survival.

Political theory is the focus of Chapters X, XI and XII. Chapters X and XI examine critically the major approaches in modern political science and their effect on the possibility of doing politics for human beings. Chapter XII presents a phenomenological analysis of political thinking and instructions for doing such thinking, while demonstrating the bases for the authors' phenomenological philosophy as an approach toward doing a politics for human beings.

You can use this book as an introduction to politics in general. Or for studying American, comparative, or international politics, or theory. Or in your own politics for human beings. But begin at the beginning. The first chapter represents the basic experience of all politics.

DEBTS The main debt for the existence of this book we owe to publisher Bob (Sisyphus) Gormley, whose courage pushed us continually to take greater risks. As Albert Camus says, "The struggle itself toward the heights is enough to fill a man's heart. One must imagine Sisyphus happy."

We hope that consulting editor Dick Young got at least partial fulfillment of his wish that he had written this book through the humorous, enthusiastic, and painstaking reviews that he delivered on every sentence.

We owe critical debts to reviewers of earlier drafts who kept us from taking wrong paths. We hope our many revisions have satisfied the criticisms of Anthony Athos of Harvard. Our gratitude extends to Rollo May, whose personal influence and encouragement confirmed our faith in the definition of politics as a social act to resolve the tension between human needs and social facts. We are thankful for the constructive criticism of Alan Saltzstein of the University of Houston, and Barry Ames of the University of New Mexico.

We incurred previous intellectual debts with Harold Lasswell, Sigmund Freud, Max Weber, Karl Marx, Immanuel Kant, Peter Berger and Thomas Luckman, Alfred Schutz, George Lukacs, Herbert Marcuse, Juergen Habermas, Ronald Laing, B. F. Skinner, Abraham Maslow, Gabriel Almond and G. Bingham Powell, Anatole Rapoport, Kenneth Boulding, Kalman Silvert, H. Mark Roelofs, Kyung-Won Kim, Thomas Kuhn, and Albert Camus.

Peter Gillard, a graduate assistant at Fordham University, deserves thanks for being helpful in a human way (from Lenin to the index).

Bea Gormley's careful copy-editing and reordering suggestions made the authors less blind in spots, letting the reader more easily in on their intended meaning.

Self-actualization is possible only with and through others. Each of the authors knows that this book could not have been written without the other. Defying conventions of priority, we decided to list authorship by the flip of a coin.

R.A.I.
R.P.H.
New York City
1975

1 Wherein two characters called Alphonse and Balthazar create a nation-state and illustrate the political cycle. The reader is cautioned to read what comes easily slowly, taking nothing for granted.

1 Understanding Politics

Each morning Alphonse went down to the water to dig clams for breakfast. So did Balthazar. Alphonse dug his clams, went to a rock, broke them open, and ate. And so did Balthazar. Island life for Alphonse and Balthazar was one in which each lived in his own separate world.

One morning, after guzzling coconut wine all night, Alphonse and Balthazar arrived at the beach, each tired and unusually hungry. As they wearily made their way through the sand to the water's edge, Alphonse stopped dead in his tracks.

CREATION

Politics begins with an idea.

He thought, if Balthazar would dig the clams and I crack them, we would get to eat twice as fast! At the same moment Balthazar looked at Alphonse.

Politics means perceiving a common need and sharing it.

"Hey," said Alphonse, "why don't we . . ."
"Yeah," said Balthazar, "why don't I throw you the clams and you crack 'em, and we'll get to eat twice as fast."

Politics is talking toward action.

So Balthazar threw the clams to Alphonse, who cracked them. Sooner than ever before, they ate. Together.

Politics is social action to satisfy human needs using social facts.

"Why don't we do this every day?" asked Alphonse.
"Okay, let's!" said Balthazar, with an expansive burp.
And they did.

A political act repeated becomes a social relationship.

Months later, everyone else on the island perceived that Alphonse and Balthazar were different: they always seemed to eat sooner. The others began to give Alphonse and Balthazar an unusual amount of respect—as if they had become an institution.

A social relationship that lasts is made an institution by the perceptions of the many.

People from all sides of the island came to ask the two for their secret. Basking in the deference accorded them, Alphonse and Balthazar decided to keep the secret to themselves.

Elites are formed when a few monopolize access to values.

Of course, there came a time when an unknown upstart tried to beat the secret out of Alphonse. Alas, the upstart was struck by a huge clam that came flying out of a bush. Some say the mysterious avenger was the hand of Balthazar, others that it was the hand of the Clam God.

Legitimacy of elites comes from deference produced by force and awe.

isaak

Soon it dawned on the two organizers that there was more to get than deference. While others were frantically digging and cracking, Alphonse and Balthazar found time to think. Thinking led them to imagine a fuller and easier lifestyle: more deference, more leisure, more power, more goods, more variety.

Political men seek to maximize their values.

In order to get more of what there was to get, Alphonse and Balthazar decided to sell their skill. They figured they could do so because their skill was of value to others. To sell their skill, they decided to organize others.

Political organization is done to protect what you have and to get more.

To protect their secret and still get the most out of it, they decided to create special social relationships. Only they would control the whole secret: cooperating in digging *and* cracking. Some others would be allowed to know half the secret: supervised digging *or* cracking. The rest would know nothing.

Class and status are often based on the distribution of knowledge.

To make their organization appear real and permanent, they decided to give it a respectable name: The Alphonse and Balthazar Clam Digging and Cracking Corporation. They had discovered that by giving names to relationships they could make them seem more concrete.

Names make social relationships more real.

To protect against imitators with false claims and false names, they hired enforcers.

Force helps keep relationships real.

Alphonse and Balthazar liked the setup all of the time. The Diggers and Crackers liked it some of the time—when they got paid. The Know-Nothings didn't like it. Since you can't fool all the people all the time, the Know-Nothings revolted. But Alphonse and Balthazar circulated the myth of the deadly Clam-Throwing Hand. And the revolting masses surrendered in fear and awe. The Corporation appeared all-powerful. Alphonse and Balthazar had discovered the power of making relationships appear to be things—and getting a deity to back it up helps.

Reification turns social relationships into things.

To prevent future revolts and maintain their security, Alphonse and Balthazar decided to make their corporation into a one and only nation-state based on the religion of the Clam God.

**A nation-state includes
all the people in a given territory
who believe in the same reification.**

MAINTENANCE   Five years later, at the annual rite of the Great Clam God, King Alphonse and High Priest Balthazar sat on the balcony of Clam Castle, reminiscing about the days of creation. Below them strutted the grand procession, banners waving, each class wearing its traditional costume. The Enforcers goose-stepped in their clam-shell helmets, Diggers and Crackers sang the national hymn, "Inlandia," and the Know-Nothings plodded behind in a stupor of fermented clam sauce.

"They're happy," said King Alphonse.

"And they've really learned how to stay in line," said High Priest Balthazar.

isaak

**In a reified society people
stay in line—and love it.**

And then came the time for the annual achievement awards. For the most courageous Enforcer, the Order-Keeping Award; for the most efficient Digger/Cracker and family man, the Order-Taking and Reproductive Excellence Award; and for the quietest Know-Nothing, the Silent Service Award.

**Elites in a stable society define
behavior, distribute roles,
and allocate rewards.**

King Alphonse congratulated High Priest Balthazar for a well-organized celebration. At that moment, a runner of the Royal Clam Post burst onto the balcony and shouted, "Disaster! The clams are dying!"

Balthazar turned to Alphonse and cried, "I told you we shouldn't have run the Royal Sewage System into the bay!"

**Narrow solutions to problems often
lead to crises in the political system.**

Gloom. Scarcity. Hunger.

In desperation, Alphonse and Balthazar held a meeting of the Clam Council at the beach. Both members were there. Suddenly the High Priest was struck by an idea: If Inlandia is running out of clams, why not send an expedition to the outlands?

**Scarcity of resources
is the mother of expansion.**

Chief Enforcer Colombo led the first expedition. Several weeks passed. At home tension and hunger mounted. At last a look-out spotted Colombo's boat riding low in the water. A great cheer rose from the beach in expectation of Outlandish clams. "Eat up!" shouted Colombo, heaving the first clam off the boat. "Today the Outlands, tomorrow the world!"

After the great feast, all the available boats set out for the Outlands. The beaches of the Outlands were raided of every clam in sight.

"Such a rich harvest for so little effort!" said Colombo to Raz Putin, the Royal Recorder.

"Exploitation!" muttered a native of Outlandia, observing from the bushes.

The meaning of a social event depends on who looks at it.

Leaving it to the Enforcers to supervise the work of the Diggers, Colombo and Raz Putin rowed toward a shady grove of trees on the beach.

The Outlandian lookout scurried off to inform the Outlandian Democratic Assembly, which happened to be meeting in a shady grove of trees on the beach.

Physical settings provide the objective place for the meeting of subjective perceptions.

"What a pleasant place to philosophize," said Colombo, on the beach. "Could not Inlandia have been spared many troubles if more of us had been consulted in decision-making to begin with?" "Yes," Raz said. "While pretending to be their deputies, the few are often the despoilers of the many."

"Disaster!" cried the lookout. "Someone's stealing our clams!" As was typical, all the Outlandians were on their feet and speaking at once. The chairman of the weekly meeting, Honest Abraham, called for order. Beaming Benjamin broke in, "I told you we should have organized a navy instead of talking so much!"

Government by the many can mean too many delays in solving problems; government by the few can mean too few.

"I wonder if all the clams in the world are ours," said Colombo, sidestepping the thought of treason. Raz had just started to reply, as the two neared the grove, "Of course they are, In-

"So let's stop talking and call out the militia," proposed Melissa Mayflower. The idea was unanimously adopted. Honest Abe was just closing the meeting with the words, "Every

landia is all there is,"
when . . .
they walked into
the grove—filled with strangers.

man to his clam-shooter!"
when . . .
two strangers
walked into the grove.

Perceptions of "Us" and "Them" begin with the presence of an "Other."

"Who are you?"

"We're from Inlandia," said Colombo and Raz Putin. "The clams are ours."

"Who are you?"
"They're the clam stealers!" the lookout shouted.
"We're from Outlandia," shouted the assembly. "The clams are ours."

Identification of self with national interest becomes nationalism in an international context of "Others."

Seeing they were out-
numbered, the
Inlandians
beat
a
hasty
retreat.
Back at their boats, the Inlandians perceived they had three
options: to flee, to wait, or to
fight.
"We're right, so we'll fight!" ordered Chief Enforcer Colombo,
his courage lifted in the presence of his countrymen.

Momentarily confused
by the sudden
disappearance of
the Others, the
Outlandians
spread news of
the invasion.

Back at their huts, the Outlanders perceived they had three
options: to hide, to vote, or to
fight. They voted . . . to fight,
their will strengthened by their
greater numbers.

When values are seen as incompatible, fights result.

At sunset, the Inlandians stormed in one side of the coconut grove just as the Outlandians rushed in the other. In disciplined columns, the Inlandians strove to overwhelm clusters of clam-flinging Outlandians. After an indecisive skirmish, the clam-munitions being exhausted, the leaders recalled their troops.

Length of violent conflict depends on technological limits of force.

With will and resources exhausted, all that was left was talk. Disgruntled, the two leaders sat down under a scarred coconut tree.

**Diplomacy is the extension
of war by other means.**

After a heated debate, Raz Putin and Beaming Ben discovered a compromise: each nation would get what clams there were to get every other day. The agreement was carved on the back of two old clam shells. The Outlandish Assembly ratified the agreement immediately.

**International treaties are problem-
solving agreements frozen in time.**

At the head of the armada, Colombo and Raz Putin thought they were returning home in triumph. But they were arrested for selling out the nation. As Alphonse said to Balthazar, "Unless approved by the sovereign, a treaty isn't worth the clam shell it's written on."

DECAY

**Sovereignty is where
legitimacy lies.**

When the Outlandians heard the news, they immediately blockaded their beaches. The Know-Nothings came to know more every day: hunger hurts, wine-guzzling won't help, their lifestyle was falling apart, the Alphonse-Balthazar monopoly no longer made sense. From their prison cells, Colombo and Raz Putin issued a manifesto proclaiming a new order: "Clams for one and all; all as one for clams!"

**Revolution occurs when
legitimacy is undermined with
visions of a new social order.**

The Know-Nothings freed Colombo and Raz Putin and jailed the old elite. A new nation was created—Overlandia. Colombo and Raz Putin, the Know-Nothings and the other classes, Outlandish Ambassador Beaming Ben, and all other interested parties sat down to face their problems. . . . The political cycle had begun again.

2 In which we see how we can regain control over the politics of our daily lives by defining what is political for us—instead of letting others define us out of politics.

2 Defining Politics

Some time ago, we read the story of Alphonse and Balthazar to a little girl—without the comments in boldface. Afterwards we asked, "What do you think the story was all about?"

"Oh, that's easy," she said. "Two guys get together. They form a monarchy. Things start falling apart and then there's a revolution."

Not having been little ourselves for a while, we sat back amazed. Grownups would not have responded so quickly.

Then she added, somewhat concerned, "That's all there is to it, isn't there?"

Well, Virginia, we have to admit we didn't tell you the whole truth. There was a bit more to it, although you grasped one of the essentials—that it is *people* who set up political systems.

We live in a world that is preconstructed for us. We are born into other people's systems of doing politics as we are born into our whole culture—language, counting with Arabic numerals, loving by kissing (unless you are an Eskimo and rub noses), and so on. Like it or not, we are forced to experience an infinite number of systems of living life created by others.

The result is that we tend to accept our way of doing politics in our own country as the only proper one. We often perceive foreign systems to be "wrong" just because they are foreign to us. For our own political institutions appear to be concrete and solid—especially when we try to move them to go our way. And people who run political institutions often look giant-size.

But in fact—as Alphonse and Balthazar demonstrated—politics is man-made and changeable. And so are institutions like Congress, the United Nations, and the City Council. And so are the giants called congressmen, mayors, and secretaries general. *We* have made men and institutions giants. *We* have raised them to their self-defined untouchable height. In fact, we have raised them so high that they no longer look man-size, and we stand in awe, forgetting who put them there. When people begin to stand in awe of their political institutions and politicians, they begin to lose control over their own lives.

Politics begins when you take nothing for granted.

The first chapter exposes the basic building stones out of which politics is constructed. In this sense, learning about politics is similar to learning how to use an erector

isaak

set. The picture on the box of skyscrapers, giant bridges, and elevated highways is awesome until you read the instructions that tell you how to simply add one piece of the set to the next. This book is meant to be a political erector set, beginning with the simplest elements to build more complex structures. It assumes that knowing how to think politics is prerequisite to doing it.

Taking politics apart into its pieces helps to *give us control over politics.* If we know which pieces, put together in which way, give us a desired political result, we have a better chance of making things happen. Explaining politics the better to do it, is one purpose of political analysis.

Also, if we know that one piece in the political process usually follows another—for example, frustration of the expectation of having clams for breakfast may be followed by revolution—we can predict what may happen next when we observe that first piece. Predicting future political events is a second purpose of political analysis.

In other words, the purpose of the first chapter and of this book is to put the individual human being back in the driver's seat of politics—even in a time when it seems little people like ourselves can't do very much. To restore man's power to engage creatively in political problem solving, it isn't enough to assert our right to do politics. We also have to find tools to assess our chances of success in the face of seemingly overwhelming social obstacles. Take things apart before they take you.

By clearly seeing where he stands in his society, every individual can use his political powers up to their limits: the powers of others.

In the following chapters—proceeding from smaller to larger situations—we try to show how to use our political power in America, *in* other countries, and *with* other countries. Finally, we suggest rebuilding our own political system to get rid of some detrimental limits to man's power.

All this activity has to begin by staking out the boundaries of what we mean by politics. We need to define what we include out of all of human activities when we speak of politics.

We believe a broad yet focused definition, relevant to the problems of our technological times, will keep others from defining our power away. Any political system always defines some people in and some people out. In Inlandia, Alphonse and Balthazar defined themselves in and defined the Know-Nothings out. The problem is to define yourself into politics.

THE DEFINITION OF POLITICS

Politics is a social act that attempts to resolve the tension between human needs and social facts.

Human beings are born and die with needs. Needs are food, security, love, self-esteem, and self-actualization. Social facts are conditions that limit or support the satisfaction of needs. The perception of tension is political consciousness. Acting out of this consciousness is politics.

The study of politics for human beings attempts to solve tension problems wherever human beings suffer them.

These are the basic ideas through which this book offers an understanding of politics. Politics begins with an idea—and must be understood through ideas that fit political behavior. Here is how these ideas can be used to understand the politics of Alphonse and Balthazar, which represent the nature of politics everywhere.

Begin with understanding needs.
The initial need of Alphonse and Balthazar was food.
Understand the social context of needs.
The social fact that at first limited Alphonse and Balthazar was their routine of getting food separately.
Find out how politics arises by pinpointing the tension between needs and social facts.
Political consciousness and action arose when Alphonse and Balthazar perceived a tension between their routines and their desire to eat faster. In this case, a change within Alphonse and Balthazar —the hunger-making action of too much coconut wine—produced disharmony between perceived needs and established routines. Later tensions in Inlandia arose from other sources: environmental challenges of clam pollution, the addition of Others from Outlandia to the original problem, and the extension of the solution to a private problem across a vast public, for the majority of whom the "solution" of Alphonse and Balthazar solved nothing at all.

Take all assumptions with a grain of salt—including these.

But before noting these further problems, notice how Alphonse and Balthazar solved their first tension that morning on the beach.
Politics as a social act began when the two communicated the idea of cooperating to solve their tension.
We now have the elements of politics. Politics begins with:

  ] at least two people [
  ] who perceive and communicate [
  ] a shared tension [
  ] between human needs and social facts [
  ] and who initiate a relationship [
  ] to solve that tension [*

Beyond this, politics can become more complex. The elements of politics can be used to analyze such complexity, but other concepts may have to be added.
Alphonse and Balthazar could easily solve their first problem, since they lived in a time and space in which social conditions were still flexible—a period of creation. A period of creation is possible

---

*The reverse brackets are used here to bracket out all circumstances and facts not relevant to a basic definition of politics. What is left are the components of political action without which politics is not thinkable.

when there are few hindering social facts to get in the way of solving tensions.

But such periods pass. The corporation and state that Alphonse and Balthazar created became rigid social facts. They found their self-ish interest in maintaining their solutions as institutions. Institutions are patterns of behavior continued over time to regularize and repeat problem solving. But one man's solution limits another's freedom to create other solutions. By enforcing their institutions, Alphonse and Balthazar introduced a period of maintenance for their reality. So, from the viewpoint of others, darkness set in—for the problems of the Diggers and Crackers were only partly solved, while the Know-Nothings had none solved at all. Periods of maintenance pass slowly.

One reason is that once social reality is created, it defines the perception of human needs. Even Alphonse and Balthazar, snugly at home in their own self-made institutions, became deadened to the perception of new problems. They became mere maintenance men.

Smug in having solved one kind of tension, they neglected the long-term consequences of their political acts for themselves and others. The tendency toward such neglect is tempting, because it feels so comfortable to believe you have solved all your problems.

Comfortable? Beware of being consumed by your social reality!

Finally an ecological crisis resulted that couldn't be papered over by the apparent security of class divisions and the symbolic satisfactions of parades and awards. Someone ran the sewage system into the Royal Bay, and the clams died. The economic basis of the political system was threatened. Even the Know-Nothings could smell that something was wrong.

It is typical that Alphonse and Balthazar, like most maintenance men, had to find out from below that their social facts were no longer meeting human needs. Perhaps it was just coincidence that a lowly messenger from the Royal Clam Post informed them of trouble at their water gate.*

Also typical is that even as maintenance men expand into other territory to save their institutions, minorities of others already perceive an era of decay. Decay is people's subjective experience that social conditions no longer fulfill human needs. Thus as Inlandian imperial expansion in search of clams met with opposition from the Outlandian social reality, the regime of Alphonse and Balthazar went from a period of maintenance to a period of decay. Finally, a revolution threw the louts out. Revolution is an objective consequence of the subjective perception of decay.

Raz Putin and Colombo and other revolutionaries moved to the center of attention by persuading others that they could resolve the

---

*In medieval castles, the "water gate" was the outlet for used water and sewage. For a man to be "caught at his watergate" meant for him to be caught with his pants down.

tension between human needs and social facts. But politicians are full of promise.

Chances are that the commonwealth of revolutionaries and Outlanders will create its own institutions, that new elites will be isolated by self-interest, that new tensions of social fact and human needs will be ignored until forcefully exposed by the perceptions and acts of others. Thus the political cycle of creation-maintenance-decay reappears.

Politics, including the politics of setting up a political system, as **Defining Terms** did Alphonse and Balthazar, thus involves *people* who have *needs* and who engage in *social acts* to meet these needs—even in the face of *social facts* that satisfy someone else's needs.

We can begin to understand how politics works if we keep in mind the scenario of Alphonse and Balthazar as an example. Then we can test for the politics of any situation simply by asking, Who are the people involved? What are their needs? What social acts do they engage in to satisfy their needs? What are the social facts they have to face in trying to fulfill their needs?

The answers to these questions give us the political actors, their goals, their style of doing politics, and their chances of succeeding against the opposition of social reality.

INVITATION

To get an idea of the kind of politics going on around you, take any newspaper story in which people are trying to solve a problem.

Ask yourself these questions:

Who are the people involved?
What are their needs?
What social acts do they engage in?
What social facts do they face?

You now should have a general picture of this political situation. If the story doesn't give you answers to these questions, it may not be the complete story.

In asking such questions, it helps to know what the terms you use mean.

A *social act* is a joint action by two or more people undertaken for similar reasons or with the same intention. It is *political* if the people involved are aware of a shared need and join in an arrangement to satisfy that need.

Needs are what it takes for your body to *be* human and what it takes for your head to *feel* human. They are physiological and psychological requisites for human existence. The failure to satisfy needs can result in death or becoming less than human—illness or pathology of the mind or body. The many cases of premature death and pathology in our times indicate that existing forms of politics aren't meeting human needs. As the psychologist R. D. Laing points out, "normal" man has killed one hundred million of his fellow normal men in the last fifty years of this century.

Many people want more than they need. *Values** are what people want, whether they need it or not. Values include things such as refrigerators, new cars, glass-bead games, and chess sets; they include feelings such as love, revenge, joy, and pain; they include ideas such as freedom, order, truth, and salvation.

What's your hottest need at the moment? Do you really *need* it?

Social facts are old social acts that have become conditions. Social facts often frustrate human needs. For example, although people set up a corporation to satisfy their own needs and wants, as soon as their act becomes a condition, it frustrates the needs of others who share more in the pollution than in the profits created by the firm. Thus the social acts of one group of people to satisfy their own needs often frustrate the fulfillment of needs perceived by other groups. As soon as such tension between social facts and human needs is perceived, political consciousness comes into being.

Politics takes place when people act out of political consciousness to reduce the tension between their perceived needs and the social facts that frustrate these needs.

RECOGNIZING POLITICS

Everyone is doing politics. Everyone says they know what they're doing when they do politics. But try to get someone to define it!

Why bother to define politics?

Because you might want to succeed at doing politics. Without knowing what it is to "do politics," it's impossible to know whether you are doing it. It's also impossible to know whether someone else is doing politics to you. Worse, it's impossible to know *how well* you or anyone else are doing it. And in politics, as in all action, doing it well means success.

Count the number of people who lived you today by doing politics. Do it yourself and live!

Through politics you and I try to resolve the tension between our human needs and social facts. Since we all have human needs, there is no way for us to avoid doing politics. We might as well learn how to do it well.

*A value is generally considered in political science as any goal toward which human beings strive. This general use is accepted here. Values are here divided into *needs* (understood as goals derived from man's nature) and *wants* (understood as goals whose satisfaction people *think* necessary, quite aside from real needs).

Politics is everywhere.

We have been conditioned not to recognize it. It goes on in the schools, on the job, in the family, at the supermarket, over the media—wherever people trade in human needs or package and sell social reality.

Much of our conditioning is not in our interest; it prevents us from recognizing our human needs and using our own political power to fulfill them. Such conditioning *is* in the interest of people who already have political power. The Alphonses and Balthazars of this world, having set up a system to satisfy their own needs, would be happy if we were all Know-Nothings. Through the family, the schools, and official politics they impose their view of the world on us.[1] Such training is called "socialization." It is the handing down of ways of getting along in any society. Not surprisingly, such ways of life are so designed as never to challenge the powerful, who already have the most of what any society considers worth getting.

Think of a totally nonpolitical social event. Think again.

Escape your conditioning by knowing this: *What you think is what you see. What others teach you to think determines what you get to see.* Our mind works like a computer—it processes only what it is programmed to take in. Try the following experiment on yourself:

INVITATION

Write down this definition of politics:

"Politics is a struggle for power."

Now write down whatever activities you associate with that definition.

(Don't read on until you have finished.)

Now write on another piece of paper the following definition of politics:

"Politics is people getting together to solve their problems."

Write down any activities you associate with this definition. (Don't read on until you finish.)

Now compare the two lists. Do definitions determine what you think about? Could they determine how you handle politics?

When this experiment was undertaken in some of our classes, our students offered us these words and thoughts associated with "politics as struggle": "Battling, competing, position, command, desire to rule, scheming, crooked, imposing your own ideology, dominance, ruling, struggling to the top, moving up the ladder, bootlicking, money, putting people beneath you, phony, control." And there were many less polite words.

The other half of each class, asked to associate terms with "politics as people solving problems," wrote typically: "cooperation, getting the job done, togetherness, love, concern for others, getting into the other guy's head, feeling out others' needs and desires, community, compromise, parties, uniting to solve problems, alliances, representation, people making themselves feel worthy."*

Cooperative politics means doing it with others (*everybody* needs it)!

Experts in the problem of understanding reality[†] have learned:

1. That it is dangerous to confuse the impression *in one's head* with the reality *out there,* as if one's own impression were the only one possible *about* reality.

2. That the words we use to describe politics limit what we get to see of it. We must be very careful that our language actually describes those parts of reality that are relevant to us.[2]

3. That definitions are arbitrary but never accidental. My definition of politics picks up what is relevant to me. Yours picks up what is relevant to you. To get where you want to go, pick your right definition.

If you are taught to think that politics is possible only as a struggle with others over scarce goods, then you will recognize as political only those human actions in which people claw at each other to rip off things that are hard to get.[3] This is the politics of pain. It is one kind of conditioning. It encourages you to see individuals and groups in conflict, but blinds you to seeing them in cooperation. Yet some human needs can be satisfied only through cooperation: the needs for love, for self-esteem, for self-actualization.

If you are taught to think that politics is going to someone in authority for the goods you want, then you will bow and scrape, inveigle and contrive to get access to the Man. The problem then is getting to the guy who has the goods, and the political system becomes a maze through which we run like rats to get at the cheese.

That you and I ourselves have the power to decide what goods are worth going after and how to go about getting them, and that people now in authority were put up there by people like us—such ideas rarely occur to us. Nor are they supposed to occur to us. The definition of politics as the process of the "authoritative allocation of values"[4] encourages powerful people to demand that we learn

---

*Special thanks to the students of Introduction to Semantic Analysis, fall 1973, Jersey City State College, who gave their cooperation to the political act of trying out this experiment.

[†]Begin with Immanuel Kant, *The Critique of Pure Reason*, Mueller, translation, 2nd ed. (New York: Doubleday, 1961; original 1781), p. 357 ff. For a lucid explanation of the fact that where you stand colors what you see, see Peter Berger and Thomas Luckman, *The Social Construction of Reality* (Garden City N.Y.: Doubleday, Anchor Books, 1967) p. 45 ff.

how to fit in with the system and play the game their way. This is the politics of power. It means *accepting* those in authority as the sources of our satisfactions: police protection, food stamps, tax rebates, minimum wages, revenue sharing, schools, sewers, transportation, and so on.

Does not respect for authority begin where self-respect ends?

Finding a Useful Definition

Somehow the politics of Alphonse and Balthazar in their creative problem-solving stage fits into neither of these views of politics. Alphonse and Balthazar did not fight over the goods, the clams in their desert-island bay. And they did not have a man in authority to tell them how they might get breakfast faster or how the goods satisfying hunger needs might be distributed.

In fact, our two heroes (before they became powerful bums) acted out a politics that involved neither fighting nor asking for help from the powerful. They perceived a problem, they did their own thinking about how to solve it, and then went about working together to solve it.

There was no system to turn to. In fact, all systems of doing politics—including our own, the Russians', and the Eskimos'—exist now only because they were set up by people like Alphonse and Balthazar.

Fighting about the clams would only have muddied the water —and delayed breakfast. Even political systems in which fights take place rest on an initial agreement to stop fighting long enough to set up rules. Within these rules legitimate political problem solving (whether through cooperation or conflict) takes place.

What politics is essentially all about, then, turns out to be not conflict or authority, but cooperation and creativeness aimed at problem solving. What we normally see as politics is merely the style of politics, the superficial form of what is basically cooperative, creative, and problem-oriented. But if we set our minds to thinking merely about style, we may forget that there can be many styles of politics. Worse, we may forget what politics in its essential sense is all about—satisfying human needs through whatever style may fit those needs.

Thinking about politics in this way turns out to be a real eye-opener. Suddenly we see politics wherever it is taking place. And suddenly we realize that politics is a human activity created and under-taken by people like ourselves. We recognize our individual power and right to do politics to solve our problems.

Mindful of the dangers of accepting someone else's definition of politics, we asked ourselves what politics everywhere could be reduced to—regardless of the languages or modes of politics used by different people.

What did politics essentially involve?

First, people. People with intentions. People who felt a need to act to reach a goal.

Second, people who *interacted*. You don't do politics by yourself—you solve your problems with others.

Third, people who interacted in a certain way. Even where people were bound politically to each other in unequal positions of dominance and submission, even where politics seemed to consist of little more than fighting modified by "civilized" rules, people seemed to see their *needs* represented in politics. Or, at least, they often complained that politics *didn't* fulfill their needs—as if they had a right to expect need fulfillment from politics.

The longer we thought about this third aspect of politics, the more we recognized two facts:

First, where politics works best for the most people, those interacting in politics seem to be taking each others' needs into account.

Second, even where politics is done through a style of conflict, initially and continually people recognize each others' basic need to understand how the political fight is to be conducted. That is, they at first agreed on *rules* about how to fight politically. And now they maintain these rules, even when they fight. Their conflict thus takes place *within a framework of cooperation.*

**Imagine a game of conflict
without any rules at all
(you've got a good imagination!).**

So even if we took the most bleakly realistic view of politics, politics was still an act between at least two people, done against a background of rules of cooperation.

Also, in its most perfect form, politics was interaction between people to fulfill their human needs.[5]

Out of this conclusion emerged a useful way of defining politics:

Politics is a social act through which human beings try to fulfill their human needs.

Later we saw a need to amend this definition. Political activity always takes place within a social framework. This framework is composed of already finished political acts performed by others who earlier tried to fulfill their needs.

In modern times, the limits of society are so strong and binding all around us that a relevant definition of politics has to take account of them:

Politics is a social act to resolve the tension between human needs and social facts.

This means politics involves at least two human beings. Each has his or her own needs. Each tries to understand the other's needs. Then they try to work together to satisfy them—always conscious of the limitations that social facts (the past political acts of others) put on such need-fulfilling interaction.

Some curious insights confront the reader who holds this definition in mind. Only two need be mentioned right away.

First, politics now appears to be going on everywhere, even where one may least expect it—in economics and the family, in love and in marriage, in the classroom and the board room. Seeing this, of course, frees us to consciously act politically in those situations. We also recognize why others try to talk us out of thinking such situations are political—if they are labeled nonpolitical, we have no right to try to satisfy our needs in such situations! We are expected to submit passively to existing social facts that keep us from satisfying our needs.

Secondly, it dawns on us that a lot of activities are called political that really are not. Any interaction in which people try to *frustrate* one another's need fulfillment is a rung below creative politics on the ladder of human interaction. It is what other political scientists have called "pseudo-politics," "non-decision-making," and "symbolic politics."*

Before looking into the possibility that most of what is called politics today is a phoney facsimile of real politics, let's see how our definition is useful for identifying potentially political situations.

You can know politics when you see it by keeping in mind three essential questions. These questions are summarized here in a "tool for recognizing politics." With this tool you can test *any* situation for political content. Try out the tool in the following invitation:

Using the Definition

INVITATION

A tool for recognizing politics:

About any situation you suspect of being political, ask these questions:

1. Are there at least two people involved?
2. Do they recognize shared needs?
3. Do they interact to satisfy those needs?

The first question allows you to identify the political actors. Politics always takes place between two or more persons.

The second question allows you to spot what they are doing politics about and whether they are capable of doing politics. Without recognizing our shared needs, what we are likely to engage in is unthinking battle, not politics as mutual problem solving.

The third question allows you to identify what the actors are doing about their shared needs. Interaction need not be egalitarian. One person may give the orders on how to dig clams, while the other does the digging. Nevertheless, mutual interaction for problem solving is taking place.

Questions: How many different political situations can you think of, using this definition of politics?

Would any of these situations normally be defined as non-political?

---

*See "Recognizing Pseudopolitics," page 25.

If you accepted the preceding invitation, you should suddenly be able to discover politics everywhere. This is the first step of liberation from those who would tell you there is only one game of politics—theirs—and that you have to play their way. This liberation is necessary both for the political scientist, who must learn to study games of politics from the outside, free of old biases, and for the citizen who wants to regain his natural power to be political, in the sense of doing his own problem solving. Suddenly we find politics not only in the election booth or in Congress, but also in . . .

. . . the politics of the family:[6] When Mom and Pop send the kids out to a movie so they can have an evening to themselves, or when Mom quarrels with Pop over who takes the garbage out;

. . . the politics of sex-role liberation:[7] When a female business executive convinces a client that her paying the lunch bill really can satisfy the needs of both; or when members of the women's liberation movement picket the Miss America contest because they feel it strips the contestants of their human dignity;

. . . the politics of insanity:[8] When a human being labeled "patient" and a human being labeled "psychiatrist" try to convince each other that their respective outlooks on life are reality;

. . . the politics of salvation:[9] When Catholic women try to stop having more children but also to stay within the grace of the Church, or when Jesus People organize their own communities to find ultimate meaning in life;

. . . the politics of education:[10] When black Americans demand the chance to win self-esteem for their children by indoctrinating them in black values, or white Americans reject busing because it's too "expensive."

. . . the politics of social security: When middle-American Democrats back a Republican president because he keeps alive the American dream: Hard work will get you a chance to climb the social ladder of success, and I'll protect your gains once you've made them.

INVITATION

Again applying the tool for recognizing politics, ask yourself:

Is what goes on in your classroom political?
Is what goes on in your family political?
Is what goes on on your job political?
Is what goes on in the supermarket political?

In the classroom: Is your relationship with your teacher so set up as to satisfy your shared needs—"learning" from your perspective and "teaching" from his?

In the family: How does your relationship with your parents, your brother, or your girl/boy friend satisfy human needs? What are the arrangements made to satisfy such needs? Do they work?

On the job: What shared needs bring you and your employer together? Are you engaged in cooperating on a common task? Is there discussion as to how to achieve it? What style of interaction is there—cooperative politics or power politics?

In the supermarket: How close to serving shared needs does your local supermarket come? Does it serve your *real* needs, or learned wants forced into your head via television? Is there a chance to express your needs to the owner or manager?

It may be that some of these situations make politics, as an activity by which human beings mutually try to solve their problems, difficult or even impossible. To the extent that such a situation makes politics as we have defined it difficult, it also makes being human difficult. If you want to be human, stay away from or try to correct such apolitical situations.

Not only does this method enable us to recognize politics anywhere it takes place, it shows that to be political, an event does not necessarily have to be characterized by conflict. Mom and Pop getting together, liberated women organizing, middle Americans voting their way—all these are examples of the cooperative, problem-solving face of politics. Any or all of these activities may draw those cooperating into conflict with others—but that is merely another face of politics, and not the only one. Mom and Pop *may* have to face opposition if the kids would just as soon stay home and watch TV. Women picketing the Miss America contest *may* be insulted by chauvinist males. Middle America *may* run into flak from liberals who can afford to be liberal, from blacks who want the prosperity of middle Americans, from corporations that squeeze middle Americans economically.

Whether or not such conflict actually takes place, however, depends to some extent on the expectations of the people involved. Mom, Pop, women's libbers, and middle Americans may *talk* themselves into a conflict stance, or they may talk others into recognizing shared needs and doing political problem solving *with* them.

The social expectations of others are nothing to be sneezed at, but to *expect* conflict makes conflict inevitable. Remember what happened when Inlanders and Outlanders first fought over clams.

Another power that the model of cooperative politics gives us is the capacity to make some initial rough distinction between situations that are political and others that are *pseudopolitical*. A truly political situation is one in which human beings cooperate over human *needs*. A pseudopolitical situation is one in which human beings struggle or cooperate over *wants*. In both cases they may engage in a *social act* to fulfill what they are after, but there is a difference in goals.

It now becomes clear that some of the examples listed on page 24 come closer to pseudopolitics than to politics.

When Mom quarrels with Pop over who takes the garbage out, several possibilities arise from our application of our model. Each may be simply operating on the level of wants, Pop wanting to drink his

PSEUDOPOLITICS AND CREATIVE POLITICS

Recognizing Pseudopolitics

beer undisturbed while watching his favorite TV program and Mom wanting a break from housework and the kids. Neither one of them is awake enough to realize that the needs for self-esteem at stake in this situation can be resolved only through mutual cooperation, not through quarrel.

> **Pseudopolitics comes with impatience and leaves you with pain.**

In such cases, it is important to guard against condemning the pseudopolitical actors. Many official political activities—such as voting for presidents—may also be a futile exercise in pseudopolitics. Individuals and parties may struggle over perceived interests without ever getting down to the mutual definition of needs that would humanize the lives of all of them. Such activity in the public political arena may be pseudopolitics from another point of view—public political decision making may merely be a sop thrown to the mob *after* essential decisions have already been made in back rooms, often by members of the elite.[11] This "sop" may be satisfying to some extent, but it is not concerned with solving problems or satisfying human needs; it is mere "symbolic politics,"[12] or "pseudo-politics".[13]

This is pseudopolitics. What would a really creative politics for human beings be like? If we could know that, then we would have a measure of the tension between human needs and the limits imposed on us by the social facts others have created.

Toward Creative Politics

A politics for human beings starts with the insight that all the routines and norms of politics are man-made. It assumes that politics is people engaging in social relationships to satisfy human needs. The study of politics means focusing on people, instead of remaining trapped in old routines, outdated norms, and dysfunctional institutions.

This approach avoids another trap—the assumption dominant among students of politics that politics must be viewed in terms of conflict.

The fact is that when any political situation is reduced to its essentials, we find at bottom *cooperation*. All political conflict takes place on the surface of silently taken-for-granted agreements. These agreements establish the rules of the political game and the goals that may legitimately be pursued.

Only when these taken-for-granted rules and norms are themselves attacked or broken does the very foundation of politics and social life stand in danger. The profound threat of the Watergate affair was that the participants challenged the cooperative rules and norms according to which surface politics is possible. This threat is what one Senate investigator perceived most acutely when he observed that the participants were men who had almost stolen America. Without fundamental agreements, human life in the company of others becomes impossible. Behind Watergate loomed the anarchy of philosopher Thomas Hobbes's war of all against all.*

*See Chapter 12, pages 274 to 276.

If you recognize only the surface conflicts of politics, you deny ethics automatically—for then you do not recognize the necessity to maintain the cooperative foundation of politics, which makes problem solving possible. People who see only the surface patterns of political conflict risk becoming madmen who know no limits to political behavior and recognize no responsibility.

A politics for human beings must offer two tools: knowledge of basic human needs and knowledge of conditions under which human beings can begin to fulfill these needs.

Over the long term, no one can permanently define human needs. In the short term, however, research into human needs has brought about some basic agreement. One synthesis of what human beings need has been placed before us by the psychologist Abraham Maslow.[14] Some such synthesis will have to be the basis for any future politics of human survival, for it encompasses the whole range of conditions for existence, from the physical to the spiritual. Beginning with the most basic, this is Maslow's hierachy of needs:

1. Physiological needs (food, water, rest)
2. Safety needs (physical and psychic security)
3. Love needs (warmth, affection, inclusion)
4. Esteem needs (positive evaluation of the self by the self and by others)
5. Self-actualization needs (creative expression of the self based on fulfilling the other needs as the foundation for meeting the challenges of one's time)

When we ask ourselves how many of these needs our system of politics—or anyone else's—fails to fulfill, we have a measure of the pathological nature of politics seen as conflict. This list suggests what politics should begin to do.

Those who want to do politics for human beings must also analyze politics as others see it to understand the basic conditions that make politics possible.* What assumptions are necessary in order for people to engage in a politics for human beings? The answer, we suggest, begins with:

] at least two people [
] who perceive and communicate [
] a shared tension [
] between human needs and social facts [
] and who initiate a relationship [
] to solve that tension. [

This approach identifies the highest political moment. Politics takes place in its purest form when two people first *perceive* a shared need and *initiate* some kind of relationship to resolve that need.

---

*A method for such analysis has been provided by the phenomenologists, especially the philosopher Edmund Husserl and the sociologist Alfred Schutz. The phenomenologist asks one question: "What are the fundamental assumptions of everyday life without which such life is not thinkable or doable?"

As such relationships are repeated, they may become routine and fall back into the less consciously political. Much of what we think of as politics is merely the ritualized repetition of procedures created by men long since dead to solve problems that died with them. Such political routines become less and less workable as prescriptions for need fulfillment because the problems of the social and natural environment change. As this happens, new tensions between human needs and the routines of social facts arise, and—with new consciousness—the political cycle begins anew.

Pure politics is the most creative act a human being can engage in. It is a different activity altogether from the conflict-prone cookbook politics we have unthinkingly accepted in the past. Even though it is unsettling to locate ourselves again and again in the tension between human needs and the limits of social facts, only those who focus their consciousness on that tension will find the place to stand for humanistic political action.

INCONCLUSIONS We have redefined politics as social action that attempts to resolve the tension between human needs and social facts. Human needs include physiological, security, love, self-esteem, and self-actualization needs. Social facts are existing conditions that support or frustrate the satisfaction of such needs. When we become *aware* of tension between our frustrated needs and social facts, we become *politically conscious*. Hence accurate perception of what we need and where we are in social reality becomes crucial if we are to satisfy our needs and get what we want. The simple technique of the phenomenologists helps us to sharpen our perception, bracket out unessential aspects of reality, and get down to the brass tacks of how we might cooperate with others to solve our problems.

Further, it appears that all social relationships develop historically into social facts through a universal pattern of creation, maintenance, and decay. That is, two or more human beings get together to satisfy mutual needs and *create* a social relationship for political action. If this relationship works, it becomes institutionalized and *maintained* in routines over time. Finally, when such institutionalized relationships become so hardened and cold with age that they no longer satisfy the needs for which they were designed, *decay* sets in, and rebellions and revolutions often occur. Old social facts are then overturned by fresh, creative political action, and the cycle of politics commences again.

This view of politics does not deny the existence of conflict. Rather, it assumes that constant tensions between human needs and social facts are inevitable. But notions of politics that are limited *merely* to conflict in present social reality are actually pseudopolitics, in that they are blind to the cooperative basis that made the initiation of such conflict possible in the first place. Conflicts can be resolved by going back to this original basis of agreement to find an acceptable solution to common needs. To see politics merely as materialistic conflict is to dehumanize it, taking social facts for immovable objects rather than for the results of human creativity.

If you can see politics in terms of human needs, you find a basis to motivate people to change social facts, the better to satisfy human needs through social action. Although tensions are inevitable, by slipping into the shoes of others to find ways to cooperate, we can make them more livable. And we become more human in the process.

1. For a description of the socialization mechanism, see Peter Berger and Thomas Luckman, *The Social Construction of Reality* (Garden City, N.Y.: Doubleday, Anchor Books, 1967), pp. 129–147, and R. D. Laing, *The Politics of Experience* (New York: Ballantine Books, 1968).

2. On how the words we use determine our actions, see S. I. Hayakawa, *Language in Thought and Action,* 3rd ed., (New York: Harcourt, Brace, Jovanovich, 1972), especially Chapter I, "Language and Survival." On how different views of reality lead to the formation of different "languages of politics," which lead to different political behaviors, see H. Mark Roelofs, *The Languages of Modern Politics* (Homewood, Ill.: Dorsey Press, 1968).

3. See Harold D. Lasswell, *Politics: Who Gets What When How* (Cleveland: Meridian Books, 1958). Lasswell, a leading political scientist, defines politics in that way.

4. David Easton, another leading political scientist, defines politics as "the authoritative allocation of resources." See Easton, *The Political System: An Inquiry into the State of Political Science* (New York: Knopf, 1964), Chapter V.

5. In *The Republic,* Plato defines man as a socio-political animal whose tendency is to join and interact with fellow human beings in the city to fulfill his human needs.

6. Begin reading in this area with R. D. Laing and A. Esterson, *Sanity, Madness and the Family* (Baltimore, Md.: Penguin Books, 1970).

7. A basic book on the politics of sex roles is Kate Millet's *Sexual Politics* (New York: Avon Books [Equinox Edition], 1971). See also the collection of essays and statements gathered by the City of New York Commission of Human Rights in *Women's Role in Contemporary Society* (New York: Avon Books [Discus Edition], 1972).

8. On the politics of insanity, see Thomas S. Szasz, *Ideology and Insanity: Essays on the Psychiatric Dehumanization of Man* (Garden City, N.Y.: Doubleday, Anchor Books, 1970).

9. For another example of a creative politics of salvation, see Carlos Castañeda, *Journey to Ixtlan: The Lessons of Don Juan* (New York: Simon and Schuster, 1972).

10. Jonathan Kozol, *Death at an Early Age* (New York: Bantam Books, 1968).

11. Peter Bachrach and Morton S. Baratz, *Power and Poverty: Theory and Practice* (New York: Oxford University Press, 1970). For a summary of their concept of non-decision making, see especially pp. 44–46.

12. Murray Edelman, *The Symbolic Uses of Politics* (Urbana, Ill.: University of Illinois Press, 1967).

13. Christian Bay writes: "I would define as *political* all activity aimed at improving or protecting conditions for the satisfaction of human needs and demands in a given society according to some universalistic scheme of priorities, implicit or explicit. *Pseudopolitical* in this paper refers to activity that resembles political activity but is exclusively concerned with either the alleviation of personal neuroses or with promoting private or private interest-group advantage, deterred by no articulate or disinterested conception of what would be just or fair to other groups" ("Politics and Pseudopolitics: A Critical Evaluation of Some Behavioral Literature," *The American Political Science Review* 59, no. 1 [March 1965]: 40).

14. Abraham Maslow, *Motivation and Personality* (New York: Harper & Row, 1954).

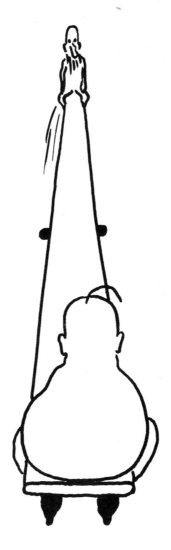

isaak

3 In which the potentially political human being sees:
What makes politics so tough to do.
How to become politically conscious.
How to do politics.

3 Doing Politics

How well you do politics depends on how well you understand what you mean by politics. But it also depends on the obstacles of misunderstanding that others throw in your way.

In modern society, these obstacles weigh heavy on anyone trying to fulfill his or her needs by doing politics. This is why our definition stresses that politics is a social act *to resolve the tension between human needs and social facts.*

**Social facts keep men down
to keep traditions up.**

Social facts have been piling up around us in America for about two hundred years—since the Founding Fathers set up a political language and political system to fulfill their needs. Wherever people get together to do politics, they first establish a political language; the political system comes next. Such language contains the meaning of politics: the needs considered proper for satisfaction through politics, the methods considered proper for interacting politically, and the needs and methods that are excluded from politics.

The American language of politics has a deep historical heritage. We still face social facts and ideas created to resolve other people's tensions that go back at least to 1588, the birthdate of political philosopher Thomas Hobbes. From him we took the definition of what most of us consider to be our most basic need: security, or staying alive in spite of the other people out to "get" us. This fear for survival comes in part from our acceptance of Hobbes's assertion about human nature: man is an animal engaged in a "war of all against all." Given this assumption, we accept negotiation and compromise as our basic political style—suggested by another British philosopher, John Locke. Since others who occupied our world before we were born believe in this language of politics, every baby raised to become an American is confronted with that language as an inescapable social fact. We become our heritage.

The language of politics is a recipe for political action. When the way we think and talk politics is translated into action, we construct the political system. The political system is a maze of institutions, channels of behavior, and routines that see to it that politics is done the way our language of politics tells us to do it. Individuals who "speak out of turn" run up against the police, the Internal Revenue Service, and the entire local, state, and federal bureaucracy, to say nothing of the disapproval of their neighbors.

But since our language and system of politics were set up to satisfy the needs of others in other times long ago, the social facts that channel our inherited way of doing politics may get in the way of satisfying our needs today.

To free ourselves for political action, it pays to be aware of such obstacles.

This chapter is divided into three parts that show:

What makes politics so tough to do.
How to become politically conscious.
How to do politics.

WHAT MAKES POLITICS SO TOUGH TO DO? Politics in the society of others is understandably more complex than the politics of Alphonse and Balthazar, working in the void of their prepolitical world.

What are the facts of life that anyone wanting to do politics must face?

Any political system is composed of basic social facts that the politically minded cannot ignore. We suggest that any human being can orient himself for doing politics in any system, if he or she recognizes that any system involves

1. Rules of the game
2. Values
3. Social institutions
4. Political institutions
5. Personality

Motivated by *personality,* human beings strive after *values.* In doing so, they can take advantage of the existing distribution of values, represented by *social institutions* like *class* and *status,* and of direct political power, which they possess through access to organizations administering *rules of the* political *game —political institutions.*

These are the reference points within which politics takes place—whether a pseudopolitics or a creative politics for human beings. As political scientist Michael P. Lerner says, "Human beings make their own history, but not in circumstances of their own choosing."[1]

INVITATION

Try to find the five variables at work in any political situation.

How do personality, values, class or status, and political institutions enter into the following situation? Find out by having two volunteers act out this problem:

There are two individuals, Al and Bal.
They are hungry.
Between them they have enough money for one corned beef sandwich.

Let the two solve the tension between their need and social facts. Which social facts dominate their interaction? Which political style?

In the preceding invitation, as in any political situation, we can grasp the outcome if we ask five questions about the facts of political life:

1. What were the *rules of the game?* If "Al" and "Bal" conducted a reasonable argument rather than coming to blows, they chose a game of reason and talk as opposed to a game of unreason and violence. Entire political systems are constructed on such choices. The American system emphasizes reason and talk, negotiation and compromise; the Nazi system in Germany was a deadly game, played according to unreason and violence.* *Rules of the game are the taken-for-granted routines within which politics is done in any community.* [2]

> **How much of your life do you spend obeying someone else's rules of the game? Politics is what happens when you try to change such rules.**

2. What were the *values?* Values are the goals individuals strive after. An example of personal value is the corned beef sandwich. Political values likely to be referred to by Americans trying to persuade each other are "equal rights" or "fairness" or "democracy" or "free and open discussion."† *Political values* refer to the goals and conditions that the game of politics enshrines and is set up to protect. They are the elements of the rules of the game. *Social values* are the goals toward which society as a whole may strive, using the game of politics as a means. [3]

Values act as norms that guide behavior

3. Did the players use access to the resource of social institutions?

Social institutions are relationships set up long ago to regulate the satisfaction of needs among human beings. Social institutions represent a previous distribution of access to values—of who gets what. As such they can be used as counters—or a basis for power—in the game of politics.

The two social institutions most closely related to politics are *class* and *status*. *Class* is how much you've got of what your society considers important to get. *Status* is· how much others think you've got. In America, class usually is used to refer to how much material goods (money, property, and so on) a person has got. Status refers to the degree of deference others give to you on the basis of how you got the goods or go about getting them. A highly skilled steelworker and a young doctor may have, for a while, the same income, yet the doctor is accorded higher status—when it comes to getting a parking place,

---

*Americans usually tend to choose the traditional rules of the American game of politics for any problem-solving situation. For a discussion of the American dynamics of politics, *see* Chapter 5, 75 to 109.

†American political values include the following: respect for life, liberty, and property, though not necessarily in that order; work as a measure of human dignity; individualism; competition (especially as in "free enterprise"); faith in reason (come let us reason together!); majority rule balanced by minority rights; mistrust of big government (checks and balances and the federal system); and the universal applicability of these values. See Chapter 5, pages 79—81, 88—92, and 102—103 for a further discussion.

airplane reservations, or invitations to prestige parties. Both class and status denote social position relative to others.*

How are the class and status of your parents social facts that frustrate your needs and determine your values?

If Al offers Bal a check for $10, he is using class as a resource. Or Bal might obtain sole use of the sandwich from Al by claiming the status of a priest—assuming that Al holds the metaphysical status of priests in higher esteem than his physical hunger.

Institutions can be used as resources to play the game of politics. This is also true of political institutions.

4. Did the players use access to political institutions?

Political institutions are problem-solving relationships solidified over time into more or less permanent organizations. They were originally designed to solve other people's human needs.

Some political institutions are organizations that allow a citizen to express his needs; others allow people with similar needs to join resources for making demands on government, another political institution. Organizations that express or articulate needs can be *political parties* or *interest groups*. Often they also accumulate or aggregate similar needs. The institution of *government* can sometimes be subdivided into distinct organizations that make rules to satisfy needs (the *legislative*), that apply rules (the *executive*), and that review rules (the *judiciary*). Different systems tend to have different political institutions.

What political institutions do you have access to? Why or why not?

The players in our invitation may cite access to political institutions to enhance their relative power position. For example, Al may say, "I know a guy in the Welfare Department (an *executive* body), and unless you give me that sandwich, I'll squeal on you for getting your welfare illegally." Or both Al and Bal may say to the deli owner, "Give us a corned beef sandwich or our uncle in the Health Department will close you down."

Political institutions are standard arrangements for administering the solution of typical problems or needs. (They are, by definition, not much good at handling new problems or needs.)

If social facts keep you from access to political institutions, should you die to preserve such rules of the game? Why or why not?

*These two ways of allocating social position are often referred to as social-economic status (SES), in which "social" refers to prestige and "economic" to possession of material goods or income.

5. To what extent did the players utilize personality in the game?

The extent to which any player involves himself in the game of politics depends on his personality, specifically on the degree of his *motivation* to solve his needs through interaction with others. *Personality* is the sum of all those personal characteristics an individual brings to bear on his public relationships. Cognitive capacities indicated by *intelligence* refer to the individual's ability to calculate rationally a solution to a perceived tension between his human needs and social reality. Affective capacities—expressed in *emotional responses* —refer to the individual's tendency to allow noncognitive feelings to rule his behavior.

If a player in our game determines the other player has less intelligence, he may be able to use his knowledge of the other's personality to talk him into miscalculating the division of the sandwich. Example:

Al: Okay, let's divide the sandwich according to the rule of fairness and equality.
Bal: Okay.
Al: All right, here's a third of the sandwich for you, and two thirds for me. That's fair because I should get extra credit for thinking of the idea that we ought to divide equally.
Bal: Duh—okay.

Here Bal, a none-too-swift thinker, has allowed Al to slip in an external consideration while the logical division of the sandwich according to agreed-on rules was in progress.

Similarly, Bal might play on the well-known emotionality of Al by throwing a crying fit to arouse Al's sympathy and thus get the sandwich.

INVITATION

Consider another political problem.

With what you have learned about the five variables —rules, values, social and political institutions, and personality—try to utilize them to your advantage in the following situation (two players again):

It is raining. Two of you have to get home. But only one of you can get a ride in my car because my girl friend, my dog, and several suitcases already nearly fill it up. *Task:* **Using the five variables, try to talk the other guy out of taking the ride.**

Cooperative Politics and Power Politics

Whenever a player of the game holds a social fact over the head of another player in order to make him play his way, the relationship is one of *power politics. Cooperative politics* aims at the common perception of a shared need and the satisfaction of that need through a mutual arrangement. But politics does not take place in a vacuum.

Our partner in politics may see satisfaction of the new need to be a danger to old satisfactions of other needs. The blue-collar auto worker at one time may have truly wanted to cooperate with blacks on wage increases to fulfill everyone's self-esteem needs, but when these needs seemed to conflict with his social status, he turned against blacks. This is the history of modern middle America.[4]

Usually the makings of power politics can be understood if we think of what people want (*values*) as arranged in order of importance. I may surrender a corned beef sandwich to a demanding friend because I value his friendship more and am afraid of losing it. Unfortunately, the order of values differ from individual to individual and from group to group. If my friend values the sandwich more than my friendship—in the situation just cited—he may take my offer of the sandwich. He ranks his values 1. Satisfaction of hunger; 2. Preservation of friendship. I rank mine 1. Preservation of friendship; 2. Satisfaction of hunger.

> **What would *you* trade for the value of friendship? What do the rules of the game in your culture force you to trade?**

Sometimes professional politicians engage in trade-offs to get what they value. A Southern senator may trade a favorable vote on civil rights legislation to a Northern liberal senator for his vote on a new naval base to provide jobs for the Southerner's constituents. But always there is the threat that a value important to one will be withdrawn unless he surrenders on a less important value. In this case what makes the horse-trade possible may be a political value important to both: that the system of horse-trading or vote-swapping itself be maintained.

Whenever one individual is willing to risk one value in order to win the surrender of another value from another individual, power politics may be said to be in progress.

Power politics is conducted by
] two individuals [
] one of whom threatens to withhold [
] a primary value [
] unless the other surrenders [
] a secondary value [*

Take the following example:

Student, Nina: (to instructor after class): Do you remember you told us that in power politics one partner in a relationship holds a value over the head of the second partner?

*The reverse brackets are used here to indicate we have "bracketed out" all incidental behaviors and orientations not necessary to a basic definition of power politics.

Instructor: Yes, a primary value like friendship, for example, which both partners want, can be used by one to bluff the other partner into giving up something else, a secondary value.

Nina: That's exactly what I mean. That's what happened to me. Since the beginning of the semester I've been a slave to my roommate. She kept asking me to get her hamburgers and milkshakes at midnight. I didn't want to lose her as a friend, so I did it.

Instructor: I see. She probably figures you wanted the value of friendship worse than the value of your comfort around midnight. So she was willing to take a chance. She threatened to take away your primary value—friendship—unless you gave her what to you was a secondary value—the service of getting her hamburgers and milkshakes.

Nina: Yes. But that's different now.

Instructor: Oh?

Nina: I told her I was through. I told her unless she started getting me some things when I want them, I wouldn't be *her* friend anymore!

Instructor: You called her bluff.

Nina: Right. Now she gets me hamburgers and milkshakes at midnight.

Power politics often seems to be the order of the day. But it is one thing to be realistically aware of what power politics can do to you and quite another to make it happen because you expect it to happen that way. What makes it so hard to create a cooperative politics for human beings? What can be done to move power politics in the cooperative direction?

Human beings often submit willingly to pseudopolitics, which deceives them into believing they are engaged in creative politics, and to power politics, which enslaves their will power by appealing to their lower-level needs and values. Pseudopolitics and power politics are both used by those in power to maintain the status quo, existing social reality. In part, this preservation of social reality is accomplished by tricks that a person's own mind plays upon him. To free an individual's power is to unmask these tricks. The five basic tricks that keep human beings enslaved psychologically in modern society are *one-dimensionality, reification, alienation, stasis,* and *pathological ideology.*

One-dimensionality One-dimensionality of the mind is a tendency to think that there is only one way of solving problems or doing politics: the way we learned on our mother's knee, in school, and in political campaigns. By thinking in only one dimension, we flatten out the tension between our needs and social facts.

We see social facts as inevitable conditions to which our needs must always be submitted. Thus we lose ourselves by submerging in the traditional system of doing things.

BECOMING POLITICALLY CONSCIOUS

Political Unconsciousness: Submitting to Social Facts

> **A clam that goes only one way
> is one-dimensional.**

Reification   Reification is believing that a social relationship (especially social and political institutions) is more real than the men and women that made it. Reification is attempting to make something real or concrete that is not.* Typically, reified thinking turns people into things and human relationships into inevitable conditions. Philosopher Alfred North Whitehead called this error the "fallacy of misplaced concreteness." If we think that relationships are more concrete than they actually are, we become blind to other aspects of reality that are just as real and important. An example is the tendency of journalists and scholars to turn nation-states into god-like beings, speaking of "England" outmanipulating "France," rather than of certain decision makers in power in England outbargaining certain policy-making humans in France. To get at the human origins of such behavior between nation-states, we have to dereify the language used to describe such interactions—expose the human details that make social facts possible. The most obvious political use of reification is propaganda.[5]

> **A clam that thinks himself into
> being a clam-god commits reification.**

Alienation   Alienation is the psychic process by which we become totally estranged from our own needs and the hope of satisfying them in our society. To become alienated is to become a stranger to yourself. One-dimensional thinking in modern society can even lead to a curious alienated state of feeling that one is happy and therefore that one is living a truly human life. But often this "happiness" is a superficial and anxious mask for the failure to satisfy one's highest needs of love, self-esteem, and self-actualization. By accepting society's popular media-advertised "needs" and their satisfaction in the consumption of consumer goods, people become alienated from their real needs and become identified and possessed by the products they buy, save for, own, and consume. As philosopher Herbert Marcuse noted, this alienation can lead to one-dimensionality when the alienated subject is swallowed up by his alienated existence and becomes indistinguishable from his society.† Such alienation results in perceiving all social values as personal values and social facts as absolute conditions of life. The individual thereby becomes unconscious of his actual human needs, and self-actualization becomes impossible.

> **A clam that forgets who he is
> suffers from alienation.**

*The word *reification* comes from the Latin term for "thing," *res.* Thus it literally means "thingification."

†For more details on the thought of Marcuse, see Chapter 12, pp. 277–281.

Stasis Stasis is the assumption that the state of the world is steady and unchanging. This leads to the belief that because it was difficult the last time you tried a politics for human beings, it must always be difficult again. Such a "things-will-always-be-the-same" attitude leads to an habitual rigid response to social facts rather than to a flexible and perceptive adjustment, countering changing conditions with changed strategies. The alienated person who believes in stasis can become completely impotent to satisfy his needs. And the successful, conservative individual believing in stasis can lose the whole game he is playing very quickly by acting as if events in the future would closely follow the pattern of events in the past. Stasis-thinking leads to mental rigidity that makes the satisfaction of the full range of human needs impossible.

**A clam that swims all waves
the same way is sick with
stasis.**

Pathological Ideology Ideology tends to freeze the human mind into believing in one unchanging set of values as eternal guides for proper behavior. This can feel very comfortable. In fact, most ideology can be defined as reified value-clusters that produce distorted images of reality. Ideologies are static and narrow ("All forms of democracy are good, all forms of communism are bad"; "All Catholics are virtuous, all Protestants are sinful.") Quite clearly, the rigidities of ideological thinking often lead to racism, nationalism, and war.

Any condition is pathological that prevents a human being from using social facts to satisfy his needs. The more basic the need that goes unsatisfied, the more extreme the pathology.[6] In political ideology there are two dominant kinds of pathology. One comes from the fixation on ideas, the other from fixation on action. The first is *pathological idealism*. Pathological idealists are so enchanted with their ideas or ideals that they neglect the practical considerations necessary to bring them about in the real world. The second is *pathological realism*. Pathological realists are so immersed in action that when they do obtain power they lack ideas to put in practice. The outcome of pathological realism is that power corrupts; the outcome of pathological idealism is that powerlessness corrupts.*

**Both clams that believe
they'll never meet clam-eaters and
clams that believe they always will
have pathological ideologies.**

The five tricks of the mind described above are all used by politicians and others to preserve existing social facts or to sell revolutionary,

**Political Consciousness:
Unmasking Social Facts**

*See Chapter 4 for examples of the pathological realism and idealism of the 1972 presidential campaign.

utopian programs based on social facts that are "bound" to come. In either case, if we are to be creative, we must be aware of these tricks that encourage us to submit to someone else's version of social facts, and we must know how to combat them. Political consciousness of the tension between human needs and social facts begins only when we unmask social facts and expose the tricks that maintain them for what they are. Philosopher Albert Camus wrote, "Beginning to think is beginning to be undermined. Society has but little connection with such beginnings."[7] Society discourages original thought and covers up human origins of social facts in order to maintain itself in all its imperfection. Political consciousness begins only when we become aware of society's cover-up and oppose its conditioning to the extent that it represses our human needs.

To Fight One-dimensionality: Know When Not to Take Reality for Granted   Living in the world as we know it as if it were the only world possible is a perfectly natural attitude—though dangerous in times of crisis. The sociologist Alfred Schutz describes this attitude:

> Thus, the social world into which man is born and within which he has to find his bearings is experienced by him as a tight knit web of social relationships, of systems of signs and symbols with their particular meaning structure, of institutionalized forms of social organization, of systems of status and prestige, etc. The meaning of all these elements of the social world in all its diversity and stratification, as well as the pattern of its texture itself, is by those living within it just taken for granted. . . . [They are] the good ways and the right ways for coming to terms with things and fellow-men. They are taken for granted because they have stood the test so far, and, being socially approved, are held as requiring neither an explanation nor a justification.[8]

Such taken-for-grantedness has serious political consequences. Each of us treats the world as he sees it as if that were the only way of seeing it. When someone else tells us of his own different impression of the world, we either manage to explain his different perception by utilizing our view ("You say the red traffic light is green, because you're color blind!") or we regard him as deviant and, perhaps, put him away ("You're nuts! Off to the booby-hatch!"). So persistent is our view of our reality as the only reality that entire nations have gone to war with other nations over different views of reality. The conflict between East and West, "libertarians" and "communists," turns around such different definitions of reality. The West claims, "Each man is human only to the extent that other men leave him alone to work out his own destiny"; the East claims, "Each man is human only to the degree that he works cooperatively with other men to construct the destiny of society."

The reason for all this onesidedness is that children in any society are taught to believe at an early age that there is one and only one set of rules and routines for getting along in the world. This process is called *socialization*. It makes American-born infants into Americans, French infants into Frenchmen, and so on.

These rules and routines include some for doing the official politics of the system. Political rules and values are sold to us as necessary to solving any tensions or problems we may perceive. That is, even when we have a problem *with* social reality, we are asked to use the norms and routines that keep that reality going to think our way *out* of that reality.

Often using official channels can result in small adjustments of social reality; but this procedure is like trying to make an omelet without cracking eggs. Taking the routines and norms of the everyday world for granted is useful, of course, as long as they work. But the need for politics arises proportionately with the degree to which such routines and norms do not work. One way to overcome this trick our mind plays on us—the smug taking for granted of our surroundings as the only possible reality—is to become aware that each of us has this tendency built into him.[9]

In stable times, standard operating procedures for evaluating what is important to us (norms) and for achieving what is important (routines) spare us from having to problem-solve creatively every time we scramble eggs, take the subway, or vote in an election. These procedures are conveniently left over and passed on to us by others who have solved similar problems. When the procedures stop working, however, it is good to remember that totally new problems often imply new ideas as to what is important to us (norms) and therefore new ways of achieving that which is newly important (new relationships with others, which later may become routines again).

A way of consciously escaping a less-and-less working reality is to try purposefully to look at the situation through the glasses of new norms and then try to determine what methods have to be constructed to achieve these norms. This method will be outlined later in the chapter.

To Fight Reification: Dereify Social Facts to Their Origins Another trick of the mind that discourages political action in the face of what seem to ·be overwhelming social facts is *reification*.[10] Reification makes us forget that all of social reality is man-made. When our minds reify social facts like social relationships or social institutions, these facts appear as things with a life of their own, rather than as mere arrangements to solve human needs.

Any social fact can become reified. When two hungry clam diggers, Alphonse and Balthazar, create a social relationship to dig more efficiently and call that relationship the Alphonse and Balthazar Clam-Digging and Cracking Corporation, they have merely turned a relationship into an object that seems more real than it is. Its origin and purpose is well known to them. When, however, they palm off this institution to others as the product of the Great Clam God, they are trying to reify the institution to safeguard it against interference. The human tendency is to respect relationships more when they can be portrayed as things. It helps if their origin can be ascribed to a nonhuman or superhuman source. Of course, that tendency also robs human beings of their power and will to revise or reconstruct such reified relationships in a way that would make them more in tune with their needs.

Reification is an extreme distortion of the natural product of man's expression of his needs: the social facts that are intended to make life easier and more meaningful.

In politics, a reified institution is a Congress that goes through the motions but no longer makes laws to satisfy human needs; a presidency to which subordinates feel loyalty even when the office or the incumbent engage in frustrating or destroying needs; or, in the politics of everyday life, a marriage in which the partners go through the routines although all meaning has long since vanished for them.

The way to overcome reification is to remember that no matter how superhuman or superpowerful an institution may seem, it is man-made—and that men can therefore unmake or remake that institution.[11]

To Fight Alienation: Leave Phoney Happiness to Create Your Own World   The concept of alienation first enters modern discourse through Karl Marx's sociological work, in which he argues as follows: Human beings have certain capacities and potentials. Among them is an individual's capacity to use his labor to create his own social world. When this social world takes on a reality outside and opposed to men, something that originally has belonged to them has been taken from them. They have become alienated from their own labor and product of their labor and therefore from themselves as world-creating beings. "The *alienation* of the worker in his product," said Marx, "means not only that his labour becomes an object, assumes an *external* existence, but that it exists independently, *outside himself,* and alien to him, and that it stands opposed to him as an autonomous power. The life which he has given to the object sets itself against him as an alien and hostile force."[12]

Some recent sociologists have interpreted this insight socio-psychologically.[13] They see alienation as a state of mind produced by accepting social facts as concrete and unmovable. Since it is a human tendency to escape from the burden and insecurity of creativeness into the comfortable belief in absolutes, the man who accepts the reification of society may actually think himself *happy* in his alienated state of mind. Just as uncertainty accompanies the act of social creation, like that which Alphonse and Balthazar undertook, false security and even apparent happiness may accompany life in a reified society.[14] In such a state of mind, people like ourselves and the Know-Nothings of Inlandia (befuddled by too much clam sauce) may never raise the question of whether reified social reality actually fulfills our needs.

The tendency toward accepting the world as it is and being "happy" in it is understandable, since we are born into a world that is already a "finished" product. We are taught, as children, the meaning of that world's routines and norms and even that world's meaning of "happiness." But we do not remain children forever. Creative adults have further needs than mere security—for example, as psychologist

Abraham Maslow suggested, gaining self-esteem and moving toward self-actualization. Such needs imply the desire to at least partly create one's own world. For this purpose, it is important to recognize and consciously reject the childhood tendency to accept the world as it is. To find yourself, create your own world.

To Fight Stasis: Use the Three-Stage Cycle of History   While it is healthy to respect the power of social institutions in order to calculate that power as an obstacle or tool in one's own political efforts, it is not healthy to give up on politics if once set back by powerful social institutions. The fact of the matter is that social institutions, because they are made up of people, do not have an infinite reservoir of power. Also, not only social institutions but whole societies change in terms of the amount of power they can muster against the individual seeking to do a politics of human needs.

Societies are no more than complex sets of arrangements among human beings, created to solve their tensions and satisfy their needs. As such, societies go through a three-stage process:

1. Men *create* societies as answers to their needs.
2. Societies, once created, become social facts that structure the daily lives of individuals. (When these objects seem to take on a life of their own, independent of human origins or purposes, we call them *reifications*.)
3. Once created, a society is then presented to newcomers as a reality to be accepted and learned.

The sociologist Peter Berger labels these three steps *externalization* (because the individual expresses the needs inside him); *objectivation* (because the products of externalization become objects in daily life), and *socialization* (because newcomers—usually babies—are socialized into the norms and routines of this man-created social world).[15] Socialization is an essential method of maintenance.

But what makes socialization go on from one generation to the next? Socialization is successful if the routines and norms taught serve as successful recipes for conducting daily life. When these recipes fail, socialization is eventually shucked off.

The alternative to socialization is the *decay* of society. This also holds true for political systems. In the sense that routines followed and norms held by individuals change, all social systems—defined as the complex of routines and norms in effect at any time—eventually decay. When the new routines and norms that succeed the discarded ones are perceived as radically different, it may be said that the old social system— including its political system—has been replaced.

It makes sense, then to speak of the creation, maintenance, and decay of social and political systems. Historians and philosophers—Oswald Spengler, Arnold Toynbee, and Pitirim Sorokin, for example—have suggested such a three-stage theory of history for years.[16] But while there has

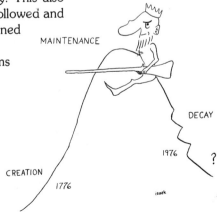

been a tendency at times to consider the cycle the result of barely comprehensible forces, we suggest that it is merely the result of the interaction of social systems and human problems. When men have problems, they create; when they believe their problems are solved, they maintain; when they believe their problems are *not* solved by their system, they allow it to decay—and perhaps try to create a new one.

If this is so, then the task for political individuals is to find their place in the cycle before committing themselves to doing politics. Their place in the cycle will determine to a large degree what kind of political strategy can succeed.

To Fight Pathological Idealism and Realism: Take a Critical Stance for Action A *pathological belief* is a rigid image of the world that does not fit reality.[17] Human beings have two important tendencies in regard to politics. One, *pathological idealism,* is to believe that one's own goals or ideas can be translated into reality without considering the opposition of already existing social facts. The other, *pathological realism,* is to believe that social reality is so strong that nothing except power can avail against it.

A typical pathological realist is the man whose view of politics is restricted to conflict situations. This individual, expecting only conflict in politics, will create conflict even if there is none to begin with—a self-fulfilling prophecy. He will know only how to mobilize power to bludgeon his enemies—never how to use ideas to win their cooperation. Similarly, the men who restrict their notion to cooperation only are also pathological. Their rigidly optimistic image of the world blinds them to realities of opposition from social facts, such as existing institutions and existing personalities. Their view of politics may be called pathological idealism.

The response to both these tendencies is to remember constantly that man is indeed the creator of his world, but that this world, once created, is a solid reality that must be taken into account in further attempts to externalize our ideas or needs.

The stance to take toward one's own needs and toward society's demands is a critical one—in the sense of evaluating the gap between the two and the chances for narrowing that gap.

Critiquing Political Reality It is difficult to bring our mind to question political reality as it is. We are born into political reality. We are taught it is good (socialization). We accept its institutions as if they were made by the gods themselves (reification). And, even in the face of contradictory evidence, we believe we ought to be happy in it (alienation) because this reality is the only possible one (one-dimensionality) and will always be around (stasis).

But how then can we tell at any given moment whether we are really involved in a politics that tries to fulfill human needs in the face of social facts? How can we be sure we are not prisoners of pseudopolitics that engages us in surface activity without solving problems based on our needs?

How can we escape pseudopolitics, and how can we begin to rethink the world as it might be?

To stage this escape, we must get an outside perspective on ourselves—become critics. Becoming a critic requires the mental exercise of stepping outside our involvement in daily life. The critic steps to the periphery of his daily world and onto a platform of ideas *about* that world, against which he measures the performance of that world.

There are at least three kinds of critics.

The reformist critic measures his world with the ideas that his founding fathers used to create that world. In America he asks, "Life, liberty, property—these are the Founding Fathers' ideals. Have they been fulfilled in America?"

The revolutionary critic steps totally ouside the norms and routines of the world he seeks to criticize. Taking a different set of values, he tests his reality's performance against these standards. A humanist Marxist looking at America, for example, may admit widespread material well-being. But he will ask to what extent well-off Americans are really "happy," in the sense that the work they do is creative and the lives they live are loving.*

The scientific critic, finally, bases his criticism on the latest discoveries about human nature. Recognizing that in America the views of reformists and Marxist revolutionaries tend to be at least 100 years old, he will measure his society's fulfillment of human needs according to a modern view of human nature based on recent scientific findings. One set of such needs are those proposed by the psychologist Abraham Maslow: physical needs, safety needs, self-esteem needs, love needs, and self-actualization needs. The scientific critic, using this set of needs, would ask of any political system, "To what extent does it work to fulfill these needs?" He would find that few systems make any effort at all to fulfill all five.†

INVITATION

Practice being a critic—reformist, revolutionary, or scientific.

To be a reformist critic, **take any of the ideals stated in the United States Constitution and ask, To what extent is this ideal practiced in the political reality I live in? For example: freedom of the press rights in the First Amendment—does even a Communist have the right to say anything he wants to? Or equal protection of the laws—who can afford a lawyer? What quality of lawyer? Are the courts available to the poor? (See also Chapter 4.)**

To be a *revolutionary critic,* read up on the values of a different political system—for example, a Marxist system. Then analyze to what degree these ideals are not met in the American system.

---

*See Chapter 12, pp. 277 to 281.
†See Chapter 6, pp. 122 to 125, for details on Maslow's set of needs.

To be a scientific critic, read up on Abraham Maslow's five needs (see Chapter 6). Then ask to what extent your system is set up to fulfill those needs. Does politics in America work to fulfill love needs, for example? Do self-esteem needs nullify satisfaction of love needs? Can power politics possibly be a politics of love?

DOING POLITICS

Doing politics involves five steps. Remember that politics is always a social act between at least two people who mutually try to resolve the tension between their needs and social facts. This definition already suggests the steps necessary to do politics:

1. Know what you want (*values* based on needs).
2. Identify and mobilize others who want it (political colleagues).
3. Determine how badly you want it (factor of *personality*).
4. Know where you are—locate yourself in political time (stage of the *cycle*) and space (environment of *social* and *political institutions*).
5. Find the rules for your game—and engage.

Knowing What You Want

What you want is not necessarily what you need. Values are the goals that people strive after. But some values are socially determined, and society usually provides standard rules of the game for getting these values. Other values are goals based on human needs; since no society fulfills all human needs, some of these values will be harder to obtain.

To assess how tough it is to reach your goal before you start:

1. Determine to what extent your values are related to human needs—physical needs (food, water, sleep), safety needs, self-esteem needs, love needs, self-actualization needs.*
2. Determine to what extent your social situation or society is set up to deny fulfillment of these needs.

The gap between your values, as defined in terms of human needs, and the values of society will indicate the degree of tension that your political action will have to overcome.

Identifying and Mobilizing Political Colleagues

The basic needs of human beings are more easily satisfied through cooperation with others; some, in fact, cannot be satisfied without others. A designer of political systems as pessimistic about human cooperation as Thomas Hobbes had to admit that even basic physiological and security needs can be fulfilled only through collaboration. The other choice—the isolation of each individual from every other—is no longer possible in a mass society, and is also more inefficient. Even if physiological and safety needs might be achieved through isolation, the other three—self-esteem, love, and self-actualization—cannot be achieved except with and through others.

*See Chapter 6, pp. 122 to 129, for details.

The fact that most politics in America today is not cooperative politics is merely evidence of the underdevelopment of our country in achieving love, self-esteem, or self-actualization.

To enhance your chances for fulfilling your needs, therefore,

1. Find others who share your perception of needs, or
2. Persuade others to share your perceptions;
3. Identify others who do not share your perceived needs and who cannot be persuaded to share them; these people are social facts arrayed against you.

Above all, find out first with whom you can cooperate to do a politics for human beings before looking for enemies with whom to do the power politics of conflict.

Psyching Out Personality

Finding out how badly you and others want to reach your goal—and how badly opponents want to prevent you from reaching it—gives you a measure of the intensity of commitment or conflict that you can expect. Psyching out the personality of others is a very complex task, but for practical purposes it is crucial to understand yourself and others in at least two respects:

1. Of yourself, ask, How important in my order of values is the value I am trying to obtain? (If low in the order, I can expect my own commitment to falter when more important values are endangered by my political action).

Of yourself, ask also, How committed am I to working with others to reach my goals—that is, how political am I? If the goal doesn't seem worth the effort, perhaps you had better not engage the energies of others.

2. Of others, ask, to what extent do their values coincide with mine? (If their order of values differs markedly from mine, I can expect desertions from our effort at crucial points. If their order of values differs radically, I have found an opponent.)

Of others, ask, How committed are they to political action? (This can be determined by inquiring where on their order of values our specific goal stands, and by finding out how committed they were in similar past situations.)*

In regard to both self and others, these questions test for priority of values and motivation.

Locating Yourself in Political Time and Space

Political time is your place in the historical creation-maintenance-decay cycle. *Political space* is your position relative to others in *class, status*, and *access to political institutions*. These are the social facts within which every one of us is committed to do politics. To let such facts overwhelm our spirit is pathological realism; to ignore reality is pathological idealism. In the 1972 presidential election, one candidate succumbed to pathological realism, amassing money and

*On specific psychological approaches to the role of personality in politics, see Chapter 5.

sabotaging the opposition, believing only the exercise of naked power could win. The other candidate believed pure ideas could triumph, evidenced in an appeal to conscience and good will in his constituents. Richard M. Nixon won the presidency and power—but began to lose out when it became clear he had no understanding for those ideas that make political life worthwhile for Americans. George McGovern lost the presidency and power—but his ideas remained a model of what political life might be like and how it could be made worthwhile. Clearly the man who knows how to tune in to the ideas of his time and balance power with them would be at an advantage—a man subject to neither the pathology of realism or the pathology of idealism.

A sound political evaluation of the chances for success for your goals begins with recognizing your location in political time. Location in political time is never clear-cut, but is constant motion from one stage to another.

To locate yourself in political time, ask these three questions:

1. What social relationships have been created for me that I cannot affect? Or, Whose victim am I?

2. What social relationships do I partly control? Or, to what extent can I work the system to get my values?

3. What social relationships am I free to totally create? Or, Am I free to create my life with others?

Depending on which of these questions gives you the most relevant answers at this time, you will find yourself in (1) an era of maintenance or reification, (2) a period of partial institutionalization (partial maintenance) or partial decay, or (3) a period of revolution or creativity.

Where you are in political time and what your chances are for doing anything about it can be envisioned on a chart like Figure 3.1.

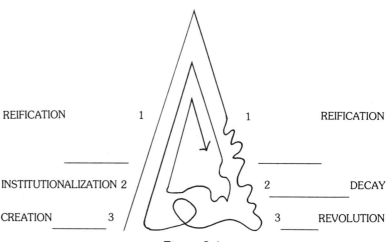

REIFICATION 1   1 REIFICATION

INSTITUTIONALIZATION 2   2 DECAY

CREATION 3   3 REVOLUTION

Figure 3-1
The Cycle of Politics

To locate yourself in political space, ask these three questions:

1. In regard to *class:* How many resources (money, property, skills) can I muster in relation to others—either those who work *with* me or those who work *against* me? The answer partly determines your chances for leadership among colleagues and your chances of success against the mobilized resources of others. In other words, the answer indicates your economic power position.

2. In regard to *status:* How much deference do I get, as compared with others? Status again affects the chances that others (who are with you) will let you lead and that others (who are against you) will put you on "enemy" lists. The answer to this question indicates your social power position.

3. In regard to *political institutions:* What is my relative access to political institutions that might work in my favor—compared with the opposition's access to political institutions that might work against my goals? Access to political institutions determines your political power position.

What you can do to get what you want depends on where your political space and time intersect. This intersection is also called your social role.* Accurate perception of where your political space and time intersect will also logically tell you by what rules to play to win.

Choosing the Rules for Your Game

If you live in a time of maintenance and are of low class, low status, and low access to institutions, it is in the interest of just about everyone else above you to have you play by *their* rules of the game. The *rules of a political game* are usually set up to keep the distribution of values where it is. To play by the rules of others may mean to always lose the game. But in a time of maintenance, *not* to play by the rules of others usually means not to play at all.

In all societies, people who don't play by the rules when everyone else is happy with the rules are killed, imprisoned, or put in insane asylums. Nevertheless, a human being may choose to die rather than live by rules that deny the value of living like a human being. Such a choice can only be made rationally, however, after thorough evaluation of your position. If the choice is death with dignity, the problem still remains to make that death a political one, with the widest possible impact on others who might empathize with your values and be stirred into action by this final act. Such acts of self-immolation have been practiced recently in seemingly hopeless situations like South Vietnam and Czechoslovakia.

If you live in a time shifting from the maintenance of political and social institutions to their decay, the evaluation of your position becomes extremely delicate. Finding colleagues for coalition building will often involve dealing with people whose values are not clear, who are in the process of changing their minds. Similarly, behavior patterns of personality are changing, and colleagues have to be selected with both

*Here "role" is used to mean a specific pattern of social conduct that provides the basis for potential political power.

courageous confidence and cautious trepidation. It is crucial in such a time to identify social and political institutions that are weaker than others for possible conversion into machinery for seeking your goals —or for neutralization.

Similarly, the opportunities for changing your relative power position through manipulating class and status can be enhanced. As to the rules of the game, this is a good time to use those rules of the game that favor your goals and to try to alter others that don't. Those for whom the old rules still work can, of course, be expected to defend them—ultimately by force.

The best time for conducting politics like a human being is a time of creation. Even then the social facts that have to be taken into account are other human beings with their personalities and their ideas. But social and political institutions in such times tend to be weak or broken down and are not easily mobilized against you. What we are left with in such times are the challenges of the environment, which must be met if we are to survive, and the obstinacies of human nature—tendencies toward emotionalism, low consciousness, reification, and seeking a smug home in an alienated state.

The most difficult thing for those who do politics in a time of creation is to convince one another that politics must be an ongoing creative process, and that they should not escape into the tempting comforts of over-institutionalization, in which politics becomes subordinate to society. In such times human beings are lucky to be able to create their own rules for the game of politics. If they are also forward-looking, they will see to it that these rules contain one rule against any other rule ever becoming frozen. Politics must never stop trying to resolve ever-new tensions arising from changing human needs and changing social facts.

INCONCLUSIONS If you accept the definition of politics as social action to resolve the tension between human needs and social facts, it becomes apparent that politics goes on everywhere that human needs are frustrated by social facts—from family politics to international politics. But such political awareness is not enough to satisfy needs. To *do* politics, you must be able to unmask the social facts of everyday life and see how they work. At least five kinds of social facts support or frustrate human needs: rules of the game, values, social institutions, political institutions, and personalities. Effective political action depends upon being able to work with these five variables. *How* one uses such social facts results in political style. Cooperative and power politics are, perhaps, the most distinctive styles.

It is to the advantage of those in power who use the style of power politics to maintain existing social facts by rendering the masses below politically unconscious. To be politically unconscious is to submit to social facts and to be unaware that these facts frustrate human needs. Five mental tricks help to make people politically unconscious: one-dimensionality, reification, alienation, stasis, and pathological ideology. To regain political consciousness, it is necessary to fight against these mental tricks continuously.

I fight one-dimensionality by not taking anything for granted —including the way I was brought up, the way I have been carefully taught to do things, the way society has seemed to map out my future. Fresh alternatives can open up if I unmask reifications or frozen mind-warps that make abstractions seem like unchangeable things—abstractions such as "The State," for instance. The propaganda surrounding such reifications can easily dupe me into alienation from myself and others, but I can fight alienation by recreating myself and new social relationships to solve my needs. To rid myself of alienation, it helps to reject the mental trick of stasis—the idea that social facts never change and that therefore I must take everything as it comes. By refusing to be taken and accurately locating myself in the continual social cycles of creation, maintenance, and decay, I can catch creative waves when they come and learn to take one step back when it is a time for silence and waiting.

Without this ability to get out of my own way, and see things as they are, I may fall into the last mental trap: pathological ideology. Pathological idealists keep running into brick walls of social fact without learning how to penetrate or scale them, whereas pathological realists pursue power for its own sake to the point that they become indistinguishable from existing social facts. Both are pathological in that they hold rigid mental images of the world, which they don't change even when new information comes in. Thus, they can never adapt creatively to the real world.

Once I have learned to avoid these mental tricks by becoming a social critic, I can organize to do politics in five steps: knowing what I want, mobilizing others who want it, knowing how badly I want it, locating myself and others in political time and space, and discovering the rules of the game. Three questions then serve as useful guides to political action: (1) What social relationships have been created for me that I cannot affect? Or, Whose victim am I? (2) What social relationships do I partly control? Or, to what extent can I work the system to get my values? (3) What social relationships am I free to totally create? Or, Am I free to create my life with others?

The answers to these questions will tell me whether I am in a period of maintenance, decay, or creativity in social relationships and help to focus political action where it does the most good. And if all three questions apply to some extent to my situation, I will know which political style to use with which kinds of social facts, and I will be prepared to change styles as the political drama casts me into different parts. For how dehumanizing it would be to have to wear the same mask all the time!

REFERENCES

1. Michael P. Lerner, "The Future of the Two-Party System," in *1984 Revisited: Prospects for American Politics,* ed. Robert Paul Wolff (New York: Knopf, Borzoi Books, 1973), p. 137.

2. An excellent book on the rules of the game of politics as played in the United States, Britain, and the Soviet Union is H. Mark Roelofs, *The Language of Modern Politics: An Introduction to the Study of Government* (Homewood, Ill.: Dorsey, 1967).

3. On American social and political values, see also Roelofs, *The Language of Modern Politics;* Louis Hartz, *The Liberal Tradition in America: An Interpretation of American Political Thought Since the Revolution* (New York: Harcourt Brace Jovanovich, 1955); and Robin M. Williams, *The American Society: A Sociological Interpretation,* 3rd ed. (New York: Knopf, 1970).

4. See Richard M. Scammon and Ben J. Wattenberg, *The Real Majority* (New York: G. Putnam's Sons, Berkley Publishing, 1972).

5. On how reification dehumanizes individuals in international politics, see Robert A. Isaak, "The Individual in International Politics: Solving the Level-of-Analysis Problem," *Polity* 7 (Winter 1974).

6. In social and political behavior, the social scientist Kenneth Boulding has defined pathological belief as a rigid image of the world that does not fit reality. See Kenneth Boulding, "Learning and Reality-Testing Process in the International System," in *Image and Reality in World Politics,* ed. John C. Farrell and Asa P. Smith (New York: Columbia University Press, 1968), pp. 1-15.

7. Albert Camus, *The Myth of Sisyphus* (New York: Knopf, Vintage Books, 1955), p. 1.

8. Alfred Schutz, "Equality and the Meaning-Structure of the Social World," in *Collected Papers,* vol. 2 (The Hague: Martinus Nijhoff, 1964), pp. 230-231.

9. People cling to their reality even when it is challenged by incontrovertible facts. See, for example, Leon Festinger, H. W. Riecken Jr., and S. Schachter, *When Prophecy Fails* (Minneapolis: University of Minnesota Press, 1956). This is a fascinating account of people clinging to their view of reality, which involved a prophecy of the end of the world, even after the world did not end on the appointed day.

10. The term is said to have been used first by the German philosopher Georg Wilhelm Friedrich Hegel in the word *"Verdinglichung",* which literally means the process of turning some event into a thing. In contrast, *"Versachlichung"* refers to turning something into an object (*Sache*) of human manipulation. This term has been translated by the sociologist Peter Berger as "objectivation," a perfectly acceptable process of turning human needs into social relationships for the satisfaction of those needs. See Peter Berger and Thomas Luckman, *The Social Construction of Reality* (Garden City, N.Y.: Doubleday, Anchor Books, 1967), p. 34 ff.

11. See the discussion on reification in Berger and Luckman, *Social Construction of Reality,* pp. 88-92.

12. Karl Marx, "Alienated Labour," in *Karl Marx—Early Writings,* ed. and trans. T. B. Bottomore (New York: McGraw-Hill, 1964), pp. 122-123.

13. Berger and Luckman, *Social Construction of Reality,* pp. 200-201ff.

14. Peter Berger, unpublished lectures, The New School for Social Research, 1968. See Berger and Luckman, *Social Construction of Reality,* pp. 89-92, for a thorough treatment of the concept of reification.

15. See Berger and Luckman, *Social Construction of Reality.* The entire book is divided into three parts, corresponding to these three steps.

16. See Oswald Spengler, *The Decline of the West,* trans. C. Atkinson (New York: Modern Library, 1965); Arnold Toynbee, *A Study of History* (New York: Oxford University Press, 1961); and Pitirim Sorokin, *Social and Cultural Dynamics,* 4 vols. (New York: Bedminster Press, 1937).

17. See Kenneth Boulding's lucid theory of knowledge for the everyday human being in *The Image: Knowledge in Life and Society* (Ann Arbor, Mich.: The University of Michigan Press, Ann Arbor Paperbacks, 1956), Chapter V: "The Public Image and the Sociology of Knowledge," pp. 64-81. Elsewhere, Boulding writes that "what we ordinarily think of as mental disease is the inability to perform reality-testing—the progressive elimination of error—on the folk-learning level. If a person's image of the world is entirely self-justified and self-evident, he will soon get into serious trouble. . . . Such

a person is incapable of learning, and it is this incapacity that really constitutes mental disease." Kenneth Boulding, "Learning and Reality-Testing Process in the International System," in *Image and Reality in World Politics,* ed. John C. Farrell and Asa P. Smith (New York: Columbia University Press, 1968), p. 3.

isaak

4 In which the reader sees how it is possible to be actively political by applying five steps for doing politics. The Watergate affair and the McGovern grassroots campaign serve as examples and warnings.

4 Executing Politics

Knowing how to do politics is inseparable from actually doing it. Theorists remain mere theorists unless they put their ideas into practice. Practitioners remain doomed to failure unless they think while doing. With political executions going on all around us, this inseparable connection between political theory and practice confronts Everyman every day. The Watergate affair that surrounded the American presidential election of 1972 demonstrated what happens when people have either too much or too little faith in the traditional rules of the political game. Social reality *is* the execution of ideas.

Moreover, despite the shame of Watergate, the 1972 election also demonstrated that it is still possible for little people to do politics in America—up to a point. The McGovern candidacy, through the primaries and even up to the Democratic National Convention, showed that one can organize little people with little money to achieve big results. But the McGovern campaign's dogmatic idealism and insensitivity to the needs of others which alienated the traditional power blocs of the Democratic Party illustrated the dangers of ignoring the variables of social fact: rules, values, personalities, socio-economic status, and access to institutions.

The history of the 1972 presidential election shows that unless you resolve the tension between existing needs and facts, you can win and still lose. George McGovern's grassroots organization succeeded in taking over the Democratic Convention but lost the support of traditional Democrats. Richard Nixon's political machine won the election but lost the confidence of the country.

This chapter discusses how to make the social facts surrounding you work for you politically. The mistakes of McGovern and Nixon provide a basis for understanding how to execute politics without being executed by it. First, consider the following invitation:

INVITATION

Judging from the facts of the Watergate investigation, what social facts did Nixonites ignore?

Judging from the disaster of his election campaign following his successful primary effort, what social facts did McGovern's managers ignore?

Now consider our analysis of the McGovern and Nixon campaigns as tales of success and failure in doing politics. Knowing what you now know about politics, could you have avoided their mistakes?

The campaign of 1972 led to disaster for both parties—and for the country—because of the Nixonites' pathological realism and the McGovernites' pathological idealism.

People who freeze or reify their perceptions of the political process tend to end up as pathological idealists or pathological realists—pathological in the sense that their rigid images of the world do not fit reality.* Pathological idealists believe that men can do politics by ideas alone. Pathological realists believe that politics is done by power alone. Think of the Watergate affair surrounding the 1972 presidential election. What about McGovern and Nixon? Who was hung up on ideas and who was hung up on power?

KNOWING WHAT YOU WANT—MAINTAINING THE SYSTEM VS. CHANGING IT

The Appeal of Maintenance

In 1972 many people saw America going from maintenance to decay. McGovern tried to sell this idea as the basis for his campaign: "Come Home America." Nixon countered that people were already at home and promised "Four More Years." How one sees social facts depends upon where one is standing. People who didn't have very much—the blacks, the poor, some youth, and some women—responded to McGovern's appeal, along with those whose conscience was stirred by guilt concerning the war in Vietnam and other social problems. People who thought they had something significant to maintain—middle Americans afraid of losing what they had—went for the man who promised at least four more years of it. Most people perceived Nixon as a maintenance man and McGovern as a radical (in the sense of changing things at their roots).

INVITATION

To find out what "radical" is for Americans, try this experiment on a group of friends or a class.

First, ask for a show of hands of those who think they'll make more than $50,000 a year at any time in their lives.

Then ask who would support a proposal that all income in excess of $50,000 a year should be taxed 100 percent—so that money could go to people who need it. This proposal was attributed to McGovern in 1972. For one group's experience with this invitation, see Chapter 5, p. 91.

Ironically, both McGovern and Nixon perceived themselves as maintenance men. McGovern saw himself as calling for a return to original American ideals. Nixon aimed his pitch at maintaining the style and level of life to which middle Americans had become accustomed.

Middle Americans—those who had climbed into the middle of the American social and economic pyramid—thought that when

---

*See the discussion on pathological realism and pathological idealism in Chapter 3, pages 41 to 42.

Nixon won they had won the election. Actually, they failed to achieve security in their social and economic position because of three misconceptions of what the election was all about:

1. They perceived McGovern as un-American, when actually he was most traditionally American, right down to his idealistic roots.

2. They perceived Nixon as preserving for them the goods they had gained through traditional politics, whereas Nixon actually strengthened the new politics of a rule by "experts" and powerful corporations that had begun a takeover of America.[1]

3. They perceived as worth putting on their enemy list the poor, the black, and the strange—when these people actually were also trying to use traditional politics to get the goods. In black-listing such "enemies," they overlooked their real foes, corporations who had already gotten most of the goods—and were trying to get more by riding an economic boom. The results of this boom, for the little guy, were unemployment, devaluation of the dollar, rising prices, tight loans, and high mortgage costs.

Middle Americans voted out of fear of losing the goods they barely possessed (the house the bank owned, the job the corporation controlled, and the savings drifting in the winds of inflation) and out of fear of losing the American dream (the belief that you can always climb upward to get more of what there is to get).[2] There is at least one lesson in the McGovern-Nixon experience with the problem of values: you can start with your needs, but if you overlook the needs or wants of others—which are *social facts*—you can't win.

Fear in Middle America

INVITATION

To understand what it means to be a middle American, imagine you have worked hard all your life to get a home, that you have to stay on the job every day to support your wife and three or four kids, that any extra expense that comes along (illness, taxes, tuition rises) cuts into your money for food, mortgage payments, and clothing.

Now ask yourself the following questions, answering first the left-hand segment of each question and then the right-hand segment.

Jobs

Are you for giving every youngster in America the right to an apprenticeship? . . .

Even if giving one to a black youngster means taking one away from a white youngster? Yours?

Housing

Should every family in America have the right to a decent home? . . .

Even if you have to pay higher taxes to give it to them?

Schools

Shouldn't there be a right for an equal education whether you are poor or not? . . .

Even if bringing poor people into your school system means importing a lot of social and economic problems that poor people have?

Middle Americans are especially aware that there isn't an unlimited number of jobs, or apprenticeships, to go around. When there is scarcity, how liberal do you want to be with your son's future? So-called liberal union members have recently become conservative on this issue, especially when the effects hit close to home.

Property taxes in many states are perceived as too high by owners of small family homes. "Reform" movements, which used to pledge an increase in city services, are now promising tax cuts, which mean *reduction* in city services—and they are succeeding in appeals to voters. A "reform" administration recently took over Jersey City, New Jersey, infamous for being one of the most corrupt cities in the country, and immediately delivered a 10 percent tax cut.

Traditionally "liberal" groups, such as Jewish voters in New York City, are now taking conservative stands against opening up their schools to poor newcomers, such as Puerto Ricans and blacks.

The Changing American Creed

Typical answers to questions like those in the preceding Invitation show that many Americans are split in their own minds as to what they believe.

The traditional American creed exalted *property* as the goal and insisted on the use of one's *life* and *liberty* to *work competitively* against others, asserting one's *individualism* and human worth on the way to attaining property.* That used to be a revolutionary acquisitive creed, stemming from the revolt of English entrepreneurs against the feudal system. It was imported by our founding fathers to America.[3]

Today most Americans—those who see themselves as the middle class—believe they have gained a modicum of life, liberty, and property, according to public opinion surveys.[4] Their problem now is to hold on to what they have gained. That means also that their values must change.[5] Liberty, for example, no longer means the freedom of all to work unhindered in the acquisition of property. To the property-owner, the man who already has made it, it means being free and secure in the use of his property. When others claim the old American liberty to get their own property, he feels his new liberty, of the security brand, endangered.

*Until quite recently, the italicized words were unquestioned basic goals of Americans and were understood in the sense of this sentence.

When people's basic worries change, often because of a change in where they stand in their society or economy, their values may change. Most Americans feel they have achieved some success in the acquisition of the primary value of property, and the security that implies. Their feeling may account for the fact that they continue to deny use of the same values—job opportunities to acquire property—to those still poor, especially when this connotes the insecurity of redistributing property. Knowing that property arrangements are not settled once and for all means liberty to the propertyless, for it promises hope of attaining property. That same knowledge, or the threat of it, means insecurity to the property owner, for it suggests that someone may take away what he owns. While both may talk of liberty, liberty to the poor means freedom to move up the ladder, while liberty to the better off means freedom to block a couple of rungs of that ladder so as to keep the poor at a distance.

There is a collision here between two value systems that are becoming rapidly more different, despite the echoing rhetoric of life, liberty, and the pursuit of happiness. The politician who does not tune in to this difference, or who refuses to use social researchers whose tools can help him tune in, is doomed to defeat.

ORGANIZING OTHERS WHO WANT WHAT YOU WANT

Idealist and Realist

Your strategy of organizing personnel depends on how you see the world. Idealists tend to construct their own social reality out of little people (they know that human beings interact to create their social world). Realists tend to maintain social reality by obtaining political support from big people (they know that big people control social facts—money, institutions, skills).

McGovern was an idealist who became pathological. Nixon was a realist who stayed pathological. McGovern's idealism gave him confidence in ideas. By using the idea of grassroots organization, he managed to construct the political reality of winning the primaries. He then became a *pathological* idealist when he failed to broaden his support for the election by taking in enough big people. Although his idealism won him the support of some young, some women, most blacks, and many poor, his lack of realism lost him the traditional Franklin D. Roosevelt coalition of the Democratic Party—big labor, the big city vote, the South, and the minimum of at least some big corporations.

Nixon's realism gave him confidence in power. By using power, he succeeded in the primaries without even running. For a while it even seemed that his pathological realism had worked—after all, he did win the election. But then came the Watergate affair and the exposure of just how he had won the election. Normally his pathological realism in overinsuring his election by all means possible could have led to instant disaster. Within weeks after the Senate began the Watergate hearings, 71 percent of the people believed Nixon either planned or knew of the Watergate affair, or was involved in the coverup. What saved him in the immediate aftermath of the scandal was the still-persisting concern of middle Americans for security—a fear which he in his realism had manipulated for the election. As a result, a few weeks into the hearings, only 18 percent of the electorate believed he should be compelled to leave office.[6]

The McGovern Strategy   To see how McGovern's idealism worked in doing politics successfully at first, read an interpretation of a *New York Times* report on his primary campaign:

McGovern's Route to the Top   "Revolutions" can be planned by political men who know their time and place: *Choosing the rules of your game.*

> "I honestly don't think there has been a major surprise in the last two years," said Gary Hart, the 34-year-old manager of Senator George McGovern's Presidential campaign, speaking calmly of a revolution in Democratic party politics that caught almost everyone else unawares.

Political relationships begin with lonely figures looking for others to share a problem: *Knowing what you want and organizing personnel.* Political success means to *know what you want* and to find enough others to help get it.

> He suffered one dark moment last January, Mr. Hart confessed. Watching the virtual parade of Democratic leaders to endorse Senator Edmund S. Muskie, he had looked ahead to the first primary and pictured himself and Joe Grandmaison, his New Hampshire coordinator, standing alone on a street corner passing out leaflets as the candidate drove his own car around to the state's college campuses.

Also know *who else wants what you want* and what their chances are of getting it.

> But depression passed quickly, and only three days after Mr. McGovern's remarkably strong second-place showing in the March 7 New Hampshire primary, Mr. Hart finished a reconnaissance of Florida and declared unemotionally: "It's all over. Ed Muskie has got to get off the ground here and he isn't doing it. John Lindsay has got to get off the ground and he isn't doing it either. That means the race through the rest of the primaries is going to be us against Hubert Humphrey, and that means we're going to win."

Political mysteries are reifications that can be unraveled by asking, What's the problem? Who shares it? What arrangement has been created to solve it? Obviously there are people out there who share the problems of a rural, radical, baldish former minister and are willing to engage in a relationship with him. *Analyzing personality is seeing some of yourself in others.*

> George McGovern's candidacy was still being widely discounted three months ago when the feeling of anticlimax settled on Mr. Hart. Even now the blossoming of George McGovern—a baldish, former minister and rural radical who campaigned for a full year without exceeding 5 per cent in the Democratic preference polls and is now on the verge of winning the nomination—is generally considered mysterious. How did he do it?

By asking himself often enough, "Whose victim am I? To what extent can I work the system? Am I free to create myself with others?"—the questions for positioning oneself in political cycles—McGovern was able to find a successful political formula for the primaries.

> Some of the critical elements in the emergence of this one-time 500-to-1 long shot were beyond his control, including the acceleration of the war in Vietnam at the culmination of his all-important drive in Wisconsin; the heavy damage that Gov. George C. Wallace of Alabama inflicted on the Democratic establishment, and Senator Humphrey's inroads against Senator Muskie.
>
> But George McGovern, who suspects that but for his own hesitation in 1967 he might be President today, had decided, at all events, to be prepared for opportunity this year. And he was.
>
> The most obvious of the ironies about Mr. McGovern's unheralded triumph is that the candidate and his staff predicted almost all of it—early, often and in detail. It is also striking that the same professionals who laughingly dismissed his chances last winter say now that it has been a triumph of basic political skills—the political equivalent of the late Vince Lombardi's "back-to-fundamentals" football.

Of course, it also helped for McGovern to have rewritten the rules for delegate selection several years earlier, as chairman of a convention reform committee. Using McGovern's ideas to rewrite the rules seemed like idealism that might work. Idealism becomes pathological when your own rules restrict you to a commitment to the powerless, whereas commitment by the powerful (the big people in the FDR coalition) is needed to win. Watch out for what your ideas do to social institutions that you need—like big labor.

> "McGovern understood something that Muskie and Humphrey didn't: that the way you win conventions is to win delegates," says Joseph Napolitan, the political consultant and author. "He went after delegates in the nonprimary states. In addition to grass-roots organization, he had the best commercials on television—and more of them. He mastered the mechanics."

If the machinery of the existing political system won't work for you, go to the people . . . and organize (just don't ignore the reality of the system).

> The premises that Gary Hart outlined to disbelieving newsmen last summer, where Senator Muskie was widely thought to be unbeatable for the Democratic nomination, proved sound and relevant.
>
> "Jack English can talk to country chairmen till hell freezes over," Mr. Hart said of Mr. Muskie's chief delegate scout. "But Big Ed isn't going to excite those housewives and those students who spend nights and days organizing their neighborhoods. That's what wins primaries."

Political organization involves the following steps:

1. Know what you want (*values*).
3. Know who else wants it (*personnel*).
3. Psych out yourself and others (personality).

4. Know where you stand (political time and space . . . the *cycle* and *institutions*).

5. Choose a strategy (*rules of the game*).

The main lines of the McGovern strategy were agreed upon at a meeting at the Senator's Maryland farm on July 25, 1970, and they were never significantly changed.

Unlike Senator Humphrey, who planned originally to enter the race later, after his opponents had destroyed each other in the early primaries, Mr. McGovern knew he had to start early, and announced formally on Jan. 18, 1971. A single winner would emerge from the primaries, he thought, and the real meaning of party reform, in which he had played a large part, was that the man with the best primary score could not be denied the nomination.

Primaries would be won by grass-roots organization, he and his staff decided, not by familiarity and the endorsements of local officeholders and party officials, as Senator Muskie's managers seemed to expect, nor by television, as Mayor Lindsay planned.

"Ours would have to be the best organization in the field," Mr. Hart said, and its power should be decentralized—outside Washington and outside the capitals of each of the key primary states.

The vital primaries, they decided two years ahead of time, would be in New Hampshire, Wisconsin, Massachusetts, Nebraska, Oregon, California and New York—Ohio would be added later, and Oregon subtracted—but not Florida, where Mayor Lindsay gambled almost all to win only 7 per cent of the vote.[7]

INVITATION

To test how important the five steps are to doing politics successfully, try out versions of the McGovern gambit in political situations on the job, at school, in your family. McGovern's gambit was to organize Democrats from the grassroots up to win the nomination, excluding traditional Democratic power centers. He then turned around and asked these power centers to support him for the contest with Nixon.

Simplified versions of the McGovern gambit:

On the Job

Organize a union or protest committee, beginning with your closest friends. Exclude some powerful supervisors, telling them they can't be trusted. Develop an antisupervisor platform.

Then, when you realize your group alone can't win, ask the supervisors to support you.

At School

Join with other nonsmokers to turn the cafeteria into a nonsmoking area. Engage in a virulent campaign against all smokers.

When you discover the college requires a democratic majority vote—and you alone can't win—beg for support from the one-cigarette-a-day crowd but still insist on total victory.

In the Family

Demand a later curfew for the older kids.

When Father insists on a majority vote, ask the younger kids to go along with you—even though there is nothing in it for them.

Question: **Which of the five steps for doing politics are ignored in each of these examples?**

In retrospect, we can see how picking the wrong people for organizing your campaign can lead to fatal mistakes in designing your campaign in all other areas. Idealists tend to pick men for their ideas; realists pick men for their devotion to the empty pursuit of power, characterized by the absence of ideas. As psychologist Rollo May has said, Watergate is the outcome of President Nixon's collecting around him cleancut public relations men who understood only the pursuit of empty power. These smooth, respectable images, outwardly representing all that once was good and clean in America, now became the facade covering a moral vacuum.[8]

Mistakes in Organizing Others

Organizing with men of ideas does not become pathological as long as you keep one foot in the world of social facts. The social facts that McGovern's idea men mainly ignored were the power and persistence of social institutions whose support they needed—for example, labor unions. Organizing with men of power is not pathological as long as someone provides ideas on behalf of which power can be exercised. Nixon's administration demonstrated that men without their own ideas and more power than they can handle tend to fall back on old ideas and weave them into pseudosolutions. Watergate proved that pseudopolitics could cover up pseudosolutions only for so long.

The pathological realism of deceptive cover-ups may be explained psychologically in terms of different personalities. So can the optimistic rigidity of pathological idealism portrayed by George McGovern. Philosopher George Santayana has said, "The mass of mankind is divided into two classes, the Sancho Panzas who have a sense for reality but no ideals, and the Don Quixotes with a sense for ideals but mad."

When it comes to the question of personality in the 1972 election, almost everyone failed to live up to the requirements of a rational politics by psyching out the other guy. As citizens, most of us failed to size up either McGovern or Nixon as pathological types. The press did its usually sloppy job of labeling—and even then only labeling one candidate. Nixon was portrayed as a chameleon empty on the inside but ready to change his colors on the outside to win—"the new Nixon," "tricky Dick," and "Would you buy a used car from this man?" Curiously, particularly in the face of accusations by Nixonites of a biased press, no newspaper ever did a psychological analysis of George McGovern.

Not even the candidates did well. If McGovern had figured out

PSYCHING OUT YOURSELF AND THE OPPOSITION—KEEPING IT ALL IN VS. LETTING IT ALL OUT

Nixon as well as did political scientist James Barber, he might have anticipated that Nixonites might be tempted to manipulate the election.[9]

Nixon's Personality   Barber evaluated Nixon's personality as an active-negative one—a president who is activist but takes no real joy from his successes. Barber traced the negative character cast to a childhood of trauma and insecurity, in which Nixon the boy could never take joy in his successes but had to constantly watch out for the next challenge from father and mother. The activist attitude Barber traces to Nixon's experience that he could win relief from insecurity by hard work, which brought him relative independence from others.

Barber predicted that in his presidency, if his personality remained fairly constant, Nixon would tend to be a loner, compulsively driven to act but preserving his independence by making decisions free of the control of others. Flexible in his values, Nixon would be able to sustain defeats on issues, but his concern with preserving an independent identity would lead to rigid responses when he saw his identity and control threatened. We have labeled this deliberate and rigid isolation pathological realism when it leads to an aggressive power response devoid of any ideas besides the immediate assertion of the realist's own existence.

In his special ninety-five page study entitled "The Nixon Prediction," Barber wrote before the 1972 election:

> Nixon's is a special variant of the active-negative character. With his remarkable flexibility regarding issues and ideologies, Nixon can be "defeated" any number of times on specific questions of policy without feeling personally threatened. His investment is not in values, not in standing fast for some principle. . . .
>
> But let the issue reach his central concern, the concern of self-management, and the fat may go into the fire. . . .
>
> As the election approaches, Nixon's Presidential fate will clarify itself. If the uncertainties fade in the light of the polls, and the probability of a defeat for Nixon rises sharply, this President will be sorely tempted to do what he feels he must do before it is too late. The loss of power to forces beyond his control would constitute a severe threat. That would be a time to go down, if go down one must, in flames.[10]

Such presidents tend to collect personnel sensitive to their needs. Even when other objective indicators are in their favor, such power-oriented personalities may select one negative sign through which to justify their habitual insecurity and rigid response. Despite all the facts in Nixon's favor for re-election, his one-time attorney general, John N. Mitchell, described the pseudocrisis syndrome before the 1972 election as follows at the Senate Watergate hearings:*

> **Q.** At the time that the break-in occurred, what was your professional political judgment as to how the President stood with regard to his chances for re-election?

*In response to a question asked by the chief minority counsel of the investigating committee, Fred D. Thompson.

A. Well, we go back to the middle of June and, of course, he had improved substantially from his previous lows vis-à-vis the then front-runner, Senator Muskie. That looked like he was on the ascendancy.

Q. Had not some polls indicated that at one time or another, Mr. Muskie was ahead of Mr. Nixon? **A.** Yes, but I believe, if my recollection is correct, that this was somewhat earlier than in June.

Q. You didn't consider him in trouble at that time?

A. When you are running a campaign, you consider anybody who is likely to get the nomination against your candidate, you may have a substantial amount of trouble with them.

Q. The extent of the problems you might visualize might have something to do with the measures you might take to confront it, would it not?

Pathological realists look for the worst possible outcome.

A. I don't believe that anybody thought the election was locked up, certainly with respect to the time element of June 17, with the potentials of the people that might become the Democrat candidate at the convention that was taking place in July. There were a great deal of uncertainties as to who the candidate might be and as to what the circumstances might be vis-à-vis the incumbent who was seeking re-election.[11]

Pathological realists tend to overestimate the power potentials of others.

The degree of pathological realism is expressed in the following exchange between Mitchell and Democratic Senator Herman E. Talmadge of Georgia, at the same session:

Q. Am I to understand, from your response that you placed the expediency of the next election above your responsibilities as an intimate to advise the President of the peril that surrounded him? Here was the deputy campaign director involved, here were his two closest associates in his office involved, all around him were people involved in crime, perjury, accessory after the fact, and you deliberately refused to tell him that.

Would you state that the expediency of the election was more important than that?

A. Senator, I think you have put it exactly correct. In my mind, the re-election of Richard Nixon, compared with what was available on the other side, was so much more important that I put it in just that context.

Pathological realists are willing to destroy all rules of the game and all moral values in order to maintain their own positions of power.

Q. Do you think anything short of a trial for treason would have prevented his election?

A. Well, it depends on what areas we are talking about. Mr. Thompson and I went through that, and of course, depending upon what time and what area it was in.[12]

What makes attitudes like these pathological is the assumption that one can destroy society and still have power. This assumption neglects a basic truth about power—that you have it only as long as you allow others to exist in a social relationship. Power outside society is naked force; the ultimate outcome of pathological realism is war.

McGovern's Personality

Similarly, a study of a pathological idealist such as McGovern would have exposed a rigid personality willing to make the same mistakes even after experiencing the reality of losing the election. In statements after his defeat, McGovern persisted in his idealism, saying he would have felt a moral obligation to make the Vietnam war an issue, even if he had known it would cost him the election. The contradiction of the pathological idealist is that he wants power to realize his ideals without compromising his ideals at all to obtain power.

Personality and values are decisive in locating yourself in political time and space.

DETERMINING WHERE YOU STAND IN TIME AND SPACE

Political Time: Maintenance vs. Decay and Creation

Realists are predisposed to tune in to other realists. Nixon tuned in to middle-American realists who feared America's transition from maintenance to decay.

Similarly, idealists are especially sensitive to the origins of change, which always begin in ideas. Both periods of decay and periods of creation begin with changes in the subjective perception of the world. McGovern appealed to people who were breaking out of the rules of dehumanizing maintenance America. Moved by their subjective experience of decay, these people were beginning to create their own ideas of what America should be like. Politics begins with an idea.

As many voters vaguely perceived, 1972 was not just another election. It was the collision between the world of people who had made it in the past and the world of people who hoped to make it in the future.

Both candidates were sensitive to their constituencies, but one of them overestimated the number of people looking for change. As two political sociologists concluded: "Throughout the 60's, and especially since 1965, many Americans felt that they were experiencing an enormous amount of cultural change, and the last man they wanted for President in 1972 was one who was identified with those who proposed to carry cultural change further, when the social order was already a-tremble."[13]

Political Space: Standing Up vs. Standing Down

Political space is where you place yourself relative to others for the purpose of doing politics. Nixon worked harder than he needed to stay up. He misplaced himself. Political space is where you stand after perceiving how your needs can be satisfied in relation to others.

The way to take your stand in political space is to become conscious of how others place you in social space. Social space is where others would like to leave you standing. Indicators of your position in social space are class, status, and access to institutions.

Class: Measured by money, Nixon had high class. Beginning with a hidden surplus from the last campaign, he used his contacts with economic institutions to collect at least $40 million (as far as anyone is willing to tell). In contrast, McGovern began with almost nothing, got most of his primary contributions in sums of less than $20 from little people—at one point standing on a New York City sidewalk to sign autographs in exchange for $1 bills—and never achieved much access to economic institutions.

Status: Nixon was always envious of those who went to prestige law schools and entered establishment law firms. After his 1960 defeat by John F. Kennedy, Nixon worked very hard to gain the status and contact with influential people associated with being in a prestigious law firm. In status perceptions of others, McGovern remained a baldish former minister and rural radical. Nixon, in the company of his millionaire friends, achieved the status of a man who had made it; McGovern, in the company of the little people, retained the status of a man unlikely to make it.

Access to Institutions: Any incumbent president has superior status because of his tenure in the institution of the presidency. Not satisfied with this, the White House made use of the CIA, the FBI, the IRS, a campaign sabotage unit, and the ill-fated burglary-and-bugging bunglers of the Watergate affair. No countercandidate can win against an incumbent willing to subvert the electoral process, using the entire machinery of the United States government, to stay in power.

CHOOSING A STRATEGY—MAKING OTHERS PLAY BY THE RULES OF THE GAME WHILE BREAKING THEM YOURSELF

The masterminds of the Watergate affair offended against both private and public rights. Their raids against private citizens may have inconvenienced some, but their assault against public rights threatened to destroy the political system altogether.

Specifically, the perpetrators of the Watergate affair committed an act of war against the American system of politics. While they claimed to be acting politically on behalf of the system, what they did was most profoundly subversive. They attacked the very foundations of the game of politics in America.

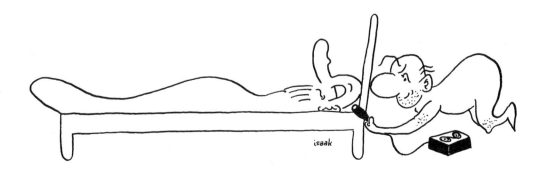

isaak

The rules of the American game are laid down in law and in political institutions. Behind them stands the American assumption that politics is a process of negotiation and compromise designed to suppress the alternative recognized by philosopher Thomas Hobbes: the war of all against all.

The extent to which President Nixon himself misunderstood the nature of American politics is revealed in his own transcripts of the tape recordings made in his office. One such transcript*—of a conversation on September 15, 1972, between the president and his assistants H. R. Haldeman and John Dean—reads:

> THE PRESIDENT: We are all in it together. This is a war. We take a few shots and it will be over. Don't worry. I wouldn't want to be on the other side right now. Would you?
>
> DEAN: Along that line, one of the things I've tried to do, I have begun to keep notes on a lot of people who are emerging as less than our friends because this will be over some day and we shouldn't forget the way some of them have treated us.
>
> THE PRESIDENT: I want the most comprehensive notes on all those who tried to do us in. They didn't have to do it. If we had a very close election and they were playing the other side I would understand this. No—they were doing this quite deliberately and they are asking for it and they are going to get it. We have not used the power in this first four years as you know. We have never used it. We have not used the Bureau and we have not used the Justice Department but things are going to change now. And they are either going to do it right or go.
>
> DEAN: What an exciting prospect.
>
> THE PRESIDENT: Thanks. It has to be done. We have been [adjective deleted] fools for us to come into this election campaign and not do anything with regard to the Democratic Senators who are running, et cetera. And who the hell are they after? They are after us. It is absolutely ridiculous. It is not going to be that way any more.[14]

The Watergaters offended not only because they fought "dirty," but because they fought against the very possibility of rules about how to do politics. Such rules can call for either conflict or cooperation in the attempt to satisfy human needs—or for a combination of both. But such rules are absolutely necessary. They satisfy a fundamental safety need of man in the company of other men—the need for some sort of order.

The American system of politics calls for majority rule balanced by minority rights. The Watergaters attempted to nullify the right of even finding out through elections who was in the minority.

The American rules call for negotiation and compromise, for giving a little and taking a little—but never putting the other party out of business permanently. By collecting funds illegally, by sabotaging the

*A different version of this conversation has been published by the House Committee on the Judiciary. The reader may want to judge for him or herself how the committee version reflects on Richard M. Nixon's conception of politics. See "Comparisons Between Passages in the White House and Committee Transcripts," *The New York Times*, July 10, 1974, p. 18.

Democratic campaigns so that the weakest opposition nominee for president was selected, by covertly using the FBI, CIA, and other government institutions, the conspirators offended not only against the rule of fairness but against a further rule—rationality.

American leaders are supposed to be selected according to the rule of rationality. Now, it is true that irrationality creeps into many campaigns. But the Watergaters tried to remove the decision as to what candidate could be nominated from the realm of public choice altogether—either by smearing candidates, or by sabotaging their campaigns, or by acquiring a monopoly of funding. Such tactics end all possibility of rational public choice.

Finally, to shroud the whole rule-breaking subversion of the system in secrecy offends against the American rule of popular sovereignty. Philosopher John Locke, upon whose ideas the Founding Fathers based their concept of sovereignty, argued that only the people can be ultimate judge in a libertarian politics. Sovereignty is the right of being ultimate judge. Nevertheless, faced with requests to make public his tapes of conversations with those implicated in Watergate, President Richard M. Nixon claimed a right of executive privilege not to reveal these tapes.

Although he accepted the president's need for protection of confidential and frank conversations in his conduct of the presidency, the first trial judge, Chief Judge John J. Sirica of the Federal District Court in Washington, cited the priority of popular sovereignty:

> A search of the Constitution and the history of its creation reveals a general disfavor of government privileges, or at least uncontrolled privileges. Early in the Convention of 1787, the delegates cautioned each other concerning the dangers of lodging immoderate power in the executive department. . . .
>
> I assert, that it was the design of the Constitution, and that not only its spirit, but letter, warrant me in the assertion, that it was never intended to give Congress, or either branch (i.e., Congress or the Executive), any but specified, and those very limited, privileges indeed.[15]

Some of the Watergate witnesses admitted they were so frustrated by dissent within the rules of the game (demonstrations and civil disobedience) that they were willing to break those rules. But without adherence to rules of the game the cooperative foundation for politics collapses, and the result is total war.

INCONCLUSIONS

Faced with the choice between a pathological realist and a pathological idealist in the 1972 election, many voters seemed to know what they *didn't* want. Asked in a poll in October of 1972 whether they thought Nixon or McGovern had "a more attractive personality," most of them favored a third candidate identified as "Neither."

REFERENCES

1. For further reading on the dominant role of corporations in American political life, see Andrew Hacker, *The Corporation Take-Over* (Garden City, N.Y.: Doubleday, Anchor Books, 1965); and John Kenneth Galbraith, *Economics and the Public Purpose* (Boston: Houghton Mifflin, 1973).

2. Richard Scammon and Ben J. Wattenberg, *The Real Majority* (New York: Coward, McCann & Geoghegan, Capricorn Edition, 1971).

3. For information on that creed's origins and impact, see Louis Hartz, *The Liberal Tradition in America* (New York: Harcourt, Brace, Jovanovich, 1955).

4. William Watts and Lloyd A. Free, *State of the Nation* (New York: Universe Books, 1973).

5. For a discussion of changing American values, see Louis Harris, *The Anguish of Change* (New York: W. W. Norton, 1973).

6. "Poll Shows 71% Feel Nixon Knew," *The New York Times*, Sunday, July 8, 1973, p. 23 (citing a nationwide Gallup poll).

7. The *New York Times*, June 10, 1972, p. 1.

8. Oral communication with Rollo May, July 8, 1973.

9. See Barber's prediction that Nixon might attempt to seize tighter control of the election in *The Presidential Character: Predicting Performance in the White House* (Englewood Cliffs, N.J.: Prentice-Hall, 1972).

10. Barber, *The Presidential Character*, pp. 441–442.

11. "Excerpts from Mitchell's Testimony Before the Senate Committee on Watergate," *The New York Times*, Wednesday, July 11, 1973 (Late City Edition), p. 23.

12. "Excerpts from Mitchell's Testimony," p. 24.

13. Seymour Martin Lipset and Earl Raab, "The Election and the National Mood," *Commentary* 55, no. 1 (January 1973), p. 50. For a best-selling study of the physical and mental effects of rapid change in America, see Alvin Toffler, *Future Shock* (New York: Random House, 1970).

14. Cited from the first press printing of the transcripts in *The New York Times*, Wednesday, May 1, 1974, p. 27. Printings of the complete tape transcripts as issued in May 1974 by the White House are also available in editions prepared by the government, *The Washington Post* and *The New York Times*.

15. "Text of Chief Judge Sirica's Opinion Ordering the President to Submit Tapes," *The New York Times*, Thursday, August 30, 1973, p. 20.

5 Wherein the reader discovers three games of politics—public, corporate, and private—played in America, and what his chances are in each game.

5 Playing the American Game

Beneath the official game of politics in America, other games are played. Many Americans believe that big politics goes on only in the big leagues—the White House, Congress, the courts. But everyone has political problems. Everyone has tensions between his needs and social facts. The needs of corporation managers run into tension with the social facts of labor unions, environmental and consumer protection groups, and tax law changes. The needs of small businessmen, farmers, and nature lovers come into tension with the social fact of corporations. Citizens might well suspect that if the federal government does not resolve such tensions, they either stay unresolved or are resolved somewhere else.

Solutions for the tensions of politics crop up everywhere. The game of American politics is at least three games: public politics, corporate politics, and private politics.

Public politics is where officials want the game to be played and where traditional Americans *think* the game is played.

Corporate politics is where businessmen *know* the game is played.

Private politics is where many human beings *hope* the game might be played.

To understand the games of American politics is to know how these three arenas function. Understanding can lead to doing politics more competently, to criticizing forms of politics that don't work for us, and even to changing politics to make it work for us.

The history of American political science has been to a large part the development of more and more precise and powerful ways of taking hold of American political reality for the purpose of trying to make it work.

This development has included several approaches:

Constitutionalism, in which students of politics look at political reality through the "eye-glasses" of state and federal constitutions and city charters to see how the system was designed to work.

Institutionalism, in which we trace the structures through which government is supposed to take place.

Behavioralism, in which, to see who actually does what in politics to get what there is to get—whether within constitutional limits or institutional frameworks or not—we look for political behaviors in and out of government, find them, and try to explain them.

Interest group theory, in which we look for centers of power outside of government that would explain how different demands were made on government. We find the NAM, the AFL-CIO, farm organizations, sports clubs, professional organizations, and later consumer groups, ecology groups, and new and old ethnic groups, all pressing government to produce goods or satisfactions for them.

Political psychology, through which we explain why especially politicians act as they do, including why they act politically at all.

Political sociology, through which we explain why citizens in different social strata and different situations tend to vote differently from one another.

By adding approaches it became possible to widen the horizon of politics from strictly government to all citizen activity that led up to claims on government. Today it no longer sounds outrageous to suggest that corporations as citizens can be included in the political arena. Further, noninstitutional definitions, such as political scientist Harold Lasswell's of politics as a struggle over "who gets what when how" perhaps unintentionally opened up other possibilities. If such a struggle went on in the nongovernmental spheres of activity—as, for example, inside corporations or inside the family—then these activities could also be politics.

As usual in the development of new paradigms as distinct ways of looking at reality, competition set in between proponents of different perspectives. For a while it was contended that constitutional approaches were obsolete and institutional approaches obsolescent. Recent events, specifically Watergate, have sent political scientists using more modern perspectives scurrying for help. They found they needed to dig up legal and institutional scholars for an understanding of the constitutional and structural implications of the system crisis induced by governmental self-subversion. As the problems change, we discovered once more, the perspective must change.

This chapter was constructed to yield experience in the use of a number of approaches: constitutionalism, institutionalism, and behavioralism, including group theory, political psychology, and political sociology.

Some of these are more useful than others in trying to understand the three arenas—public, corporate, and private—of American politics. In one case we have had to borrow an additional approach—the sociology of knowledge—for the understanding of corporate politics. In another we have borrowed from the sociology of religion to understand the counterpolitics of hippies, artists, and new sectarians. What approach you use, what glasses you wear, doesn't matter as long as the approach helps you find facts relevant to the problem you are studying.

What you get to see of American politics in the following pages will shift as you change approaches and your perspective shifts. But note how each approach uncovers different layers of political reality. Which approach you use depends on what you want to know. For example, institutional approaches may neglect the behavior of less organized groups; a group approach may serve as a smokescreen for the growing impotence of individuals; a simple individualistic approach tends to neglect the social context within which the individual has to function.

These are continuing problems in political science. Since change is the only constant of the present era, the best any student of politics can do is to guard against clinging to any single frozen approach.

Public politics is done according to traditional American rules. The motivation behind traditional American politics is fear.* Americans have always been afraid of anyone having too much power. But they have been equally afraid of no one having enough power to prevent chaos. The result: *American politics is a system that fragments power and requires negotiation and compromise.*

Motivated by this fear, the Founding Fathers accentuated the negative in the Constitution, stressing what government could not do as well as what it could. The outcome is a network of institutions appearing so complex that everyday human beings are kept in awe by them and don't know how to use them.

Despite such appearances, institutions are merely rules of the game made concrete in permanent social relationships.

Saving such appearances is to the advantage of those who know how to use political institutions—the elites. An idea as simple as tic-tac-toe (Figure 5-1) can be used to undo such appearances.

	LEGISLATIVE	EXECUTIVE	JUDICIAL
FEDERAL	Congress	President	Supreme Court
STATE	Legislature	Governor	State Court
LOCAL	Council	Mayor	Local Court

Figure 5-1
Political Tic-Tac-Toe

To use the tic-tac-toe idea as a tool for power, assume that institutional roles are represented in the vertical columns: legislative, executive, and judicial. Further assume that each horizontal row represents a distinct institutional level: federal, state, and local. Each square represents a center of power. Relationships between roles traditionally represent the *checks and balances* between branches of government. Relationships between levels have been called *federalism.*

*This motivation rests on our acceptance of a concept of man's nature developed by the political philosopher Thomas Hobbes, who saw fear as man's main drive. See Hobbes's *Leviathan*, various editions.

The Rules of the Game   Many games are played within the basic game of tic-tac-toe. As in tic-tac-toe, a player needs three in a row to win.

To pass a bill into law: Fill in three boxes in a horizontal row. At the federal level, get Congress, the president, and the Supreme Court to agree; at the state level, the legislature, governor, and state court; at the local level, city councils, mayors, and local courts—with variations in towns, townships, or counties.

To get laws carried out: For federal laws, fill in the three executive boxes. Get the president, governors, and local officials to act in harmony.

To appeal a law: Move up the judicial column.

Checks and Balances   To get the most of what there is to get in the game, the best winning combination nation-wide is the tic-tac-toe "T"—total cooperation between all branches of the federal government (Congress, president, Supreme Court), plus total cooperation between executive roles at all levels (federal, state, local). This strategy works best because no one is checked or balanced out of action at the federal level, and all powers reserved for the states and the people are harnessed through their executives.

Federalism   A recent illustration of a nation-wide "T" strategy is that utilized when Claude Kirk, then governor of Florida, and President Richard Nixon clashed over the desegregation of a Florida school. In 1954 in the *Brown v. Topeka* decision, the Supreme Court filled in one square for school desegregation. The congressional square was neutralized when Congress didn't object. The presidential squares were filled over time by Presidents Eisenhower, Kennedy, Johnson, and Nixon. Occasionally some gubernatorial squares were occupied with federal troops and marshalls—by Presidents Eisenhower and Kennedy.

In the Kirk-Nixon dispute, a local Florida school board had filled in its square by agreeing to integrate. But the governor ordered the county sheriff to prevent black children from entering school. Deciding not to use force, the president was left with having to negotiate and compromise. The negotiation was quiet. No one knows for sure if there was a compromise. But black children started going to white schools, and Governor Kirk got Nixon's support at the next election.

**Give and take quietly
if you don't want to use force.**

Force   Force is possible within the American game. The Founding Fathers went back at least to the seventeenth-century philosopher Thomas Hobbes for this idea. In *Leviathan,* Hobbes argued that without government's right to use force, the people would live in a state of war of all against all.

> **Police remind lawbreakers
> every day that Hobbes is alive
> and well in America.**

Individual Rights The eighteenth-century philosopher John Locke furnished the Founding Fathers with a defense of individual privacy against the monopoly of public force. In his *Second Treatise on Government* Locke asserted every man's God-given right to life, liberty, and property. These individual rights were installed in the Declaration of Independence: "We hold these truths to be self-evident: that all men are created equal; that they are endowed by their creator with certain unalienable rights; that among these are life, liberty and the pursuit of happiness . . ."

> **Rights balance individual freedoms
> against the forces of social facts.**

Fragmentation of Power In fact, Thomas Jefferson, who wrote the Declaration, used Locke's treatise as his main source of inspiration. He and other Founding Fathers adopted Locke's division between executive and legislative powers as a safeguard against any one holding a monopoly of public force, and added to the executive and legislative the third division proposed by Montesquieu, the judicial branch.

However, the diffusion of power does not stop here. There are more than 100,000 governments across the United States, many again divided into subgovernments. Obviously this is a system well designed to prevent government from doing very much *against* any individual. But such a system is also not likely to be able to do very much *for* individuals.

Many politicians fondly point out that the United States is one of the most stable political systems in the world. Fragmented as we are, things can go very wrong with government at one level—for example, at the federal level in the Watergate crisis—and other levels and subdivisions will still keep working. But while a system of a hundred thousand power barons, each with his own political base, may be difficult to rock, there is a price for such stability: it is never easy to get these power barons together to solve national or even regional problems.[1]

Traditional public politics focuses on the tensions between official barons rather than unofficial barons. A recurring issue that draws the headlines in official politics is the constitutional crisis over the powers of Congress and the president. Typically, Americans see the growth of executive power as a crisis not because they don't want the president to use his power, but because if he really uses his power to solve

**Institutional Conflict:
Congress vs. the
President**

problems, he's doing what other baronies were set up to prevent government from doing.*

In America, failing to deliver the goods is not a constitutional crisis. Grabbing for too much power is.

Not to do things is not perceived as crisis. In 1971, for example, when Congress defeated or ignored every single one of President Nixon's six major legislative proposals, there was no public outcry. But doing something powerful that threatens this do-nothing stability *is* perceived as crisis. Witness congressional reaction to Nixon's setting up do-something super-cabinet agencies to replace traditional do-little baronies (for instance, Henry Kissinger replacing the State Department). Or Nixon's impounding of funds allocated by Congress, or Nixon's expansion of presidential power through executive agreements in international affairs and executive privileges in domestic administration.

How can the following news clips be analyzed in terms of the traditional rules of American politics?

Nixon says aides will not testify before Congress In a policy statement on the use of executive privilege, President Nixon said today that members and former members of his personal staff would decline to make any formal appearances before Congressional committees.

The statement indicated that Mr. Nixon was ruling out an appearance before Congress of John W. Dean 3d, the President's counsel, and Dwight L. Chapin, a former White House aide, in the continuing inquiry into political sabotage during last year's Presidential race.

"A member or former member of the President's personal staff normally shall follow the well-established precedent and decline a request for a formal appearance before a committee of the Congress," Mr. Nixon said.

"At the same time," he continued, "it will continue to be my policy to provide all necessary and relevant information through informal contacts between my present staff and committess of the Congress in ways which preserve intact the constitutional separation of the branches."

Status of Top-Level Aides
President Nixon said that the four super-Cabinet members, who hold White House and Cabinet titles, would be required to testify as is customary under their Cabinet designations, but not concerning their White House duties.

---

*In the words of Justice Brandeis: "The doctrine of the separation of powers was adopted by the Convention of 1787, not to promote efficiency but to preclude the exercise of arbitrary power. The purpose was, not to avoid friction, but, by means of inevitable friction incident to the distribution of the governmental power among three departments, to save the people from autocracy." Cited in Raoul Berger, *Impeachment: The Constitutional Problems* (Cambridge, Mass.: Harvard University Press, 1973), p. 262.

The four are James T. Lynn, Secretary of Housing and Urban Development; Caspar W. Weinberger, Secretary of Health, Education and Welfare; Earl L. Butz, Secretary of Agriculture, and George P. Shultz, Secretary of the Treasury. Mr. Shultz is assistant to the President and the other three are counselors to the President, in addition to their departmental duties.

The use of executive privilege has become a heated issue recently, not only in regard to Congressional efforts to find out about possible White House involvement in last year's Watergate bugging and break-in case but also in the evolvement of Presidential government—the drawing of more authority and decision-making away from the departments and into the White House, where the President can curtail the extent of Congressional and public access.[2]

INVITATION

Assuming that stability is the main goal of traditional politics, and using what you know about the rules of checks and balances, how might you resolve the following dispute, on which no clear-cut rules have yet been made? The dispute arose out of the Watergate investigation.

Remember the tic-tac-toe squares. How you stand on the issue depends on which box you stand in.

As the president saw it:
EXCERPTS FROM PRESIDENT'S STATEMENT
Special to The New York Times
Washington, March 11—*Following are excerpts from a statement issued today by President Nixon on his use of executive privilege:*

The doctrine of executive privilege is well established. It was first invoked by President Washington, and it has been recognized and utilized by our Presidents for almost 200 years since that time.

The doctrine is rooted in the Constitution, which vests "the executive power" solely in the President, and it is designed to protect communications within the executive branch in a variety of circumstances in time of both war and peace.

Without such protection, our military security, our relations with other countries, our law enforcement procedures and many other aspects of the national interest could be significantly damaged and the decision-making process of the executive branch could be impaired.[3]

As others saw it:
Executive Privilege
A BASIC POWER COLLISION
Washington—Congress and the President had been sparring for months over such weighty matters as control of the public purse and the use of war powers. Last week they were slugging it out over a little-understood and seemingly mundane issue called executive privilege.

Behind both sparring and slugging hovered a basic constitutional question: Could the Congress, weakened over the years by a steady erosion of authority, again become an effective check on a power-ful, highly centralized Presidential Government? It was not without irony that the incident which brought the mighty issue to a head was a chapter out of last year's dirty politics—the Watergate caper.[4]

Who defines the national interest?

Some say that, since the president is the only man in government with a national constituency, he should be the one. But once he defines it, who can hold him accountable? In Great Britain, a prime minister can be ousted on a vote of no confidence by Parliament. In America, because of four-year presidential terms, the legislative branch does not have that power—except for lengthy impeachment procedures.* What is the purpose of checks and balances, if one branch can no longer be checked?

Nixon:

The general policy of this Administration regarding the use of executive privilege during the next four years will be the same as the one we have followed during the past four years: Executive privilege will not be used as a shield to prevent embarrassing infor-mation from being made available but will be exercised only in those particular instances in which disclosure would harm the public interest.[5]

Others:

The Senate Judiciary Committee had reopened the Watergate case in the course of confirmation hearings on L. Patrick Gray 3d, President Nixon's choice to become permanent director of the Fed-eral Bureau of Investigation. Mr. Gray testified that as acting director he sent reports from the F.B.I.'s inquiry into the matter to John W. Dean 3d, the President's counsel who had been delegated by Mr. Nixon to see if White House staff members were involved in the espionage.[6]

Who checks a president when embarrassing information is what the issue is all about? Who guards the guardians?

Nixon:

Under the doctrine of separation of powers, the manner in which the President personally exercises his assigned executive powers is not subject to questioning by another branch of government. If the President is not subject to such questioning it is equally inappro-priate that members of his staff not be so questioned, for their roles are in effect an extension of the Presidency.[7]

Others:

On Thursday, President Nixon spent more than half of a 40-minute press conference defending his position and reiterating that Mr. Dean would not be permitted to testify, even under threat of Congressional subpoena. Suggesting that he was willing to face a test in the Supreme Court on the issue, Mr. Nixon said: "Perhaps

*As the British historian J. H. Plumb noted, any Prime Minister in Eng-land who had his Attorney General and nearly thirty top aides indicted would be forced by the unwritten constitution to resign within a week. Plumb thought Nixon should have resigned immediately. (In an interview on Bill Moyer's Journal, April 4, 1974, Channel 13, New York).

this is the time to have the highest court of this land make a definitive decision with regard to this matter."

"This matter" has been periodically in dispute since George Washington was President. There is nothing in the Constitution about it. No court of any significance has ruled on it. The only precedents are what Presidents have got away with and what checks Congress has been able to bring to bear. Everyone agrees that the President in the conduct of his office and of foreign and military affairs has to have some freedom from Congressional interference. Everyone also agrees that Congressional oversight is needed over the execution of the laws by strong Presidents.[8]

To work out your position in this dispute, consider the following:

Separation of powers: This is what the tic-tac-toe game is all about. Article I of the Constitution begins: "All legislative powers herein granted shall be vested in a Congress . . ." Article II says: "The executive power shall be vested in a President of the United States of America." Article III states: "The judicial power of the United States, shall be vested in one Supreme Court, and in such inferior courts as the Congress may from time to time ordain and establish." The separation of powers is the division of government into three branches: legislative, executive, and judicial.

Checks and balances: But as you saw in the tic-tac-toe game, a power baron cannot simply play politics within his own little box. As Justice Oliver Wendell Holmes of the Supreme Court said in 1928, "The great ordinances of the Constitution do not establish and divide fields of black and white." The official intentions of the Founding Fathers are to be found in *The Federalist Papers.* In paper No. 47, James Madison notes Montesquieu's argument for the separation of branches to protect liberty. But Madison argues Montesquieu could not have meant that these branches should exercise no control over the acts of each other. The idea of checks and balances provides that no branch can act unless in concert with other branches, accepting the limits and powers that come along with such give and take.

Power of judicial review: Although the Constitution was mute on the Supreme Court's powers over the other two branches, the power of judicial review was first stated in *Marbury* v. *Madison* (1803), in which the Court asserted jurisdiction over an act of Congress. The theory for the Court's action can also be found in Alexander Hamilton's No. 78 of *The Federalist Papers.*

Even when political power barons fight over fundamental issues, like how the government should be run, the tendency is not to let the conflict come to a head, but to compromise. Here is how Senator Samuel J. Ervin of the Senate Watergate investigating committee suggested a way to avoid head-on confrontation when the president again denied access to information on the basis of executive privilege:

Dear Mr. President:

I acknowledge receipt of your letter of July 6, addressed to me with a copy to Senator Baker.

The Committee feels that your position as stated in the letter, measured against the Committee's responsibility to ascertain the facts related to the matters set out in Senate Resolution 60, present the very grave possibility of a fundamental constitutional confrontation between the Congress and the Presidency. We wish to avoid that, if possible. Consequently, we request an opportunity for representatives of this Committee and its staff to meet with you and your staff to try to find ways to avoid such a confrontation.

We stand ready to discuss the matter with you at your convenience.[9]

INVITATION

In the above controversies, the issue was whether members of the White House staff would be allowed to testify before Congress in the judiciary committee case, and whether the Watergate committee should have access to White House information (papers, diaries, and, later, tapes).

To what extent were compromise or a fight to the finish involved in either case?

When power barons of official politics argue, the talk is of social facts—how other people in other times resolved their tensions into arrangements that became institutions, constitutions, legal precedents, and footnotes from Founding Fathers. But where does this talk refer to the needs of everyday political man? Take the example of the power baron most successful in responding to domestic needs, President Lyndon Baines Johnson, who at his high point in 1965 had 68.4 percent of his proposals approved by Congress. Johnson left a legacy of 30 to 40 million poor, 10 million malnourished or undernourished, 20 million blacks still segregated in ghettos and poverty pockets, soaring inflation, unemployment—and, internationally, the Vietnam war. Some people say these and other needs unfulfilled by official government can be expressed through interest groups and political parties.

Interest Groups, Political Parties, and Elections

Traditional politics does not seem to satisfy most needs. How can Americans still hope that it might? One reason for hope is pluralist theory.

Pluralist theorists assume that people begin with different interests around which they establish their own little power baronies. Unlike the official institutional baronies of government, there are unofficial baronies of like-minded citizens. What holds each barony together is the shared interests of its members. What brings different baronies together in politics is the need to negotiate and compromise if different interests are to be reconciled. In America, public policy springs from the conciliation of interests so that each barony or group gets a little of what there is to get. The rules are, give a little to get a little, never asking for so much as to put another group totally out of business. No wonder no one ever gets all they want to get! The advantage of pluralistic politics is that while no one ever wins totally, no one ever loses totally . . . so these theorists argue. They also maintain that since interests of most Americans are represented by organized groups, the interests of most get a hearing in the political process.

> **Pluralists see politics as conflicts and compromise over interests. Interests are what people think they want.**

Pluralism could be democratic if each group were equal in power. But the social fact is that some groups are more equal than others. That often means that the needs of groups with lots of clout (money, access to policy makers) are met more often.

Also, interest groups must be "legitimate." That means they must be recognized as justified and proper by other groups.[10]

In practice the requirement of legitimacy has led to some ironies of political life, challenging the claim of pluralists that anyone can form an interest group and thus fulfill at least part of his needs. For example, the major proponent of the interest-group view of American political life has been political scientist David B. Truman.[11] However, when radical students started to organize on the Columbia campus where he was dean, he refused to recognize this group as legitimate, and the university called in the police.

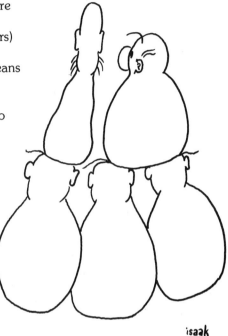

isaak

Typical successful interest groups in America are the National Association of Manufacturers, representing industrial interests, and the American Federation of Labor and Congress of Industrial Organizations (AFL-CIO), representing long-established labor unions. These groups have large funds with which to organize themselves and with which to seek access to policy makers in government through lobbying.

Among less successful and less funded, though still legitimate groups is the National Association for the Advancement of Colored People (NAACP), representing mainly blacks who can't afford to pay high dues to organize. Similarly the American Association of University Professors, representing college teachers who often could afford to pay to organize and lobby, has been restricted because teachers value their professional status more than salary and "dirty" politicking.

Groups like the Black Panthers and Students for a Democratic Society have been unsuccessful. Their values were believed to differ from the values of the rest of the interest groups, and they were never granted legitimate status. They were often prevented from playing the American game of politics—to the degree that they even wanted to play it. Groups that want values different from those which the system is set up to distribute are often denied the legal opportunity to organize.

Most political scientists today look at American politics through interest group theory. Ironically, they are not immune from the temptation to hinder the success of new and not-so-legitimate interest groups among themselves. In 1968—1969, after more than sixty years of uncontested elections for officers of the American Political Science Association, an opposition group was formed. The majority of the APSA then found it necessary to change its democratic rules of procedure to make it more difficult for a small group to win votes at the annual national conventions. Instead of a convention vote, a mail ballot was introduced for crucial issues.

INVITATION

Pick any interest-group dispute in your local newspaper. What kinds of social facts are apt to allow one group to win as opposed to others?

Does the size of the group matter? Money? What values are implied by each group's interests? Does access to political institutions—whom you know—play a role?

To play at any political game—including the pluralist version—it pays to evaluate your power in terms of the five standard variables: *rules of the game, values, social institutions, political institutions, and personality.*

Rules of the Game Rules of the game are the taken-for-granted ways in which politics is done in any community—how you are used to playing the game of politics. The rules that were found to apply to the politics of government institutions also apply to the more informal politics of interest groups. *The American rules of politics provide for negotiation and compromise between semi-independent centers of power, in which each gives a little to get a little, never asking so much as put others permanently out of business.* Interest groups are big and little clusters of neighbors that translate some of their needs and wants into goals. Such groups include unions for laboring people, manufacturers' associations for industrialists, consumer's unions for housewives, rifle associations for sportsmen, sierra clubs for conservationists, civil rights associations for those discriminated against, and neighborhood protective associations for those who want to keep what they have.

Values Values of the political game are norms into which people are socialized and according to which they guide their political actions. Social and political *values* are society's definition of your wants. *Attitudes* are values positions that people take on concrete issues. *Interests* are attitudes translated into action. Riflemen have rugged individualistic values, shooting attitudes, and politically fire away in groups at other groups with other interests.

Traditional American political and social values are:

Life

Liberty

Property

Majority rule and minority rights

Rule of reason

Rule of law, not of men

Work as an activity that gives men human dignity and worth

Egalitarianism

Individualism

Competition

Doing in nature before it does you in

Puritan ethic: one wife, one God, sex for procreation, no art for art's sake

Universalism: the belief that all men must believe in these values, like it or not

To hold these values is to be traditionally American. To hold or not to hold these values has become the pivot point of American political life.

Tradition-oriented Americans hold these values as self-evident truths. To the extent that they do, these clusters of values have become ideology. *Ideology* is the ultimate reification of value clusters—giving them a reality of their own separate from their utility.

Ideology is ultimately pathological. For its intent is to preserve previous solutions or nonsolutions of tensions between human needs and social facts, not to cope practically with current tensions. To the extent that all value clusters—*political cultures*—are ideological, they too are pathological. Interest groups most apt to use ideology as a political tool are those most satisfied with old solutions or afraid of new ones; see the following example.

ADS TO PUSH WORK ETHIC HERE

A massive advertising campaign will begin soon warning Americans they are about to lose something they were never sure they really had—their work ethic.

"America didn't get rich by goofing off," reads one of the ads designed to convince the public that work for work's sake has been and still should be one of its most cherished virtues.

Or as Commerce Sec. Peter Peterson put it: the $10-million campaign by the National Advertising Council will try to persuade workers that "productivity is not a 12-letter dirty word representing certain people getting exploited by others."

When the rate of increase in productivity—output per worker —slowed in the past few years, a theory developed among many sociologists, business leaders, politicians and others that America has lost its work ethic, that workers just don't enjoy work as they once did.

There is, indeed, substantial evidence to prove that America, like other highly industrialized nations, does face a revolutionary attitude toward work.

Less Fearful

Today's workers have far higher educational achievements than their parents and grandparents; they are less fearful of permanent unemployment, more confident of their ability to find work. So they are more willing to move from job to job in search of satisfying occupations than were the young of past generations. . . .

Seriously Contended

President Nixon has said that the work ethic holds that labor is good in itself, according to religious teachings and American tradition, and "that is why most of us consider it immoral to be lazy or slothful."

In one speech to Republican governors, Nixon seriously contended that "scrubbing floors and emptying bedpans have just as much dignity as there is in any work to be done in this country—including my own."

But some persons believe there is a greater tendency today to treat work more casually than in the past, and that this represents a new "the-hell-with-it" feeling. Some people blame this change on television.

"TV is more of an agitator today than any of the radicals who preached revolution to workers in the past," said Stanford poet and professor, Al Young.

"Workers who see the 'good life' on TV are ready for it now, not in years to come," Young said, "and that stirs more demands for quick changes than the revolutionaries ever managed."[12]

INVITATION

In whose interest is it to maintain the work ethic?

Values have political consequences. If a politician can get people to see issues in ideological terms, he can prevent new solutions to social problems. If a politician can keep the rhetoric of ideology out of an issue, he may win public support for innovative solutions to public tensions.

The basic interest groups that use ideology as a tool in the political game are *political parties*.[13] Two political parties—Republicans and Democrats—have a monopoly on official politics in the United States, and constantly struggle to maintain and create compatible coalitions of interest groups to keep their power. For example, in the 1972 presidential campaign, Senator George McGovern and the Democrats, after party reform, tried to put together a coalition encompassing youth, blacks, the poor, and women. But by stressing the rhetoric of traditional ideology—especially the protection of property—President Nixon and the Republicans put together big business, big labor, and most of the middle class.

McGovern frequently appealed to voters with practical issues, like raising the taxes of the rich to relieve the burden of the less wealthy and the poor. In contrast, Nixon raised an ideological issue. To take money from those who earned it through work, he said, would be an attack on norms this country was built on—the work ethic, property, competition, and stability through old laws and orders.

INVITATION

On what ideological grounds could you have anticipated the outcome? Note the issues the candidates raised in newspaper stories.

One political scientist acquainted with the conflict between individual interests and ideological beliefs was able to use values to predict the outcome months ahead of the election.* Professor Howard Smukler asked his students at a business college in Providence, Rhode Island, how many thought they would ever make more than $50,000 a year. None raised their hands. Then he asked how many would favor a proposal (attributed to Senator McGovern) to tax heavily anyone's income over $50,000. None raised their hands. As one student explained: "I know I'll never make $50,000. But if you take that away, there's no hope." Survey researchers who surveyed the whole country on such issues might count this as an example of their over-all observation that Americans display a "schizoid combination of operational liberalism with ideological conservatism."[14]

Figure 5—2 shows how Americans stack up on an ideological spectrum based on what they deeply *believed* versus an operational spectrum based on what they wished to be *done* on practical issues.

Figure 5-2
Ideological and Operational Spectrums

	Ideological Spectrum	Operational Spectrum
Completely liberal	4%	44%
Predominantly liberal	12%	21%
Middle of the road	34%	21%
Predominantly conservative	20%	7%
Completely conservative	30%	7%
	100%	100%

Source: Lloyd A. Free and Hadley Cantril, *The Political Beliefs of Americans: A Study of Public Opinion* (New Brunswick, N.J.: Rutgers University Press, 1967).

Note: The term "ideological spectrum" refers to values people say they prefer when referring to their deep-seated political or social beliefs. These preferences may differ from their choices on the "operational spectrum," in which people are asked to state preferences of action in relation to specific practical issues. What people believe and what they will do on a practical issue may be two different matters.

*Professor Smukler has since graduated to a politics for human beings—he is now an apprentice electrician whose only complaint is that his tool box is too heavy.

Figures like these show that "liberal" or "progressive" solutions to human problems, such as those related to social welfare, are made difficult by the bias of the traditional set of American values. Also, some values within each set can contradict others. For example, Americans' liking for practical solutions, a part of the American political culture, can be and often is offset by their commitment to values such as individualism and competition. Thus policies and plans that involve social cooperation and obligation can often be stymied, no matter how practical or plausible they may be.[15]

Values of the political culture define the limits within which citizens make political decisions. In a country with a libertarian ideology, solutions requiring adaptation to nonlibertarian values—for example, social welfare—have great difficulty being accepted.[16]

Social Institutions: Class and Status   Values and issues—even personality—can make a difference, but everyone who runs for office has to be able to pay the admission price. This depends on his ability to mobilize his own class resources or the socio-economic status perceptions of others. *Class* is how much you've got of what there is to get; *status* is what others think you've got.

Stressing the relationship between parties, elections, and money, President Dwight D. Eisenhower said in 1968:

> . . . we have put a dollar sign on public service, and today many capable men who would like to run for office simply can't afford to do so. Many believe that politics in our country is already a game exclusively for the affluent. This is not strictly true; yet the fact that we may be approaching that state of affairs is a sad reflection on our elective system.[17]

For playing, locate yourself in class. If out-classed, don't play.

Consider the following report on the 1968 presidential election:

> Mr. (Lawrence F.) O'Brien, who managed former Vice President Hubert H. Humphrey's campaign for the Presidency in 1968, said that President Nixon's supporters had spent almost three times as much as he had been able to spend. At a crucial stage of the campaign, he added, he was obliged to trim $3 million from the television budget, because the networks insisted on being paid cash before selling air-time.
>
> "I'm not crying crocodile tears," said the sandy-haired, deep-voiced party leader. "But it cost us the election. It's really as simple as that."[18]

Clearly, he who is able to mobilize his class resources has a better chance of manipulating the beliefs of others, simply because he can buy the chance to be heard.

**He who has something of value plays; the rest watch from the sidelines.
—Rules of the game.**

Yet the winner in American official politics is not always the one with the most money or property. Take the record of television spending by some candidates in the 1970 congressional elections:

In Indiana: Senator Vance Hartke, (D), $246,000, won against Representative Richard L. Roudebush (R), $441,000.
In Texas: Lloyd M. Bentsen, Jr. (D), won with $115,540 spent at five major television stations in a race for the Senate against representative George Bush (R), who spent $184,000 at the same stations.[19]

Socio-economic status achieved on the basis of skills used to acquire what is valued most in a society has always been a potential base for political power everywhere. Until recently, what was valued most in America was property. But as control over property slipped from those who possessed it to those skilled in managing it, property was no longer enough of a base for power. In order to exercise the power of property, the owner must have the skill to employ those who know how to manage it (private managers) and the permission of those publicly charged with overseeing that management (public administrative officials).

Political Institutions Access to political institutions has become an important condition of economic success. Whether you are a hotdog vendor in New York City or an airlines executive, you must get the agreement or license of public officials to operate. Fortunately for you as a businessman, many of the agencies charged with supervising you are insulated from public political control—for example, the president cannot give orders to the vast array of independent regulatory agencies. As one report on such agencies prepared for President John F. Kennedy noted:

> Irrespective of the absence of social contacts and the acceptance of undue hospitality, it is the daily machine-gun-like impact on both agency and its staff of industry representation that makes for industry orientation on the part of many honest and capable agency members as well as agency staffs.[20]

Working in secrecy, agencies such as the Civil Aeronautics Board have set airline fares in consultation with airlines, while excluding the public and even members of Congress from their hearings.[21] Another regulatory agency, the Interstate Commerce Commission, allowed the Pennsylvania Central Railroad to broach bankruptcy. The Commission had ignored for fifteen months a report by its own staff cautioning against a growing trend among railroads to reorganize as conglomerate corporations, a step the Pennsylvania Central was taking. The staff report had warned, "The conglomerate holding company provides a convenient means for the transfer to other industries of assets now devoted to transportation."[22]

A new arena of corporation-run politics has existed for decades created by the effective insulation of supposedly public regulatory agencies from all parts of the body politic but that which they were to control. Since private decisions with enormous public consequences

Bureaucratic Politics and Depoliticization

are made in this private and secretive arena, it is no longer sufficient to study merely official politics. Private corporation politics has to become a subject matter for those concerned with politics, no matter how defined: as the authoritative allocation of resources, the struggle over who gets what when how, or as the attempt to resolve tension between human needs and social facts.

Access to institutions, however, is also important in what is left of the relatively public and open part of the shrinking arena of official politics.

If, for example, you want to get elected to office, it may help to have a friend in Washington. "The President asked me 'what do you need?'" explained Representative Thomas Kleppe, who outspent his opponent Senator Quentin N. Burdick two to one in the most expensive political campaign to date in North Dakota history. He received $200,000 from individuals outside North Dakota. "I got the money because of White House help," he said of the 1970 campaign. Even so, he lost. In the traditional political game, money isn't everything.

On the other hand, direct access to financial institutions can ease the road for many a politician. Access can short-circuit the official route of having to drum up widespread public support for one's campaign efforts. Financial access is effective in the same sense that knowing someone in a regulatory agency conveniently relieves a businessman of the burden of doing official politics through the public political process.

Well connected to relatives and friends of great fortune, former Governor Nelson A. Rockefeller of New York was able to raise $260,000 to finance each "lovely little word," as the *National Observer* called it, of the 1967 gubernatorial oath of office: "I do solemnly swear that I will . . . faithfully discharge the duties of the office of governor according to the best of my ability."[23] Rockefeller engaged

isaak

in the most expensive state-wide election effort ever put together in this country.

Personality   What kind of personality succeeds in the official American game of politics? The answer depends on whether you mean citizen personality or politician personality.

After a long and futile search for a "leadership personality," those studying the personality of leaders now tend to believe that leadership success comes out of the interaction between personality and environment. Neither totally determines the outcome.[24]

A most striking example is political scientist James David Barber's explanation and prediction of success and failure among United States presidents, including Richard M. Nixon.[25] Barber draws attention to three major components of leadership success: *character* (what a person basically is), *style* (the way he relates to his environment), and *environment* (the kind of challenges his role as a leader presents him). Incompatibility or conflict between any of these can lead to disaster.

For example, Herbert Hoover evidenced a compulsive character in his driving energy, depressed mood, orientation toward manipulating his environment, his ambition, and his problems with controlling aggression. Also, Hoover never developed a convincing speaking style—a fact that may be related to Hoover's failing English four years in a row when he was at Stanford University. When the time came to react to the disaster of the Great Depression, Hoover's style was so out of tune with the realities of the times that few people believed anything he said:

> Lacking the guidance of successful experience in rhetoric, he drew upon his character-rooted sense that words are essentially devices for persuasion—propaganda weapons rather than symbols for realities or terms of commitment. The result was a rhetoric of reassurance, a pollyanna optimism so obviously out of line with national conditions that its main effect was to increase, not allay, national anxieties.[26]

For another example of dissonance between style and environment, President Lyndon B. Johnson developed over decades of playing political roles the style of the middleman between politicians who wanted different things. Thrust into the topmost position in the land, where he was expected to take stands or provide guidance, he tried to act as middleman—and failed. That style did not suit the new environment. It was one thing to compromise away votes on issues that could be compromised—for instance, housing for the elderly versus tariff protection for cotton farmers. But when different interests made irreconcilable demands about the Vietnam war, Johnson could not simply promise an aroused youth "a little bit of peace" while promising hawks "a little bit of war."

> Put crudely: Johnson's style failed him, so he fell back on character. There he found no clear-cut ideology, no particular direction other than the compulsion to secure and enhance his personal power.[27]

Barber predicted in 1969—accurately—that, as president, Richard M. Nixon would be twice handicapped. First, his style was to take a judge-like stance in contacts with his staff. Staff members would present their cases as if in briefs, Nixon would retire to "chambers," and Nixon would hand down a decision without benefitting from exchanges with his staff about that decision.[28] A number of ill-thought-out decisions long before Watergate, like his early Supreme Court nominations, resulted. These might have been avoided by more consultation and back-and-forth communication.

While warning that only the general trend of a president's interaction with his environment could be anticipated on the basis of personality formation in childhood, Barber predicted with remarkable accuracy that an event like the Watergate affair could develop. Barber saw Nixon as particularly concerned with his own independence or "self-management." "The danger is that Nixon will commit himself irrevocably to some disastrous course of action," Barber wrote in 1969.[29] This, he reiterated in 1972, is even more likely should the issue "reach his central concern, the concern of self-management . . ." Then the "fat may go into the fire."[30] Writing just before the 1972 election, Barber anticipated prophetically what actually later took place in the Watergate affair:

> As the election approaches, Nixon's Presidential fate will clarify itself. If the uncertainties fade in the light of the polls, and the probability of a defeat for Nixon rises sharply, this President will be sorely tempted to do what he feels he must before it is too late. The loss of power to forces beyond his control would constitute a severe threat. That would be a time to go down, if go down one must, in flames.[31]

Barber's only mistake was not to anticipate that even with the polls favoring Nixon by a landslide, the White House's mere perception of threat would lead to burglary, bugging, sabotage of the opposing party's campaign, and the collection of huge and unnecessary amounts of money to double- and triple-assure Nixon's re-election.

Another aspect of personality in politics is the personality of the citizen. From the viewpoint of the politician, the ideal citizen is the type easily swayed from his values by those appeals in which a politician is expert. The demagogue, who sways by appeals to emotion, prefers an emotional citizenry. He succeeds best in times of crisis. Modern democratic politics of the libertarian kind assumes a great deal of rationality, as well as knowledge, on the part of the citizenry.[32] But while politicians who wish to appeal to reason would prefer a citizenry informed and capable of rational choice, such constituents are often hard to find.

Surveys of citizen knowledge about the system of official politics and its issues and candidates show that . . . many citizens are unaware of names and duties of the nation's political leaders . . .*

*In 1963 Elizabeth Taylor, the film actress, led an entire field of politicians, ranging from Richard Nixon (whom 88 percent recognized) to Nelson Rockefeller (88 percent), and Barry Goldwater (72 percent), and also includ-

> **In 1945, the boxer Joe Louis,
> comedian Bob Hope,
> and comics detective Dick Tracy
> were better known than
> leading members of Congress
> and Cabinet officials.**[33]

. . . most citizens don't know of anything a politician has done for them lately . . .

> **"Has he (your Congressman)
> done anything for the district
> that you definitely know about?"
> Percentage correct answers: 14%**[34]

. . . and few admit to having taken part in campaign activity . . .

> **Percent of those who "talked to
> someone and tried to persuade him
> how to vote": 31%**[35]

As a specialist in the psychology of politics comments, "Even hardened pollsters sometimes are unable to conceal their wonder at the assiduousness with which many Americans insulate themselves from the massive flow of political news and commentary."[36]

Yet it has occurred to few political scientists to explore either the island of privacy on which refugees from official politics live human, and *therefore* profoundly *political*, lives, or the island of corporate Never-never-land whence major decisions go that can't or won't be made in the official arena of politics.

How can the arenas of privately personal politics and secretive corporative politics be understood? More importantly, how can we train ourselves to successfully and consciously "do politics" in these arenas, which we are told (by whom?) are not political?

PRIVATE POLITICS OR THE POLITICS OF EVERYDAY LIFE

If politics involves human beings engaging in social acts to resolve tension, then we should be able to find politics everywhere we find human beings. Logical as this may seem, all of us have difficulty accepting that possibility. As citizens we have been trained since grade school that politics takes place in official places.[37] As students of politics we may fear that to seek—and possibly find—politics everywhere would present us with too huge an arena to study.

Yet whether we prefer such a wide scope or not, whether we tend from childhood to limit politics to its "proper" places or not, such concerns make little difference to the fellow human beings who try to satisfy their needs. If they perceive tensions between these needs and

ing George Romney (37 percent), William Scranton (32 percent), and Mark Hatfield (10 percent), all potential presidential material. Liz got 91 percent recognition. Only major crises, like Watergate, seem to change this picture.

social facts, they simply engage in the politics of trying to find solutions—whether official channels are open or not.

INVITATION

Think of any personal problem you have had involving other people—in the dorm, in the home, in the classroom, on the job.

 Was there a conflict between needs and social facts?

 Did other people's solutions interfere with your new solution?

 How were values, attitudes, or interests involved?

 Did knowing someone in power help you solve the problem (access to institutions)?

 Was money involved (class)?

 In retrospect, was your attempt to solve the problem political?

On the basis of having accepted the invitation above, do you personally feel that this problem-solving or tension-reducing interaction was *not* political? Should we, or can we, run to our city councilman or congressman *every* time we need to solve such problems? What could happen to our lives, if we had to wait for Congress to act on such matters?

Since politics is the continuing process of resolving tension between human needs and social facts, it takes place wherever human beings are alive. As new tensions arise, new solutions must be found. Who creates these solutions? It's not apt to be the maintenance men of traditional politics, bogged down in the give and take of old solutions. Nor is it apt to be businessmen, whose innovations are oriented toward the company, not the individual. Is there an island, squeezed between past solutions of traditional politics and the future shock of corporate innnovation, of private politics or a politics of everyday life?

Politics as Counterculture

To counter repressive social facts of an existing culture and its values, in order to satisfy human needs, people may create a counterculture. Culture is the label we give to shared values and behavior patterns acted out by people over time. A counterculture is the refusal to share or be shared by such values and behaviors, ending in the creation of new lifestyles.

Listen to a founder of a commune modeled on the book *Walden Two*, by the psychologist B. F. Skinner:

> "If I hadn't got involved in living in community," says Kathleen Kincaid, "I would probably be an office manager—some responsible job a person can get without an education. And I wouldn't like it . . . Living at Twin Oaks changed the way I relate to people. I pay a hell of a lot more attention to the way other people think and feel."[38]

Private political creation can bring us near self-actualization.

In America, a dominant characteristic of countercultures has been the rejection of getting property as the highest goal in life and of considering values like life, liberty, individualism, competition, and work mere tools for that acquisition. Instead, people in countercultures tend to consider work and freedom and individualism and property tools employed in a celebration of life. As one student told us recently, "Life to us is just the power to *be*." Styles include emphasis on art, on creativity, on a mixture of sociability in being with others and "doing your own thing," and generally on developing your own potential with and through others.

Original members of countercultures in the recent past—the hippies—tended to be people from upper social strata whose physical needs of food, shelter, and safety were pretty well fulfilled. Going beyond such needs, they sought self-esteem, love, and self-actualization. Recently such values have filtered down to the lower-middle-class youth, who engage in a mixture of the old acquisitive style of life and a style aiming at self-actualization beyond mere physical well-being.

Politics as Art

Since politics is creative, it can take the form of creating through art. The literary critic Richard Poirier writes that "any effort to find accommodation for human shapes or sounds is an act that partakes of political meaning. It involves negotiation, struggle, and compromise with the stubborn material of existence, be it language or stone."[39]

Although Poirier recognizes politics as an artistic act, he is limited by his conception of politics as the traditional American game involving conflict, negotiation, and compromise. In contrast, notice how the Spanish film-maker Luis Bunuel conceives of art as a political act much less compromisingly:

> In any society, the artist has a responsibility. His effectiveness is certainly limited and a writer or painter cannot change the world. But they can keep an essential margin of nonconformity alive. Thanks to them, the powerful can never affirm that everyone agrees with their acts. That small difference is very important. When power feels itself totally justified and approved, it immediately destroys whatever freedoms we have left, and that is fascism.[40]

Politics as Religion

In resolving tension, politics creates solutions that have meaning for those involved. The ultimate political act attempts to establish meanings for everything the mind can reach: religion. Whereas the politics of everyday life gives meaning to practical problems, the politics of religion sometimes attempts to mystify the consciousness of man as creator of his own social world. The philosopher George Santayana noted: "The ideal of mysticism is accordingly exactly contrary to the idea of reason; instead of perfecting human nature, it seeks to abolish it; instead of building a better world, it would undermine the foundations even of the world we have built already; instead of developing our mind to greater scope and precision, it would return to the condition of protoplasm—to the blessed consciousness of an Unutterable Reality."[41]

Despite mystification, which serves the power of those interested in maintaining existing meanings of reality, there seems to be a need in all human beings for religion as a way for anchoring their meanings outside themselves. New religions are always signs that old anchors have torn loose. The creation of such religions is the ultimate political act, for they claim to take care of *all* human needs and resolve *all* tensions.

Hear the relief in the voice of a devout believer participating in the creation of a "Christ Commune," a part of the Jesus People movement: "If I had not come to the Lord, I would either be in jail or in an institution, or maybe dead by now."[42]

Nevertheless, there are also bitter notes here. The joy of the social architect, the creative impulse of the film-maker artist, the salvation of the Jesus "freak"—these seem sandwiched between gargantuan social forces. Each refugee from these forces reports his escape as a tight squeeze.

Sometimes human beings think it possible to squeeze through to a human life between such realities as the institutions of official politics and official religion. Such an attempt is represented most recently by followers of Satguru Maharaj Ji, the adolescent Indian guru spreading his teachings across college campuses.* His "Divine Light Mission," surprisingly free of specific doctrine, emphasizes the release of human capacities (including those for love and what used to be known as religious experience) repressed by modern life. The "Knowledge" that the guru imparts is teachable only to those ready for it and is supposed to be useful for handling the problems of daily life in a state of blissful but practical transcendence.

That, despite all denials, this movement retains both political and religious aspects is made clear by the comments of the former Left-radical Rennie Davis shortly after he converted to the guru's words:

> "I was impressed by the fact that an organization like this could exist worldwide," Davis said in an interview not long ago, "and that I would have so little consciousness of it. The strength of the organization is just absolutely remarkable. It's not just a spiritual strength, either. The Guru Majaraj Ji has 5,000 mahatmas (disciples with direct experience of 'the Knowledge'). Most of them are based in India, but increasingly they're learning English and other languages and are travelling to other nations. He's in every continent now except for the Socialist countries, and He announced that next year He's going to Russia and the year after that He's going to China and by 1975 everyone on the planet will know that He's here.

*In a personal conversation, a follower of Maharij Ji repeatedly stressed to us that "This is *not* politics and it is *not* religion. The Knowledge you get is a practical Knowledge that can help you get along better in *everyday* life."

"In the United States there are now 150 centers oriented around the Guru Maharaj Ji. They're all hooked up with Telex machines and WATS lines. Next year Guru Maharaj Ji is going to build, probably in California, a city that will use all the advance methods of technology to insure that the air is pollution-free, cars will be run on electricity instead of gasoline. It will be an architectural wonder, and it will be—according to Him—a concrete demonstration of what it means to have Heaven on Earth. When you see the organization that He's assembled in two and a half years and you see the forces that are coming together for this city, for a huge festival in the Houston Astrodome next fall, which is going to launch the Divine United Organization—you realize that there is an incredibly serious force here at work that really means to have people roll up their sleeves and get down to work with the problems of this material world. I think the combination of a politics and a spirit joined together in one form led by God Itself is a very far-out vision."[43]

INVITATION

Using the tools for political analysis in Chapter 3 and further sources on the Divine Light Mission, determine to what extent the Maharij Ji movement can be considered political.

Politics as Revolution

Those who walk away from society and formal politics may be allowed to escape with slight socio-economic scars. Those who battle society and threaten official and corporate politicians may find themselves less lucky.

A father speaks to his radical daughter:

> You speak of a revolution against capitalism. This can only mean that you are developing forces against me and the rest of your family. The oldest and most reasonable form of capitalism is the ownership of agricultural land and this is what your family has been involved with for a hundred years.
>
> I will resist any effort to change the basic ideology governing my own life and it should be obvious I do not want to support any movement that would develop into violence against me and my family.

Diana Oughton, the daughter to whom these words were addressed, was killed March 6, 1970, in a bomb explosion in a Greenwich Village townhouse. She was a member of the violent revolutionary group known as the Weathermen. Police called the townhouse a "bomb factory." The doctor who examined the remains of her body said she had been standing within a foot or two of the bomb when it exploded. Diana was 28.[44]

The Politics of Everyday

Social escape artists like commune builders, film-makers, and revolutionaries may create islands of release from social tension. But what about the ordinary citizen, for whom there is no escape?

What freedom to create herself is there for the housewife? How can she create herself—with others—when she is taught by a thousand media voices fulfilling the "role of God/father figure" that a woman *is* her appearance and her household no more than an extension of that appearance? For her, "commercials reinforce . . . a neat, antiseptic, unemotional, well regulated body and mind. . . ." In the most intimate activities, in which she might design her private life politically by making her own decisions, she is controlled by corporations and their media:

> There is *Lysol* to remove household odors. *Saniflush* to kill germs in the bathroom bowl . . . *Scope* to make breath fresh for hours, *Bold* makes your clothes not just clean, but bright, *Jubilee* makes your kitchen positively shine, and there are deodorants and antiperspirants: *Arrid, Hour-After-Hour, Right Guard, Mennen E., Mum, Soft and Dri,* to name a few and not including vaginal sprays and douches, and the all-purpose deodorant *Body All.* [45]

Compared to the corporation control exerted over a woman, the degree of control of her husband's life may be even more terrifying:

A worker for a large corporation behaves for eight hours a day according to production norms of his employer. After work he spends perhaps two hours in the local bar, drinking the beer that corporation advertising has conditioned him to drink and absorbing new corporation commands through the color television he watches instead of talking to his companions. When he arrives home, he eats food that the corporative media have socialized his wife into selecting at the supermarket. Following dinner, the worker spends four more hours watching and being socialized by corporation-selected entertainment on TV, laced with corporation-designed commercials. Life with the corporation has now accounted for roughly fifteen hours of his twenty-four hour day.

Everyman's Tension: Surviving Social Change

Assume this individual dimly perceives a tension between his human needs and his social surroundings. Where does he get his ideas—his guiding norms—according to which he is likely to design a solution to this tension? Figure 5–3 shows the configuration of Everyman's guiding norms.

**Remember:
Politics begins with an idea.**

Naturally, our average worker is a little confused when it comes to making political decisions—whether in his private life or in the official political arena.

**Politics begins with an idea.
But—which idea?**

As a result of that confusion, he is easily manipulated into affirming the work ethic against the poor but not against corporations.

FIGURE 5—3
Everyman's Social Norms

First, he believes, of course, in:			Second, he believes, equally of course, in:
Life Liberty Property Individualism Competition The work ethic.	}	being replaced by	Life Security Skilled management for property Teamwork Cooperation . . . and both the work ethic and the spend ethic.
That much he has been taught at mother's knee and in school.			That much he has learned from the corporation and its media.

Money spent on the poor is "the dole"; money spent on the rich corporations is "a subsidy."

> **"The upside-down welfare state
> helps the rich get richer
> and the poor, poorer."**
> —Justice William O. Douglas[46]

When asked whether he thinks the government has gone too far in regulating business and interfering with the free enterprise system, the average American mustered 42 percent of his ranks to agree and 39 percent to disagree, with 19 percent in the don't-know category.[47] In 1972, given a chance to vote for a president who was the first to institute price and wage controls since World War II, the same average American turned out nearly 70 percent of the vote for Richard M. Nixon.

It is difficult to find where the average American uses norms that are self-determined or that are derived from his personal human needs. Left to himself for a reasonable length of his day, he might be expected to develop a fairly consistent set of norms for behavior.

But he is not left to himself. His experience is government-propagated, corporation-conditioned, and media-mediated. On the one hand, he believes in this God-given obligation to pull himself up by his bootstraps. On the other, he demands the values of the modern industrial and business corporation: job security, income stability, and even welfare guarantees (at least for those willing to work).

American political man was conceived free. But everywhere he lies in chains. How did this become so?

Originally individuals solved their tensions through private relationships—private politics. When new tensions developed between private groups over different solutions, government was called in to do public politics—now traditional or official politics. As the ideology of science fostered the belief that only specialists with skills in technology

APOLITICS: POLITICS IN A CORPORATION WORLD

could solve tensions, the average citizen turned in awe to corporations to make decisions for him—apolitics. *Apolitics is the ideology that asserts the superiority of technical problem solving over the common-sense solution of human needs.*

Traditional Politics vs. Apolitics

In traditional politics, as in traditional economics, the emphasis is on the *product.* In apolitics, as in modern corporate economics, the emphasis is on *internal efficiency,* whether that leads to better products or not. General Motors is constantly increasing internal efficiency—and having to recall more and more cars as the quality of its product declines.

Recall that under President Nixon the United States Post Office was removed from the traditional political arena, redesigned into a government-held corporation operated according to business expertise, and relabeled the United States Postal Service.

Notice how the tension between traditional politics of amateurs (represented by a senator) and the new corporate apolitics of "experts" (represented by the postmaster general) comes to a head in the following article:

> KLASSEN TOLD BY A SENATOR THAT MAIL SERVICE IS A JOKE
> Postmaster General E. T. Klassen was told at a Senate hearing today that despite a major reorganization the mail delivery service has deteriorated to the point where it was a national joke.
> "Postal service jokes have become a national pastime," said Senator Alan Cranston, Democrat of California, in asserting that the reorganization of the Post Office Department into the United States Postal Service had failed to speed service or to slow down rate increases.
> Mr. Klassen, meanwhile, apologized to the Senate Post Office Committee for remarks that he made to a reporter before the opening of the hearings yesterday when he said, "I don't give a damn what politicians say."
> "I want to apologize for it," he said today. "It was not my intent now, nor has it been my intent, to show disrespect for Congress."[48]

What the *New York Times* may have considered a filler piece is not simply a color story on two personalities, but an example of the growing conflict between the cultures of yesterday and tomorrow: traditional politics and apolitics. The attitudes of senators versus the postmaster general quite typically represent the concern of the old-time politics for satisfying human needs, or at least interests, versus the concern of the technician for running a well-oiled machine, regardless of whether the machine produces anything or not.

Science and Apolitics

Apolitics can be seen as the result of a long process in which science plays a key role.

In ordinary human politics, people perceive needs, set goals, and design means to reach those goals. Before the scientific era, such politics, when it existed, revolved around "the central questions of men's collective existence and of individual life history. Their themes are justice and freedom, violence and oppression, happiness and gratification, poverty, illness and death. Their categories are victory and defeat, love and hate, salvation and damnation."[49]

But science rejects such themes.* It takes us away from a life in which people concern themselves with people and forces us all to concern ourselves with the "life" of the technological-economic machine. Unconcerned with what is good or bad in the conduct of human beings, the doctrine of scientism held people could build and run machines to produce things they needed. As science became reified into technology, people were assigned roles in technology and economy to keep the machines and the systems running, whether they delivered any worthwhile product or not. High priests of scientism like the psychologist B. F. Skinner, counting on the efficacy of their status, then tell human beings they must go beyond such concerns as freedom and dignity—the very qualities that make human beings human.[50]

The result is apolitics. Apolitics is both an ideology and a human condition in the postmodern era. It is a condition in the sense that people engage in symbolic politics in the official political arena within limits already set by engineers, technicians, and bureaucrats in the administrative segments of government and corporations. It is an ideology in the sense that people believe that technical and expert decisions are superior to decisions made by the mere citizen. Ultimately the system of apolitics requires that the citizen be totally depoliticized—that he collapse into apathy.[51] With barely half the citizens in the United States voting in the last presidential election, apolitics appears on the upswing.

The Ideology of Apolitics

Yet public politics, despite its dominant concern with responding to mere selfish interests, is one of the last defenders of human beings interested in human needs. As such it is an obsolescent form of activity, but some of its politicians seem determined to go down fighting. While having willingly relegated much of their political power to administrative organs—the executive and the separate independent agencies—politicians responded swiftly when the technicians of purposeless power in the White House declared total war on the political process in the subversive operations of the Watergate affair.

At the same time, the power of private corporations remains essentially untouched by attempts from the traditional political arena to control it. Corporations such as International Telephone and Telegraph are supernations of their own that transcend national borders, have their own law, and run their employees' lives from cradle to

The Growing Domain of Apolitics

---

*We are not critical of creative science, but of the taken-for-granted routine of scientism which has become sacrosanct in America's technological society. To see how the creative scientific *process* differs from the stale, *Maintenance* paradigms of scientism, see Thomas Kuhn, *The Structure of Scientific Revolutions* (Chicago: University of Chicago Press, 1962). Also see Chapter 12.

grave.[52] Because both the managers and technicians of corporations and administrative governmental agencies share the same technique-oriented mentality, they frequently exchange personnel. Together these two centers of power control without appeal our daily lives.

As the codirector of the Institute for Policy Studies, Richard J. Barnet, comments:

> Because of their power over technology, finance, communications and markets, the mature corporations function like a government. . . .
>
> . . . economics is a branch of politics. Once demystified, the dismal science (economics) is nothing less than the study of power.[53]

And, as the social scientist Martin Peretz notes:

> The top 500 industrial corporations in America control 70 percent of the production of the non-agricultural economy, which is approximately half of the manufacturing done in the world. . . .
>
> Essentially, what this concentration entails is the establishment of formally and effectively irresponsible private government over public problems. The corporation's psychological test for employment, its country club, its "school tie," its psychoanalysts, its residential clusters, its chaplains, its implicit demand for conformisms of all sorts constitute impositions of power we would resist from government.[54]

What characterizes the era of apolitics is the absence of ultimate norms and the emphasis on technique. In the apolitical system, thinking, especially about human needs, is discouraged. Government and private corporations both focus on carrying out blindly the functions and on repairing malfunctions of a system designed long ago for forgotten purposes.

As this system changes daily life, even the categories for the analysis of political and social life are becoming obsolete. The *socialization* of *values* is replaced by *conditioning*, in which the individual does not measure his actions against learned normative standards, and action becomes its own reward or punishment. Social scientists will have to find analytical tools for studying conditioning.

The study of *personality*, another current tool of analysis, deals with the whole man. But in the system of apolitics, the technological machine requires that each role-playing individual perform only a limited number of functions. The system cares nothing for the whole man and how he feels, as long as he puts a bolt in the proper place in a car on the assembly line. The analysis of *role* and *function*—the study of fragmented man—will tend to replace studies of personality.

Even *class* or *social-economic status* are no longer as useful, because actual social action and differentiation cuts through class and income lines. When the space program of Boeing Aircraft closes, all employees are fired—from engineer to janitor. These are problems of analysis that a future political science will have to confront.

Until such analysis takes place, the individual will find himself increasingly trapped in a seemingly chaotic world.

Despite occasional efforts at government trust-busting, the individual will perceive his private sphere permeated and opened up to such corporate giants as General Motors, International Telephone and Telegraph, and General Electric. At the same time, politics conveniently diverts our private energies into arguments over old values like individualism and competition, which we have already been forced to surrender as we work in noncompetitive, docile teams at the corporate assembly line and office.

Opened up like a clam shell, the individual is now forced to accept quietly as a clam the fact that corporate policies determine the shape and content of his private life. These policies affect him primarily through three contact points: his job, where he is conditioned into new behavior tailored to corporative technical needs; the media, through which he is conditioned to value those goods that corporations make; and the market, where his conditioning is expected to pay off in proper support behavior for the corporate state.

No wonder that under such conditions some Americans see the irrelevance of traditional public politics and try to flee into an unfortunately already penetrated private sphere. Other Americans are looking to other countries in search of solutions to be imported from abroad.

REFERENCES

1. See H. Mark Roelofs, *The Language of Modern Politics* (Homewood, Ill.: The Dorsey Press, 1967).
2. *The New York Times*, Tuesday, March 13, 1973, p. 1
3. *The New York Times*, Tuesday, March 13, 1973, "Week in Review" section, page 16.
4. *Loc. cit.*
5. *Loc. cit.*
6. *Loc. cit.*
7. *Loc. cit.*
8. *Loc. cit.*
9. *The New York Times*, Friday, July 13, 1973 (City Edition), page 1.
10. Robert A. Dahl, *A Preface to Democratic Theory* (Chicago: University of Chicago Press, 1956), p. 137.
11. See David B. Truman, *The Governmental Process: Political Interests and Public Opinion*, 2nd ed. (New York: Alfred A. Knopf, 1971).
12. *The New York Post*, December 27, 1972, p. 48.
13. For a basic book on voting behavior, see William H. Flanigan, *The Political Behavior of the American Electorate*, 2nd ed. (Boston: Allyn & Bacon, 1972).
14. Lloyd Free and Hadley Cantril, *The Political Beliefs of Americans* (New Brunswick, N.J.: Rutgers University Press, 1967), p. 37.
15. See also Joe R. Feagin, "Poverty: We Still Believe That God Helps Those Who Help Themselves," *Psychology Today* 6, no. 6 (November 1972), pp. 101 – 110.
16. See Louis Hartz, *The Liberal Tradition in America: An Interpretation of American Political Thought Since the Revolution* (New York: Harcourt Brace Jovanovich, 1966).
17. Dwight D. Eisenhower, "The Ticklish Problem of Political Fund-Raising—and Spending," *Reader's Digest*, January 1968, cited in Morton Mintz and Jerry S. Cohen, *America, Inc.—Who Owns and Operates the United States* (New York: Dell, 1972), p. 200.
18. Interview with R. W. Apple, *The New York Times*, March 28, 1970, cited in Mintz and Cohen, *America, Inc.*, p. 215.
19. Mintz and Cohen, *America, Inc.*, p. 214.

20. James M. Landis, *Report on Regulatory Agencies to the President-Elect*, cited in Mintz and Cohen, America, Inc., p. 295.

21. See Mintz and Cohen, *America, Inc.*, p. 299.

22. Mintz and Cohen, *America, Inc.*, p. 295.

23. James M. Perry, "The Almost Perfect Political Campaign: Nelson Rockefeller's Last Hurrah," *The National Observer*, January 9, 1967, reprinted in Robert T. Golembiewski, J. Malcolm Moore, and Jack Rabin, eds., *Dilemmas of Political Participation* (Englewood Cliffs, N.J.: Prentice-Hall, 1973), p. 256.

24. In recent work on leadership, one of the authors suggests that in fact only a few functional characteristics may qualify an individual for leadership in terms of the expectations of followers—so that a number of different personality types might qualify for the same position. See Ralph P. Hummel, "The Psychology of Charismatic Leadership," paper presented at the Ninth World Congress of the International Political Science Association, August 1973, Montreal.

25. See especially his major work, *The Presidential Character: Predicting Performance in the White House* (Englewood Cliffs, N.J.: Prentice-Hall, 1972).

26. James David Barber, "The President and His Friends," paper delivered at the annual convention of the American Political Science Association, September 1969.

27. Barber, "The President and His Friends," p. 23.

28. Barber, "The President and His Friends," pp. 24–25.

29. Barber, "The President and His Friends," p. 28.

30. Barber, *The Presidential Character*, p. 442.

31. Barber, *The Presidential Character*, p. 442.

32. It is not technical know-how that makes the good citizen, but the fact that he is an amateur at decision making who knows what he needs, in the normative sense, and is aware of the social facts that oppose or facilitate satisfaction of his needs, as well as of rules of the game that can help him gain his satisfactions politically. For an excellent exposition of the role of the citizen and the type of knowledge he needs, see Alfred Schutz, "The Well-Informed Citizen," in *Collected Works*, vol. 2 (The Hague: Martinus Nijhoff, 1964), pp. 120–134.

33. Fred I. Greenstein, "The Citizen Base of the American Political System," in *Dilemmas of Political Participation*, ed. Golembiewski, Moore, and Rabin, pp. 297–298.

34. 1965 AIPO survey, reported in the *Gallup Opinion Index*, November 1965, cited in Greenstein, "The Citizen Base," in *Dilemmas of Political Participation*, ed. Golembiewski, Moore, and Rabin, p. 298.

35. John P. Robinson et al., *Measures of Political Attitudes* (Ann Arbor: Survey Research Center, Institute for Social Research [University of Michigan], 1968), cited in Greenstein, "The Citizen Base," in *Dilemmas of Political Participation*, ed. Golembiewski, Moore, and Rabin, p. 295.

36. Golembiewski, Moore, and Rabin, p. 296.

37. See Robert D. Hess and Judith V. Torney, *The Development of Political Attitudes in Children* (Chicago: Aldine Publishing, 1967). See also David Easton and Jack Dennis, *Children in the Political System: Origins of Political Legitimacy* (New York: McGraw-Hill, 1969).

38. Peter Koenig, "Kat Kincaide of Twin Oaks," *Psychology Today* 6, no. 8 (January 1973): 40.

39. Richard Poirier, *The Performing Self* (New York: Oxford University Press, 1971), p. viii.

40. Carlos Fuentes, "The discreet charm of Luis Bunuel," *New York Times Sunday Magazine*, March 11, 1973, p. 93.

41. George Santayana, *Interpretations of Poetry and Religion* (New York: Harper Torchbooks, 1957), p. 15.

42. Mary White Harder, James T. Richardson, and Robert B. Simmonds, "Jesus People," *Psychology Today* 6, no. 7 (December 1972): 110.

43. Reported in Andrew Kopkind, "Mystic Politics," *Ramparts* 12, no. 1 (July 1973), pp. 26–28, 47–57. Especially useful for understanding such movements in the light of the sociology of religion are Peter Berger, *The Sacred Canopy: Elements of a Sociological Theory of Religion* (Garden City, N.Y.: Doubleday, 1967), and *Rumor of Angels: Modern Society and the Rediscovery of the Supernatural* (Garden City, N.Y.: Doubleday, 1969).

44. From Lucinda Franks and Thomas Powers, "Making of a Terrorist," in Golembiewski, Moore, and Rabin, *Dilemmas of Political Participation*, pp. 24–42.

45. Beth Aroyo, "Menage a Trois: Women, the Cleanliness Syndrome and the Media," unpublished student paper, SUNY, College at Fredonia.

46. William O. Douglas, *Points of Rebellion* (New York: Random House, Vintage Books, 1970), p. 70. Among other statistics from Justice Douglas's book: "In one year, Texas (oil) producers, who constitute .02 percent of the Texas population, received 250 million dollars in subsidies, while the Texas poor, who constitute 28.8 percent of the Texas population, received 7 million dollars in food assistance." Ibid, p. 72.

47. Lloyd A. Free and Hadley Cantril, *The Political Beliefs of Americans: A Study of Public Opinion* (Rutgers University Press, 1967), Clarion edition, pp. 24–25.

48. *The New York Times*, city edition, March 9, 1973, p. 14.

49. Juergen Habermas, *Toward a Rational Society: Student Protest, Science and Politics*, trans. Jeremy J. Shapiro (Boston: Beacon Press, 1971), p. 96.

50. B. F. Skinner, *Beyond Freedom and Dignity* (New York: Bantam Books, Vintage, 1972). Skinner's ideology may be acceptable as description of the fact that under the reign of apolitics human beings are increasingly *conditioned* into behavior rather than being capable of *thinking*. When Skinner asserts that conditioning describes the functioning of man's mind in all eras, his psychology becomes ideology that serves the technicians and managers of apolitics.

51. "The solution of technical problems is not dependent on discussion. Rather, public discussion could render problematic the framework within which the tasks of government action present themselves as technical ones. Therefore the new politics of state interventionism requires a depolitization of the mass of the population. To the extent that practical questions are eliminated, the public realm loses its political function." (Habermas, *Toward a Rational Society*, pp. 103–104).

52. See specifically Anthony Sampson, *The Sovereign State of ITT* (New York: Stein & Day, 1973). For a general treatment of the power of corporations: Andrew Hacker, *The Corporation Takeover* (Garden City, N.Y.: Doubleday, Anchor Books, 1965). On life and work inside the corporation: *Work in America: Report of a Special Task Force to the Secretary of Health, Education and Welfare* (Cambridge, Mass.: MIT Press, 1973).

53. *The New York Times Book Review*, September 16, 1973, p. 1. This is a review of John Kenneth Galbraith, *Economics and Public Purpose* (Boston: Houghton Mifflin, 1973), on public and private bureaucracies as "the decisive force in economic and political life."

54. Martin Peretz, "Some Notes on the Present and Future of Power and Wealth in America," in *The Endless Crisis: America in the Seventies*, ed. Francois Duchene (New York: Simon and Schuster, 1970), pp. 199–200.

isaak

6 **Wherein the Inlandians learn that to satisfy their needs they must communicate with foreigners and compare political ends and means. To do so, they go through four steps for comparing politics.**

6 Comparing Politics for Outsiders

When things go wrong at home, people look to other cultures for solutions. We can look at foreign cultures from the outside or from the inside or both. Most of the time we view these cultures superficially, from their outermost structures, processes, and colorings. We remain as strangers in a strange land. To get inside a culture, to see things as a native would in order to learn from him, is more difficult. We must learn not only his language and traditions, but also how he thinks, perceives, loves, and hates. We must temporarily try to shed our own skin and biases and take up his.

To get inside the meaning of a foreign culture, we begin by identifying what we have in common with the foreigner. Which needs and values do we both have in common? Which ideas, elements, or variables are universal enough to cut across both of our cultures and be meaningful to both of us? And once we identify similarities, we then look for differences.

This is what writer Carlos Castaneda did when he described his progress toward learning the esoteric way of life of the mystic don Juan in *Journey to Ixtlan: The Lessons of Don Juan:* " . . .as a teacher of sorcery, don Juan endeavored to describe the world to me from the very first time we talked. My difficulty in grasping his concepts and methods stemmed from the fact that the units of his description were alien and incompatible with those of my own. His contention was that he was teaching me how to 'see' as opposed to merely 'looking,' and that 'stopping the world' was the first step to 'seeing.'"[1]

Stopping the world means getting off my own world and onto another's. In short, to understand the culture of another, we begin with universal needs and then move towards his particular historical situation—both the position of his culture in the creation-maintenance-decay cycle and his own unique interpretation and life-style in that culture. As similarity leads us to differences, universality leads us to uniqueness.

This chapter discusses the need to compare problems and perspectives across cultures, the universal concepts or variables that make such comparison possible, and specific ways of thinking or tools for understanding cultures caught in creation, in maintenance, or in decay. The chapter represents only a general beginning—a way to move from the outside of a foreign culture to the inside. To actually experience the uniqueness of a foreign culture, the reader must go out on his own to learn a foreign language and a foreign tradition and live and work with "foreign" human beings until he no longer feels foreign to them or they to him. Only then will he truly know how to solve his problems or tensions in *their* way.

Recall that when things went wrong in Inlandia, the political leaders looked to another culture for a solution. Because of a lack of the
resources (clams) on which their economy was based, Alphonse and
Balthazar, the governing elites, sent an expedition to exploit the outlands. Inlandians discovered that Outlandians also depended upon
clams as a solution to their universal survival need. A brief armed
clash resulted. Afterwards, the leaders of both forces sat exhausted
under a battle-scarred coconut tree and struggled to communicate. . . .

Raz
Putin: (breathing heavily) Puff, puff. What—puff—were we fighting
        about?
Beaming
Ben: (not-so-beaming just then) Clams!
Raz: That's right. Our clams died from pollution, and we came here
       to get some more. We didn't know they belonged to you.
Ben: (suspiciously) Hmmmmmm.
Raz: You know, we both have the same problem: getting clams for
       food . . .
Ben: That's right.

> **The study of comparative politics
> begins with the perception of
> a shared problem.**

Raz: (continuing his thought musingly) . . . and I've been won-
       dering how you kept your clams alive while ours died.

> **The study of comparative politics
> involves discovering alternative
> arrangements for solving
> similar problems.**

Ben: (hedging) Well, how did you use to get your clams?
Raz: I don't know. Our King Alphonse and our High Priest Bal-
       thazar set up the arrangement. Only they were allowed to
       know the secret techniques.
Ben: Well, here we do everything by mutual agreement. When
       two of our people discovered how to do clamming, they told
       the entire population. We then set ourselves up in pairs, with
       one person of each pair digging and the other cracking.

> **Different cultures use different
> techniques to solve problems —
> for example, different RULES
> OF THE GAME.**

Raz: (aghast) B—b—but how did the Great Clam God like that, Mr. Benjamin?

Ben: Call me Ben. What Great Clam God? We believe all men are created equal. Everyone had a right to know how to survive by getting clams!

What people want or believe in—VALUES—differs from culture to culture.

Raz: Oh.

Ben: May I call you "Raz"?

Raz: Please do. But tell me one more thing. How were you able to pay your Enforcers to keep the Know-Nothings down if everyone knew . . . the . . . secret? (Suddenly astonished at a thought that has just occurred to him) Say, you're not going to tell me you don't *have* Know-Nothings?!

Ben: That's right. I was going to tell you just that.

Raz: (aside) I had hoped you wouldn't.

Ben: Well, if everyone knows all there is to know, you can hardly have a class structure, can you?

Some SOCIAL INSTITUTIONS favor creative solutions; some don't.

Ben: (continuing) And besides, by not having a lower class, we were able to encourage participation by all in our system. That came in very handy one day when an ordinary member of a digger-cracker team saw where our sewage was going and had an idea. You may have heard of the saying that politics begins with an idea? (Continues without waiting for an answer) Well, he saw some clams moving very sluggishly around the sewage pipes. Thought they might be sick. Came to the next assembly meeting and told us. That sounded bad to our medicine men; they ran some tests and found the clams might die, so we invented the "latrine."

Different POLITICAL INSTITUTIONS can lead to different social techniques for solving problems.

Raz: (confused) Latrines? Assembly? How can a mere Digger or Cracker be so smart? Ours are sodden clods. Give 'em some coconut beer and a girlie show at night and their minds are out of commission for days. Unimaginative types. Reprehensible personalities.

Ben: Maybe personality has something to do with how people are trained to live and what class they're in.

> **Policy-makers shape PERSONALITY
> and get from their creations
> what they deserve.**

Ben: (continuing) . . . anyway, we were pretty lucky to have planned for thorough popular support by getting everybody into a cooperative and informed state of mind. Otherwise we might never have heard about the clams until it was too late.

Raz: (thoughtfully) So that's how you kept your clams alive . . . .

TOOLS FOR GENERAL COMPARISONS

Human beings study comparative politics—how others solve their problems—when things go wrong in their own political situation. Problems perceived depend on the values and needs of a culture. In fact, culture may be defined as the shared values acted out by a population over time. How human beings solve problems to satisfy their needs and values depends upon the techniques that their culture allows.

For example, the authoritarian culture of Inlandia prevented the population from solving its hunger problems over the long run. Restrictive class structure and personality manipulation prevented the possibility of creative solutions from the lower ranks. In the democratic culture of Outlandia, the creation of equal social opportunities for inventive personalities led to a solution of the hunger problem before it arose. On the other hand, Outlandia was almost overrun by the class-based efficiency of the Inlandian military. Different problems require different techniques for their solution.

Cultures may borrow techniques from others for their survival. Likewise, survival and self-actualization for the individual depend on his being able to use the proper techniques to solve his problems. When his culture prevents the rational use of such problem-solving techniques, the individual may perceive it to be pathological. Recall the revolution of Raz Putin, Colombo, and the Know-Nothings. In such revolutionary situations, we can expect individuals to go to other cultures for ideas to solve their problems.

How does the individual know what techniques to use to solve his problems? First, he determines his location within his own culture—within the historical stages of the cycle, within the limits of social class, political institutions, his personality, and socially accepted values. The power of the individual to solve his problems depends on his ability to use the tools of his own culture to get what he wants. Second, when he meets obstacles in his own society, he locates other individuals with similar problems in other cultures. He looks at their location in the cycle of creation, maintenance, and decay, their location in social space, and their problems. Then he sees if they have been able to use different techniques to solve their problems.

From the distant perspective of looking abroad, some universal variables that affect problem-solving techniques emerge. As they were illustrated in the scenario, these variables are rules of the game, values, social and political institutions, and personality. The appearance of these variables was not accidental. Politics everywhere is problem solving through social relationships. In any social relationship, human beings are motivated by *values*, create rules and patterns (*rules of the game, social* and *political institutions*) to fulfill their needs and are socialized into these patterns (*personality*).

Accepting that the comparative study of politics is useful, the individual goes through **four steps for comparing politics:**

1. Know what variables make the comparative study of politics possible.

2. Identify your needs and ends compared with those of other cultures.

3. Locate yourself in your historical problem-situation and find others elsewhere in a similar position.

4. Learn how and when to use standard tools for finding variables relevant to your needs and discovering techniques developed elsewhere for solving your problems.

IDENTIFYING VARIABLES FOR COMPARING POLITICS

The meaning of the variables that emerged in the scenario depends on their relationship to the problem solving of everyday human beings—the many I's and you's that make up the social worlds being compared. Unless they are related to concrete human beings, abstract concepts get in the way of meaningful communication and problem solving. Let's see what these variables mean *personally*. What do "I" from Inlandia have to know about "you" from Outlandia to learn how to use your techniques to solve my problems?

The Five Variables

VALUES How you see your problems—your values. These determine what perceptions you have of your world, what you feel your needs are, and what techniques you think proper to satisfy your needs. Values are outcomes of your past and are norms that guide behavior.

RULES OF THE GAME How you are used to do doing politics—the rules of the game. Rules of the game are the taken-for-granted procedures of the routine problem-solving relationships of any political world. Most of us are born into rules of the game; only in times of creation do we get a chance to make them. Every game has rules—baseball has rules for playing baseball; America has rules for playing America. In baseball, the rules are well known. In America, the rules emphasize that politics is a process of negotiation and compromise between independent groups of "I's" and "you's," in which every player gives a little to get a little of what there is to get. In the Soviet Union, the rules require integrating each "I" with every "you" in collective labor towards social goals prescribed by elites.

POLITICAL INSTITUTIONS The patterns of problem-solving you usually perceive as relevant to your public problems—political institutions. Institutions are arrangements between people that are used again and again to solve problems. Political institutions are repeated patterns that relate more or less directly to the problem of how you go about solving public problems.

Take the unemployment problem—in the United States and in the USSR. In the United States, the problem is referred to Congress, in which individuals are encouraged to represent the needs or interests of independent centers of power. In contrast, in the Soviet Union the problem is referred to the Supreme Soviet, in which individuals are socialized to acclaim a general interest defined by a central elite. The result is likely to be that unemployment is only partly solved in the United States, because fragmented interests deadlock one another in Congress. But in the Soviet Union the problem is apt to be totally solved, because centralized political institutions do not allow individual interests to get in the way. In both cases, the idea of "solution" is defined by people in power.

SOCIAL INSTITUTIONS The patterns in your social environment that constrict or reinforce what you can do to satisfy your needs—social institutions. Whereas your personal values express your ideal chances in life, social institutions determine your real chances in life. *Social class*, for example sets certain objective limits on what you can make of yourself relative to others. Class is your location in social space as compared with others who also want what you want. Class is measurable by how much you've got of what there is to get. Where others *perceive* you to be in social space is *status*. Status is measurable by the deference accorded you by others. Often people mistake status for class—what they think of others (subjectively) for what they've got (objectively). It's one thing to have the clams and another to have others think you have them. But, as every poker player knows, having others think you have it can give you as much power as really having it. Social institutions such as status and class are the bases for political power.

PERSONALITY To find techniques from other societies to solve my problems, I have to find comparable individuals. The analysis of such individuals into characteristics of similarity and uniqueness is called the study of personality. The universal determinants in all societies are social conditioning, the human animal's needs, and the human individual's capacity (or will) to make value choices.

Social institutions impress individuals with the need for similarity in behavior; social pressures work to create *social personalities*. In doing so, society encourages the individual to satisfy certain needs created by others. To the extent that a society leaves the individual's human needs unsatisfied, the society is pathological. And indeed social institutions often do not satisfy human animal needs. For the individual human animal, the prime political act is to create himself as a unique human being through applying his will to resolve the tension between society and human needs. The result of this interaction is *individual personality*.

Note, for example, the influence of personality on politics in the Case of the Observant Clam Digger. Encouraged by his society to recognize the tension between his individual needs and society's habits, he recognizes that a mistake of his society is killing off the clams and might kill him off with starvation. By engaging in the political act of complaining to others, the Observant Digger is able not only to persuade others that human animal needs should be society's needs, but to demonstrate the effectiveness of his unique personality. The creation of unique personality comes out of a political act resolving the tension between socially prescribed needs and actual human animal needs.

In summary, all personal problems are potentially political, and the use of social relationships to solve them necessarily involves the use of the five interacting variables: values, rules of the game, social and political institutions, and personality. The comparative study of politics shows us how to use these variables for borrowing the techniques of others to satisfy our needs. This is not always an easy task, as we see in the following scenario.

Raz Putin and Beaming Ben continue their peace talks. Now they turn to the reasons for their mutual lack of success in the Skirmish of Coconut Grove.

Problems in Borrowing Techniques

Raz
Putin: . . . so that's how you kept your clams alive. I guess achieving one's goals depends on using the right methods.

> **What techniques you use determine what goals you can achieve.**

Beaming
Ben: (in a conciliatory gesture) Perhaps we were just lucky in hitting on the kind of political and social structure that suited our needs. . . .

> **Variables hooked up together can become techniques.**

Ben: On the other hand, we admired the way you seemed to be able to launch a quick attack; we didn't even have a chance of digging in. How did you do that?

> **Inquiring after others' techniques is useful for reaching similar goals.**

Raz: (cheered up by the other's interest) It was simple. Our Chief Enforcer, Colombo, just gave the order, and we marched.

> **Forced total CORRELATION between POLITICAL INSTITUTIONS and individual PERSONALITY is called totalitarianism.**

Ben: (confused for once) Yes, I understand that's what happened. He gave the orders, you marched—but why did you follow his orders?

Raz: In Inlandia, whenever orders are given, Enforcers obey. They're taught that from childhood.

> **Socialization in CLASS shapes
> PERSONALITY for class work.**

Ben: In our society we are taught the Three Steps.
Raz: The three steps?

> **The meaning of
> the techniques of others
> should not be taken for granted.**

Ben: Yes. Think, Consult, Act. We never do anything before
        thinking about its consequences for a long time. We talk with
        all others about it, especially if the consequences might affect
        all others. Then, if we can agree on action, and only then,
        we act. We believe that way we get everybody's whole-
        hearted support.

> **POLITICAL INSTITUTIONS
> that represent conflicting NEEDS
> of autonomous PERSONALITIES
> produce libertarian politics.**

Raz: Hmm. Yes. Your troops did seem to fight with considerable
        esprit de corps. On the other hand, our system gave us
        the jump on you before you were ready, even though
        there's been some grumbling in the ranks. . . . Now if we
        could put your system and ours together, we'd have an
        army that would be both courageous and lightning-fast.

> **Certain techniques fulfill
> specific NEEDS and preclude
> the satisfaction of others.**

Ben: I doubt it could be done. The reason we Think, Consult, and
        Act is that we believe the highest good of society is to enable
        individuals to achieve their true potential through interaction
        with other individuals—self-actualization through social rela-
        tionships. To be lightning-swift in our decisions, we'd have to
        drop that.

> **Some needs are better and
> tougher to actualize than others.**

Raz: You mean you wouldn't drop your goal of self-actualization,
        even if it meant you'd have a better chance to survive a
        war?!
Ben: Well, we didn't do too badly. We fought you to a standstill.
Raz: For us, survival is the highest good—you might say, the
        basic good. Without it, you can't very well self-actualize.
Ben: Yes. But there must be more to life than just taking orders.

Borrowing techniques from other worlds is not always easy. Note what happened when Raz Putin tried to borrow morale-building techniques for his army from Benjamin. Thoughtful participation to build commitment and morale is incompatible with mindless conditioning designed to produce lightning-swift reflexes. The borrower soon learns that to introduce a new variable into the problem-solving techniques of his world may be to move or displace other variables. He finds he needs a tool to study the relations between social facts. The concept of "correlation" is such a tool.

The idea of correlation asserts that when one piece of reality, or variable, is moved, another piece may move also. There are two standard forms of correlation: "If-then" and "the more-the more (or the less)." "If-then" correlations imply definite relationships; "The more-the more" correlations imply probable relationships. Take the example of military training. *If* I threaten a Know-Nothing with death, *then* he will respond to my orders with lightning speed. This statement implies that *every time* a Know-Nothing is threatened with death, he will respond swiftly, because he values life even under slave conditions more than death.

The same statement could also be made in the terms of probabilistic correlation: *the more* I threaten the Know-Nothing with death, *the more* he makes like lightning. This statement implies the more often a Know-Nothing is threatened with death, the more often he is *likely* to respond quickly. *Comparative politics means finding typical correlations between variables so that you can import from the outlands those variable clusters useful for solving your problems.*

Say your problem is to maintain iron-clad discipline in your society. Through comparative study you find that all other societies with iron-clad discipline have rigid educational systems (social institutions) that produce submissive human beings (personality). According to the idea of correlation, you have every right to expect that importing rigid educational techniques will yield submissive personalities fit for accepting iron-clad social structures—such as rigid class stratification—in your own society. If this theory works out in practice, you've got a useful cross-cultural correlation.

isaak

INVITATION

There are many examples of correlations that can be borrowed to help solve problems. Take any two of the five variables—values, rules of the game, political institutions, social institutions, personality—and find correlations between them in:

Your local newspaper's coverage of problems shared by a foreign country and ourselves.

For other examples of cross-cultural correlations see:

Bernard Berelson and Gary Steiner, *Human Behavior: An Inventory of Scientific Findings* (New York: Harcourt, Brace & World, 1964).

Roy C. Macridis and Robert E. Ward, eds., *Modern Political Systems: Europe* (Englewood Cliffs, Prentice-Hall, 1972).

COMPARING YOUR NEEDS AND ENDS WITH OTHERS

To identify the variables and correlations that are similar in different cultures is not enough for comparing politics. The second step is to compare your own needs and ends with those of the people you are studying.

Recall that politics is a social act by which human beings try to resolve tensions between their needs and their social facts. The variables of politics define the existing *social facts* in a culture. These are residues of past attempts at need-satisfaction that eventually get in the way of satisfying some people's present needs. They include social or political institutions like class, status, and traditional problem-solving machinery, and old personality and value systems.

By human *needs* we mean those prerequisites to existence without which human beings cease to be human. Such needs are universal for all people everywhere by definition. However, most of us live in societies governed by interests and values that do not always relate to human needs and even frustrate their satisfaction. If we do not perceive the gaps between our human needs and dehumanizing interests, values, and social facts, we lack political consciousness. Political consciousness comes into being when we become aware of such tensions.

Without knowing what we really need, it is not possible to learn what it is worthwhile to borrow from other cultures. And disagreement over what human needs actually are still lurks behind all attempts to compare the politics of different cultures.

Indications of Universal Needs

Until this question is conclusively settled by science, all we can do is to adopt a tentative set of needs established with the best scientific backing we can find. Here it will be assumed that the ultimate test of such a set of needs is whether or not this set is more or less in tune with man's ultimate value—human life.

Before listing the set of needs we assume to be relevant for all human beings everywhere, it is intriguing to cite a few of the many scientific findings that support this set of human needs.

> —Deprived of food, prisoners of war abandoned all activity and thought except that centering around food.[2]
> —Sleep deprivation in a man who stayed awake for 220 hours produced irritability, paranoid thinking, hallucinations, and rage; he also revealed cycles of deficits in thinking and visual-motor performance, ending in virtual untestability on the ninth day.[3]
> —Religious hermits, prisoners of war, and castaways display a strong tendency to hallucinate other people after reporting an unbearable "pain" of isolation. One typical report by a prisoner: "Gradually the loneliness closed in. Later on I was to experience situations which amounted almost to physical torture, but even that seemed preferable to absolute isolation."[4]
> —Even prisoners in a concentration camp tended to display a drive toward order and meaning by developing strong relationships and orientations toward their guards and potential executioners. One of the rare causes for rebellion was the "capricious rule" of criminal prisoners over political prisoners, disrupting the orderliness of starvation and death.[5]

—These and other scientific findings were summarized into twenty-eight types of "needs" as early as 1928—ranging from "need acquisition, need conservance, need order, need superiority, need recognition . . ." to "need abasement, need affiliation, need play, need cognizance, and need exposition."

Consider the difficulties that founders of a new political system might experience if they wanted to design values, personalities, behavior, and structures in such a way as to meet all possible needs of everyone in society. The representatives of former Inlandia and former Outlandia are trying to create a Super-State to be called Overlandia. Typical problems at the first Constitutional Convention of Overlandia indicate the necessity for political people to come to some agreement on a basic set of need priorities.

THE PLAYERS:

Making Needs and Ends Meet

From
Inlandia:
Colombo, formerly police chief. Raz Putin, former cabinet minister.
From
Outlandia:
Beaming Benjamin, ambassador. Melissa Mayflower, ambassadress.

Raz Putin: If I may say so, it seems to me our major task will be to design goals for Overlandians.

Beaming Ben: And ways to reach to those goals.

Raz: Right. But what goals? We've had some bad experiences with an elite system in our late unlamented country—before the revolution, that is. The elites couldn't satisfy the most basic of all needs—survival. We almost starved.

Ben: And we failed to satisfy our need for security. Your army almost overran us and stole our food supply. We should be able to improve on that.

Raz: Yes, but how? Remember, we discussed that before. How can you have your democratic rule of the political game and simultaneously have our lightning-swift discipline in the armed forces? And how could we have a state with our disciplined way of life that keeps us fit for war and yet allow imagination for the lower and middle classes? But it's imagination that permits the people to adjust to new problems and stimulates Know-Nothings to know enough to see solutions. We have run into a basic conflict between needs and have to find a standard for ordering them in value priority. Does anyone have any suggestions?

Melissa Mayflower: I have one that might work. My husband, Maslow May-

	flower, and I have developed a theory of five basic human needs and the order in which they must be satisfied. As a matter of fact, he stayed home to scrub the kitchen floor and look after our fourteen children so that I could present the theory to you today. If you decided to adopt it, all you would have to do is find ways of meeting all five needs one by one so that they do not lead to unnecessary conflicts.
Ben:	(who had eighteen mistresses in France looking after his illegitimate children and was therefore skeptical of this liberated woman) What five needs? And if they really exist, why doesn't Maslow come to address us himself?
Melissa:	I came here after we both agreed that I was the more gifted at oral expression. Besides, he needs the exercise at home—exercise it looks as if you could use as well, you tubby male chauvinist—
Raz:	Now, now. This must remain a peaceful meeting. And our state must allow various life-styles to let men and women fit their needs together as they see fit. What are these five needs or ends, anyway?
Melissa:	We think people have to satisfy their physiological, safety, love, self-esteem, and self-actualization needs, in that order. I suspect the love need may be more important than he thinks, but otherwise we are in total agreement. Put simply, without food, water, and air—our physiological needs—we couldn't exist at all. Clearly without security from bullets, knives, and other physical threats, we wouldn't have much time for love, self-esteem, and self-actualization. Without love, self-esteem would never be complete. And without self-esteem, we wouldn't be able to live up to our greatest potential as human beings—self-actualization. So there you have it: the psychological need scale in a clam shell.
Ben:	Hmmm . . .
Raz:	How do you expect us to apply these needs to politics?
Melissa:	Well . . . we haven't finished our book yet. Perhaps we could adjourn until . . .

Maslow's Need Hierarchy

Several millenia later, the psychologist Abraham Maslow, perhaps a descendant of Maslow and Melissa Mayflower, finished a book containing an integrated list of human needs.[6] These are (1) physiological needs, (2) safety needs, (3) love needs, (4) esteem needs, and (5) self-actualization needs.

It should be possible to estimate the success of a society by measuring the degree to which its political institutions provide for the satisfaction of all five of these needs.

Before looking at the problems such measurement creates, let us define these needs more closely:

Physiological needs include the need of the body for food, water, and rest. Man's higher needs presuppose a body.

Safety needs include two types: (a) bodily safety, and (b) psychological security. The first refers to the need to live in the absence of serious physical threat, the second to the need for a predictable and orderly world.

Love needs refer to the desire for warmth, affection, and inclusion by desired objects. Children whose love needs are not satisfied may grow up, but they will be emotionally and cognitively underdeveloped.

Esteem needs include the need for positive self-evaluation and the positive valuation of the self by others. They are based on "real capacity and achievement," which "leads to feelings of self-confidence, worth, strength, capability, and adequacy, of being useful and necessary in the world."[7]

Self-actualization needs motivate the individual to do what he is fitted for. "A musician must make music, an artist must paint, a poet must write if he is to be ultimately at peace with himself. What a man *can* be, he *must* be."[8]

How Bad Are Contemporary Societies?

In his search for the best possible society, the philosopher Aristotle studied more than 150 city-states. If a modern researcher were to apply Maslow's five needs to the study of as many nations, it is doubtful that he would find a single one that did more than partly take care of the two basic needs—physiological and safety—and none at all that is designed to take care of everyone's needs for love, self-esteem, and self-actualization.

Political scientist Bernard Crick noted that though it is difficult to find a good society, almost everyone can recognize a bad one. If so, it may be possible to use Maslow's five needs not in a search for the society that fulfills them, but in a negative process of elimination. Anyone who seeks to borrow something from other systems that seems useful for his own can ask what the costs of such borrowing might be. If one or several of the basic human needs that any society should fulfill are not satisfied in a given society, we have clues as to such costs.

Consider the following news report from Greece:

In the story below, it might seem that no one's needs are being met. Certainly neither the students being beaten nor the police doing the beating seem to be receiving satisfaction of physiological, safety, love, self-esteem, or self-actualization needs.

But put yourself into the shoes of the police: are you sure beating up students may not help protect your self-esteem?

And besides, read the end of the story. *Somebody's* need for safety and even self-actualization seems to be taken care of: the "needs" of the faculty on the academic senate!

How can we make needs compatible?

Athens Police Storm University To End Sit-In by 800 Students

ATHENS, March 20—Policemen swinging clubs stormed into the Athens University Law School today to break up a sit-in by 800 students demanding greater academic liberties.

Small groups of protesters emerged spattered with blood, clutching their mid-sections or heads, trying to support each other.

Most of the protesters ran out screaming "Murderers!" at the policemen who pursued them. Some were beaten to the ground. Others were taken away in police cars.

How many were injured was not immediately known. The police put the number at 11, but this was disputed by witnesses. A woman student was said to have suffered a brain concussion. . . .

Gen. Vassilios Tsoumbas, the Public Order Minister, who directed the raid, told newsmen outside the law school that the Athens University Senate had asked the police to clear the building. The university senate said tonight that the raid had been staged after the students had defied its ultimatum to evacuate the school.

Onlookers were also beaten by the police.

John Rigos, a United States citizen who is a correspondent for United Press International, was roughed up by a policeman although he identified himself. He said the policeman told him: "Go to the devil! What will you dirty journalists write?"

A Dutch journalist was beaten by policemen and a family with an evidently retarded child was roughed up, the father screaming that it was a medical emergency. Ioannis Koutsoheras, a poet and a former member of Parliament, was seriously injured in an eye and was hospitalized.

Later, the security police picked up Prof. Ioannis Pesmazoglu, former deputy governor of the Bank of Greece who is regarded by the Government as an instigator of student unrest. He was arrested as he left the house of a friend and was reportedly detained for questioning at Athens security police headquarters.

Agitation by Greek students—pressing for greater participation in educational policies and programs—has been building up in the last three months as the Government, in an attempt to curb unrest, decreed that student strikers would lose their student draft deferment and be forced into the army at once.

Protests More Vehement

The decree triggered more vehement protests and more police crackdowns. In an effort to allay the developing crisis, Premier George Papadopoulos promised not to interfere in university affairs unless requested by the rector.

Athens University then banned protest meetings. But today some 800 students from the schools of law, physics, philosophy and medicine massed on the upper floors of the three-story law school in downtown Athens, and some climbed to the roof.

They chanted slogans for democracy and against the military-backed Government of Greece, calling on the Premier to go. They also chanted slogans against the United States, whose warships have homeport facilities here, and they spread out a banner demanding "Out with the Americans."

When the large force of uniformed policemen entered the two gates of the school, students could be heard singing the Greek national anthem. Suddenly there was silence. Then shrieks could be heard along with the shattering of window panes.

"There was no way for us to escape," said one student. "We had to run the gantlet on the stairs and the choice was either to get beaten on your backbone running away, or to get your skull smashed if you stayed."

The Athens University Senate, after an extraordinary session, denounced the protesters as "a minority trying to deny the majority of students their unalienable right to study" and ordered them to evacuate the building by 5 PM.

"When they refused to comply to the urging of the university authorities and of the district attorney, order was restored through the intervention of the state," the senate announcement said.[9]

Safety needs of some are here satisfied by the State. Are *you* willing to pay *this* cost to gain your safety needs?

Now consider this story:

Privilege Invoked for 11 Priests in Basque Dispute with Madrid

The Roman Catholic Archbishop of Pamplona has invoked the church's special privileges in Spain to protect 11 priests of his diocese against legal proceedings for having delivered some of the strongest public attacks in recent times on Spain's political leadership.

The action of the Most Rev. José Méndez Asensio and recent incidents involving the church in Bilbao have revealed a state of deep hostility between the Spanish Government and the hierarchy in the Basque country of northern Spain where the Basque people have been at odds for centuries with the central authorities.

The Spanish hierarchy as a whole recently issued a declaration calling for the independence of church and state and the dissociation of church doctrine from that of the authoritarian regime. The bishops called in particular for revision of the concordat between Spain and the Vatican among whose privileges is one that protects priests against prosecution except with the consent of their bishops.

Defended Kidnapping

Paradoxically, it was this privilege that Archbishop Mendez invoked to reject prosecution of seven priests who gave sermons early last month that justified to some extent the kidnapping in January by a group of Basque terrorists of Felipe Huarte, a prominent industrialist, from his home in Pamplona.

Four priests who delivered similar sermons were given the choice between prison and fines in legal proceedings that did not involve a trial. The priests having chosen prison, the Archbishop exercised his right to place them in a nearby monastery for the three-month period.

The Archbishop said that while he favored revision of the concordat between the church and Generalissimo Francisco Franco's regime, he was applying it fully in this case because "we firmly believe that allowing the prosecution of these 11 priests would gravely damage the peace of our Christian community."

Official Violence Seen

In one typical sermon the priest told his parishioners that they must distinguish between acts of violence and what he termed a permanent state of violence attributed to the political leadership.

"A permanent state of violence," he said, "is one in which the majority of citizens are deprived of their liberties and which prevents them from exercising their full rights. The most serious aspect of a state of violence such as ours is that it has the appearance of legality and legitimacy."

Acts of violence, such as the kidnapping of Mr. Huarte, were described by the priest as "the reaction of the oppressed, the protest that is raised by the people when it begins to awaken from its submission." The priest said the kidnapping had been commented upon by all those able to speak in public "but the people have said nothing, at least in public, because they cannot say anything."[10]

INVITATION

In this story, first define what needs are involved.

Then define whose needs are being met and whose needs are being attacked.

How does this story show that it helps to have a powerful institution back you up if you want to self-actualize?

The illustrations show that Maslow's cluster of needs can be used as a norm against which to judge how bad societies are in satisfying each of the five needs. In looking at countries this way, we uncover some interesting ironies.

People in "highly developed" societies flatter themselves that their really important needs are satisfied.* But a look at Maslow's need hierarchy shows that the values they are most anxious about are the needs at the bottom of the list (physiological and safety needs). Ironically, people in "underdeveloped" countries, in which people die because of the failure to meet bodily and safety needs, often seem to better satisfy love and self-esteem needs. People in India starve for salvation, refusing to eat sacred cows.

No society in the world is really developed in Maslow's sense. Human beings in "lesser developed" societies are socialized into holding values that are ineffective for satisfying certain basic needs (for example, family loyalty often conflicts with achievement motivation). "More developed" societies have conditioned their people to be so technologically efficient that they no longer have time or ability to satisfy affective needs (making time into money on the job takes time away from making love together at home).

Anyone who says his own society is healthy is pathological, to the extent that his needs are not being met but his social values say they are. The use of social value clusters to cover up real needs is ideology.

*Typical is a recent listing of "national hopes" of Americans gathered by the Gallup Organization. Most Americans showed intense concern for material and safety needs including peace, employment, law and order, economic stability, pollution, national unity and political stability, and an improved standard of living. Only a few were concerned with issues of self-esteem—social justice was cited as an issue by eight percent. None mentioned any love needs. And five percent cited "public morality (ethical standards, religion) as a concern. Cited in William Watts and Lloyd Free, *State of the Nation* (New York: Universe Books, 1973), p. 257.

All human beings are pathological to the extent that they assume their value clusters are self-evident truths. Therefore, they think they see the world the way others see it. In order for the stranger in a strange land to borrow the techniques of the native, he must temporarily suspend his ideology. He must think himself into the other person's shoes.

Understanding how difficult it is to empathize, the sociologist Alfred Schutz commented that "except in the pure We-relation . . . we can never grasp the individual uniqueness of our fellow-man in his unique biographical situation."[11] But we can understand him in terms of his similarity. We can ask him how he stands in terms of the five needs—physiological, safety, love, self-esteem, and self-actualization—and the five standard variables—rules of the game, values, social institutions, political institutions, and personality.

One difficulty that the borrower of others' techniques experiences is that the world of others usually looks so chock full of interesting facts and correlations that it is hard to know where to begin. Usually, the borrower does what comes naturally—he selects from the infinite stream of available information those pieces which coincide with his interest. Sometimes the investigator wonders about this procedure, Am I being objective when I pick data according to what interests me?

Not only is there nothing wrong with this procedure, as long as the same field of interest is maintained throughout the investigation, but it may be the only possible procedure. As one of the founders of sociology, Max Weber, pointed out, "There is no absolutely 'objective' scientific analysis of culture . . . [or] of 'social phenomena' independent of special and 'one-sided' viewpoints according to which —expressly or tacitly, consciously or unconsciously—they are selected, analyzed and organized for expository purposes."[12]

In fact, only if the investigator admits to himself what his perspective of interest is can he clearly define what he is looking for in his research. After he has defined his problem and field of research, he only has to adhere to two rules of research in order for other investigators to check up on him, making his work useful:

1. Having defined his field of research, he will not allow himself to change his perspective arbitrarily while looking at the reality of others. That is, he will maintain a clear-headed and consistent logic of inquiry.*

2. When defining what it is in the world of others that can possibly be of interest and use to him, he will make every attempt to see if the behaviors or structures of others have a similar meaning to them as comparable structures or behaviors have to us in our world. He will ascertain that similarity of meaning by asking others what their actions mean to them.

The final test of whether his definition of his field of interest was better or worse than that of other investigators lies in the results. If the

*When you start to chase butterflies, don't open the net wide enough for elephants; butterflies will escape.

LOCATING YOURSELF AND YOUR VALUES IN POLITICAL TIME AND SPACE

Selecting from Others

would-be borrower of techniques from others has adequately attuned himself to the world of others, he will find that he *can* borrow their techniques. To the extent that he has not so attuned himself, his borrowings will fail.

Worse, it will be impossible, without such tuning-in, to even understand what others are talking about. In the following examples, the would-be borrower in the first case fails to tune in, while in the second case a borrower does quite well. Note the different approaches.

Tools For Studying Creation: An Application

Assume you have heard that two people in your own society have discovered a faster way of making a living. For old times' sake, let's call the two Alphonse and Balthazar. Let's pick two approaches for understanding the new technique Alphonse and Balthazar have developed for getting clams for breakfast—literally "making their living." Which approach in the following scenario provides more understanding, and why?

Macro-level Approach

Interviewer
for KNMN: (Know-Nothing Major Network) We are here at Ever-Splash Beach, where for generations Inlandians have come for their health. We've heard a lot of rumors about some strange activity going on here. Our sources have it that two Inlandians have invented a new wrinkle in Ever-Splash recreation. There they are now . . . Balthazar and Alphonse. Uh, hello, Mr. Balthazar!

Alphonse: (who is addressed) I'm Alphonse! *He's* Balthazar.

Interviewer: Now, now, all our records show that members of the Alphonse family are allergic to rock-handling. But I see that you, Balthazar (he is addressing Alphonse), are handling rocks. You *must* be a Balthazar.

Alphonse: But, I—

Interviewer: Now what is this new recreation technique you've both worked out?

Alphonse: It's not a recreation technique—

Interviewer: For centuries the pattern on this beach has been that people come here for recreation. Why, it's never been known for anyone to do anything else. Now don't be coy, tell me what you've been up to!

**Understanding new events
in terms of old patterns
often doesn't work.**

Balthazar: No really we . . .

Interviewer: Seems to me you're engaging in a new version of the water cure. One of you is acting out the role of STAND-IN-THE-WATER, while the other plays FEET-IN-THE-

SAND. Of course, you're not alternating roles the way we used to . . . Say, I bet that's your new idea. But don't your feet get water-logged, Alphonse?

Balthazar: (whom the interviewer mistakenly addresses) I'm Balthazar. He's Alphonse . . .

> **Trying to fit new people
> into old roles prevents
> understanding their newness . . .
> . . . furthermore, new behavior
> can't be understood in terms
> of old institutions.**

Alphonse: (hysterically cracking clams at twice his usual speed) You've got it all wrong!!! We've invented a new way to . . .

Interviewer: (interrupting) Now, now, don't get excited! It's quite obvious that you're performing the function of social deviant and hysteric. They tell us about functional analysis back at broadcast school.

Now let me summarize for our viewers what this is all about . . .

FADEOUT SHOT OF ALPHONSE AND BALTHAZAR SLOWLY SINKING INTO THE WATER.

> **Final note:
> Even functional analysis won't work
> if your set of known functions
> doesn't include the meanings
> of what social innovators do.**

Moral: To learn techniques others use to solve their problems, it helps not to assume their problems are the same as yours, nor that what they do has the same meaning for them as for you.

Micro-level Approach

Interviewer
for CSB: (Cycle-Sensitivity Broadcasting) Hey, what're your names?

Alphonse: Alphonse.

Balthazar: Balthazar.

> **It helps to know
> who people think they are**

Interviewer: Hmmm. What are you guys up to?

Alphonse: We're trying to eat. We're hungry.

Interviewer: And what do you think you're doing? Looks to me like you're just throwing clams around.

Balthazar: Well, I'm picking up the clams out of the water and throwing them to him . . .

Alphonse: . . . and I'm cracking them with these rocks as soon as he throws them. We figure this way we split the labor and we'll have breakfast twice as fast.

Asking what meanings others ascribe to what they do may help understand their reality.

Interviewer: Wow, that's really different from the old individual get-your-own technique. But what makes you think, Balthazar, that Alphonse will still be waiting for you out there when he gets all the clams? He could just crack 'em and run . . .

Balthazar: Well, I've been watching Alphonse a lot. We used to go down to the beach together, each to do his own thing. He never missed a morning. Looks pretty reliable to me.

Watching behavior may tell you something about personality.

Alphonse: And besides, I value his friendship more than anything else. Isn't that right, Balthazar?

Balthazar: We've been doing our digging-and-cracking scheme on this beach for two weeks now, and he still hasn't run off with the goods.

Hearing of people's values and seeing them acted out gives you both a picture of behavior and what it means.

Interviewer: Boy, this'll be good news to the folks on the Cycle-Sensitivity Broadcast circuit!

Alphonse: What circuit? We figure on keeping this secret to ourselves and taking over this joint. I just cut your cable with one of my clam shells.

**Final note:
When working to understand revolutionaries, try also to understand how to get back to the old social reality.**

Macro-investigators look at macro-politics. They assume that systems and patterns are more meaningful than people. Micro-investigators look at the source of politics—micro-politics. They know that it is always people who make politics.* The illustration above focused on a historical period of creation in a foreign culture. Clearly the "Macro" and "Micro" investigators came from a culture in a different historical phase—most likely a phase going from maintenance to decay, like American society.

The "Macro" investigator could have avoided some of his misinterpretations if he had (1) attempted to see the world of the foreigner as the foreigner did and in his terms, and (2) identified the difference between his own historical perspective and that of the foreign culture he was observing. By locating yourself and your cultural subject in the historical cycle of creation, maintenance, and decay, you become more aware of historical distortions caused by your own limited circumstances.

Such psycho-social mapping also helps one to step into a foreigner's shoes for the moment and see things as he does. To do this the investigator must learn the language of the foreigner, his history, his traditions, and his habits. It also helps, in the beginning, to limit the field of inquiry. As social scientist and mathematical biologist Anatol Rapoport has pointed out, "It is possible to see the 'here and now' clearly only if the field of vision is sufficiently small and properly focused. . . . The expert is one who successfully orders or manipulates a portion of the world which he understands."[13]

In sum, the third step of comparing politics involves identifying your values and interests openly, locating your historical situation compared with that of the other culture, limiting your subject of research, and trying to understand foreigners in their own terms. In doing all this you evolve tentative theories, explanations, or hypotheses, which are then tested with the relevant tools.

After locating one's values and limitations in historical perspective in terms of the foreign culture, the last step of comparing politics comes naturally to mind. Which conceptual tools or methods of analysis are most appropriate to investigate this particular problem in this culture at this time? The illustrations on pages 130 to 132 of an inquiry into how Alphonse and Balthazar earned a living showed the errors that can result from using the wrong tools to analyze a culture in a period of creation. Similarly, there are specific methods or tools that are particularly appropriate for studying cultures caught in decay, maintenance, and revolution.

LEARNING TO USE TOOLS THAT FIT THE PROBLEM YOU CHOOSE

A culture is a pattern of values and behavior patterns modeled on those values. When people no longer believe in these values or start engaging in behavior contrary to these norms, decay begins.

Decay is the subjective perception by people living in a culture that its rules and norms no longer apply to them.

Decay can be perceived at many levels. President Richard Nixon at one time perceived that "most Americans today are simply fed up with government at all levels." His perception was shared by everyday Americans, who expressed themselves slightly differently on the same

Tools for Studying Decay

*See Chapters on "self" versus "system," Chapters 11 and 10.

issue. In 1972, half of them agreed with the statement, "The people running the country don't really care what happens to people like yourself."[14]

Another recent survey indicates that many Americans feel a detachment not only from the official political patterns for problem solving, but also from the most sacred norms and beliefs of society in general. In 1965, 44 percent agreed with the statement "The trouble with the world today is that most people really don't believe in anything," while 82 percent agreed with the statement, "With everything so uncertain these days, it almost seems as though anything could happen."[15]

The attitudes reported in the political realm are measures of political alienation; the attitudes reported in the social realm are measures of anomie. *Political alienation* is the feeling that control over political decision making has escaped people's hands. *Anomie* is the feeling of the individual that the rules and norms of society have become meaningless and no longer apply to him.

What tools are available to test for such feelings of decay?

A basic tool is *to ask people how they feel.* This can be accomplished through a number of techniques. *Survey research* asks a small representative number of people how they feel and draws conclusions about how others of their type feel—usually questionnaires are used. The *personal interview* is another way of getting at the same information—but in greater depth, because there is a personal give and take between researcher and respondent.

Specific tools may be designed around two types of questions—questions centering on attitudes toward the official political arena, and questions centering on attitudes toward society and culture in general.

Attitudes Toward Politics—Survey Research　A Gallup Poll was carried out on this question:

> Taking into account what you would want America to be like ten years from now, do you think a basic change will need to be made in the way our governmental system is now set up or organized or don't you think this will be necessary?

One thousand, eight hundred and two individuals, a slightly larger number than the average sample, were polled. These individuals represented all different groups, socio-economic strata, races, ages, and sexes in the country as a whole. Their responses to the question were as follows:

Change needed	54 percent
No change needed	36 percent
Don't know	10 percent[16]

A potential borrower of techniques and institutions of political problem solving, looking at these American data, might understandably hesitate to adopt any American means of politics to resolve problems in his own country. Feelings of decay are not rampant in just a small minority in this case.

Attitudes toward Politics—Personal Interviews In the same series of polls, individuals were asked to write their own feelings about the need for basic change. The interviewers considered the following responses typical of the general mood:

> We just don't have the government up there that can handle the problems that need taking care of.
> —A hospital employee in Kentucky.

> We, the people are losing control. The vote doesn't mean anything anymore. A form of dictatorship may be coming. We have little to say now.
> —A female hairdresser in a New York suburb.

Groups especially dissatisfied included Easterners, young people, the very poor, manual workers, people living in smaller cities, independents, the very liberal, and black Americans (seven out of ten opted for fundamental change).[17]

INVITATION

Create your own questionnaire of some questions that explore the meaning of decay in American society today. Focus questions on correlations between social facts that interest you (see pages 121 and 129) or upon the tensions you believe exist between certain social facts and the human needs of the people you intend to interview. Try to relate all of your questions to an overall thesis or theory of how you think the people will respond and why you expect such a response. Finally, distribute ten copies of your questionnaire to people willing to answer them and compare the results with your original thesis or expectations. How do you think the personal and social circumstances of those you polled affected the results? What effects do you think social class, age, sex, and occupation had upon the answers?

(For sample questions, see the Anomie Test questions in Chapter 7, page 159.)

Once political systems are set up, patterns or routines of solving people's needs are developed, and people are taught to behave according to these patterns. To the extent that they learn well, it is possible for the researcher to avoid the personal approach—which is especially time-consuming in large systems—and study how well the general patterns of behavior fulfill the needs taken on by the political system.

Looking at these general patterns provides a quick overview as to how systems different from our own work. Contrasting their patterns with ours may also help to pinpoint breakdowns in our own system, just as a doctor can tell what's wrong with an ill person by keeping in mind the workings of a healthy one.

Tools for Studying Maintenance: The Structural-Functional Approach

Structural-Functional Measures One way of looking at general patterns of political problem solving, the structural-functional approach, suggests that we focus on a few standard patterns. These patterns are said to express necessary functions that any system must perform; if it does not perform these properly, it is said to be an unhealthy system. Here are the functions:

Interest articulation. Any system must provide its citizens with structures (patterns or institutions) through which an individual's interests, demands, or needs can be expressed.

Interest aggregation. Structures that collect interests must be provided. Unless citizens have a chance to join those with similar interests, they may have difficulty putting pressure on government to satisfy these interests, and a chaos of interests might result.

Rule making. Any system needs structures to process and hand down rules regarding whose interests will be satisfied.

Rule application. Any system needs structures through which specialized personnel enforce or apply rules.

Rules adjudication. In any system there has to be a regular structure to which people can appeal when they find a rule or its application unjust.

Communication. In any system, the people must be told what rules have been made so that they may know how to behave. The regular passing on of this information can be assured by institutionalizing a specific structure for this purpose.

Recruitment and socialization. If a political system is to survive from generation to generation, it must recruit newcomers to the system (for example, children who then become adult citizens) in standard political patterns and teach them what these patterns mean (socialization).

Two additional measures of functionality are *integration* and *differentiation*. *Integration* refers to the smooth meshing of different structures performing the seven functions. For example, if there is no meshing between structures performing the function of interest aggregation and the function of rule making, there will be a bottleneck in the system, and no outputs of rules related to people's demands can be expected. *Differentiation* refers to the separateness of each structure performing each distinct function. Structures with overlapping functions are likely to produce a muddled operation of the system. As in a well-functioning watch, each cog in the system must be designed to perform its assigned function clearly (differentiation) and yet must be so placed as to interact with other cogs and wheels to make the whole system go (integration).[18]

Consider how well the legendary Inlandia fulfills these functions:*

Structural-Functionalists in Inlandia Two well-known political scientists representing the structural-functional approach have arrived in Inlandia to determine how the Inlandian system functions. They are

*For an example of structural-functional analysis applied to the development of Russia, *see* Chapter 7, pp. 155–158.

equipped with the knowledge of the Famous Seven Functions, which they immediately begin to apply.

Professor
Rigor: Well, Mort, here we are in Inlandia. Looks like a God-for-saken place.

Professor
Mortice: (ducking a flying clam that has just been launched from a nearby bush)
Maybe we'd better leave our cultural biases home. Let's unpack the Structural-Functional Objective Test, Rig.

Rigor: Okay, Mort. Let's begin with "interest articulation." From what I hear, the last time anybody articulated any interest around here, he got hit in the head with a flying clam. Hey, let's ask this dude with the flowing beard some questions. Hey, you sir!

Raz
Putin: You called?

Rigor: Yes. Who are you?

Raz: Raz Putin, sir, the Royal Recorder.

Mortice: (nudging Rigor) Just the fellow we need. He can show us some of the local sights . . . er, I mean structures.

Rigor: (to Raz Putin) We're from Project Paidalot. New here. Mind answering some questions?

Raz: Sure.

Rigor: We're interested how you do politics in this place—er, Finlandia, you call it?

Raz: Inlandia.

Rigor: Well, anyway. For example, where does a fellow like that go when he wants to express to the government what he wants? (Points at a shabbily dressed native.)

Checking for interest articulation.

Raz: Him? To the filling station.

Mortice: No, no, you misunderstand. Not where he takes his car to get gassed up. Where he goes to express what he wants!

Raz: Sure. I got ya. He goes to the filling station to get gassed up!

Mortice: Uh—(he is at a loss.)

Rigor: (to Mortice) Remember, we have to leave our cultural biases at home. Maybe getting gassed up means something else down here in Inlandia.

Raz: (having overheard) Nope. Means the same thing it does up North. We get your TV reruns, you know. When one of those Know-Nothings—that's our lowest class, you know—feels like he's got an interest, we send him to the filling station. There he gets gassed up with coconut wine, and that usually keeps him quiet for a few days.

Mortice: Oh! In other words, you've got an institution that prevents interest articulation, but none to express it?!
Raz: You might say that.

> **Note from the**
> **Rigor-Mortice research diary:**
> **Inlandia lacks structure for**
> **interest articulation function:**
> **looks like they're going to be**
> **in trouble.**

Rigor: Now, don't tell me, Mr. Putin, let me guess. My guess is you probably don't have a place for your people to aggregate—er, uh, gather together—their interests.
Raz: Yup, if they want to aggregate we send them down—
Mortice: —to the filling station?
Raz: You guessed it.

> **Note from**
> **Rigor-Mortice research diary:**
> **Reminder: Make air reservations**
> **for return trip immediately:**
> **no structures for interest**
> **aggregation. This place might**
> **blow any minute.**

Rigor: But who runs this place? Who makes your rules?

> **Testing for rule-making function.**

Raz: Oh, King Alphonse and High Priest Balthazar, naturally.
Mortice: (with mounting excitement) And who enforces the rules?
Raz: Why the Enforcers, naturally, under the command of King Alphonse, of course.
Mortice: (hardly able to contain himself) And the adjudication of rules? When somebody complains?
Raz: King Alphonse and High Priest Balthazar—
Mortice: —of course. (sighs and glances meaningfully at Rigor.)

> **Note from**
> **Rigor and Mortice's research diary:**
> **Tested for rule making,**
> **rule application, and**
> **rule adjudication functions.**

Rigor: Surely, the king consults your other people—your Enforcers, for example. Or what about the guys I've seen working at clamming on the beach?
Raz: No. The King and the High Priest rule. We obey.

> **Entry in**
> **Rigor and Mortice's research diary:**
> **Central governmental functions all**
> **centralized in king and priest;**
> **no differentiation between**
> **supreme institutions; no inputs**
> **from the people.**

> **Rigor and Mortice's private telegram**
> **to U.S. State Department:**
> **"Revolution highly probable in**
> **Inlandia. Send Marines to**
> **evacuate us immediately."**

Rigor: (to Raz) Excuse me. I had to get off a telegram on our COMSAT satellite communications system. What about communications? Who tells your people what the rules are?

Raz: Well, King Alphonse usually stands on the balcony of Clam Castle and reads the rules down to the assembled populace of Enforcers, Clam Diggers and Crackers, and Know-Nothings.

> **Rigor and Mortice diary note:**
> **Communications function controlled**
> **by King.**

Mortice: (to Rigor) Let's check for the capacities of this system and then blow. This is getting me nervous.

Rigor: (to Raz Putin) I'm curious. I see a lot of work going on. Diggers and Crackers are digging and cracking. Enforcers are cracking the whip. Know-Nothings are staggering around in a stupor of coconut wine. Who gets all the goods in this system? Whose needs does it fulfill?

Raz: Why the needs of King Alphonse and High Priest Balthazar, of course. They get all the clams everybody else produces, and then they hand back some clams to Diggers and Crackers to keep them healthy in their work, and a few go to the most noisy Know-Nothings who don't understand the clam-digging system.

Mortice: Hmmm, let's see (leafs through his Structural-Functional Test). Systems can have five types of domestic purposes or capacities: extractive, regulative, distributive, symbolic, and responsive. If I had to take a stab at it, this system looks mainly extractive.

Raz: (wisely) It certainly looks as if it's set up to let Alphonse and Balthazar extract most of the goods from everybody else. I agree, fundamentally an extractive system.

Mortice:	Hey, I see some kind of commotion going on over by the castle. What's that, Mr. Putin?
Raz:	Oh. Our annual celebration of the accession of Alphonse I and Balthazar I.
Mortice:	Aha. But I see a runner threading his way through the parade. Has a clam shell helmet on.
Raz:	A runner of the Royal Clam Post. He must have an important message.
Rigor:	Now he's disappeared into the castle.
Mortice:	There he is again on the balcony next to the king. He's yelling something—
	(Just then there is a lull in the parade music.)
Runner:	(heard shouting in the pause) Disaster! The clams are dying!
Rigor:	(to Mortice) Let's get the heck out of here!

As we leave Inlandia, we see the famous Rigor-Mortice team of political science butterfly-swimming away from Inlandia and into the sunset.

Tools for Studying Change and Revolution

Political scientists have no generally accepted theory to explain or predict revolution. The reason for this deficiency is that all social scientists lack a generally acceptable theory of change.

Gaps in Current Theories A theory of change, which would include a theory of revolution, would require knowledge of three processes: (1) The process by which individuals come to perceive a tension between their needs and their environment and therefore a need to adapt to or reconstruct the environment (whether social or natural); (2) the process by which people decide between alternative ideas as blueprints for change and will the decision into action; (3) the process by which distribution of new knowledge takes place. Further, we lack knowledge as to how these three processes are related. Social facts consist of routines and norms that express people's needs and adapt them to their environment. What we need to know is under what conditions individuals perceive these routines and norms as no longer effective and go about creating new ones.

What is available is a series of fragmentary explanations of segments of the cycle of change that rotates through the stages of the creation, maintenance, and decay of social and political systems. Most of these explanations focus on large-scale changes in institutions and behavior.[19] They therefore tend to discover change after it has already taken place, fail to detect its origins in individual thought, and have great difficulty in finding the origins of change or in predicting it.

The great dilemma of students of change has been deciding whether to focus on the objective conditions that "make" men change and on the social facts that men make in producing change, on the one hand, or, on the other, to concentrate on the individuals as they process needs for change and produce responses. The temptation has been to focus on objective conditions—because these can be more easily observed and to some extent can be measured. The trouble has been that human beings are capable of ignoring objective concrete facts and of refusing to change in the face of them, even such a blatant fact as the continued existence of the world.

For example, recall that the psychologist Leon Festinger found a number of the adherents of a recent prophetess of doom clung to her view of reality, even after her prophesied end of the world did not come about. Similarly, Marxists who take an economic interpretation of their teacher's theories are constantly embarrassed by the fact that, contrary to their expectations, people (in India, for example) do not revolt even when millions of them die by starvation. Total impoverishment does not produce revolution all by itself. On the individual level, the psychologist Milton Rokeach found that each of three insane men who believed they were Christ emerged from a confrontation with the other two strengthened in his conviction that *he* was Christ.[20]

The fact of the matter seems to be that objective conditions are *meaningless* as causes of change unless they somehow become *meaningful* to the minds of the individuals involved. The most promising theories of change—in terms of early detection, explanation, and prediction of change—seem to be those that take into account external conditions *as they are perceived by human beings*. The task of such theories then becomes explaining the differences of perception that lead one man to revolt and another to remain comfortable in the reality that "objectively" is shared by both.

Unfortunately, studies in the distribution of knowledge, the ripple effect that spreads individual need for change throughout society, are practically nonexistent in political science, though they exist in sociology, especially in the sociology of religion.[21] Until the necessary studies are undertaken, it is, however, possible to evaluate existing explanations of change according to two standards of usefulness. We can ask:

1. Does a given explanation of change take into account all three processes of change: the impact of reality, the individual's response to that impact, and the distribution of that response? How complete an explanation is and how well it works to predict and manipulate change will tend to depend on how completely the explanation covers this cycle.

2. To what extent does a given explanation of change focus on and take into account the subjective interpretation of social and political events by the individual? Only if an explanation performs this function well will it be possible to detect the origins of change early (in the mind of the individual) and to predict whether any given "objective" social fact will actually give rise to the tension in the individual that alone may lead to change.

While a thorough summary of individual explanations of change is not possible here (see the source books in "To Explore Further," pp. 303–309), it is possible to evaluate briefly some of the major theories in terms of their possible use.

James C. Davies—The Theory of Expectations One explanation of change that comes closest to taking into account subjective perceptions by individuals is that offered by the political scientist James C. Davies.[22] Davies suggests that individuals engage in revolution as a specific form of change when there is a sudden and sharp downward turn in their perceived fulfillment of their expectations.

This sequence seems to work to explain revolutions, from the Russian Bolshevik revolution to ghetto revolts. For example, it might be argued that, in the 1950s, blacks in America perceived fulfillment of their expectations to be rising as they successfully used civil rights demonstrations to gain access to the voting booth and schools. However, along with such gains they may have developed an expectation of gains in economic power and social status. By the 1960s it became clear to many blacks that economic and social expectations were not being fulfilled. This lack of economic and social gains in turn may have been perceived *subjectively* by blacks as a sudden and sharp downturn in their hopes for the fulfillment of expectations.

The example illustrates how important it is to tune in to the subjective interpretation of reality by those involved instead of imposing objective measures. According to "objective" measures imposed by white observers, it seemed that blacks should have been satisfied with the political and educational successes they had originally set out to gain.

Davies' approach, when properly applied, can take into account subjective interpretations of events, with which change starts, and does focus our attention on at least two of the three processes of change: the impact of reality from the outside and the individual's response to that impact. How that response is spread and distributed is not made clear.

Emile Durkheim—Objective Indicators of Change Political sociologists looking for objective indicators to forecast change may be encouraged by part of the findings of the French sociologist Emile Durkheim, who studied what causes suicide.

Durkheim found that suicide rates went up when there was a rapid change of economic conditions for *either* better or worse.[23] From his general understanding of man's need for routines and norms to adapt himself to the world, Durkheim concluded that human beings react sharply when there is *any* radical change in the norms and routines of social life.

If that were all there was to Durkheim's findings, and if change in behavior correlated all or most of the time with change in objective patterns of norms and routines, a theory using objective indicators to explain or forecast change might be justified. But even Durkheim found that when he *compared* reactions to social change *across* cultures, nations with Roman Catholic populations reacted less violently to external change than nations with Protestant populations.

It follows, from this comparative study, that quite possibly people's world view may alter their understanding as to how threatening any external change is, and whether the external change requires internal changes of attitudes and resulting radical response. External change, it turns out, is *interpreted* according to internal cognitive and emotional maps of the world. Differences in internal maps account for differences in response to the same stimulus.

S.M. Lipset—Differential Response by World View A telling example of how people with different beliefs change their behavior more or less radically under the impact of the same social, economic, and political pressures has been demonstrated by the political sociologist Seymour Martin Lipset in his study of the Nazi revolution in Germany.[24]

Lipset found—as had others—that those who supported the National Socialist Party's overthrow of the Weimar Republic shared one perception in common: they were being displaced from their class or status positions into lower class and status.

However, Catholics and Marxists in the same class and under the same economic, social, and political pressures resisted joining the Nazi Party more intensely and longer than did the mass of Protestants.

It may be that both Catholicism and Marxism functioned as internal maps according to which the faithful were able to interpret external pressures as less threatening and stressful than did Protestants. Catholics could retreat to the doctrine "God's in his heaven and all's essentially well with the world." Marxists could tell themselves, "After all, didn't Marx predict the fall of capitalism represented by German economic, social, and political decay?" Protestants, on the other hand, with their emphasis on each individual looking to himself for salvation, had no such recourse to pacifying doctrine, nor could they take refuge in a convenient hierarchy such as that which gave support to Roman Catholics.

Marxist Revolutionary Theory There is no single way in which Karl Marx's revolutionary theory has been interpreted. Both scholarly preferences and practical needs have produced interpretations polarized between arguing that objective material conditions bring about revolutionary behavior and counterarguing that consciousness or ideas do so.

Marxism as Materialism A materialist interpretation of Marx would emphasize objective measurable change in the condition of the working class. Crudely put, an increase in conditions producing misery brings about the proletarian revolution. This misery comes about inevitably, a materialist Marxist would argue, because of a built-in economic dynamic in the capitalist system. For efficiency and profit, industrial capitalism requires ever-expanding reinvestment of capital. Capital is material goods needed for the expansion of production. It is acquired through a social relationship in which capitalists, who control the tools of labor, tend to reduce wages to bare subsistence levels for the proletarians or laborers. When this increasing misery grows bad enough, the workers will revolt.

This interpretation, then, places emphasis on the material conditions and dynamics of the economy—on the sources of revolt in objective reality.[25] What it ignores is the question, How and when do the workers *perceive* objective conditions to be bad enough to revolt? Even Marx's colleague and lifelong partner, Friedrich Engels, barred such a simplistic interpretation based on mere level of misery.

Engels' Interpretation   Empirical observation, Engels pointed out, shows that the poorest of the working class are *not* revolutionary. He drew this fact from a study of the voting behavior of the poorest nineteenth-century workers in Germany, the Silesian weavers. They did not revolt, even during starvation, but voted as conservatively as they could![26]

Engels concluded that to be revolutionary the worker has to have acquired something to lose. To be an effective revolutionary, the worker has to be located at the site of a relatively advanced form of the production of goods; there, if he withdraws his support, his revolution will be felt most severely by the system. Revolution occurs when workers who have achieved a relatively substantial class position feel the threat of being thrown down and out of their class.

This emphasis on the individual as focus—and the individual looking outward at the conditions of his world—is quite compatible with another aspect of Marx's theories. Although he was intensely interested in the material conditions of man's life, Marx also emphasized the role of consciousness in man's actions.

Marx, Consciousness, and Revolution   In his long-lost *Early Philosophical and Economic Manuscripts*,[27] Marx emphasized the creative role of man as against his environment, noting that man both makes his world and is made by it. The later *Communist Manifesto* contains appeals to the worker to develop *class consciousness* of his true position in the world, expressed in a now-well-known slogan: the hope that once he recognized this position he would throw off his chains.

Whether Marx can be called ambivalent on the importance of objective conditions versus consciousness, or whether he is understood in terms of a dialectic of interaction between both, it is clear that he has no explicit theory of how perception of the need for revolution comes about. He thus fails to connect the first two segments of any explanation of revolution: objective facts impinging on the individual from without and the interpretation the individual gives to these facts.

Practically, this lack of connection led to quite diverse behavior by Marxist parties.

The Western Social Democrats: Evolutionary Revolution   In the West, and especially in Germany, which in the nineteenth century had the largest Marxist party, Marx's ideas of revolution were interpreted in the light of consciousness. The Social Democrats, who as their name indicates tried to achieve socialism through democratic means, placed their emphasis ultimately on the long-term evolution of workers' consciousness to bring about the revolution in routines and norms of behavior that Marxism as an ideology implies.[28] In avoiding the temptation of mere stimulus-response violence and engaging in the reasoned study of whether social facts were ripe for revolution, the German Social Democrats even received support from Marx himself.[29] As things turned out, however, the German Social Democrats achieved neither socialism nor lasting democracy when they took over Germany for a short period after the end of World War I.

The Bolsheviks: Revolution for What?   In Russia, the Bolsheviks also emphasized consciousness—but only for a vanguard of people "in the know." For the masses, objective conditions of history were held to be operative. In stressing the role of consciousness for the vanguard, the Bolshevik leader V. I. Lenin may have taken a leaf from Marx's own example. After all, did not Marx raise his own consciousness by studying the condition of the working class in the nineteenth century? Was it not therefore possible for others to do the same and become conscious early of the objective conditions moving the masses?

On such grounds, Lenin helped organize the revolution at a time when he perceived the forces of Czarist rule to be weak. Whether the leap that his organization took either actually led to socialism or could lead to Marxism's final stage, communism, is still disputed. But Lenin did demonstrate that it is possible to "make" a revolution through the use of will and consciousness—even when the correctness of his analysis of conditions was in doubt. For example, it is disputable whether Russia had reached a capitalist stage of development which, according to Marx, is a precondition for the socialist revolution.

All in all, the usefulness of the Marxist theory of revolution, if it can ever be clearly understood, is in doubt. Unfortunately, there isn't any useful, complete non-Marxist theory of revolution available, either.

Toward a Theory of Revolution?   If a full theory of revolution ever is established, it is likely that it will rest on the following grounds. All theories of revolution either turn around the problem of the individual's adaptation to changes in the routines and norms of his social environment or can be interpreted in that direction. Most simply stated, human beings may begin to make motions to readapt themselves to their environment or change it—whether to effect slow change or to revolt—when they perceive that their mental maps of the external world are no longer useful for getting along in that world.

Social change does not always result from such perception. Many responses to perceived change are maladaptive—the individual may become insane and withdraw from reality, or he may commit the ultimate withdrawal, suicide. But under some circumstances, external and internal, he may also revolt. To correctly explain the interaction between such circumstances is the first task for any future theory of revolution.

INCONCLUSIONS

The four steps of comparing politics grow naturally out of the definition of politics: the attempt to solve the tensions between human needs and social facts. First the social facts of the foreign culture to be compared are identified—the existing values, personalities, social and political institutions, and rules of the game. Interesting correlations between these five kinds of facts are noted as well—for instance, the relationship between membership in a social class and the ability to satisfy one's desires within the rules of the game.

The second step is to analyze the typical needs and values of the community, noting which of the five basic needs are least satisfied. Maslow's need scale, going from physiological needs to security needs to love needs to self-esteem needs and to self-actualization needs, is a useful tool for this part of the task.

Third, just as awareness of the tensions between existing social facts and unsatisfied needs can be called political consciousness, the way in which one selects interesting tensions to analyze can be termed *social science consciousness*. This scientific approach to social and political problems requires putting your own values honestly on the table, limiting the scope of your problem, and doing your best to see the foreign culture in the terms of the foreigner. In using this approach, you make it possible for others to check up on the meaning of your study at a later time. Normally scientific consciousness involves forming a thesis or hypothesis based on the values you have made explicit and on the possible correlation or answer that you think is most likely to explain the problem.

The fourth and final step of comparing politics is to test your hypothesis or theory by using tools of explanation appropriate to your task and to the foreign culture's historical stage of development (creation, maintenance, or decay and revolution, or their combination). Even if you should disprove your theory or hypothesis, if you have followed the four steps carefully, your work should be of interest to others, who can then avoid your mistakes.

INVITATION

Creating a hypothesis: The four steps of comparing politics in this chapter lead naturally into the creation of a hypothesis or tentative explanation of political tensions or social events that can be tested in the real world. Note how easy it is to create such hypotheses:

(1) Determine the social facts and human needs in both your own culture and that of the other. Identify which of these facts and needs are most relevant or interesting in terms of the problem you want to investigate or explain.

(2) Create plausible *correlations* or explanatory relationships between interesting social facts and human needs. This allows many possible correlations, since any one social fact can be related to any other social fact, any need can be related to any other need, and any social fact can be related to any need. Such relationships or correlations should point toward a possible explanation of the problem in question. For example, if my problem is to explain why so many people feel insecure in highly industrial societies, I might write down the following possible correlations:

(a) The higher a person's social class, the less likely he is to feel insecure.

(b) The lower a person's social class, the more likely he is to feel insecure.

(3) Find concrete *indicators* for the *variables* (Either social facts or human needs) that make up your tentative explanatory correlation or *hypothesis*. Taking the example in (2), "social class" might be indicated concretely by finding out how much money the people you are investigating earn, how they earn it, and what they spend it on relative to other people in their society and your own. You might create a psychological test or set of questions to ask people to find out how insecure or secure they think they are. Perhaps you could compare the results of this test with how insecure a psychiatrist who interviews them thinks they are. (See the anomie questions in the next chapter, pages 158 to 159.)

(4) Test your hypothesis in two or more cases and compare your results with others.*

Social science is a never-ending process of eliminating errors and finding new theories that better explain and predict social events. This process can be exhilarating and playful as well as frustrating and tension-building. Sociologist Jean Duvignaud once said, "If Balzac and Dickens were alive today, they would be sociologists." But if they lived in a highly politicized country like America today, they would be even more apt to be political scientists. For only by comparing politics of cultures existing in the same and in different historical periods can those interested in the fate of all men learn how to alleviate some of the tensions between human needs and social facts. In our mass era, it is no longer possible to be fully human without becoming political.

REFERENCES

1. Carlos Castaneda, *Journey to Ixtlan: The Lessons of Don Juan* (New York: Simon and Schuster, A Touchstone Book, 1973), pp. 9–10.

2. Ancel Keys, Josef Brozek, Austin Henschel, Olaf Mickelsen and Henry Taylor, *The Biology of Human Starvation,* vol. 2 (University of Minnesota Press, 1950); cited in Bernard Berelson and Gary A. Steiner, *Human Behavior: An Inventory of Scientific Findings* (New York: Harcourt, Brace & World, 1964).

3. Elliot Luby et al., "Sleep Deprivation: Effects on Behavior, Thinking, Motor Performance, and Biological Energy Transfer Systems," *Psychosomatic Medicine* 22 (1970), pp. 182–192; cited in Berelson and Steiner, *Human Behavior,* p. 243.

4. A. Weissberg, *The Accused* (New York: Simon & Schuster, 1951); cited in Berelson and Steiner, *Human Behavior,* p. 252.

5. Elmer Luchterhand, "Prisoner Behavior and Social System in the Nazi Concentration Camps," *International Journal of Social Psychiatry* 13, no. 4 (Fall 1964). See also James C. Davies, "Toward a Theory of Revolution," in *When Men Revolt and Why,* ed. James C. Davies (New York: The Free Press, 1971), p. 338, fn. 10.

6. Abraham Maslow, *Motivation and Personality* (New York: Harper & Row, 1954).

7. Maslow, *Motivation and Personality,* p. 91. For empirical support of Maslow, see Jeanne Knutson, *The Human Basis of the Polity* (Chicago: Aldine, 1972).

*On how to test hypotheses, see Hans Zetterberg, *On Theory and Verification in Sociology* (Totawa: Bedminster Press, 1964).

8. Maslow, *Motivation and Personality*, p. 91. For a critical evaluation of Maslow's self-actualization need, see M. Brewster Smith, "On Self-Actualization: A Transambivalent Examination of a Focal Theme In Maslow's Psychology," *The Journal of Humanistic Psychology* 13, no. 2 (Spring 1973), pp. 17–33.

9. *The New York Times*, Wednesday, March 11, 1973, pages 1 and 13.

10. *The New York Times*, Wednesday, March 21, 1973, page 12.

11. Alfred Schutz, *Collected Papers*, vol. 1 (The Hague: Martinus Nijhoff, 1962), p. 18.

12. Max Weber, *The Methodology of the Social Sciences*, ed. Edward A. Shils and Henry A. Finch (New York: The Free Press, 1949), p. 81.

13. Anatol Rapoport, *Fights, Games and Debates* (Ann Arbor: University of Michigan Press, 1967), p. 270.

14. William Watts and Lloyd A. Free, *State of the Nation* (New York: Universe Books, 1973), p. 233.

15. From a scale designed by McClosky and Schaar in John P. Robinson and Phillip R. Shaver, eds., *Measures of Social Psychological Attitudes* (Ann Arbor, Mich.: Survey Research Center, 1969), p. 171.

16. Watts and Free, *State of the Nation*, p. 247.

17. Ibid., p. 248.

18. For a full presentation of the structural-functional model, see Gabriel A. Almond and G. Bingham Powell, *Comparative Politics: A Developmental Approach* (Boston: Little, Brown, 1966). See also the specific country studies in the Little, Brown Series in Comparative Politics.

19. For a summary of theories of change focusing on institutions and policies, see Samuel P. Huntington, "The Change to Change: Modernization, Development and Politics," *Comparative Politics* 3, no. 3 (April 1971), pp. 283–322. For a comprehensive source book on such theories, see Jason L. Finkle and Richard W. Gable, *Political Development and Social Change* (New York: John Wiley, 1966). Useful as a survey of studies on violent rebellion is Ted Robert Gurr's *Why Men Rebel* (Princeton, N.J.: Princeton University Press, 1971).

20. Milton Rokeach, *The Three Christs of Ypsilanti* (New York: Random House, Vintage Books).

21. For an introduction to the sociology of knowledge as a tool for tracing the spread of change, see Peter Berger and Thomas Luckman, *The Social Construction of Reality: A Treatise in the Sociology of Knowledge* (Garden City, N.Y.: Doubleday Anchor Books, 1967). For an introduction to the sociology of religion, see Peter Berger, *The Sacred Canopy: Elements of a Sociological Theory of Religion* (Garden City, N.Y.: Doubleday, 1967). The classical case study of the social distribution of a new idea is still Max Weber's *The Protestant Ethic and the Spirit of Capitalism* (New York: Charles Scribner's Sons, 1930).

22. See Davies, *When Men Revolt and Why*, p. 187, fn. 3.

23. See Emile Durkheim, *Suicide* (New York: The Free Press, 1951).

24. Seymour Martin Lipset, *Political Man: The Social Bases of Politics* (Garden City, N.Y.: Doubleday, Anchor Books, 1963), pp. 138–139.

25. The internal dynamics of the capitalist economy were investigated by Marx in his three-volume magnum opus, *Das Kapital*. See, in English translation, Karl Marx, *Capital: A Critique of Political Economy*, vol. 1, *The Process of Capitalist Production*, ed. Frederick Engels, trans. Samuel Moore and Edward Aveling (New York: International Publishers, 1967).

26. Friedrich Engels, letter to the German Social Democrat Eduard Bernstein, "Engels an Eduard Bernstein," in Karl Marx and Friedrich Engels, *Werke*, vol. 35 (Berlin: Dietz Verlag, 1967), pp. 237–238; see also p. 270.

27. Not rediscovered until just before World War II. Since these manuscripts, which emphasized the construction and analysis of social and economic life in terms of relationships, were not available to the leaders of the major Marxist movements before the 1930s, the rest of Marx's work lent itself easily to a materialist interpretation with emphasis on objective conditions. Those

who, like the German Social Democrats, emphasized the humanist aspects of the early Marx without knowing the manuscripts, could be justifiably accused of revisionism until the early works were found. However, at least one sensitive scholar detected Marx's humanism even before that discovery: George Lukacz, in his classic *History and Class Consciousness.*

28. See Carl E. Schorske, *German Social Democracy, 1905–1971: The Development of the Great Schism* (Cambridge, Mass.: Harvard University Press, 1955).

29. Karl Marx, *Critique of the Gotha Programme* (New York: International Publishers, 1938).

7 Wherein the reader observes how to compare politics through the viewpoint of insiders in a foreign culture. We use the theories of anomie, charisma, and psycho-history illustrated by insiders like Lenin, Stalin, and Mao.

7 Comparing Politics Through Insiders

Comparing politics can appear to be a mind-boggling job. It is hard enough to find your own position in social reality and to estimate the chances of satisfying your own needs and values, much less compare your position with millions of others in strange lands.

Indeed, the complexity of this task makes many political scientists tense. To simplify the process of comparison, they often create reified, abstract models of how other systems are supposed to work, rather than focusing upon everyday human beings who make up and are made up by other nations. The capacity of such models to encompass great complexity is superficially attractive. But they often create unnecessary distance from the people of the everyday world and the meaning everyday life has for them. Such models of thinking too often stay outside the culture they are studying—outsiders coolly writing outside impressions in outsider's language for other outsiders. Theoretically speaking, when it gets too cold in terms of human needs and values, it's time to go inside.

In comparing politics it is necessary to select carefully both tools that depict large patterns of behavior (to give a rough, outside overview of other nations) *and* tools sensitive to the meaning life has for individuals inside other nations. Indeed, without knowing the meaning a problem situation has for those inside it, we cannot really know whether their problem situation is comparable with ours. And without such knowledge, borrowing from others to solve our problems is not rationally possible. Done irrationally, it can become downright dangerous.

Borrowing from others requires understanding the meaning of others.

The ideal tool for gaining access to the meaning of the world of others is a phenomenological approach. Phenomenology—the science of appearances—goes behind the surface appearance of social and political events or structures and asks what these events or structures mean to the people involved.* This approach is based on the insight that human beings construct their social and political worlds and endow them with meaning from the inside. The problem then becomes to understand their meanings so as to understand their world.

The meaning of the world of others radiates out from inside that world.

*See Chapter 11 for an exposition of the phenomenologist's method.

A number of existing tools in the social sciences can contribute to a phenomenological approach to the meaning of the worlds of others.*

Among these, the most useful available tools for studying politics comparatively, or otherwise, are those that link system and self. In doing so, it is important to dereify (unmask "concrete" abstractions) a political system to understand how it is made up of others. Three tools for dereifying are the theories of anomie, charisma, and psycho-history. Without such theories it is impossible to understand the cycle of creation, maintenance, and decay.

The faster your time-space intersect moves, the more you need tools grasping the meaning of change.

The theory of anomie (people drop out when rules fall apart) explains decay's meaning for masses.

The theory of charisma (in crisis, masses surrender their egos to create a superego for one leader) explains whose meaning will prevail in times of severe crisis that lead to creation or maintenance.

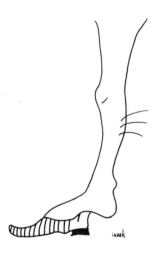

The theory of psycho-history (slipping into the shoes of creative human beings to look out at their world) shows how to compare the development of leaders from the inside in relation to their historical situation.

To illustrate how these theories can be used as tools, we begin comparative analysis by focusing on one other country—in this case, Russia. This act of focusing forces the political scientist to take the most difficult step first: slipping into another's shoes. It also allows us to come back to our own country from a foreigner's perspective. Only once you have at least two perspectives in mind does comparison really become possible. To avoid the danger of having loaded the dice by the choice of a particular country, it is useful to simultaneously consider third countries in related situations.

Combining these considerations, we selected Russia as our central focus, America the home to which we return for comparisons, and China as a checkpoint. In addition, time comparisons are also instructive; Russia can be viewed at different points in history, adding a new range of possible comparisons.

The other country you study will be colored by where you stand— a question for the sociology of knowledge.

*These tools are no more than possible fragments of a logically consistent future phenomenology of politics. But they are preferable to the large-scale pattern-describing models used in comparative politics, especially in those instances when patterns of behavior are undergoing rapid change and when, as a result, it becomes crucial to determine the meanings with which human beings actually endow their behavior. See Chapters 11 and 12.

As Americans, we tend to color the Soviet Union red. To enter and understand the perspective of someone in another culture, one must try, as Dag Hammarskjöld noted, to divest the *eye* of all color. At the same time, we must be aware that this is not totally possible, for our socialization limits what we know. To use the sociology of knowledge is to ask, "Says who?" We assume that a person's perception of knowledge in the world depends on where he or she stands in social and cultural space.

Sociology of knowledge looks for the origins of knowledge — asking, "Says who?"

How do we begin the study of another country? The first principle, if you want to detach yourself from your prejudices, is to assume you know nothing. For this purpose, and to go beyond it, the approach of structural-functionalism is just right. Even Max Weber, the sociologist who first focused a science on the meanings of events to others, urged that if we know nothing we should begin with a functional analysis of what others *do*. Then we can ask what it means to them. Keep in mind also Weber's warning that we may mistake our functional *model* of what others do for the *reality*. The reality becomes accessible to us only if we come to know with what meanings others illuminate their reality from within.[1]

Americans who travel abroad usually take a lot of snapshots. For investigators studying other countries in decay, structural-functionalism provides a way of taking snapshots of the condition of such countries over time.*

DECAY
Decay Within the System: Structural-Functional Snapshots

Structural-functionalism assumes that all political systems, if they are to have a long and healthy life, have to provide patterns of relationships between human beings (*structures*). These patterns enable human beings to live together for the purpose of satisfying their needs. The activities of living together are called *functions*.

Among such functions for which structures have to be developed are those of interest articulation and aggregation—through which individual and group needs are expressed. Further, such structures, once they exist, must be integrated with the governmental structures of rule making, rule application, and rule adjudication—which are to provide satisfaction of individual and group needs.†

Look ahead at Figures 7–1, 7–2, 7–3, and 7–4.

---

*See Chapter 6, pp. 136 to 140 for a description of structural-functionalism as a tool of analysis.

†Unfortunately, structural-functionalists often forget that what is important in a political world is the needs of its human beings and pervert the emphasis to the needs of systems; that is, what functions do human beings have to perform to keep the *system* alive. That systems were created to satisfy needs of human beings then becomes a forgotten fact relegated to the prehistory of structural-functionalism. See Chapter 10 for details.

Read comparatively, the charts show that in 1812, Napoleon's time, Russian peasants—the mass of the people—were blocked from access to structures for interest articulation and aggregation. In fact, for them, such structures did not exist.

By 1900, such blockage continued for the mass—except that now the mass had differentiated itself into three segments: peasants, working class, and middle class. It can be assumed that economically these levels of society played a key role, and especially that the newly rising working and middle classes in the cities would begin making demands for political participation. Nevertheless, the elite refused these classes access to the *political* system.

When such access was granted through the creation of political parties and a parliament (Duma) in which individuals and groups could express their needs and wants, the blockage was shifted into the political system itself. The Czar and the rest of the elite simply ignored the demands of the Duma. With people mobilized into political action through the articulating and aggregating structures, it could also be assumed that pressure for the meaningful satisfaction of that mobilization would increase. No citizen whose pressure tactics had resulted in the creation of parties and parliament could be blamed for holding high expectations that he could now gain a meaningful set of political satisfactions—the goods of politics.

These rising expectations continued until 1917, at which point the lack of fulfillment of expectations suddenly produced two revolutions. The second of these revolutions destroyed the previous political system.*

Note how these developments can be understood comparatively over time from a bird's-eye view by drawing the structural-functional categories of a political system and placing people and their needs and pressures in the picture. The resulting snapshots *cannot* in themselves indicate *why* people actually engaged in change or revolution, but they *can* indicate at what points major change resulted. To some extent, such an overview may also give an early warning of the build-up of pressures for change by noting breakdowns or blockages in the integration (or differentiation) of parts of the system.

Note that in snapshots covering 105 years, Figures 7−1 to 7−4 show only two major changes: (1) the appearance of new classes and (2) the shift of the blockade against the pressures from the lower and middle classes from the entrance to the political machinery to a bottle-neck within the machinery. The structural-functional model assumes that any stable political system must have structures that fulfill seven basic functions: socialization and recruitment, interest articulation, interest aggregation, rule making, rule application, rule adjudication, and communication.

This simplified overview of the Russian system shows that despite the build-up of pressures from huge new classes, the system maintainers refused for ninety-three years to provide structures for the articula-

*Note how this analysis uses the approach to understanding revolution suggested by James C. Davies. See Chapter 6, "Tools for Studying Change and Revolution," page 142.

Figure 7-1
Russia in 1812

Socialization & Recruitment	Interest Articulation	Interest Aggregation	Rule Making	Rule Application	Rule Adjudication	Communication
			Czar Aristocracy	Czar Aristocracy	Czar Aristocracy	

```
    B L O C K A G E
     ↑
     └-----Peasants
    [pressure]
```

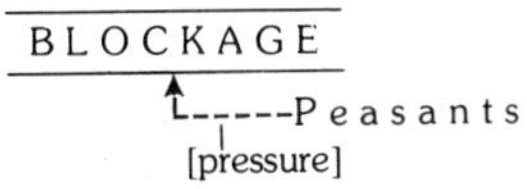

Figure 7-2
Russia in 1900

Socialization & Recruitment	Interest Articulation	Interest Aggregation	Rule Making	Rule Application	Rule Adjudication	Communication
			Czar Aristocracy	Czar Aristocracy	Czar Aristocracy	

```
    B L O C K A G E
   ↑   ↑  ↑
   |   |  └---MIDDLE CLASS----   a) merchant
   |   └--------WORKING CLASS--   b) industrial
   └------------PEASANTS           a) industrial
                                   b) other urban
  [pressures]
```

Figure 7-3
Russia in 1905

Socialization & Recruitment	Interest Articulation	Interest Aggregation	Rule Making	Rule Application	Rule Adjudication	Communication
Parties Illegal groups	Duma Parties Illegal groups	Czar Aristocracy	Czar Aristocracy	Czar Aristocracy		

```
                        /[pressure]
   Parties   Duma—→ Czar    Czar     Czar
   Illegal   Parties Aristo- Aristo-  Aristo-
   groups    Illegal cracy   cracy    cracy
             groups |B|
                    |L|
             ↑  ↑ ↑ |O|
             |  | | |C|
             |  | | |K|
             |  | | |A|
             |  | | |G|
             |  | | |E|
             |  | └------ MIDDLE CLASS
             |  └-------- WORKING CLASS
             └----------- PEASANTS
```

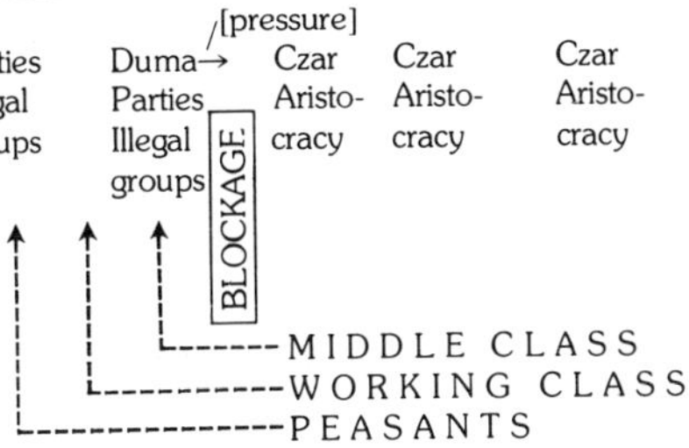

Figure 7-4
Russia in 1917
(February)

Socialization & Recruitment	Interest Articulation	Interest Aggregation	Rule Making	Rule Application	Rule Adjudication	Communication
Parties Illegal groups	Duma Parties Illegal groups	Czar Aristocracy	Czar Aristocracy	Czar Aristocracy		

```
                        /[pressure]
   Parties   Duma—→ Czar    Czar     Czar
   Illegal   Parties Aristo- Aristo-  Aristo-
   groups    Illegal cracy   cracy    cracy
             groups |B|
                    |L|
             ↑  ↑ ↑ |O|
             |  | | |C|
             |  | | |K|
             |  | | |A|
             |  | | |G|
             |  | | |E|
             |  | └------ MIDDLE CLASS
             |  └-------- WORKING CLASS
             └----------- PEASANTS
```

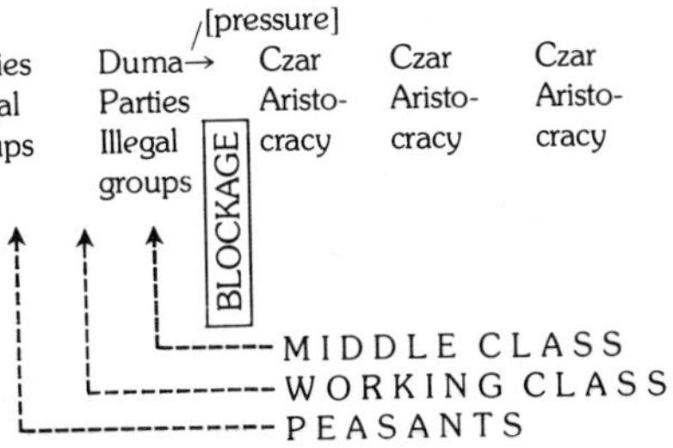

tion and aggregation of these classes' interest. Superficially, such elite power might appear to be evidence of stability—if you don't count the cost in rubles and human lives and the explosion at the end. When the maintainers finally created the Duma—an advisory parliament that functioned on and off for the last twelve years—the result was only the illusion of participation. Until hours into the revolution of March 1917, the Czar still refused to appoint ministers who would be responsible to the Duma.

Static snapshots can show how pressure builds up against static maintainers.

Revolution Against the System: The Psycho-sociology of Meaning

Structural-functional snapshots are sufficient at a distance to catch the movements of large masses of people as if they were objects. But people aren't objects. And at certain points in the cycle, their humanity becomes decisive. At such times they actualize themselves for values—for example, times of creation and revolution. At those points it becomes necessary for political scientists to step inside the perspectives of human beings. One way to do this is to do a psycho-sociology of meaning—to get at the tension between individual selves and social systems that catches us all. Three handy tools for getting at this tension are the theories of *anomie, charisma,* and *psycho-history.*

To get at the sources of change, move from externals to internals.

Testing for Anomie Early in the history of Russian revolutions, the secret police looked at Lenin's writings. They believed him when, in 1905, he said that the time was ripe for the bourgeois revolution but not for the proletarian one. They mistook the external for the internal. They mistook the weakness of external actions for objective reality, forgetting the human potential to transform disillusionment into revolt. If, instead of looking at the objective power of the middle class, they had looked at Lenin's psycho-history and at the disillusionment (anomie) among his followers, they would have located the real threat to the regime.

How do you test for disillusionment or anomie among dissidents? First one must know the psychosociological meaning of anomie. Anomie theory was first put forward in the late nineteenth century by the French sociologist Emile Durkheim.[2] He contended that society is made up of meaningful rules and behaviors. In Greek, the word for such meaningful order is "nomos." When the meaning goes out of the rules of behaviors, you live in the opposite situation of a "nomos." You live in an "anomos"—you are "anomic." When meaning goes out of people's lives and they become trapped in the psychic state of anomie, they drop out of society.

Tests for anomie have recently been developed by American

social scientists. Some sample questions getting at internal attitudes related to anomie are given in the following invitation.

INVITATION

Just as a rough measure of anomie among your friends, a college class, or people who work with you, ask them to answer "yes" or "no" to the following questions. Figures in parentheses at far right indicate the percent of a national sample who agreed with each statement in a 1965 survey.[3]

1. With everything so uncertain these days, it almost seems as though anything could happen. (82)

2. What is lacking in the world today is the old kind of friendship that lasted for a lifetime. (69)

3. With everything in such a state of disorder, it's hard for a person to know where he stands from one day to the next. (50)

4. Everything changes so quickly these days that I often have trouble deciding which are the right rules to follow. (49)

5. I often feel that many things our parents stood for are just going to ruin before our very eyes. (48)

6. The trouble with the world today is that most people really don't believe in anything. (44)

7. I often feel awkward and out of place. (37)

8. People were better off in the old days when everyone knew just how he was expected to act. (27)

9. It seems to me that other people find it easier to decide what is right than I do. (27)

But to determine which leaders will be motivated to turn anomie into positive revolutionary action, a tool that encompasses a man's whole personality and his time is required—a tool like psycho-history.

Psycho-History as Tool   Psycho-history is a tool that explains the relation between an individual and his actions through the study of his personality growth in his social situation. In a typical psycho-historical study, Erik Erikson analyzed the sources of Mahatma Ghandi's historical actions against owners of industrial capital.[4] These sources were found in the development of Ghandi's personality from childhood on. Using a Freudian approach, Erikson discovered a parallel between Ghandi's attitude toward his father and his attitude toward property owners. A mixture of guilt and hate characterized Ghandi's attitude toward his father, which he then transferred onto property owners. Erikson claimed that this parallel explained why Ghandi took an ambivalent political stance, alternating between attack and submission, risking alienating property owners in the drive he led for India's national independence.

Similarly, the police might have learned much about Lenin's motivations in political action by using psycho-history on him. In 1905 these maintenance men erroneously judged his party to be less dangerous than the middle class.

Lenin in 1905—Elite and Mass   [A young Bolshevik from Russia visits Lenin in London for instructions on how to meet the near-boiling situation in Russia]

Lenin: (springing to his feet, pacing up and down his room, thumbs tugging at his vest, speaking rapidly) What is to be done? One thing—an armed uprising—an immediate armed uprising!

Visitor: (hints that Bolsheviks in Russia still doubted that an uprising could bring victory.)

Lenin: (standing still for a moment) Victory? What do we care about victory?

Visitor: (visibly astonished, stands gaping.)

Lenin: (speaking as if addressing a large gathering, clenching his right fist and hammering away with it) We do not live by illusions! Tell that to the comrades in my name. We are sober realists. Let no one believe that we shall necessarily win. We are still very weak, but this is by no means a question of victory alone. We want the uprising to shake the foundation of the autocracy and set the broad masses into motion. Our task then will be to attract those masses to our cause. That is the main point! *The uprising is what matters.* Talk that "we can't win" and therefore don't need the uprising is the talk of cowards with whom we must have no relations.[5]

Psycho-history, placing an encounter like this one in the context of a man's early development, provides us with a basis for understanding the meaning of his later acts.

For example, we know that Lenin always had a strong streak of icily controlled will. When the young Lenin was informed that his anarchist brother Alexander had just been hanged for plotting to kidnap the Czar, he is reported to have said, "No, we shall not take this road. This is not the road to follow." And then he returned to his studies for his high school comprehensive exams.

His callousness was well developed in 1892, when as a youth he rejected a proposal to feed peasants starving in a famine. The "famine today," he said, "fulfills a progressive function: It destroys the peasant economy and throws peasants from the village into the city. Thus the proletariat is formed. . . . It will destroy his faith in the Tsar and in Tsarism and will in time speed the victory of the revolution."[6]

His intolerance of others emerged in the first party cell he joined. He took it over, forcing others to leave. At twenty-four he was already known as "the old man" and addressed by the deferential patronymic "Ilyich." Alexander Potresov, an early associate, commented: "There must have been an inner reason, springing from his emotional make-up, that was responsible for the complete suppression of youthfulness in the man."[7]

Recall the rigid and callous social and political system that evolved in Russia after 1917 under Lenin's command. Note also the disciplined and organized fighting party structure he put into the field against the loosely organized, democratic Mensheviks.[8] Contrasting Lenin's case with the psycho-history of Mao Tse-tung, keep in mind how the comparative study of psycho-history can lead to comparative insights about different means to achieve the same end—revolution. Let Mao speak for himself:

Mao in 1936—The Making of a Revolutionary Leader [On relations with his father]

Mao: One incident I especially remember. When I was about thirteen my father invited many guests to his home, and while they were present a dispute arose between the two of us. My father denounced me before the whole group, calling me lazy and useless. This infuriated me. I cursed him and left the house. My mother ran after me and tried to persuade me to return. My father also pursued me, cursing at the same time that he commanded me to come back. I reached the edge of a pond and threatened to jump in if he came nearer.

In this situation demands and counterdemands were presented for cessation of the civil war. My father insisted that I apologize and k'ou-t'ou as a sign of submission. I agreed to give a one-knee k'ou-t'ou if he would promise not to beat me. Thus the war ended, and from it I learned that when I defended my rights by open rebellion my father relented, but when I remained meek and submissive he only cursed and beat me the more.

Reflecting on this, I think that in the end the strictness of my father defeated him. I learned to hate him, and we created a real united front against him.[9]

Although this is just one example in the early development of Mao, there is evidence of comparative differences with the psycho-history of Lenin. Mao, even in the agony of anomie as he left the order of his father's house, refused to totally cut off the relationship, demonstrating tolerance and ability to compromise. But Lenin's intolerance of differences with others consistently pushed others out of his life. Whereas Mao self-actualized himself *with* others, allowing them to maintain their identities as human beings, Lenin either absorbed others or crushed them with his all-encompassing ego—a clear-cut case of megalomania (the belief of being all-powerful).

Recall what Lenin said about the starving peasants trapped in famine, and now note what Mao said about a similar situation:

Mao: At this time an incident occurred in Ilunan which influenced my whole life. . . . There had been a severe famine that year, and in Changsha thousands were without food. The starving sent a delegation to the civil governor to beg for relief, but he replied to them haughtily. "Why haven't you food? There is plenty in the city. I always have enough." When the people were told the governor's reply, they . . . drove out the governor.

This incident was discussed in my school for many days. It made a deep impression on me. Most of the other students sympathized with the "insurrectionists," but only from an observer's point of view. They did not understand that it had any relation to their own lives. They were merely interested in it as an exciting incident. I never forgot it. I felt that there with the rebels were ordinary people like my own family and I deeply resented the injustice of the treatment given them.[10]

Like Lenin, Mao also was aware of the significance of famine and disillusionment for making revolutions. But unlike Lenin, he also not only demonstrated a humane insight into the injustice of the situation but showed awareness that what affects others also affects yourself.

INVITATION

What insights does the tool of psycho-history suggest regarding the relationships between the early development of personality, leaders, and the structures they create in their historical situation?

For Mao's structures: Investigate his later claim that he established "democratic centralism" in China, in which "the organs of state must practice democratic centralism and must rely on the masses," that "democracy operates within the ranks of the people," but that "this freedom is freedom with leadership and this democracy is democracy under centralized guidance not anarchy."[11]

For Lenin's structures: Consult any of several works on the political and social structure of the Soviet Union,[12] and see how the following statement by him on structures reflects his personality: "Classes are led by parties, and parties are led by individuals who are called leaders. . . . This is the ABC. The will of a class is sometimes fulfilled by a dictator. . . . Soviet socialist democracy is not in the least incompatible with individual rule and dictatorship. . . . What is necessary is individual rule, the recognition of the dictatorial powers of one man. . . . All phrases about equal rights are nonsense."[13]

One of the strongest arguments for doing psycho-history has been made by Erik Erikson in *Young Man Luther* and *Gandhi's Truth.*[14] As political scientist Dankwart A. Rustow remarked:

Erikson showed a keen awareness that the role of a major innovator in religion or politics must be explained concurrently on distinct levels: the personal or psychological and the social or historical. Only where personal and social need, each following its distinct logic, broadly coincide does that rare opportunity arise when "an individual is called upon . . . to lift his individual patienthood to the level of a universal one and try to solve for all what he could not solve for himself alone."[15]

The historical situation is cold if experienced to be outside of oneself. Psycho-history provides a warm, human way of viewing it. We perceive the time-space concept as cool because it means necessity, implying determinism. But actually human existence or activity can take place *only* in time and space. Psycho-history makes this clear by beginning with the psychological development of a human being and relating these aspects of personality to the external constraints of his social space and time.

Severe disjunction between inner individual meanings and outer social conditions gives rise to the need to reconstruct a network of meaning between the individual and society. One way to do this is to regress to second youth and learn new meanings by accepting the authority of a charismatic leader.[16]

Initially, charisma is a response to anomie. When the social world is perceived to be in chaos, a need arises among people to find new meaning. Sometimes this need can be satisfied by ascribing the possession of new meaning to a single individual, who then becomes a leader. This constitutes a charismatic relationship. Often it does not matter whether the chosen individual had intended to provide such meanings, but he must at least have the capacity to crystallize answers to the dominant concerns of people in his historical situation, and he must state them with self-assurance.[17]

**CREATION
Founding the Faith:
Creating Through
Charisma**

**Charisma is in
the eye of the beholder,
but leadership qualities help.**

Take the example of Lenin. A worker who heard him speak said of him:

> There was nothing extraordinary in his manner of speaking, no rhetorical phrases, unless he wanted to underline his thought. He would step back, then come toward the listeners, his arms stretched out before him as though to serve them that thought on the palm of his hand. The manner in which one listened to him was far from indifferent. As soon as he saw that attention was flagging, he would throw out a lively, striking word and immediately take the audience in hand again. . . .[18]

Similarly the author Maxim Gorki, who knew Lenin intimately, said of one encounter:

> It was the first time I had heard complicated questions treated so simply. There was no striving after eloquent phrases with him, but every word was uttered distinctly, and its meaning was marvelously plain. . . . His arm was extended with the hand slightly raised, and he seemed to weigh every word with it. . . . He gave us a shorter speech than the orators who spoke before him, but he made a much greater impression. I was not alone in feeling this. Behind me was an enthusiastic whispering: "Now, he has got something to say."[19]

All descriptions of Lenin, including these two, indicate that, except for his greater clarity and certainty, he was not in any objective sense a figure transcending ordinary men in the god-like stance often attributed to charismatic figures. Yet many of those who followed him did so as if they perceived in him just such god-like transcendence. Their loyalty was unswerving, their faith total. Comparisons over time with other charismatic situations reveal that the making of a charismatic leader depends not on what the man says and how so much as the presence or absence of the one crucial social condition that produces in the mass the *need* for charisma.

Selection of a leader from several potential charismatic figures who offer themselves occurs often by accident and more frequently on the basis of the content of their message. In the case of the pre-Exile Judaic prophets, for example, true prophets were told from false prophets on the basis of the fact that the "true" ones prophesied doom, which was in accord with fundamental religious beliefs, while "false" ones prophesied better times during the foreign invasions that shook Israel's faith in God.

If comparison can lead to insights into the social conditions preceding charisma, it should also illuminate the personality type of charismatic leaders, as indicated in the following section.

The Revolutionary Personality: Mao and Others

One of the gains sought from the comparative study of politics is the discovery of better means towards similar ends. Finding better means for successful revolution is as legitimate a goal in such studies as unraveling better means out of the knotty problem of maintaining a system. A comparative comment by the China expert Edgar Snow on the personalities of Chinese and American revolutionary leaders suggests that comparative studies can lead to insights for a theory of revolutions and how to make them. Although Snow focuses upon Mao, notice how his analysis becomes richer as he compares Mao to others.

INVITATION

As you read the following paragraph, ask, What can I learn about the kind of personality that best fits the task of revolution by looking at individual revolutionaries in a comparative way?

Mao's childhood resentments seem to have been well-founded protests against tyranny and ignorance, but we have only his side of the story. On his later years there is much more information. It is difficult to separate Mao's adult behavior or writing from the whole Chinese revolution. Should that be considered one vast delusion of persecution? Is everyone who disdains to compromise with the intolerable a paranoid? That would put Patrick Henry in the vanguard. If, after a nation has been exploited, robbed, opium-soaked, plundered, occupied and partitioned by foreign invaders for a century, the people turns upon its persecutors and drives them from the house, along with the society whose weakness permitted the abuses, is it suffering from paranoia? Or would it be schizoid if it did otherwise? Some grave miscalculations in Mao's later years suggest delusions of grandeur. Could they not readily be matched by blunders of bigoted "normal" statesmen elsewhere which are rationalized as bad judgment? Erik Erikson has described Martin Luther as a great man whose personality found maximum stability only when he discovered his *adult* "identity" in reasonable heresy; in his rebellion against Rome he found truth in a fully justified good cause. Similarly, Mao had little difficulty in uniting his personality as leader of a "just war" of liberation. . . .

It was Mao's ability to analyze the experience common to his generation—rather than the uniqueness of his own experience—plus his messianic belief in the correctness of his own generalizations of that experience, which distinguish him from compatriots who became his followers.[20]

What does Snow's comparative statement regarding Mao Tse-tung and others suggest?

First, we observe that leaders in similar situations (for Henry and Mao, situations of decay and revolution) manifest similar personality characteristics. If we can find further evidence in other leaders, we may conclude that individuals who would exercise leadership in times of decay had best be "paranoid." We cannot come to such a conclusion here, without investigating the personality of many others. But the possibility of learning something about the personality type best suited for revolution from a comparative study of revolutions strongly suggests itself.

Secondly, from such comparative study we may well learn something about the concept of personality that may correct our understanding of that concept. Mao did have strong resentments in childhood. He did have strong feelings of persecution, which were not alleviated by the fact that a certain warlord tried to arrest him and possibly kill him several times when he was still a young man beginning to organize Communists in his home province. But Mao reacted to such feelings of persecution by working out an adaptation. Against the disorder and conflict of his time, he worked out a life plan for himself and others of ordered conflict through which to adapt himself to his environment. Can such an individual be called psychologically sick? After all, Mao did adapt to and finally control his environment.

The insight we may tentatively derive from this is that the psychological concept of personality—especially that of abnormal personality—must be understood within its environmental setting. An individual can be called paranoid if he has delusions of persecution in a normal, ordered life situation. But he should not be given that label if he is living in a world filled with actual persecutions, disorder, slaughter, plunder, and exploitation. In fact, the individual who feels persecuted in such a situation is the *sane* individual.

As psychologist R. D. Laing critically states: "The condition of alienation, of being unconscious, of being out of one's mind, is the condition of the normal man."[21]

What we may be observing in individuals everywhere who break out of the "normality" of imposed anticreative patterns of behavior is their coming into their own mind after being out of it. But this is a question for a philosophy of mind or a philosophy of being. Nevertheless, it is a point in favor of the comparative study of behavior—political or otherwise—that such study can bring us to such ultimate questions, even to the hint of some answers to these questions.

MAINTENANCE
Working the System: Tools for Explaining Dehumanization

As systems continue in time, they tend to become more and more dehumanized. To build the revolution, Lenin felt he had to detach himself from the question of how individuals might feel about making sacrifices and being killed in the service of the idea with which all politics begins. Perhaps the lesson to be learned from the Russian experience is that the design of the idea for a political system is the most crucial event in making the system. It may be true that, as the Social Democrats in Germany discovered, a humane idea for a humane system cannot be institutionalized in a maintenance society that uses force to resist that idea. Such force must be met with force, which is contrary to the humane idea.

At the same time, the history of the Soviet Union demonstrates that while it is possible to overthrow an existing system by the use of inhumane activities—especially killing—this overthrow does not transform the humane aspects of the idea of Marxism into reality. In fact, it has seemed in the history of the Bolshevik revolution that the tactics of the revolution determined the face of the succeeding political culture and institutions more than did the original idea of Marxism.

Since the individual becomes less important in times of maintenance than he or she is in times of creation, it may be possible to understand the workings of a system in the stage of maintenance with tools reflecting social institutions rather than with those stressing individual behavior in the mass of followers, who are routinized into enforced patterns of behavior. But the meaning of such a period in terms of human needs and values may be bypassed, using such large-scale tools.

For example, although the maintenance era under Joseph Stalin may be roughly comprehended without understanding individual personalities of the masses of people involved, a personality study of the leader of the society may be extremely useful.

The following section illustrates how both impersonal tools tapping social structures and more sensitive, individual tools tapping personality can be used separately to yield insights into Stalinist Russia. An investigator using the tool of psycho-history would, of course, weave the evidence from the psychic and social sources together in historical context.

Stalin: The Detached Personality as Systems Builder and Maintainer

The advantages of personal detachment from the fate of others have already been indicated above. Such detachment does not make us more humane, or for that matter, human, but it is an effective tool for manipulating others for our own purposes.

As the main leader in the Soviet Union's first period of maintenance, Stalin managed to develop such detachment. Analyze the following conversation with Winston Churchill, then prime minister of Great Britain, in 1942:

Stalin and the Kulaks   [Churchill and Stalin are meeting at the latter's apartment in the Kremlin, in which Stalin's rooms, according to Churchill, were "of moderate size, simple, dignified, and four in number—a dining room, working-room, bedroom and a large bathroom." The two have been talking since 7:00 p.m. It is now past midnight.]

Churchill: Tell me, have the stresses of this war been as bad to you personally as carrying through the policy of the Collective Farms?

Stalin: (perhaps remembering the millions of peasants killed, at his orders, for resisting collectivization) Oh, no, the Collective Farm policy was a terrible struggle.

Churchill: I thought you would have found it bad, because you were not dealing with a few score thousands of aristocrats or big landowners but with millions of small men.

Stalin: (holding up the fingers of his two hands) Ten millions. It was fearful. Four years it lasted. It was absolutely necessary for Russia, if we were to avoid periodic famines, to plough the land with tractors. We must mechanise agriculture. When we gave tractors to our peasants they were all spoiled in a few months. Only Collective Farms with workshops could handle tractors. We took the greatest trouble to explain it to the peasants. It was no use arguing with them. . . .

Churchill: These were what you call Kulaks?

Stalin: (not repeating the word) Yes. (Pausing) It was all very bad and difficult—but necessary.

Churchill: What happened?

Stalin: Oh, well, many of them agreed to come in with us. Some of them were given land of their own to cultivate in the province of Tomsk or the province of Irkutsk or farther north, but the great bulk were very unpopular and were wiped out by their labourers. (There is what Churchill later calls "a considerable pause." Then Stalin resumes) Not only have we vastly increased the food supply, but we have improved the quality of the grain beyond all measure. All kinds of grain used to be grown. Now no one is allowed to sow any but the standard Soviet grain from one end of our country to the other. If they do they are severely dealt with. This means another large increase in the food supply.

[Churchill, commenting later in his memoirs: "I record as they come back to me these memories, and the strong impression I sustained at the moment of millions of men and women being blotted out or displaced for ever. A generation would no doubt come to whom their miseries were unknown, but it would be sure of having more to eat and bless Stalin's name. I did not repeat Burke's dictum, 'If I cannot have reform without injustice, I will not have reform.' With the World War going on all round us it seemed vain to moralise aloud.''][22]

**A politics for human beings
requires humane means for
humane goals—
but what if humane means
require the starvation of millions?**

Structural-Functional Analysis of Stalinist Russia   How was it possible for such a policy to be carried out? A quick structural-functional analysis of the Soviet Union in Stalin's time presents an answer in snapshot form (Figure 7–5).

Figure 7-5

Stalinist Russia

Socialization & recruitment	Interest articulation	Interest aggregation	Rule making	Rule application	Rule adjudication	Communication
The Party	The Party	The Party	Stalin	Stalin	Stalin	The Party

The picture is one of the centralization of the rule-making, rule-applying, and rule-adjudicating functions under one man—Stalin. The apparatus of the Communist party was used not only to train newcomers to party ranks but to channel any and all expression of popular demands. To a large extent, that party's communications machinery was used to socialize members into voicing demands or interests previously defined by the elite, specifically Stalin.

Superficially, the structural-functional snapshot of the Soviet system of politics might seem to resemble that of the Czarist system, excluding large segments of the population from participation in the political system. But a more careful comparison shows that the party political system excluded no single major group in the society. Representatives of both the industrial workers and the agrarian workers are present in the party structure. The bourgeoisie, the aristocracy, and land-owning peasants have been "liquidated." The dead don't aggregate and articulate.

And all those not allowed into the party still fall under the control of a second system, the government. This system is mainly administrative but also has interest-articulating and aggregating structures—at the top, for example, the Supreme Soviet and the Soviet of Nationalities. While "expression of interests" no longer meant expression of individual interests but of socially approved general "interests," *participation* in articulating and aggregating structures was more intense than in democratic nations (because attendance was required).

The degree of at least symbolic opportunities to articulate and aggregate interests mounted a considerable distance above the level of Czarist times, even for groups low in social or economic position. But to a large extent, the articulating and aggregating structures were simply used as socialization and communications structures that channelled national goals set by the elite downward, inculcated them in the mass, and then allowed these learned interests to be "articulated" and "aggregated" and chanelled upward again.

INCONCLUSIONS

With the establishment of Stalin's dictatorship for maintenance of the Soviet system, the cycle of decay-creation-maintenance has gone through all three phases. So has our use of different tools for the analysis of different phases. Just as we began using the structural-functional tool of snapshots to understand the development of Russia's revolutionary crisis over 105 years, we ended using a snap-shot of the maintenance system under Stalin to indicate the reason for the extent of his control. Such purposeful choice of tools would have to be continued if we were now to look at the period of decay to be expected in the Soviet system. And, according to our toolbox, the first test for decay would involve use of a tool that would enable us to step into the shoes of the Russians, to get the first inkling of ideas in their minds that might lead to systems-crumbling attitudes and actions— tests for anomie, for instance.

The toolbox provided here is far from exhaustive. Nor is the treatment of the Russian subject exhaustive. Rather, it is an introduction to how the study of comparative politics can be undertaken with three purposes in mind: learning how to deal with others, learning about others' goals—their means and the cost—and obtaining a perspective on ourselves through the others' looking-glass.

REFERENCES

1. See Max Weber, *Economy and Society*, vol. 1 (New York: Bedminster Press, 1968), Chapter 1, on the fundamental concepts of sociology.
2. Emile Durkheim, *Suicide* (New York: The Free Press, 1951).
3. Scale by McClosky and Schaar in John P. Robinson and Phillip R. Shaver, eds., *Measures of Social Psychological Attitudes* (Ann Arbor, Mich.: Survey Research Center, 1969), p. 171.
4. See Erik H. Erikson, *Gandhi's Truth: On the Origins of Militant Nonviolence* (N.Y.: W. W. Norton, 1969).
5. Scenario created on the basis of David Shub, *Lenin: A Biography* (Baltimore, Md.: Penguin Books, 1967), pp. 100—101.
6. Cited in Shub, *Lenin*, p. 39.
7. *Ibid.*, p. 41.
8. See M. C. Morgan, *Lenin* (Ohio University Press, 1971), p. 191. Note not only what happened to the democratic-idealistic Mensheviks in Russia in the Bolshevik Revolution of October-November 1917, but what happened to them later in the Georgian Republic, where they permitted unrestricted Bolshevik activity.
9. Edgar Snow, *Red Star Over China*, first enlarged and revised edition (New York: Grove Press, 1968), pp. 132–133.
10. *Ibid*, p. 135.

11. Mao Tse-tung, "On the Correct Handling of Contradictions among the People," in *Communist China: 1955–1959—Policy Documents with Analysis*, editor anonymous, with a foreword by Robert R. Bowie and John K. Fairbank (Cambridge: Harvard University Press, 1965), p. 277.

12. Ellsworth Raymond, *The Soviet Government* (New York: Macmillan, 1968), for example.

13. V. I. Lenin, *Collected Works*, vol. 18 (Moscow: Foreign Languages Publishing House), p. 89.

14. See Erik Erikson, *Young Man Luther* (New York: Norton, 1958) and *Gandhi's Truth*, cited in footnote 4.

15. Dankwart A. Rustow, "Introduction to the Issue 'Philosophers and Kings: Studies in Leadership,'" *Daedalus* 97, no. 3 (Summer 1968), p. 688.

16. See Peter L. Berger and Thomas Luckman, *The Social Construction of Reality* (Garden City, N.Y.: Doubleday Anchor Books, 1967).

17. On the psychology of charismatic leaders, see Ralph P. Hummel, "The Psychology of Charismatic Leaders," paper delivered at the World Congress of the International Political Science Association, August 1973, Montreal, and Ralph P. Hummel, "Freud's Totem Theory as Complement to Max Weber's Theory of Charisma," *Psychological Reports*, vol. 35 (October 1974), pp. 683–686. For a standard discussion of charisma, as well as other types of authority, see Max Weber, *The Theory of Social and Economic Organization*, ed. Talcott Parsons (New York: The Free Press, 1964), especially Part III, "The Types of Authority and Imperative Co-ordination."

18. Cited by Nina Gourfinkel, *Lenin*, trans. Maurice Thornton (New York: Grove Press, 1961), pp. 130–131.

19. Maxim Gorky, *Days with Lenin* (New York: International Publishers, 1932), p. 16.

20. Edgar Snow, *Red China Today* (New York: Random House Vintage Books, 1971), pp. 164–165.

21. R. D. Laing, *The Politics of Experience* (New York: Ballantine Books, 1968), p. 28.

22. Winston Spencer Churchill, *The Hinge of Fate* (New York: Bantam Books, 1962), pp. 434–435.

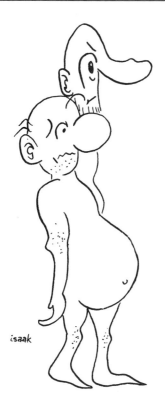

isaak

8 **Wherein Bismarck, Kissinger, and Hammarskjöld illustrate to the reader how to create and maintain national political systems in international politics.**

8 Internationalizing Politics

How human beings view the cycle of creation, maintenance, and decay depends on where they are standing. They can see politics *nationally, comparatively,* or *internationally.* As the observer widens his vision, he moves increasingly from a human to a bird's-eye view. These three perspectives, or *levels of analysis,* depend upon the number of nations and the geographical scope involved.

**To internationalize politics,
widen the focus of relationships
between human beings to relations
among groups of human beings
called nations.**

Many approach international politics by counting the history of social facts and national systems for much and individual wills and values for little. Such a viewpoint can lead to a pessimism of historic proportions, sapping all individual will to control world politics for the sake of human needs. This chapter will not begin with the conventional view but will rather focus on the principles of international politics as shown in the views and actions of individual world leaders.

The social facts of nation-states always appear bigger than the men who would control them. Nations are created, expanded, and corrupted as leaders come and go in the cycle. The system of nation-states remains, though in its detailed events it changes daily like a kaleidoscope. This ominous shifting of world events has caused many experts in international relations to become gloomy conservatives, counting human beings for little.

**The more a person studies
international politics,
the more pessimistic and
conservative he often becomes.**

But human beings exist who refuse to let the conservative atmosphere of international politics swallow them up in determinism. Some human beings refuse to be totally put down by the cycle. They live in the spirit of Friedrich Nietzsche, who said: "I want to teach men the sense of their existence, which is the Superman, the lightning out of the dark cloud man."

**The will to power in your life
can open the cycle to a new phase of
social and self-creation.
Or, powerlessness corrupts.**[1]

Anyone can do local politics and have some faith in his power to affect events for his values. But when politics gets big—national, corporative, or international—most people let feelings of powerlessness corrupt their wills and render them impotent.

There are some human beings who see themselves as bigger than that. They refuse to be sapped by feelings of powerlessness, and they put themselves on the line to alter the cycle of nations. They strap the fate of Sisyphus to their shoulders, the Sisyphus of Greek myth condemned by the gods to struggle forever to roll a rock up the mountain, only to see it fall back each time to the depths. As Albert Camus wrote: "The struggle itself toward the heights is enough to fill a man's heart. One must imagine Sisyphus happy."[2] Human beings who take on that legendary burden are living proof that not only do systems create people, but people *can* create systems.

Among those who use their spot in their cycle to will their values are *nation makers, coalition makers,* and *peace makers.* Each of these types of "great men" illustrates how human beings can internationalize politics.*

CREATING SYSTEMS
Nation Makers: Bismarck

Some Founding Fathers or nation makers are born great, become greater, and thrust their greatness upon others. Usually they are high self-esteem personality types. But as Alphonse, Balthazar, and Otto von Bismarck Schoenhausen learned, great plans of strength often carry the seeds of future failure in them.

**Greatness inflates the ego
and deflates others—
until something pops the balloon.**

Bismarck was born in 1815, the year Napoleon was banished to St. Helena. His parents represented the Junker aristocracy and bureaucracy—he was born with class and the potential power to create his own social relationships with whom he wanted.

**Men with class can create social
relationships with whom they want.
. . . Low class means no class.**

Like many great leaders, Bismarck was a bad student who enjoyed getting into trouble. Called "the mad Junker," he proudly tried to outdress, outdrink, and outduel everyone. Typically, his parents tried to cure him by making him transfer—from the University of Goettingen to the University of Berlin. To no avail. In Berlin he continued to rebel, to drink, and, in his own words, to "sit in the first tier of the opera and behave as rowdily as possible."

---

*This is not to endorse a one-factor analysis such as Carlyle's. It *is* to assert that the power of individual men can be great in some given situations, based on their correct estimate of their location in such situations.

**Forming yourself and your own
social relationships often involves
aggression against others and their
relationships.**

But the woman behind the man—Bismarck's mother—wanted
greater things from him, and her connections helped him get a civil
service job in Aachen.[3] Yet the routine of the job was too much for
him, and he left without notice after a year:

> I had every prospect for what is called a brilliant career . . . had not
> an extraordinarily beautiful Briton induced me to change course
> and sail in her wake for six months without the slightest leave. I
> forced her to come aside; she lowered her flag, but after possession
> of two months I lost the booty to a one-armed colonel fifty years of
> age with four horses and 15,000-dollar revenue.[4]

Beneath the love affair was another reason for Bismarck's decision: he did not want to play third fiddle in a Prussian bureaucracy. He
wrote a friend: "I want to make music as I consider proper or none at
all."[5] And Bismarck did exactly that later—he used a ten-year stint as
Prussian ambassador to work out a foreign policy through which he
united Germany almost single-handed.

**All great conductors must learn
how to say "no" to make the music
go their way.**

Bismarck was able to create a policy of great political power
because he was aware of his position in the political cycle of his time.
This awareness enabled him to use facts to get what he wanted.

One can use the three questions or locating tools introduced in
Chapter 3, page 50, to place Bismarck (or any other human being
of that time) in the political cycle of mid-nineteenth-century Europe:

1. What social relationships had been created for him that he
could not affect at that time? Or, whose victim was he?
Answer: Bismarck was the victim of the Metternich system of international politics, named after the Austrian foreign minister who created
and used it to keep European states balanced off against one another
for the sake of Austrian security between 1815 and 1848. As Henry
Kissinger has pointed out, this system was based on (1) a general
balance of power in Central Europe (especially in Germany), strong
enough to resist pressures from the East and West; (2) an equilibrium
within Germany that gave the German states enough unity to
mobilize against outside threats, but not so much centralization as to
become an offensive threat to neighboring regions; and (3) a moral
consensus, allowing most disputes to be settled by appeal to a "higher
principle" rather than by force.[6]

**If you want to keep the present
international system going,**

Metternich was so successful at imbuing his diplomatic system with legitimacy that the Prussian king refused the crown of a united Germany from the National Assembly at Frankfurt because he thought only Austria had an historical claim to it! Bismarck found the legitimacy of Metternich's system (and probably of anybody *else's* system) to be stifling. Once again he found himself kowtowing to a bureaucracy that he couldn't stand. And Prussia was being kept down as well.

2. What social relationships did he partly control? Or, to what extent could he work the system for his values?

Answer: Bismarck used his role as ambassador of Prussia to influence others with a flood of memoranda.

**Power grows out of
the barrel of a pen.**

He attacked the Metternich system, rejecting its axiom that Prussia's security depended on subordination to a unity of conservative monarchs. His thesis was that Prussia had a unique tradition that could be turned into a politics of invulnerable strength.

**A nation maker often advocates the
belief that his would-be nation-state
is unique and invulnerable.**

isaak

This German nation maker placed political "facts," force, and nationalism before Metternich's notions of balance of power and bowing to superior principles. Many German writers at that time, such as Herder, Fichte, and Hegel, conceived of each people as being a separate distinct entity, and they saw the State as the embodiment of national identity and ultimate values. Bismarck transformed such beliefs into *nationalism*—the ultimate We-They reification—to integrate Germany under Prussian leadership.

3. What social relationships was he totally free to create? Or, was he free to create himself with others?

Answer: Like most would-be nation makers, Bismarck was not in a position to start from scratch. There existed in Europe a conservative balance-of-power system that he had to exploit for his ends. But the spirit of the nineteenth century was one of nationalism combined with liberalism. By persuading the elite among his countrymen that Prussian nationalism could be based on traditional conservatism rather than liberalism, Bismarck was able to exploit the existing social relationships of states to unite Germany through Prussian power.

**To lead a nation, go in the door
of the spirit of the times . . .
and come out your own.**

Bismarck was by no means totally free in his choices. Once in office as Chancellor, he found it necessary to use tactics of *ambiguity, secrecy,* and *surprise* to accomplish his ends.

> **Ambiguity is to create an image with at least two meanings.**
> **Secrecy is sharing the one meaning you choose with friends.**
> **Surprise is springing your meaning on others when they least expect it.**

To protect Germany from France, Bismarck refused to return Alsace-Lorraine, taken in the *(surprise)* war of 1870—71 that unified Germany. And he negotiated unannounced treaties with Austria and neighboring states *(secrecy)* to insure German security from a possible Russian attack or Russo-French alliance. The strategy of forming secret alliances was called "employing one's neighbors to pull out each other's teeth" by Britain's Lord Salisbury. Whenever he could, he remained aloof until other powers were committed *(ambiguity)*.

An artist of the possible, Bismarck combined three speedy wars with moderation in victory to create the German nation and undo Metternich's entire system of European politics. He was an archetypal pathological realist who was to inspire other aggressive realists in the future. And he undoubtedly helped to sow the seeds for the German tragedies in the century to follow.

Bismarck, like many strong leaders, was replaced by mediocre successors. Henry Kissinger wrote about Bismarck's Germany: "A system which requires a great man in each generation sets itself an almost insurmountable challenge, if only because a great man tends to stunt the emergence of strong personalities."[7] But did not Kissinger himself become such an irreplaceable great man in a system going from maintenance to decay?

Coalition Makers: Kissinger

For thirty years, Metternich manipulated Europe in a time of maintenance to maximize Austria's national interests. Then, in 1848, Metternich was undone when revolutionary upheaval in Europe indicated that a period of maintenance had entered into a phase of decay. Bismarck was able to manipulate social relationships in this transition from maintenance to decay to consolidate Prussian power, unite Germany, and change the rules of the game in European diplomacy. He created. *He saw his position in time and space in the political cycle, obtained an effective role with his class, status, and personality, and then created policy that maximized his values at least cost.* As decay unsettled the balance-of-power Metternich system, Bismarck increasingly found that he had to create secret coalitions to preserve German interests and get what he wanted. In the late twentieth century another diplomat has sought to maximize national interests by secretly forming coalitions in a period in which international relations move from maintenance to decay. His name: Henry Alfred Kissinger.

Unlike Bismarck, Kissinger did not have an upper-class background. He was born into the middle class in Fürth, Germany, in

1923. His father taught in a girl's high school; his mother was a housewife. From the day of his birth, Kissinger's political environment deteriorated as the Nazis gained ground in Germany and anti-Semitism spread. He was beaten up by classmates for being Jewish and forced to go to an all-Jewish school. His father was dismissed from his job. As in the case of Bismarck, his mother played a crucial role in his development. Largely at her prompting, the family left Germany for New York in 1938—just before it would have been too late.

In New York Kissinger went to high school at night and worked to earn money for his family—squeezing acid out of brush bristles in a Manhattan shaving-brush factory. Soon he was promoted to delivery boy. Then he was drafted—a lucky break, it later turned out. At first it didn't seem that way. In the army's regular testing program, Kissinger was discovered to have an I.Q. high enough to qualify for a special group of 3,000 men whose minds, the military thought, might later be useful in the war. He was sent to college for six months. But then the army dropped the program and sent all the men into the infantry.

A few months later, Dr. Fritz Kraemer, a thirty-five-year-old lawyer with two Ph.D.'s, was ordered to explain why America was in the war and teach optimum strategies to an army unit lead by Buck Private Kissinger, who was nineteen years old. Soon thereafter, Kissinger sent Kraemer an enigmatic note, carefully worded, complimenting him on his speech:

Dear Pvt. Kraemer:

I heard you speak yesterday. This is how it should be done. Can I help you somehow?

Pvt. Kissinger[8]

Impressed by Kissinger's style, Kraemer used his influence to have Kissinger made an interpreter in case the Eighty-fourth Division should be sent to Germany. It was. And Kissinger became interpreter for a general.

Stroking a strong man's ego can bring rewards and create an invaluable social relationship. *

Soon Kissinger's division took over the city of Krefeld and discovered that the city government had vanished along with the Nazi soldiers. Kraemer again intervened and suggested that Kissinger, since he spoke German and was extremely intelligent, should be placed in charge of reorganizing the government of the city of 200,000 people. It took Kissinger three days to have the city running smoothly again.

---

*This principle is perhaps best understood as an inversion of the neologism: "If you are not stroked, your spinal cord will shrivel up." Many social psychologists worry about what happens after the child is separated from the ego-stroking of "mother-power." Great men often create intimate social relationships to replace motherly ego-stroking with more mature varieties. Such substitute relationships cannot help but bolster the backbone and self-confidence.

As a result he was made administrator of the Bergstrasse district, a job he did so well that many German people in the area begged him to stay when he was transferred.

Kraemer then helped Kissinger, now a sergeant, to be appointed to the faculty of the European Command Intelligence School, where he taught colonels and officers of higher ranks how to root out Nazis who had gone underground. When the war was over, some people in the army were so impressed that they asked Kissinger to stay on at the school as a civilian teacher for a high salary.

**Show competence at small jobs
to bring deference and
the confidence of others for big jobs.**

In 1946, Kissinger applied late for study at Harvard. He was accepted and did brilliantly. William Elliott, a professor of government, told him that he had the makings of a "great philosopher." Kissinger eventually wrote his Ph.D. thesis on—guess what—the creation of the Metternich system of balance of power between 1812 and 1822 (later turned into a book, *A World Restored*).

The turning point in his career, however, was a book he wrote in 1957, *Nuclear Weapons and Foreign Policy,* which became a best seller and attracted the attention of statesmen as well as scholars. In this influential book Kissinger argued that the use of nuclear weapons did not have to be merely *strategical* (the popular belief at that time), but could be *tactical* as well. He introduced new flexibility into the theories of nuclear strategy at a time of "big bomb or bust" thinking.

**Little books with dangerous ideas
can increase deference
and political power.**

After serving as Director of Nuclear Weapons and Foreign Policy Studies for the Council of Foreign Relations, Kissinger became a professor at Harvard University and an adviser to then Governor Nelson Rockefeller of New York. In 1968, with Rockefeller's help, Kissinger found his pivotal role in international politics: National Security Adviser to President Richard M. Nixon. His job was to preselect the optimum foreign policy options for the president of the United States and to serve as the chief adviser on policies linking domestic and international security.

**Foreign policy decision making
is done under the cloak of
national security; or,
policies of fear inspire deference
for authority among the masses.**

Kissinger, who has been called "the Metternich of the Bronx," is almost an ideal example of how a human being can combine historical situation (place in the cycle), chance, personal ability, and perception to create a role of great power in international politics. After an unbelievable career of upward mobility, he located himself in a national system moving from maintenance to decay in the political cycle and obtained perhaps the best possible role for maximizing his values domestically and internationally (he could not become president, failing to fulfill the *native* American requirement). It is undoubtedly no accident that he did detailed scholarly studies of Metternich and Bismarck, who were both political geniuses at maximizing their values in periods moving from maintenance to decay. Both were adept at forming secret coalitions or temporary alliances with other states for national profit.

> **To make a political role**
> **work best for you,**
> **study those who have used**
> **such roles best before.**

Kissinger, however, has more in common with Metternich than with Bismarck. Bismarck's primary aim was to use Prussian nationalism to break Prussia out of Metternich's balance-of-power system to unite Germany. Metternich, on the other hand, sought to maintain Austria's power in the status quo by using the principle of *legitimacy* (that is, for Metternich, "the higher moral principle" beyond force) to keep the major powers of Europe—Austria, Prussia, Russia, France, and England—in balance. Kissinger was not in a position historically (or cyclically) to create a nation as did Bismarck; but he, like Metternich, matured in a time in which someone had to work to maintain the great-power status of a nation. His was a time of maintenance, not of creation.

From the time he was nineteen onwards, Kissinger accepted the reality of his social world only to the extent that he could create himself within it. For instance, he initiated his relationship with Fritz Kraemer, the man who did so much for him so often. At each point, Kissinger seemed to accept the authority of those above him only to the extent that he could become an authority—part of an elite due to knowledge, university status, publication, and administrative and intellectual efficiency.

> **To become great politically,**
> **accept the authority of elites**
> **only to the extent that you can**
> **become one and create**
> **social relationships accordingly.**

Kissinger's philosophical gifts and intellectual incisiveness attracted politicians who either did not have those abilities or had not taken the time to develop them. It was not accidental that Henry Kissinger chose important foreign policy issues as topics for his books: nuclear weapons strategy, national security, American foreign policy decision making, and the Atlantic Alliance.

> **Perceive where political time
> and space meet in your everyday
> world and make yourself needed
> for a significant role at exactly
> that intersection.**

When he took over his most significant political role, National Security Adviser to President Nixon, Kissinger knew that the maintenance of American power in the world was threatened by decay. Vietnam had made foreign policy a controversial domestic issue. Even in a democratic country*, such controversy means an attack upon the legitimacy of the governing elite if no domestic consensus is achieved.

> **In democratic countries,
> controversial foreign policies
> undermine the legitimacy of elites;
> hence, good diplomats are seen
> but not heard.**

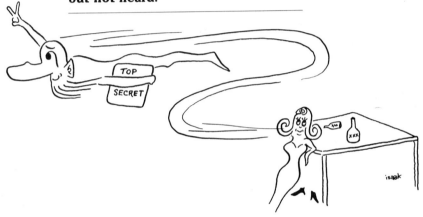

Kissinger, like Metternich, was forced by historical events to concern himself with the legitimacy of governing elites—including himself. Also, like Metternich's, his strategy was one of quiet maintenance. He worked to maintain his country's strong position in world politics by balancing other world powers—Russia, China, Japan, and Europe —and by playing them against one another to maximize American interests. As one observer bluntly put it:

> If Henry has it the way he talks about it to interviewers, the historians may be compelled by the facts to write that during the Kissinger period the old post-war Marshall Plan foreign policy of malignant altruism was replaced with a policy that might be called benign selfishness. Henry has pointed out time and again that the world of the 1970's is no place for the rhetoric of a John Kennedy who pledged in his inaugural that the U.S. would fight anytime, anywhere, any enemy to defend liberty.[9]

*There are no countries without elites. See especially Chapter 3 for the dominance of elites in "democratic" America.

But Kissinger was faced with creating policies of national interest in a world more complex than that of Metternich. Metternich's Austria was one of five approximately equal great powers whose leaders all basically agreed to preserve the legitimacy of the status quo by preventing any one power from becoming too strong.

Kissinger's world was one of nuclear weapons dominated by two superpowers, the United States and the USSR. As Japan, China, and Western Europe became stronger, this *bipolar* world (one dominated by two powers) was being transformed into a *multipolar* world (dominated by more than two powers) on some, but not all levels. Thus Japan's strength was economic, not military; China's power was founded on the basis of agriculture, a large population, and a rather small nuclear capability, compared with the two superpowers; Western Europe's potential great-power status depended upon constant agreement on economic, military, and political strategies among a number of competing entities often too proud of their differences. So although neither American nor Soviet elites were strong enough any longer to maintain control of a bipolar world, China, Japan, and Western Europe were not strong enough to threaten the special status of the two superpowers.

Although Metternich's balance of power model served as one of Kissinger's frames of reference, he was aware of its weakness when he came into power. In *A World Restored*, he dismisses Metternich as obsolete, a leftover from the Enlightenment misled into believing in a natural harmony of international affairs. Because of such a faulty world view, Metternich "failed to achieve final greatness." And Kissinger has probably often made use of Bismarck's more flexible world view—the notion that international politics can be stabilized only with a dynamic equilibrium, manipulated by diplomats who can operate with amoral calculations of power marked by secrecy and ambiguity.[10]

But although "higher principles of morality" beyond force may be secondary in importance to amoral power calculations for Kissinger, he has nevertheless relied heavily upon two other aspects of Metternich's balancing system: the notion of legitimacy and the balance of five major power units.

> **Maintenance men threatened by decay attempt to reaffirm the legitimacy of the principles that hold the nation and their power together.**

Kissinger has insisted upon the legitimacy of American national interests, represented by himself as bargainer, in a balancing game with four other powers: the Soviet Union, China, Japan, and Western Europe. The only reason that Kissinger was able to make any use at all of the Metternich balancing model was that nations with nuclear weapons seemed to tacitly agree not to use them. This, in turn, diminished the importance of Soviet and American nuclear superiority, making these two powers more nearly equal with the other three major powers. Domestic problems within the United States and the

USSR further restrained the superpowers and tended to make them comparable with Japan, China, Western Europe and the Middle East in many day-by-day political and economic interactions.

Military and domestic restraints make superpowers less super.

Kissinger perceived his task to be to preserve the status quo and America's special status in it by making the four other powers uncertain as to when and where the United States would actually use her tremendous potential power. Noting that an image of Soviet unpredictability—such as Khrushchev's banging his shoe on a United Nations desk—became a valuable bargaining device for the USSR, Kissinger has suggested that the United States might improve its bargaining by also "banging the shoe" occasionally.[11]

Accordingly, *secrecy* and *ambiguity* were two of his favorite weapons when he made clandestine trips to China, establishing United States-Chinese relations in the form of political and economic ties for the first time since the Chinese Revolution. He then used the ambiguity of these secret negotiations as a bargaining tool to worry the Russians and get a better deal with them. Thus he was able to play Russia and China against one another for the benefit of American national interests.

Kissinger, of course, has contributed to some mistakes. For instance, American interests were not furthered when the United States joined China to support Pakistan in the India-Pakistan war, which India won with Soviet help. Nor was it wise for Kissinger to wait until the last minute to inform the Japanese of America's new agreements with China—this delay created animosity unnecessarily.

But on the whole, Kissinger used secret coalitions and ambiguity with great ability to maintain American interests at a time they were threatened by decay from many sides—domestic and foreign. And his own words demonstrate unquestionably that he was aware of his spot in the political cycle. For the models he would prefer are those "to whom it is given not only to maintain the perfection of order but to have the strength to contemplate chaos, there to find material for fresh creation."[12] Note that in this pithy statement, Kissinger not only identifies the maintenance, decay, and creation phases of the cycle but even defines his role preference: creative maintenance man.

However, no matter how successful Kissinger has been as a flexible maintenance man, he has failed to begin to touch the basic problems confronted by a politics for human beings. Indeed, his remarkable ability to maintain the superpower-dominated status quo also means he has been able to preserve many unjust social facts that frustrate the human needs of the poor, undernourished, and underprivileged in the world. Phenomenologically speaking, he enters the worlds of others only to maintain the best aspects of their interaction with his own world—"best" in Kissinger's view of America's national interest. He has frequently pointed out that the basic threat to this national interest is the presence of "revolutionary powers" that reject the basic *rules of the game* of international politics as the superpower elites understand them. Such revolutionary subversion Kissinger believes to be "illegitimate."[13]

In terms of the theory of this book, Kissinger satisfies his own needs and values by preserving the social facts of the status quo—the rules of the game of existing elites, the preservation of present social and political institutions. His chief preoccupation is not to satisfy the needs of all men in the world, but merely the needs of well-to-do men in maintenance America. As a great maintenance man, he necessarily works to frustrate the needs of people whom the maintenance of existing social facts represses.

Whether or not Kissinger made himself into an irreplaceable great man remains to be seen. His appointment by Nixon as the fifty-sixth Secretary of State in 1973 and his acceptance by President Gerald Ford confirmed his place as a dominant world figure in late twentieth-century history, yet he was perceptive enough to sense his dilemma: "I believe in the tragic element in history. I believe there is the tragedy of a man who works very hard and never gets what he wants. And then I believe there is the even more bitter tragedy of a man who finally gets what he wants and finds out that he doesn't want it."[14]

Peace Makers:
Hammarskjöld

Kissinger's notion of "peace" is one based on the maintenance of American power and maximization of our national interest in the world. If the status quo is preserved, the United States will continue to be the richest and most powerful nation. Like Charles de Gaulle, whom Kissinger always admired, he believes that all realistic notions of world peace and stability are based on the calculation and balancing of the interests of nation-states. In this sense, he assumes the nation-state system to be inevitable insofar as day-to-day diplomacy is concerned. If this is the case, nationalism will continue to be the greatest secular religion the world has ever known.

> **Nationalism is the belief that your own nation-state is the ultimate source of legitimacy and security. Corollary: nice nations finish last.**

But this "realistic" notion of world peace is not the only one. Other statesmen in the past and present have believed in an *idealistic, supranational* notion of world peace—one in which international organizations become the ultimate source of legitimacy and security.

> **Supranationalism is human loyalty invested in a universal principle of law and order beyond the nation-state. Corollary: if nasty nations are allowed to win, we all may soon be finished.**

One of the greatest supranational peace makers of all time was Dag Hammarskjöld. In some ways, Hammarskjöld was like Kissinger:

extremely intelligent, philosophically inclined, gifted in languages, competent in administration, and perceptive enough to see his position in the political cycle and to use his role to maximize his values. But even more significant, perhaps, were the ways in which Hammarskjöld differed from Kissinger. Unlike the Jewish-German American, the mystical Swede came from an aristocratic background, preferred passive anonymity to colorful action, preferred being by himself to escorting beautiful women, and believed in submission to God and world law rather than to the interests of one nation-state. Hammarskjöld's beliefs—axioms for all human beings—were revealed in his diary, *Markings:* "We are not permitted to choose the frame of our destiny. But what we put into it is ours. He who wills adventure will experience it—according to the measure of his courage. He who wills sacrifice will be sacrificed—according to the measure of his purity of heart."[14] Hammarskjöld found his frame in the cycle, experienced adventure, and was sacrificed accordingly—by accident or assassination in a 1961 plane crash.

Dag Hammarskjöld was born in 1905 in Jönköping, Sweden. His family had a long, aristocratic heritage and prided itself in selfless service to the kingdom. Hammarskjöld's father, an expert on international law, served as prime minister of Sweden during World War I.

International maintenance men often come from upper-class families with a tradition of public service.

As in the case of Bismarck and Kissinger, his mother played a crucial role in his development. She gave him a great deal of attention throughout his life and introduced him to her interests in music, poetry, art, literature, history, and politics. From childhood, Hammarskjöld discussed politics and culture with adults at the dinner table—where his most important education undoubtedly took place. He did brilliantly in school, amazing everyone with his almost photographic memory of the details of a book that he had just glanced through. Like Bismarck and Kissinger, he was a high self-esteem personality type.

At age eighteen he entered the prestigious University of Uppsala, where he majored in French, the history of literature, and practical philosophy. There he avoided social activities and preferred being alone to becoming involved with women. His shyness and iron self-discipline caused some of his friends to think he was unfriendly and aloof. Most of his friendships developed from his passion for skiing and mountain climbing. The existentialist serenity of these sports was complemented by his devotion to the music of Johann Sebastian Bach and Antonio Vivaldi, which brought him a sense of order and peace.

Effective diplomats tend to be well-primed in the world's languages, literatures, philosophies, and music.

Hammarskjöld became fluent in French, German, and English and taught himself classical Greek. Throughout his life he studied philosophy and history. He was particularly fascinated by Thomas Becket, the twelfth-century "God-intoxicated" man who served the Church and Henry II of England at the same time, and who finally was assassinated. Hammarskjöld was intrigued by Becket's philosophical dilemma, the loyalty conflict, which this chancellor resolved by adopting a life of great austerity and giving himself wholly to the needs of the Church rather than remaining subservient to the king's orders. Later Hammarskjöld found himself in a similar dilemma: loyalty to his own nation-state and the Western concept of freedom, or loyalty to the universal principles of the United Nations, held to be above and beyond any nationalism or culture-bound notions of liberty? And he too, like Becket, had a God-ache. They both thought, "Not I, but God in me" —a difficult creed.

> **The supranationalist is often ready to sacrifice his humble "I" to a higher universal principle of perfection.**

Hammarskjöld completed his B.A. in two years and then studied economics. He wrote a brilliant Ph.D. thesis, "The Expansion of Market Trends," which resulted in his being appointed Assistant Professor of Political Economy at the University of Stockholm. Simultaneously he served as Secretary of the Royal Commission on Unemployment. Word soon spread of the brilliance of his thesis and work for the Commission, and he was named Secretary of the National Bank of Sweden.

> **To gain national power intellectually, specialize in a relevant policy area and make yourself well-known and needed.**

Just as Kissinger established a national reputation for his speciality of national security and foreign policy, so did Hammarskjöld with his specialty of economics. In 1936 he was named Undersecretary of the Ministry of Finance of Sweden—at thirty-one years of age, the youngest man ever named to that post.

When reporters called, Hammarskjöld turned down requests for personal interviews politely but firmly. He became known for his passion for anonymity.

> **Anonymity and discretion are political tools that build power through confidence and are extremely useful in national and international bureaucracies.**

As an exponent of the economic theories of John Maynard Keynes, Hammarskjöld soon found himself in demand to explain them to old economic decision-making elites whose theories no longer worked and who were relatively unfamiliar with Keynesian theories.

Class and status are often based on the distribution of knowledge.

Hammarskjöld's status increased as more and more people paid him deference for his knowledge and skill. A series of appointments followed: Undersecretary of Finance, then Chairman of the Board of Governors of the Swedish National Bank, then Financial Advisor to the Swedish Cabinet, then Secretary General of the Foreign Office, and finally, in 1953, Secretary General of the United Nations—the most prestigious diplomatic post in the world.

The Cold War between the United States and the USSR was warm indeed when Hammarskjöld was chosen Secretary General of the United Nations. But the efficacy of the United Nations, its very existence, depended upon cooperation between the great powers.

The founding of the United Nations in 1945 merely confirmed the dominance of the great powers in the status quo by granting them veto power in the Security Council.

A veto by a great power in the Security Council meant that no major political decision could be made or United Nations action taken. Thus, if two such great powers—such as the United States and USSR—did not cooperate or could not be persuaded to cooperate by a neutral third party, the United Nations was helpless to act in many critical world situations.

To push antagonist We-They political relationships towards cooperative I-Thou relationships often requires the intervention of a neutral third party or arbiter.

Hammarskjöld was chosen Secretary General because of his potential utility as a neutral arbiter between antagonists in the Cold War. This potential was due to several factors: he was from a neutral country, Sweden; he was not well known to many world leaders at the time; and among those who did know him, he had a reputation for selfless service, cool diplomatic skill, and desire for anonymity. His ability in economics was also significant at a time when the United Nations was having serious economic problems. Yet Hammarskjöld's image of neutrality and effective philosophical gifts were probably the decisive factors. In a 1961 lecture at Oxford University just before his death, Hammarskjöld described what he thought should be meant by the "neutrality" of the Secretary General:

> He is not required to be neuter in the sense that he has to have no sympathies or antipathies, that there are no interests which are close to him in his personal capacity or that he is to have no ideas or ideals that matter to him. However, he is requested to be fully aware of those human reactions and meticulously to check himself so that they are not permitted to influence his actions. This is nothing unique. Is not every judge professionally under the same obligation? . .
>
> In the last analysis, this is a question of integrity, and if integrity in the sense of respect for law and respect for truth were to drive him into positions of conflict with this or that interest, then that conflict is a sign of his neutrality and not of his failure to observe neutrality—then it is in line, not in conflict, with his duties as an international civil servant.[15]

Such conflicts not only arose, but one of them (a civil war heated by superpower intervention) may have had some bearing on Hammarskjöld's death in a mysterious plane crash in Rhodesia during the 1961 Congo crisis.* Yet during the seven years that Hammarskjöld did serve as Secretary General, he imbued that office with amazing power and legitimacy through his brilliant art of quiet diplomacy.

He demonstrated this unusual act of creating social relationships for peace in 1955, when he flew to Peking to negotiate the release of eleven American fliers who had been shot down by Communist China during the Korean conflict. He succeeded against all odds, for Communist China had been repeatedly denied membership in the United Nations. The Chinese diplomats were so impressed with his quiet integrity and philosophical ability to match them at their own subtle form of diplomatic game that they announced the release of the fliers *on his birthday*. Political leaders all over the world perceived a successful formula for peace:

> **To move a We-They politics of antagonism towards an I-Thou politics for human beings, have a neutral diplomat negotiate who can beat both sides at their own diplomatic games.**

Such diplomats, as Hammarskjöld wrote in his diary, must be able "to exist for the future of others without being suffocated by their present." This ability allowed Hammarskjöld to create the first international police force within forty-eight hours to establish peace in the difficult Suez crisis of 1956. By increasing the legitimacy of the role of Secretary General of the United Nations through his own integrity,

---

*In this crisis colonized Africans won freedom from their Belgian overlords but found themselves pawns in a power game between the United States and Soviet Union.

Hammarskjöld was able to create peace in the political cycle where lesser men might have given up in despair. It takes a great deal of faith in oneself *for the sake of others* to create a politics for human beings or a just concept of peace.

MAINTAINING SYSTEMS
The Balance of Power

What tools can great men use to gain power over the politics of nations?

Everyday human beings can create nations, coalitions, and peace settlements if they are given an opportunity in the political cycle of their time and know how to use it. They are perhaps the best examples of how human beings can make the most of their intelligence and will power in international politics.

But to what extent does the international system direct people, rather than people the system? And, specifically, what is the nature of this recurring balance-of-power system that Metternich perfected, Bismarck overturned, and Kissinger tried to restore? Why are "revolutionaries" such as Hammarskjöld so often defeated by such systems in their attempts to create an alternative—such as the "collective security" system? What does "the balance of power" mean and who keeps it going?

The *balance-of-power* concept dates back at least to the seventeenth century when clusters of sovereign states developed, each personified by its prince, who tried to maximize a set of limited interests in the international game. The rules of this game were rationally spelled out in the eighteenth century, the century of the Enlightenment. The techniques of a typical prince playing this game would include bargaining, forming coalitions, marriage strategies (increasing territory with dowries and legitimacy with more royal blood), and war of a limited variety. The diplomacy of this period was carefully choreographed like a minuet and the battles executed through iron discipline, much like a traditional chess game.

As if at a grand ball, a prince would form loose bilateral alliances for a time, quickly breaking them if they did not suit his interests. Hard-fought battles were avoided—they cost too much, given the mercenary soldiers of the day, who would switch sides like ambitious American business executives. The aim was to place your armies in a position of strategic advantage, whereupon the other side normally capitulated honorably, just as a good chess player would concede.

There are four major assumptions in the classical balance-of-power game:

- The existence of a system of independent states with approximately equal potential power.
- A recognized size of the system and a limited number of states to be balanced.
- Relative homogeneity among the members of the state system.
- A rational system of estimating power.[16]

The mechanistic philosophy inspired by Isaac Newton and the rationalism of the Enlightenment underlay these assumptions. At the time, "enlightened" human beings saw the world as one giant clockwork of forces that could be harmonized.

A balance-of-power system is an equilibrium made up of approximately equal powers or nations set against each other so that no one power can predominate.

To maintain equilibrium, however, it is vital to limit the maximum number of interacting states within the system. This limit makes a rational calculation of interest and appropriate balance possible. Balance-of-power diplomats require a *limited* number of variables for the same reason that a juggler used to manipulating a half dozen eggs might be driven crazy if given a dozen.

One way to limit such a system is by the criterion of relative homogeneity. If a prospective member state does not fit, culturally or politically, it must be excluded. Thus Edmund Burke argued that Turkey should be excluded from Metternich's nineteenth-century balance-of-power system because an Asiatic empire was not culturally in harmony with Europe.

Balance-of-power systems, whether they are relatively homogeneous or not, must contain a limited number of states. One balance-of-power theorist has given the number five as optimal. With more than five too much instability and uncertainty is probable. Fewer than five allow too little flexibility for shifting alliances.[17] An international system dominated by just two powers is called *bipolar;* by three, *tripolar.* Systems of two or three dominant powers are not balance-of-power systems simply because there are not enough states to balance. When international systems really get out of hand and the number of powerful entities becomes too great to keep on counting, they are called multipolar systems. Indeed, some people call any international system with more than two major powers in it a multipolar system.

It is easy to use this systems language to describe the world at any one point in time—like a snapshot. For instance, I can argue that *from the American viewpoint* the world is going from maintenance to decay in the cycle, since bipolarity (United States-USSR dominance) is disintegrating into tripolarity (enter China) or worse (enter Japan and Western Europe). We are entering a period of decay in relationship to Them. But notice that this argument is a reification (making something more real than it really is). It freezes change and suppresses the thought that we can be an active partner in shaping reality.

Systems theory rhetoric can always be reduced to some form of "We-are-being-undone-by-Them." Human beings are thus dehumanized by collective "We's and They's."

The "We"-"They" perspective of nationalism implies that a particular nation-state and, implicitly, the nation-state system is the ultimate source of legitimacy and *collective security.* Nationalism is dehumanizing, since it assumes the nation is always more important than any individual in it, no matter what it does. Nationalism gives the individual no choice: it's "my country, right or wrong."*

**A NATION is a people
that controls a STATE—
a territory
of relationships.
A NATION-STATE is all people
in a territory who believe enough
in the same collectivity
to become things or to die for it.**

All national collectivities are reifications, since in a collectivity people are not considered as individual humans. Reification—turning relationships into things—is necessarily dehumanizing.

The logic of nationalism carried to absurd extremes of reification leads to world war—the most insecure and dehumanized condition the world can be in. In short, the more I identify myself with one nation, the more nationalistic I am; the more nationalistic I am, the more closed-minded I am likely to be concerning the viewpoints of citizens of other nations; closed-minded nationalism that refuses to compromise normally leads to antagonism and war. The more nationalistic I become, the more I become my nation's "thing." Think before becoming thingificated!

INVITATION

Imagine you are the National Security Adviser for the president of the United States *in the present or future*. You must decide whether or not the president should play the balance-of-power game or forget it.

**_The Balance-of-Power Game_
(For Very Special Occasions)**

Rules:

(1) Identify the most powerful nations around the world. If there are five, or six or seven, you are in good shape. If there are more than seven, forget it; that's too many to juggle at once. If there are fewer than five, forget it; that's too few for flexibility.

(2) The five to seven states must be relatively equal militarily and economically. If they are grossly unequal to start with, forget it.

(3) If the five to seven states do not have a similar cultural heritage, you're in for trouble. You might want to forget it.

(4) If, at this point, you're still playing the balance-of-power game, _work to prevent any one nation in the powerful group (or any one coalition) from becoming strong enough to_

---

*As Samuel Johnson said, "Patriotism is the last refuge of a scoundrel." But nationalism makes scoundrels into "great men."

overwhelm any other nation (or coalition). **If this isn't possible, forget it.**

(5) If in doubt—you guessed it—forget it! Given the rules, what would you do?

A handy way of finding out what the present international situation is like, in terms of American national interests is to read the *New York Times* for at least a month. Sources for predicting future situations are Herman Kahn's *The Emerging Japanese Superstate* or his book with Anthony Wiener, *The Year 2000*.

On the basis of this and other information, do you think the US, USSR, China, Japan, and Western Europe—and perhaps some other growing nation—do or will qualify as great powers in the balance-of-power game, given the limits of its rules? On what do you base your argument?

Collective Security Can human beings escape the pathological religion of nationalism? Is there a way out that is less likely to lead to war? The supranationalists, such as Hammarskjöld, think so. They think that human loyalties should be invested in a universal principle of law and order beyond the nation-state. They argue that only when the leaders of nation-states are restrained by world law will imperialism and world war cease to exist. But how can this international law for all of mankind be enforced?

A new concept was invented to enforce international law: *collective security.* You might call the notion of collective security a refined extension of the balance-of-power game—a more integrated, centralized, and idealistic balancing act.

> **Under the collective security concept leaders of member states of the international system view an attack upon one as an attack upon all and respond accordingly.**

The threat of such overwhelming force bearing down upon the nationalistic decision maker with aggressive tendencies is supposed to *deter* him from attacking other states. The collective security and balance-of-power ideas are similar, in that both assume the existence of a *system* of *independent nation-states* that are presumably *deterred* from attacking one another by a combination of force potentially at least as strong as that of the would-be attacker. But the guiding force of balance-of-power politics is a clique of great powers that keep the international status quo going for their own interest. In contrast, the principle of collective security is that to restrain conflict in the status quo is in everyone's interest, large or small. Furthermore, as political scientist Inis Claude puts it, "Collective security is too nervous to rely on in the hope that aggressive statesmen will be inhibited by subtle calculations of equilibrium; it is comfortable only when such leaders are confronted by the obvious fact that they are greatly outclassed."[18]

The problem that collective security theory has had so far is that too few national decision makers will support it with economic sanctions and military force. Witness the failure of the League of Nations to prevent World War II, and the reluctance of national leaders in the United Nations to support any form of United Nations police force activity since the death of Hammarskjöld. Indeed, since the People's Republic of China was accepted as a member of the United Nations, many American government officials have argued that it is in our national interest to cut back on our financial support of the United Nations.

> **As Great Power consensus
> disintegrates in the United Nations,
> "We"-"They" antagonism increases,
> funds are cut,
> and war becomes more probable.**

Nuclear Deterrence

Imagine that 135 individuals live on a city block, each possessing his own apartment, none fully trusting another. To be secure, each bolts his door with locks and double locks, bars the window, sets up burglar alarms, and keeps a pistol under his pillow. Now suppose an unfortunate drunk wanders into a building on the block by mistake and tries to get into an apartment he believes to be his own. The real owner panics and fires his pistol toward the door to ward off the intruder. The drunk, frightened half to death, runs off in great haste. In the turmoil that follows, accusations are bandied about, everyone becomes tense, and more pistols, ammunition, and locks are brought into the community. General security actually decreases for everyone as weapons pile up and nerves are stretched to the limit.

In microcosm, this rough analogy is what the nation-state system is like in terms of unilateral defense. Each of more than 130 nations is expected to maintain its own private arsenal and to be ready to defend itself against any possible attack from any other state in the world community. If one state develops new types of offensive or defensive weapons, neighboring states with the capability are expected to follow suit—not merely to create similar weapons, but to create bigger and better ones to deter any nasty neighbor from attacking. Low-class states that can't afford to create new weapons rally around a powerful neighbor in a coalition or alliance. Millions of dollars are spent on weapons research, each country or alliance trying to outdo the other, sapping resources that could be used for more constructive projects and increasing no one's security—the original goal.

> **Nations enter arms races to find
> security, but they thereby increase
> insecurity and the chances of war.**

The basic dilemma of our times is that the romantic myth of national independence just does not fit in a nuclear age. Only superpowers with arsenals of H-bombs can even begin to approach such "independence." And even they cannot achieve this goal, since they can no longer meet its prerequisite: that the nation can be stronger than its potential enemies on its home territory.

Superpowers cannot fulfill this condition because (1) modern missile technology has made it impossible for a nation to be far enough away from its adversary to be truly independent, and (2) even a superpower can no longer dominate a buffer zone wide enough to be certain to destroy an incoming deadly missile with multinuclear warheads. Thus, the ideal of secure unilateral defense is now impossible to achieve.

> **Expanding arsenals appear to bring short-run security but undermine long-run security, and so the logic of nuclear deterrence collapses.**

The weak logic of nuclear deterrence has finally forced the superpowers to the bargaining table to sign the Anti-Ballistic Missile Treaty (ABM Treaty) and to continue the Strategic Arms Limitations Talks (SALT). The consequences of deterrence logic are perhaps spelled out most clearly by game theory.

Games Balance-of-power and systems approaches to world politics dehumanize individuals by abstracting certain of their qualities—such as rationality and the desire for short-term security—and by talking in reified, collective terms. A world system of a clique of great powers blots out the role of the individual human being. The big "We's" and "They's" absorb the everyday "you's" and "me's." Moreover, we everyday human beings are supposed to accept the "rational" theories of Great Power decision makers—such as deterrence—without question. "They," the argument goes, are using the best of knowledge and sophistication to maximize our national interests.

"National," we now know, is the catchword here. Governmental elites maximizing the nation's short-term security interests may actually undermine our individual security interests in the long run—as every young man called up to serve in Vietnam knows. But advocates of short-term military security have discovered some neat "rational" theories to use to sell national elites on their views.

A "rational" technique that has become popular with many foreign policy decision makers' advisers is *game theory*. In 1955, the philosopher R. B. Braithwaite wrote: "No one today will doubt the intensity, though he may dislike the color, of the (shall I say) sodium light cast by statistical mathematics, direct descendant of games of chance, upon the social sciences. Perhaps in another three hundred years' time economic and political and other branches of moral philosophy will bask in radiation from a source—theory of games of strategy—whose prototype was kindled around the poker tables of Princeton."[18]

Indeed, game theory did emerge at Princeton in 1947 with the work of John Von Neumann and Oscar Morgenstern. These men described two basic kinds of logical games that underlie the thinking of many human beings at certain moments of choice: *zero-sum games* and *variable-sum games.*

A zero-sum game is one like chess, in which whatever player A gains, the other player, B, loses EXACTLY, and vice versa.

A zero-sum game is one of absolute antagonism between "We" and "They" (the players) within the context of rules mutually agreed upon. No cooperation is possible. Each guy is out to get what there is to get before the other guy does. Nice guys finish last. Consider the zero-sum game in Figure 8–1.

Figure 8-1

Two-Person Zero-Sum Game

		Balthazar	
		b_1	b_2
Alphonse	a_1	5	3
	a_2	6	−4

Assume that the outcomes of this game are certain. Each of the two opponents is to make just one choice between two alternatives. Each is ignorant of how the other chooses. In the game above, only Alphonse's payoffs (positive or negative) are tallied. Based on Alphonse's payoffs, Balthazar's scores would be the same numbers with the *opposite signs.*

Both are stuck in a social situation with only two choices. Alphonse can choose a_1 or a_2. If he chooses a_1, he can get either five or three clams, depending upon whether Balthazar chooses b_1 or b_2. But note that in this case, Balthazar loses either five clams or three clams (for what one player gains in this kind of situation the other player loses exactly). Like many competitive games in a social world of scarce resources, the situation is loaded against one of the players—Balthazar. For he has only one small chance of winning anything at all—if he chooses b_2 and Alphonse is so foolish as to choose a_2 (the only situation in which Alphonse can lose). It is assumed that neither player can communicate with the other, that both know the possible payoffs, and that both try to maximize their gain by attempting to anticipate what the other will do.*

*Zero-sum games include chess, checkers, coin-flipping. To the extent that people are in political situations that do not have zero-sum logic and yet play according to zero-sum rules, they are pathological. Such people believe that cooperation is not possible and that whatever they don't get now, someone else will get. Politics focusing on conflict tries to apply zero-sum logic to all situations.

In this case, decision is simple. If he chooses a_1, Alphonse can guarantee himself a gain of 3, no matter what Balthazar does. Balthazar, on the other hand, is better off choosing for himself b_2 no matter what Alphonse does; otherwise he will lose 5 or 6 to Alphonse. Therefore, we can expect (a_1, b_2) to be the outcome, the payoff being 3 to Alphonse. This payoff is called the value of the game.

In such a game, each person is encouraged to maximize his gains at the expense of the other. Note how applicable this game structure is to the perceptions of decision makers in world politics at certain points in history: "If 'We' democrats don't overwhelm the world with our philosophy, 'They' (the Communists) will." The implication of this statement is that *each side is focusing merely on the present distribution of the political pie or status quo, not upon the greater gains possible for both if cooperation did take place.*

The non-zero-sum game or variable-sum game allows for rational cooperation to take place, because A's losses do not equal B's gains in all cases.

But even in the case of variable-sum games, whether or not players cooperate for maximum gain depends upon mutual trust as much as upon mere "rational" considerations. The European Common market is an example of a variable-sum game. By cooperating, the individual member states can produce more than they could individually. Yet if they bicker too much about the distribution of the existing economic pie, such cooperation and maximum production will not be possible.

Another variable-sum game with these implications is SALT—the Strategic Arms Limitations Talks. If leaders of the United States and USSR trust each other enough to cooperate, they can save each other millions of dollars and rubles; if not, they may pay later with nuclear war for being fixated on superiority in the existing status quo.

Games and Human Beings For a politics for human beings, game theory has both positive and negative implications. Positively, the stark contrast in zero-sum versus non-zero-sum or variable-sum perceptions illustrates that by never trusting the other person's intentions, you bring about conflict situations. But by seeking out aspects of mutual benefit, you can make a politics of cooperation possible. Negatively, these mathematical models oversimplify how people think, except in moments of unusual clarity. The irrational, emotional, and all-too-human aspects of decision making are abstracted out of the equation. Furthermore, one could even go so far as to argue that zero-sum thinking is merely a description of the reactions of a pathological realist and that variable-sum thinking typifies the thought processes of a pathological idealist. If so, the human being seems forced to choose between two forms of

isaak

pathology: *either* inflexible zero-sum realism *or* inflexible variable-sum idealism.

Although such either-or choices do exist in everyday-life political situations, human beings often find themselves in more complex and muddled situations that cannot be resolved by such an oversimplified formula. Not wanting to be either a pathological realist or a pathological idealist, human beings must evaluate each particular political decision individually, rather than use the rigidly logical responses of game theory. Otherwise, inflexible images and inability to process new information—the characteristics of pathology—will blind human perceptions and make it difficult to cope with reality.

Perhaps the greatest asset of game theory exercises is that they force human beings to speculate on the *intentions* and *thinking processes* of others. To play rationally, to know the possible outcomes for a particular game, they must put themselves in the shoes of the other player. Thus, game theory forces you to become phenomenological to some extent, which is good. On the other hand, it forces you to think in terms of prescribed, abstract models, which is unnecessarily restrictive and dehumanizing. To get beneath the static logic and rationality of the games of the status quo, to see what they really mean for human beings, more revolutionary ways of thinking about international politics are needed. The complex social facts called *nation-states* cannot be understood, changed, or controlled with such simplistic tools as game theory. Other modes of thought are required as well—more revolutionary tools.

INCONCLUSIONS

International politics is different in scope but not in kind from other politics. This is not the conventional view of international politics, which begins with the global system and works downwards—only sometimes reaching the individual. In our view of international politics, politics begins, as always, when an individual organizes others into social action to solve the tension between human needs and social facts. The human needs are those of immense groups of people called nations, and the social facts include the existing values, personalities, rules of the game, and social and political institutions of the entire world. But the cases of Bismarck, Kissinger, and Hammarskjöld show how this complex game of nation-states can be unmasked to reveal the political tools for creating and maintaining political systems.

Bismarck illustrates how national power can be created and consolidated through individual initiative. Kissinger refines the tactics of Bismarck, demonstrating how and why coalitions between nation-states are formed. Going beyond the balance-of-power games of the other two, Hammarskjöld shows how peace can be created by using the tools of collective security and preventative diplomacy.

Finally, there are four popular ways of maintaining stability or peace in the international system—the balance of power, collective security, nuclear deterrence, and game theory—tools that any human being in the future may also use to maintain his own little political system if he chooses. After all, ideas are free.

REFERENCES   1. To use these ideas as tools for power, see Friedrich Nietzsche, *Thus Spake Zarathustra* (in various editions) and Rollo May, *Power and Innocence* (New York: Norton, 1972).

2. Albert Camus, *The Myth of Sisyphus* (New York: Random House, Vintage Books, 1958).

3. For a fascinating, Freudian interpretation of Bismarck's debt to and dislike for his mother, see A. J. P. Taylor, *Bismarck: The Man and the Statesman* (New York: Alfred A. Knopf, 1955). Taylor claims that Bismarck was a neurotic genius who had the sophistication of his mother but masqueraded as his heavy, earthy father.

4. Otto von Bismarck, *Die gesammelten Werke,* vol. 14, no. 1 (January 30, 1845), p. 30. This English translation and some aspects of Bismarck's story recounted here are among recent materials borrowed from the ineffable, swinging scholar-diplomat Henry A. Kissinger. See his "The White Revolutionary: Reflections on Bismarck," *Daedalus* (Summer 1968): *Philosophers and Kings: Studies in Leadership;* vol. 97, no. 3, p. 893.

5. Loc. cit.

6. Kissinger, "The White Revolutionary," p. 900.

7. Loc. cit.

8. Barnard Law Collier, "The Road to Peking, or How Does This Kissinger Do It?" *New York Times Magazine,* November 14, 1971, p. 107.

9. Ibid., p. 34.

10. See Nora Beloff, "Prof. Bismarck Goes to Washington: Kissinger on the Job," The *Atlantic Monthly,* December 1969, p. 78.

11. Statement by Kissinger at the Princeton Conference on Arms Control and Limitation, October 20–21, 1960.

12. Beloff, "Prof. Bismarck," p. 77.

13. Henry A. Kissinger, *Nuclear Weapons and Foreign Policy* (New York: W. W. Norton, 1969), p. 44.

14. Dag Hammarskjöld, *Markings* (New York: Knopf, 1964).

15. Dag Hammarskjöld, "The International Civil Servant in Law and in Fact," in *The United Nations System and Its Functions,* ed. Robert Gregg and Michael Barkun (Princeton, N.J.: Van Nostrand, 1968), pp. 227–228.

16. Edward Vose Gulick, *Europe's Classical Balance of Power* (New York: W. W. Norton, 1967—orig. 1955), Chapter 1.

17. Morton Kaplan, *System and Process in International Politics* (New York: Wiley, 1957), Chapter 2.

18. Inis L. Claude Jr., *Power and International Relations* (N.Y.: Random House, 1966—seventh printing), p. 125.

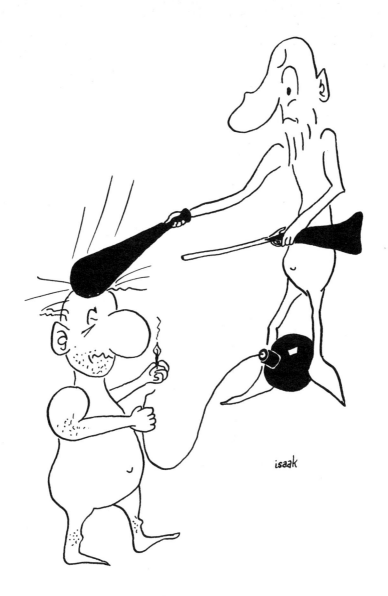

isaak

9 **Wherein the reader sees the transition of a postindustrial society from maintenance to decay from the global view. We explore some of the difficulties of revolutionizing politics in such a society to create a world for human beings.**

9 Revolutionizing World Politics

Nowhere are revolutionary tools for doing politics more desperately needed than in world politics. The use of traditional tools has brought us all to the brink of global death. Destructive policies allocate most of the world's resources to a few nations in the short run, leading to the frustration of everyone's human needs in the long run. Armaments for nuclear holocaust multiply, while natural resources for the satisfaction of basic needs decline. Narrow pathological ideologies of nationalism, stimulated by the nation-state system, threaten every human being every day with major international conflicts and the possibility of world war.

How can the tension between human needs and social facts best be understood from the global point of view? What kind of world consciousness can move people to act politically to relieve such tension? These are the questions this chapter considers—focusing upon decay and revolution, in contrast to the global view of creation and maintenance in Chapter 8.

This book began with the simplest possible political situation and slowly developed in complexity and scope to arrive at international politics. The reader first experienced chapters on understanding, defining, and doing politics. The first part of the book then flowed into chapters applying these principles—two in American politics, two in comparing politics, and now two in international politics. In this second international chapter, we bring together concepts learned earlier so that the reader can experience them from the international or global viewpoint. Only by grasping this world view of the human political condition is it possible to fully comprehend the obstacles that confront the creation of a politics for human beings everywhere. And only after experiencing this world perspective as a synthesis of all the principles introduced before can one fully understand the *human meaning* of the different ways of thinking politics, evaluated in the three chapters following this one.

This book began with one self cooperating with another to create politics and a nation-state. As a nation-state matures, moving from creation to maintenance, more tools are necessary to take social facts apart in order to change them to satisfy human needs. As more and more people become involved in political behavior, it is necessary to compare one's own culture and nation-state with others, to borrow ideas and solutions from others. And as one compares more and more cultures and nation-states, further principles and tools are necessary to take international politics apart. Yet as later chapters will show, *which* tools or assumptions you use to analyze politics determines how you see the world, whose interests you serve, and how close you come to a politics for human beings.

The following scenario highlights this development and illustrates how individuals experience political consciousness by becoming social critics of a world perspective.

TECHNOPHOBIA IN 2084

Each morning in the year 2084, Alphonse went down to the clam factory. So did Balthazar. Passing the factory gate, Alphonse saluted the five interlocking clams gleaming gold on blue on the corporation flag. So did Balthazar.

> **In technological society, the corporation replaces the nation-state.[1]**

Inside, Alphonse sat down at his console. So did Balthazar. Alphonse pushed the blue button imprinted with five gold interlocking clams. Instantly one million machines plucked five million clams from the Gulf Coast waters of Technophobia and dropped them into one million cans. Balthazar pushed the button marked "LID." Instantly one million machines clamped 999,999 lids onto the one million cans. Balthazar held his breath . . .

> **In technological society, it looks like people run machines. . .**

A video monitor above Balthazar flashed to life. "You're not giving your all to the button," cooed the blonde with the clampaste smile. "70 volts!" Balthazar ground his teeth as 140 volts passed through his left shin. "Ouch!" said Balthazar.

> **. . . in technological societies, machines run people.**

Alphonse ignored the interruption and loaded the next million cans. Technological life for Alphonse and Balthazar was one in which each lived in his own separate world. "Ouch," said Balthazar again, "they gave me twice the voltage! Fine friend you are, you just keep on loading those cans!" Alphonse pushed his button again. "Friendship has got nothing to do with getting the job done," he said, grinning happily at a banana that dropped out of a slot marked "Reward."

> **In technology, stimuli replace values.**

Five hours later, observing the daily rite of Great Clam Juice, Alphonse and Balthazar sat in a darkened booth at Techno's Clam Bar, grousing about the day's events.

"I don't see why you're giving me all this negative reinforcement about those extra 70 volts," muttered Alphonse defensively. "Machine is always right. *I'm* happy in my work."

In a reified society, alienated people stay in line and love it.

"That's because conditioning has replaced your socialization!" shouted Balthazar. "You don't even remember the time when I saved you from a Giant Clam-Picker that was putting you in a can. Then you swore you'd be my friend for life."

In technology, conditioning replaces socialization.

"Your trouble is you don't know anything about 'tics,'" Balthazar ranted on.

"Tics?" said Alphonse.

"Yeah," said Balthazar, "like it says right here on the cover of this forbidden book I got *tics for Human Beings.*"

"Lemme see that," said Alphonse, sipping his fermented clam juice and peering at the torn cover of the book. "Yeah . . . *tics for Human Beings.*"

"Inside," explained Balthazar, "they also talk about 'politics' for human beings."

"Never heard of 'politics,'" mumbled Alphonse. "So what?"

As technology advances, administration replaces politics.

"Well, for one thing," said Balthazar, "it says here that politics is a social act in which people try to solve the tension between their human needs and social facts. Today I got *high* tension. And you remember what happened to your girlfriend working the next console? You remember! Mary. She was working the cherry pickers."

"Yeah," said Alphonse, two big tears plopping down into his clam juice. "She got canned."

When technology advances too far, it represses human needs.

"Makes me damn mad when I think of it." Alphonse pounded the table.

Emotions can pierce technology to release human needs.

"Let's go smash the machine!" Alphonse shouted.

"Wait a minute . . ." said Balthazar.

Emotions do not a revolution make.

" . . . I've got an idea," Balthazar continued.

**Revolution and politics
begin with an idea.**

Next day at the clam factory, Alphonse looked at Balthazar. At the same moment, Balthazar looked at Alphonse and nodded.

**Revolution begins with a shared
understanding of a common tension.**

As one, Alphonse and Balthazar rose from their consoles. Together they walked to the console controlling the cherry pickers. Together they fed a new program into the console computer.

**A political act is setting up a
social interaction to solve a problem.**

Together, Alphonse and Balthazar pushed a button.

All along the Gulf Coast, one million cherry pickers rolled out of the orchards toward the seashore. They dropped one million cherry pits into one million cans filled with five clams each. . . .

INVITATION

Compare the historical condition of Technophobia with the state of Inlandia in Chapter I, in terms of:

The cycle of creation-maintenance-decay—compare the Alphonse and Balthazar of Technophobia with their ancestors of Inlandia, using the three locating questions from page 20. (Whose victims are they? To what extent can they work the system for their values? Are they free to create their lives with others?)

Realism versus idealism: Which political style is most appropriate for which historical situation?

Needs and values: To what extent are they the same or different in the two situations?

Social facts that prevent human beings from satisfying their needs: Contrast the social facts of both states and compare them with those of your own.

Revolutionary alternatives: Which revolutionary tools are most appropriate for Inlandia? For Technophobia? For your own state? (See Chapters 6 and 7 for suggestions.)

If you accepted the preceding Invitation, you will have noted that Inlandia was in a historical period of creation, where social facts were rather simple and clear-cut. But in Technophobia the descendants of Alphonse and Balthazar found themselves in a repressive period of maintenance in a postindustrial society, where social facts were extremely complex. This chapter will take up the points in the preceding Invitation as they apply to a postindustrial society such as our own: (a) the cycle of creation-maintenance-decay, (b) realism versus idealism, (c) needs and values, (d) alienation through social facts, and (e) revolutionary attitudes. In so doing, three vital questions will be raised for which each reader must find his own answer.*

1. What are the international implications of the priority of basic human needs?

2. What social facts limit the satisfaction of these needs, and for whom?

3. What kinds of perceptions lead human beings to become so aware of tensions between their unsatisfied needs and existing social facts that they are willing to start a revolution?

When faced with a postindustrial society going from maintenance to decay—like America today—you can react to perceptions of decay by submitting to social facts (in one way or another) or by revolting against them. Whether you submit or rebel largely depends upon how you view political cycles.

OBSTACLES TO THE REVOLUTION OF NEEDS

To view politics in historical development as a recurring cycle of creation-maintenance-decay is just one way of looking at things. And though this cycle theory is one of the ordering principles upon which this book is based, the reader should accept the notion only if he finds it useful to prevent a static view and to explain changes that go on in his own society. Indeed, if one takes the cycle theory too seriously, it can become unnecessarily deterministic, sapping the will of the individual to act politically to solve tensions between his needs and social facts that frustrate those needs. On the other hand, if such cycles are not considered at all, the individual may lose historical perspective and repeat avoidable mistakes made by others in the past.

Cyclic or Manipulator?

Human beings who perceive historical cycles to be absolutely inevitable in all spheres of activity (love, job, business, politics, history) help make them become inevitable. The typical example of such a fatalistic determinist can be called a "cyclic." The cyclic defines man as totally powerless to affect things—at least in the long run. He's the doomsday advocate who makes a mess of his own life and that of other people and claims such developments are inevitable. Cyclics are *conditions-oriented,* arguing, for example, that the socio-economic conditions you are born into will determine what you become, no matter what you try to do about it. Though there's some truth to such statements, they are too simplistic to explain the whole truth (such as the fact that a significant number of people born poor achieve high social and economic standing).

*For the approach the authors suggest, see Chapters 3 and 12.

On the other side of the argument is the "manipulator"—the individual who believes that will power can move the world. Manipulators (like Bismarck, Kissinger, and Hammarskjöld) are *people-oriented* rather than conditions-oriented. If such a person is so blinded by his will that he does not take historical conditions into account at all, his task becomes the Zen masters' definition of difficulty: the mosquito who tries to bite into the butt of an iron bull. But basically, cyclics lament over the tragic ways in which conditions mold man, whereas manipulators use ideas at the proper historical moment to mold conditions, satisfying the needs of themselves and others.

> **Cyclics become conditioned.**
> **Manipulators become conditions.**

Each human being must decide for himself whether to aid or hinder the development of civilization. Not to decide is to become a tacit accomplice in its decline. As Albert Schweitzer, the doctor, musician, philosopher, and manipulator has written: "The future of civilization depends on our overcoming the meaninglessness and hopelessness which characterize the thoughts and convictions of men today, and reaching a state of fresh hope and fresh determination. We shall be capable of this, however, only when the majority of individuals discover for themselves both an ethic and a profound and steadfast attitude of world- and life-affirmation, in a theory of the universe at once convincing and based on reflection."[2] The very survival of human civilization depends upon the creation of a politics for human beings. And in times of decay and revolution, concern for a politics for human beings often becomes explicit and ideological.

Perceptions of Social Facts: Realism vs. Idealism

How one views civilization depends upon how one views other human beings and oneself. Crises in civilization force such views of human nature to the surface, as human beings take sides according to polarized "We"-"They" belief systems. Traditionally, there are two extreme views of human nature that have had profound political consequences—particularly in times of crisis and revolution: the "realist" view of man as basically bad, and the "idealist" view of man as basically good.

> **Realists make negative aspects**
> **of human nature into**
> **self-fulfilling prophecy;**
> **idealists undermine positive aspects**
> **by becoming blind to**
> **the power of the realists.**

Machiavelli and Hobbes vs. Rousseau Perhaps the most notorious realists are Machiavelli and Thomas Hobbes. In *The Prince* Machiavelli claims that human nature is essentially selfish and that the effective statesman must manipulate people's egoistic motives—such as the desire for security in the masses and the desire for power in rulers. Living in the Italian decadence of the sixteenth century, Machiavelli became convinced that security depends upon strong government. In the fragmented Italy of his day, that strong government could come only through a strong monarch who was not hesitant to use all available means at his disposal. The extension of Machiavelli's belief in universal human egoism into a systematic psychology is the political philosophy of Thomas Hobbes's *Leviathan* (1651).

Hobbes viewed human life as "nasty, brutish and short," a natural struggle of all against all. Human survival and security could only be assured, he thought, if egoistic individuals gave up their rights completely to a state that would keep them in awe.* This view is often sharply contrasted with that of a notorious idealist, Jean Jacques Rousseau (1712–1778), who believed that man was naturally good, but had been corrupted by an imperfect society. Rousseau looked for the causes of conflict and war in the weaknesses of society—which is the reification of community—more than in the weaknesses of human nature. But Rousseau, like Hobbes, saw the need for man to affirm his loyalty to something larger than himself—in Rousseau's case, the universal "general will."

Who is more correct in describing everyday political life—Hobbes or Rousseau? Most political debates include both realists and idealists, neither side willing to give in to the views of the other. And such debates will continue as long as human civilization survives. But at least one theorist has attempted to combine both realist and idealist notions about man into a theory of culture and decay in civilization: Sigmund Freud.

Freud: Civilization vs. Nature In his *Civilization and Its Discontents,* Sigmund Freud argues that the instinctive life of man is one of aggression and egoistic self-satisfaction (realism). The whole structure of culture has been designed to put prohibitions and curbs on him, and the sense of guilt has become the maker of civilized humanity. Civilization is made possible only by individual renunciation of selfish satisfactions for the sake of a more universal principle of culture (modified idealism).

But Freud claims that although man may well be inherently aggressive, he is not inherently "bad." Civilization provides him with models to live towards (or under), and the tension between his aggressive, egoistic instincts and these cultural norms creates *civilization*—"the whole sum of the achievements and the regulations which distinguish our lives from those of our animal ancestors and which serve two purposes—namely to protect men against nature and to adjust their mutual relations." This willingness of human beings to rechannel their egos towards the creation of cultural objects outside of themselves Freud refers to as Eros. *Note how closely Freud's notion of Eros comes to an embodiment of the definition of politics as a social act that attempts to solve the tension between human needs and social facts:*

*For more on Hobbes, see Chapter 12, pages 274 to 276.

. . . man's natural aggressive instinct, the hostility of each against all and of all against each, opposes [the] programme of civilization. This aggressive instinct is the derivative and the main representative of the death instinct which we have found alongside of Eros and which shares world-dominion with it. And now, I think, the meaning of the evolution of civilization is no longer obscure to us. It must present the struggle between Eros and Death, between the instinct of life and the instinct of destruction, as it works itself out in the human species. This struggle is what all life essentially consists of, and the evolution of civilization may therefore be simply described as the struggle for life of the human species.[3]

Freud's view clearly grows out of realism towards idealism, in contrast with the self-fulfilling pessimism of Hobbes, who gives us only realism growing into realism. Whereas Freud would have us give up our individualism to create culture, Hobbes stresses the need for us to give up our egoism to create a state. No one who is aware of the two world wars of the twentieth century can deny the need of human beings to give up their egoism to a higher, universal principle. But the end must justify the means. And cultural creativity is a more appropriate end for human beings than an institutional state of force, although to some extent culture is dependent upon the security that the state provides.

Survival of civilization depends on giving up egoism to a higher principle.

Avoiding Pathology The tension between state security (survival and security needs) and cultural creativity (love, self-esteem, and self-actualization needs) corresponds to the ideological conflict between the extremes of *pathological realism* and *pathological idealism*. As indicated in Chapter 3, "pathology" in this context means a rigid image of the world that does not fit reality nor allow the believer to progressively eliminate errors in this image to adapt to social conditions.

A typical pathological realist believes that nice guys finish last and that others are always conspiring to undermine his security, and fails to perceive the human cooperation that can take place to satisfy his higher level needs. Therefore, he is usually fixated on protecting the satisfaction of his physiological and security needs (through large defense budgets or whatever) and is unwilling to risk the vulnerability of attempting to satisfy love, self-esteem, and self-actualization needs.

The pathological idealist, on the other hand, believes that virtue is its own reward, that people must always be trusted, and that survival and security needs can be more or less taken for granted—cooperation being the style for political action. Such idealistic optimists can easily lead others to stumble into conflict and war because of their failure to take the realistic, aggressive aspects of human nature into account. An example of such an idealist is Neville Chamberlain, British prime minister, who signed the Munich Pact with Adolf Hitler just before the latter launched World War II.

> **Pathological realism freezes us at the physical, material level. Pathological idealism risks physical survival for the sake of spiritual utopia.**

To avoid the extremes of either pathological realism or pathological idealism, the individual must locate himself accurately in the historical conditions or phase of the cycle of his time. He must determine how he is limited by the five variables of politics: values, rules of the game, social institutions, political institutions, and personality. In this context he must then decide how to begin to satisfy his needs, depending upon which needs are already satisfied. (The five basic needs, in order of priority, are physiological, security, love, self-esteem, and self-actualization.) Conditions in the late twentieth century appear to support a basic assumption of this book: No individual will ever be able to satisfy *all* of his needs. Therefore, the human being is fated to be a political animal, always in a state of tension between unsatisfied needs and the obstacle of social facts.

Global Needs and Values

In the time it takes you to read this sentence, at least four people will die of starvation in the world, the majority of them children.[4] In an historical period going from maintenance to decay, the question is not one of saving everything but of what to save first. There are only so many resources, pocketbooks, and people with time and ability to act politically for the sake of others. Human needs are infinite, existing resources finite. A clear-cut hierarchy of needs has to be established to make a politics for human beings possible. Luckily, some people have identified what they believe to be a universal hierarchy of human needs. Unluckily, most of these people are ignored by maintenance men ruling countries and writing political science textbooks.

In a world of scarce resources, it pays to focus on needs rather than on values. For, as was pointed out in Chapter 3, people often want more than they need. Needs—at least in principle—can be identified scientifically through biology and social psychology, and eventually the priority of one need over another can be pinned down. Consider the difference between needs and values in this newspaper article:

India Seeks to Change Her Beggar Image
by Bernard Weinraub

"We're a society of survival and we've lost the capacity to identify, to tackle the problems," says the former government official. "We can't change without paying the price, without breaking up the caste system and this hierarchal system of government. Yet who's willing to pay this price?"

Like a sluggish elephant, India is moving heavily through a dark forest that seems without end. Last week violence exploded in the poor, caste-ridden northeast state of Bihar, a state where ever-present corruption and bungling by officials have become a serious problem for the New Delhi Government. The violence in Bihar, followed by the upheaval in the state of Gujarat that toppled the leadership there, is a measure of the nation's deepening internal political and economic ferment, a ferment that also affects India's relations abroad.

Three years ago India's leaders predicted that food self-sufficiency was in sight. Now, the World Bank says in a confidential report that India will need at least ten million tons of imported grain in the next five years, a severe economic and psychological jolt. Last year, Indian officials were using a pet phrase, "zero net aid," and predicted that by 1979 the nation would be healthy enough to finally halt the embarrassing specter, at least in India's eyes, of the nation walking around the world with a begging cup. Aid here, especially from the United States which has poured in $10-billion, is a symbol of humiliation.

But, now the World Bank, in the report to a 13-nation aid consortium, says that India requires a staggering $12-billion in the next five years, and that assistance from oil-producing countries is crucial to meet the nation's needs. It is symptomatic of the nation's embarrassment about aid that when *The New York Times* published the details of the carefully worded report, the Washington correspondent of *The Times of India* said that the document had been leaked to "hostile" newspapers.

The Eternal Problems

The enduring problems for India, intertwined with the oil crisis, include food, the population spiral and the nation's perceptions about her relations to the outside world, especially the United States and the Soviet Union.

Essentially, India needs United States help but doesn't want to ask for it or even admit it. One reason for this is the past aid relationship, which many Indians have viewed as crippling. (The fact that 60 million tons of food were sent here through the 1960s to thwart famine is viewed, in current revisionist thinking, as a vehicle for American domination). . . .[5]

INVITATION

In the article on India's domestic and global needs, which values have become reified into social facts to the point of making basic needs impossible to satisfy?

Can you think of any social facts in America that might blind American diplomats to the reified self-esteem needs of the Indians?

The institutions and values of both more and less developed countries often distort the perception of human needs. Whereas in America people's values and institutions are fixated on material needs that have largely been satisfied, India is fixated on self-esteem, love, and self-actualization needs to the point where people starve to death. Pathological idealism masks the reality that without a body there can be no self-esteem, love, and self-actualization. In Gandhi's well-known words: "Man does not live by bread alone. Many prefer self-respect to food."*

Of course, when you get beyond biological and physical needs to socio-psychological needs (love, self-esteem, and self-actualization), values do become more important. One person's need can be another person's poison—especially in socio-psychological terms. Yet in a world in which more babies are born than can be fed, it does seem reasonable to focus first on fundamental needs that can be scientifically established, leaving values to those who have satisfied physiological and security needs.

Maslow's Need Hierarchy This book uses the psychologist Abraham Maslow's need hierarchy as representative of universal human needs and their priority. Although some biological and socio-psychological evidence supports this need hierarchy, it should be noted that its existence and priorities have not been conclusively established, in scientific terms. Nevertheless, like the historical cycle, it does provide a useful working hypothesis that seems to explain much of past human behavior. Furthermore, it is a theory that is eventually subject to scientific verification (or falsification), making it much more valuable than any random set of needs or values.

Maslow's need hierarchy is a positive theory of motivation, a theory that explains why men act positively to resolve the tension they perceive between their needs and social facts. Recall the five basic needs of Maslow's hierarchy, in their order of importance (defined in Chapter 3):

Physiological needs (bodily needs for water, food, rest, etc.)
Safety needs (physical and psychological security)
Love needs (warmth, affection, inclusion by desired objects)
Self-esteem needs (positive evaluation of self by self and others)
Self-actualization needs (the desire to become everything that one is capable of becoming—usually based on first fulfilling all other needs.)[6]

Maslow's need hierarchy suggests that an individual's sense of power or efficacy in social relationships depends upon his having *previously* satisfied body, security, and love needs and *going beyond them*. A human being has to have not only a full stomach, but a sense of personal strength that comes from the feeling that others recognize and even love him before being ready to risk extending himself into the world. To be politically effective, it is not enough for a human being to satisfy concrete biological and material needs. He must go beyond them *to create himself* in the eyes of both himself and others.[7]

Human power is created out of matter through the psyche and

---

*According to the 1972 World Bank estimate, of roughly 3.8 billion people in the world, 1 billion are malnourished or hungry.

> **fulfills needs to the extent it is
> recognized by significant others.**

Postindustrial vs. Third-World Needs Since power is a relationship between human beings, few people who say "If you can do it, more power to you" really mean it. People are jealous about power, for dominating social relationships strokes their ego. Most people seek to maintain the power in social relationships that they have and, if possible, create more power than they can control. Americans recognize this psychological pattern immediately. For Americans are well fed, watered, rested, secured, and even loved—in *most* cases. After meeting their body, safety, and love needs, many of them find time and energy left to strive to fulfill esteem and self-actualization needs.

Unfortunately, people in *most* countries of the world are not as well off as Americans. Many are starving. Many are fighting or preparing to fight for their very existence. If you are sick, starving, or fighting, little time is left over for trying to satisfy self-esteem and self-actualization needs. The life chances for such deprived people begin more with the belly than the ego, more with the body than the spirit. Mere physical survival becomes the first and sometimes only priority.

> **If your physical needs
> have not been met,
> they will define your priorities.**

Fortunate people in postindustrial societies cannot afford to ignore the more basic needs of lesser developed countries.

Just as media theorist Marshall McLuhan sees the communications explosion drawing us all into one Global Village, political scientist Peter Corning points out that sharing the limited resources of the spaceship Earth forces us all to engage in a *global survival enterprise*.[8] Happily some political scientists, such as Corning, are exploring the biological sciences in an attempt to better assess people's biological needs from a political policy viewpoint. At some future time, whether or not Americans eat may depend upon whether Asians are eating. Or, put another way, in a time of rising expectations, Asians with empty stomachs are more apt to revolt and make war against rich countries like the United States than are Asians whose basic physical needs have been met.

Nationalism and Security Needs However, the perception by elites in rich countries that people in poor countries may resort to violence or war to satisfy their physical needs more often causes a concern for security than a desire to help the poor. And this focus upon security is made more intense by erroneous notions of unilateral defense, by the outdated romantic myth of the independent nation-state. In a nuclear age, when the technological epidemic spawns weapons too powerful and complex to defend against effectively, no state can claim total independence or sovereignty any longer. But most peoples in the world still believe that national independence and sovereignty is possible. And political elites manipulate the insecurities that these people experience as they try to maintain nationalistic myths that don't fit the technological or ecological limits of their age.

Elites stay elite by stoking the insecurities of masses who believe in outdated myths — such as the nation-state.

Ironically, this predominant concern for physical security built into the outdated nation-state system means that even the richest peoples in the world often cannot get beyond basic physical and safety needs to satisfy love, esteem, and self-actualization needs. Maintenance men use "law and order" and "arms race superiority" ideas as tools to keep the masses insecure and thereby repress them from growing beyond basic security needs to self-actualize themselves. And the stress of Western culture upon the material and concrete helps the elite in power to keep the attention of the masses focused upon economic and military security needs—even in the richest and most secure nations of the world.

Since the short-term, selfish interests of national elites are served by increasing the insecurity of the masses, it is unlikely that peoples of rich nations will be encouraged by their governments to give a damn for the poor in poor nations in the near future. Hence, C. P. Snow's prediction that "since the gap between the rich countries and the poor can be removed, it will be" has proved to be optimistic, if not naive.[9]

Just because men have the technology and wealth to help others does not mean they will have the desire to use it for that purpose. And people in countries such as America, who perceive their societies to be going from maintenance to decay, are particularly apt to be concerned with security needs—rather than living out their decadence in a fruit-ful, generous, and humanistic way. Many so long to return to the lost stage of maintenance that they forsake their present and future for the sake of a vision of the past. And in the 1930s, Benito Mussolini in Italy and Adolf Hitler in Germany demonstrated the extreme pathology that can result when reactionary elites, or maintainers, base policies on recovering the lost national glories of the past.

INVITATION

Analyze the policies of your own nation's elites in terms of Maslow's need hierarchy, using information and quotations in newspapers and weekly news magazines. To what extent do these elites focus upon economic and security needs? To what extent do they exaggerate the importance of such needs to appeal to the nationalism and economic interests of their constituency in order to get reelected or increase their power? Do they ever refer to love, esteem, and self-actualization needs? Why or why not?

Compare the policies and need hierarchy of your own na-tional elites with that of other countries that have gone from maintenance to decay, such as Italy and Germany in the 1930s and Great Britain since World War II. Who seeks to satisfy which needs of the majority of the people, and why? (Read the relevant sections of *The Twenty Years' Crisis, 1919§1939*, by Edward Hallett Carr (New York: Harper and Row, 1964), or of any modern European history book. An extremely well-written and concise book is *This Age of Conflict*, by Frank P. Chambers (New York: Harcourt, Brace and World, 1962).

Our Age ot Hollow Men

If the energy of human beings is absorbed by seeking to fulfill real or imaginary physical and security needs, little is left over for the cultural and spiritual development implied in the satisfaction of love, esteem, and self-actualization needs. As long as elites can bamboozle the masses into pursuing merely economic and security values, higher cultural values will be neglected, and postindustrial societies will be made up of hollow men. As T. S. Eliot put it in "The Hollow Men":

> We are the hollow men
> We are the stuffed men
> Leaning together
> Headpiece filled with straw.

Human beings in the twentieth century have been hollowed out by decadent events—by world wars, concentration camps, domestic racism and violence. The experience of meaninglessness and powerlessness has become almost universal, and the experience of having the power to affect events in one's life is rare. The universal symbol of the age has become Eliot's poem *The Wasteland*, not Alfred Lord Tennyson's *Ulysses*. Indeed, the spirit of Tennyson's call "to seek a newer world" appears to have been assassinated with Robert Kennedy, who used that idea as an ideology and book title.

In the twentieth century individual powerlessness has become a universal.

As psychologist Rollo May wrote, "I cannot recall a time during the last four decades when there was so *much* talk about the individual's capacities and potentialities and so *little* actual confidence on the part of the individual about his power to make a difference psychologically or politically . . ."[10] Why have feelings of powerlessness become self-fulfilling prophecy? Why do men and women almost seek out powerlessness, preparing themselves to be put down, accepting their manipulation by others? Why don't human beings move to fill in their hollowness and rebel against the decadence of the times? These are the kinds of questions that led to the writing of this book.*

Answers to alienation are hard to come by but do exist. Our thesis is that people can overcome powerlessness by knowing how to

*See also Chapter 3, p. 40 on alienation and Chapter 7, p. 158—159 on anomie.

use ideas as tools to create power for themselves in social relationships. By becoming aware of the historical cycle of creation-maintenance-decay, a human being can set realistic goals to maximize his power in his historical situation and to satisfy his needs in social relationships. This theory assumes that if an individual passively accepts the cyclic view of inevitability, man is rendered powerless. But if he blends the view of the manipulators—using social relationships to satisfy needs—with cyclic insights, a human being can learn to create and experience power in social relationships, power that gives him the freedom to love, to feel self-esteem, to actualize himself.

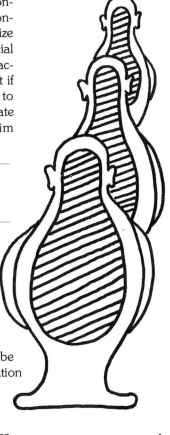

isaak

> **To create power, manipulate the cyclic views of others to maximize your values in social relationships.**

If in doubt, it pays for human beings to adopt the belief of manipulators rather than the beliefs of cyclics. *The manipulators stress the integration, order, and stability of society, states, and regions, whereas the cyclics emphasize disintegration and the recurrent comings of disorder and instability.* The manipulators see integration as a tool, a means that can be grasped to direct historical change for the benefit of man. The cyclics view integration and order as passing phenomena, to be overturned in time—empires must wither, the leaves of civilization must fall.

The choice between adopting the view of a passive, alienated cyclic or that of an active, ambitious manipulator is clearly not an appealing one. Yet not to choose one of these two strategies results in sterile hesitation, if not in a decision made by someone else. For as philosopher Karl Jaspers said, "Unconsciously or consciously, each individual chooses how he wants to live, to think, to act and to die."[11] There is no escape: the alternative to power is impotence, and those who opt out of the political game must resign themselves to seeing it decided by others.

Hollowness is relative to an experience of fullness dreamed, seen, or imagined. If I do not know that I am potentially powerful, I cannot use my power to create culture or actualize myself. And my awareness depends upon the awareness of others. If my empty way of life is seen to be "normal" by others, I may be tempted to make a routine and social virtue of hollowness. If I have never met a fully cultivated, aware, and humanistic person, it is unlikely that I will try to become one. My goals are too often limited by my limited experience. Moreover, the political goals of my society are too often limited by the narrow experience and imagination of the governing elites.

REVOLUTION AND REBIRTH

Rethinking

> **Limiting experience narrows choice and values. Or, to know one helps to become one.**

Many human beings are as politically hollow as Stepan Ar-
kadyevitch Oblonsky in Tolstoy's *Anna Karenina:*

> Stepan Arkadyevitch had not chosen his political opinions or his
> views; these political opinions and views had come to him of them-
> selves, just as he did not choose the shapes of his hats or coats, but
> simply took those that were being worn. And for him, living in a
> certain society—owing to the need, ordinarily developed at years of
> discretion, for some degree of mental activity—to have views was
> just as indispensable as to have a hat. If there was a reason for his
> preferring liberal to conservative views, which were held also by
> many of his circle, it arose not from his considering liberalism more
> rational, but from its being in closer accord with his manner of life
> . . . And so liberalism had become a habit of Stepan
> Arkadyevitch's, and he liked his newspaper, as he did his cigar after
> dinner, for the slight fog it diffused in his brain.

The sociologist David Riesman calls people like Stepan "other-
directed." Such people's need for approval and direction from others
governs their behavior to the point that they are no longer capable of
thinking for themselves or of questioning their own values. In democratic countries, other-directed types are popularly elected to become
governing elites in many situations. In authoritarian countries, inner-
directed, high self-esteem personalities often take advantage of the
other-directedness of the masses to impose their own values and political life-style on everybody.

**To be other-directed is to be
directed by others; or,
those who create their own values
create values for others as well.**

Inner-directed elites often develop coherent *systems* of value or
belief so that they can more easily and credibly impose their views
upon their community. If such beliefs also incorporate idea-systems
that are universally recognized over time in many countries and that
provide model problems and solutions to a community of practitioners, they are called *paradigms.*

**Paradigms are universally recognized
idea systems that influence many
communities over time.**

In scientific thought, two paradigms that come immediately to
mind are Newtonian mechanics and Einsteinian relativity. Likewise,
two paradigms in international politics are the balance of power and
collective security idea systems. There are also parallels between scientific and political thought in how paradigms change.

**Cracks in paradigms
cause revolutions and rebirth
in times of crisis.**

Thomas S. Kuhn has explained how scientific and political paradigms dominate societies until certain historical changes occur. In *The Structure of Scientific Revolutions* he writes:

> Political revolutions are inaugurated by a growing sense, often restricted to a segment of the political community, that existing institutions have ceased adequately to meet the problems posed by an environment that they have in part created . . . In both political and scientific development the sense of malfunction that can lead to crisis is prerequisite to revolution.[11]

Note that the awareness of crisis in Kuhn's description of revolutionary change is *an awareness of human beings that existing social relationships or idea systems are no longer adequate to solve their problems.*

Revolution occurs when legitimacy is undermined with visions of a new social order.

As Thomas Kuhn noted, a change in paradigm can be called a revolution. That is, when a paradigm such as the balance-of-power system begins to crack in times of crisis, the other-directed Stepan Oblonskys of the world begin to question their values, and perceptive inner-directed thinkers think up new paradigms with which to solve the grave tensions between human needs and social facts. If the inner-directed manipulators can come up with a useful counter-paradigm and persuade enough other-directed people that they are right, revolution may break out. Rethinking can lead to revolting at the proper historical moment in the political cycle.

Revolting

Take the example of the French revolution of 1789. At that time the dominant political paradigm in European politics was the balance of power system. The conservative monarchs who manipulated this system to keep their positions of power foisted the homogeneous ideology of the balance of power upon their populations under the guise of "legitimacy." These rulers grew so in the habit of dominating European politics with their paradigm that they never seriously entertained the possibility that revolutionary upstarts might create a counter-paradigm that would upset their applecart. Ideology, for the old maintenance men, had blinded them to forces of historical change. By seeking only stability, they failed to take political account of diversity. They perceived the threat of the French revolutionaries far too late to eliminate it before revolution rocked the international system.

And then the reactionary monarchs of Europe overreacted. The French revolutionaries created a heterogeneous ideology based on a democratic creed that reduced international stability by sharply increasing the odds of distorted perceptions, as political scientist Kyung-Won Kim has pointed out. Neither the reactionary "We's" nor revolutionary "They's" correctly perceived the strength or views of each other, causing violent revolution, bloodshed, and repressive reaction. Professor Kim has hypothesized how such breakdowns in the international system occur in *Revolution and International System*:

> The probability of a breakdown of a given international system varies directly with (1) the extent of ideological heterogeneity, (2) the degree of ideological rigidity among the essential actors, and (3) the strength of the feedback effect of the divergent actor's international action on its domestic political system . . .

In short, Kim argues that the balance of power paradigm distorted the perceptions of the conservative manipulators in power, whose rigid ideology did not permit them to see the emergence of powerful others or understand their counter-paradigm. Likewise, the revolutionaries let ideological rigidity distort their perceptions.

Rigid paradigms become ideological blinders that cause misperception, which can lead to violence.

Furthermore, if reactionary maintenance men use their political paradigm as a club, sympathy and support will spread for the idealistic revolutionaries and their counter-paradigm. Thus, when the conservative monarchs overreacted in putting down the French revolutionaries through their heavy-handed balance-of-power ideology, sympathy spread for the revolutionaries both at home and abroad. Indeed, the over-reaction of the maintainers helped cause the revolutionaries to make their political goals not only domestic but universal, and to export their revolution from France to other countries.

Overreaction on the part of maintenance men makes revolutionaries more revolutionary and spreads international violence.

Revolutionary counter-paradigms grow out of rebellion against a system that doesn't make sense to certain human beings. The old, traditional political paradigm no longer works for them; it doesn't solve their problems. The tension between human needs and social facts becomes unbearable. As Albert Camus has written, "Rebellion is born of the spectacle of irrationality, confronted with an unjust and incomprehensible condition." The old paradigm no longer fits the social facts of the historical moment for a significant number of human beings. Often this misfit only becomes apparent when economic or social crisis strips off the legitimacy in which elite maintainers have cloaked their political domination of social relationships. And the more old elites use old ideas as clubs in times of crisis, the more revolutionaries will make their counter-paradigm an all-or-nothing ideology and the more "We-They" rigidity will lead to violence.

Rebellion become revolutionary violence calls for a period of reconstruction, of re-creation. The political cycle normally goes from maintenance to decay to revolution to creation. For everyday human beings, times of reconstruction after revolution are often the most bitter and repressive of all. Albert Camus has pointed out that all modern revolutions have resulted in a reinforcement of the power of the State, in a reinforcement of that collective, dehumanizing reification based on the myths of nationalism. 1789 brought Napoleon. The revolutions of 1848 in Europe brought Napoleon III. The Russian revolution of 1917 resulted in Stalin; the Italian uprisings of the twenties, Mussolini; the Weimar Republic, Hitler. In each case, the failure of revolutionaries to limit their objectives according to their place and time in history resulted in reactionary repression and a reconstruction of State authority. Rigid all-or-nothing ideologies of revolutionaries were crushed by rigid law-and-order ideologies of maintenance men.

> **Unlimited revolutions result in**
> **repression and reaction.**
> **Or, to paraphrase Confucius,**
> **admire a large plantation**
> **but revolt for a small one.**

The Limits of Rebellion   The limits that effective rebels must place upon themselves are subtle but vital. The universality of their rebellion depends upon their willingness to accept the same limits upon themselves that they would impose upon the State authorities. Albert Camus summarizes these limits in *The Rebel:*

> Rebellion is in no way the demand for total freedom. On the contrary, rebellion puts total freedom up for trial. It specifically attacks the unlimited power that authorizes a superior to violate the forbidden frontier. Far from demanding general independence, the rebel wants it to be recognized that freedom has its limits everywhere that a human being is to be found—the limit being precisely that human being's power to rebel. The most profound reason for rebellious intransigence is to be found here. The more aware rebellion is of demanding a just limit, the more inflexible it becomes. The rebel undoubtedly demands a certain degree of freedom for himself; but in no case, if he is consistent, does he demand the right to destroy the existence and the freedom of others. He humiliates no one. The freedom he claims, he claims for all; the freedom he refuses, he forbids everyone to enjoy. He is not only the slave against the master, but also man against the world of master and slave.[13]

According to Camus, the true rebel's creed must be "I rebel therefore we exist." Rebellion is only humane and justifiable to the extent that it is *universal* in its respect for human existence and freedom. In the twentieth century, a politics for human beings can only be constructed with a humane rebellion that respects its own limits and universal integrity. Human beings must rebel for the existence and freedom of others—of *all* others.

Camus's notion of limited rebellion is consistent with the ethical principle of the philosopher Immanuel Kant: treat people as ends, not as means; or, act in such a way that you could recommend that all other human beings act in the same way. Only by acting to fulfill your own needs through fulfilling the needs of others will you be able to self-actualize in Maslow's sense. When Camus writes, "I rebel therefore we exist," he means that only insofar as I self-actualize to resolve the tension between my human needs and repressive social facts do I prove that the self-actualized "We" of humanity in social relationships exists.

**By self-actualizing,
you symbolize the self-actualization
of humanity and inspire others.**

The Ultimate Goal   Furthermore, in a world of scarce resources such as ours, *self-actualization is always political.* For scarcity *means* that existing social facts preclude the satisfaction of everyone's basic needs. Tensions riddle world politics in the twentieth century because of the social fact of scarcity of resources on the one hand and the exaggerated expectations of millions of human beings on the other. If the physiological, security, love, and esteem needs must be satisfied before self-actualization can take place, in the present world, where millions of people are starving, only the relatively wealthy can afford to self-actualize. All signs indicate that in the near future the rich will get richer, the poor poorer. The gap will make international tensions more intense and revolutionary violence more probable.

Consider the idea of self-actualization more carefully. Maslow describes the need for self-actualization as follows:

> "Even if all these needs [physiological, security, love, and self-esteem] are satisfied, we may still often (if not always) expect that a new discontent and restlessness will soon develop, unless the individual is doing what he is fitted for. A musician must make music, an artist must paint, a poet must write, if he is to be ultimately at peace with himself. What a man *can* be, he *must* be. This need we may call self-actualization."[14]

Put bluntly, it's hard to paint, make music, or write poetry if you are starving to death. And if you need to duck enemy bullets all day long, self-actualization is equally hard to come by. Social facts today make self-actualization impossible for the majority of people in the world. Only by political action can the individual help himself and others to change these social facts to reduce the tension and make self-actualization possible.

Effective Reform   However, effective political action in a postindustrial society going from maintenance to decay, such as the United States, is a subtle matter. For in such societies, creation, maintenance, and decay are often going on simultaneously, although the present appears to be dominated basically by maintenance men and the future looks like it will bring a decay of present conditions and stability.

In such a period, revolutionaries can help their cause by making their ideology flexible and now and then presenting the image of maintenance men. Otherwise, they are apt to provoke overreaction on the part of the ruling elite, as did the French revolutionaries.

Moreover, many revolutionary or reform ideologies today lack a clear-cut positive program based on human needs. Mere redistribution of income through tax reforms, for example, does not attack society's dehumanizing public problems as much as it just spreads them out in a different way. It doesn't change society's basic priorities. This is not to say that income should not be more equitably distributed, but larger, more meaningful value priorities must be included in a program for a politics for human beings. These priorities include stands on the energy and environmental crises, the disarmament and transformation of the nation-state system, and the creation of a more equitable world economic system.

Additionally, the basic survival needs of thousands of starving people in Asia and Africa will not be met unless these general world policies are translated into superpower foreign aid programs, *much more* generous and nonideological than those of the United States and Soviet Union today. And to make such reforms effective, would-be reformers must first understand how maintenance men use systems thinking to maintain old social facts.[15]

INCONCLUSIONS

Beginning with two individuals on an island, we have seen the scope of politics expand from family through American through comparative politics until it now includes the whole world—a lot of needy people and a lot of frustrating social facts. Many people don't take their eyes off of their own needs long enough to see the needs of others—much less the needs of all others in the entire world. As the globe becomes increasingly divided between the rich, industrial nations of the Northern Hemisphere and the poor, rural nations of the Southern Hemisphere, as basic natural resources dwindle and the world population skyrockets, human needs become tragically acute and existing social facts appear hopelessly frustrating. Clearly some revolutionary thinking is called for on the global level. We can no longer claim to be human unless we rebel against such inhumane conditions. Hunger spreads day by day, nuclear stockpiles expand ridiculously, violence hangs in the air. . .

Men and women are hollowed out and anxious, too timid for action. Revolutionaries burn themselves up in their own fires, failing to take the cycle of social facts and its limits into account. World Wars I and II haunt us with the possibility of a Third Coming if mankind doesn't do something to halt its destructive tendencies, and soon. We can't buy our way out—or steal our way out. We must act our way out, politically, realistically, walking the line of human limitation that Camus and other philosophers have sketched for us. We must begin rethinking, revolting, reconstructing Now. So let's see what kind of thinking and rethinking is being done by political theorists. . . . Politics begins with an idea.

REFERENCES

1. See György Adam, "Multinational Corporations and the Outlines of a Global Economy," a paper presented at the 14th Annual Convention of the International Studies Association, March 14–17, 1973, in New York City. See also Harvey D. Shapiro, "The Multinationals: Giants Beyond Flag and Country," *The New York Times Magazine,* March 18, 1973.

2. Albert Schweitzer, *The Philosophy of Civilization* (New York: Macmillan, 1953—orig. 1923), p. xiv.

3. Sigmund Freud, *Civilization and Its Discontents*, The Strachey translation (New York: W. W. Norton, 1961—orig. 1930), p. 69. For a brilliant linking of Hobbes and Rousseau with the nature of man, the state, and war, see Kenneth N. Waltz, *Man, the State and War* (New York: Columbia University Press, 1954).

4. Paul Erlich, *The Population Bomb* (New York: Ballantine Books, 1968).

5. *The New York Times*, "Week in Review," March 24, 1974, p. 34.

6. Abraham Maslow, *Motivation and Personality* (New York: Harper, 1954), and Abraham Maslow, "A Theory of Human Motivation," *Psychological Review* 50 (1943), pp. 370–396.

7. Compare Stanley Renshon, "The Psychological Origins of Political Efficacy: The Need for Personal Control," paper delivered at the 1972 American Political Science Convention, Washington, D.C. (Ann Arbor, Michigan: University Microfilms, 1972), pp. 15–16. See also Renshon, *Psychological Needs and Political Behavior* (Garden City, New York: The Free Press, 1974).

8. See, among other writings, Marshall McLuhan, *Understanding Media: The Extensions of Man* (New York: McGraw-Hill, 1965), See also Peter A. Corning, "The Biological Bases of Behavior and Some Implications for Political Science," *World Politics* 23, no. 3 (April 1971), p. 363.

9. C. P. Snow, *The Two Cultures* (Cambridge: Cambridge University Press, 1960).

10. Rollo May, *Power and Innocence* (N. Y.: W. W. Norton, 1972).

11. Thomas S. Kuhn, *The Structure of Scientific Revolutions* (Chicago: University of Chicago Press, 1962), p. 91.

12. Kyung-Won Kim, *Revolution and International System* (New York: New York University Press, 1970), p. 131.

13. Albert Camus, *The Rebel—An Essay on Man in Revolt* (New York: Knopf, 1956), p. 284.

14. Abraham Maslow, *Motivation and Personality* (New York: Harper and Row, 1954), p. 91.

15. To see what kinds of social facts stand in the way of a revolutionary world politics that would be more equitable for all people, read Stanley Hoffman's "Choices," *Foreign Policy*, Fall 1973, and David P. Calleo and Benjamin M. Rowland, *America and the World Political Economy* (Bloomington, Indiana: Indiana University Press, 1973).

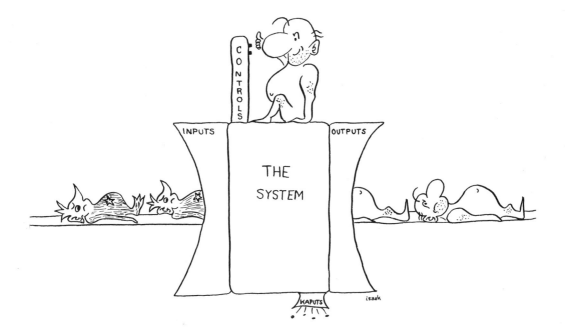

10 Wherein the reader experiences what it's like to think politics through a system—through structural-functionalism, systems theory, communications theory, and mathematical models—and feels the danger of losing one's self in the process.

10 Thinking Politics Through the System

Most people prefer to avoid thinking about thinking. After all, it's easier to think and act out of habit. But ours is an era of decadence and crisis. Old habits of thinking reveal their bankruptcy and are found by many to be irrelevant to human needs. The chapters on American, comparative, and international politics have demonstrated that old ways of thinking can make us slaves to existing social facts and fail to satisfy our needs. When Americans think about the Vietnam War and the Watergate affair, they become aware of the mistakes of old ways of political thinking.

INTRODUCTION

But rather than asking what kinds of thinking led to these mistakes, many prefer to pull back into the shell of their private existence and hope that somehow they can get away with leading apolitical lives. But as has been shown again and again, without thinking politically, without being conscious of the tension between social facts and our needs, we will never be satisfied as human beings. By giving up the political game, we give up humanity as well.

> **Human beings rethink politics
> when old ways of thinking
> no longer solve their problems.**

Modern American political thought has reflected America's movement in the political cycle from maintenance to decay. Political thinkers concerned with maintenance tend to focus on the political *system* as a whole and how to keep it stable. In contrast, thinkers most concerned with the political implications of change often focus upon the individual self and creative behavior. This fundamental difference in focus has led to one of the most important disputes in social thought: *Holism* versus *individualism*. Holists argue that in order to explain political or social events, thinkers must introduce concepts (such as "the system") that depend for their meaning precisely on the fact that they can never be reduced to a list of statements about individuals. Individualists, on the other hand, argue that any statement about a collectivity must be able to be reduced to a set of statements about the individuals of whom the collectivity is composed—at least in principle.[1]

> **Holists are theoretical
> maintenance men who focus on
> the system and stability;
> individualists think a lot about
> social change and focus on the self.**

Take the example of the Ik (pronounced "Eek") people in East Africa. The Ik adults send their children out of the hut to seek food and perhaps to starve at the age of three or four. The parents either refuse to let the children return home, or sometimes let them starve to death even if they are allowed to return. Most other peoples of the world would call them consistently inhumane. Anthropologist Colin Turnbull analyzed the Ik from a *holist* viewpoint in his book *The Mountain People*. Slowly he learned not to hate them because he understood their primitive behavior in terms of the *system** in which they were trapped and socialized.[2]

Two basic properties characterize the Ik system: a shortage of food and an administrative decision by official others, who forced the Ik to give up their cheerful nomadism to settle down and farm unfarmable land in northern Uganda. In such a basic survival system the Ik discarded kindness, generosity, consideration, and affection as counterproductive or nonfunctional. The existence of a mere survival system seemed to preclude a *social* system. Turnbull concludes that the Ik show society is not indispensable for survival, that man is not as social an animal as has been thought, and that man can associate for purposes of survival without being social. Noting that among the Ik all human association is temporary and cannot flourish into anything as dysfunctional as affection or trust, Turnbull asks: Does that sound so very different from our own society?

Turnbull's systemic viewpoint leads him to focus on the *stable* elements of Ik society—the undernourishment and inhumanity of its members—and leads him to the universal claim that there is some of the Ik in all of us. A *methodological individualist* viewing the same people would probably have been less apt to make such universal generalizations about human nature, focusing upon the transition of Ik society from nomads to starving farmers and upon Iks as unique individuals. Whereas a systems theorist tends to reify the stable, the universal, and the maintenance functions in a society, an individualist is apt to reify the changing, the unique, and the decadent aspects as they affect individual behavior. Each type of reification has its own kind of blindness and its own kind of truth—one cheating the forest for the trees, the other underrating the trees for the forest. To analyze the multi-dimensional truth in social relationships, political thinkers must be aware of both the system-oriented and self-oriented theories that have been created to explain human behavior. To explain the individual without reference to the political cycle and social collectivity is to neglect the historical situation. To stress the system to the point of eliminating all individuality is to be swallowed up in cyclic determinism.

Both the system and self orientations in political theory have a long historical tradition in philosophy. By the end of the eighteenth century, the split between the two views had become clear in modern terms—as natural philosophy became distinguished from moral philosophy. Most system-first theories became "natural," most self-

---

*"System" will be used to mean any set of interacting elements with identifiable regularities.

first theories, "moral." With the rising prestige of chemistry, physics, and biology, the names "natural" and "moral" science became popular.

Names make relationships more real. To give your theory political power, name it to match the spirit of the times.

The contemporary phrase "social science" grew out of the focus on human relationships in society by Saint Simon and August Comte in the nineteenth century. Political scientist David Easton maintains that each of these transitions—from philosophy to natural and moral philosophy, to moral and natural science, then to social science, and finally to behavioral science—represents a stage in a linear development of our understanding of man in society.[3] To the extent that politics can be analyzed as a scientific *system*, Easton may be right: individual selves become significant only to the extent that they represent verifiable trends in the context of a systematic framework. But some individualists don't like to be framed. They argue that the linearity of Western scientific thought is too limiting, repressive, and deterministic—a kind of theoretical cyclicism. They would prefer to speak about politics as an *art* or a *happening* rather than as a science.

But many people cannot tolerate the existential ambiguity of the individualist's view. They need something concrete, something systematic—the comfort of a solid reification. An individualist in political science, Henry Kariel, critically describes this desire for intellectual security:

> We do not want a variety of identities; we want more than the chance merely to *play* at being a sociologist, historian, artist, or scientist. We want to *be* someone. Perceiving our various possible identities, we diagnose our condition as "critical": we say (are taught to say) that we suffer from a type of "identity crisis" for which the best therapy is "commitment." . . . As the boundaries have been authoritatively drawn, approved and enforced, as convention ratifies them, we ultimately experience them as quite concretely *there*—as real, thank God. When not identified with God's design, we see them as inherent in the very nature of things. To cross the prevailing boundaries thus becomes utopian, sentimental, unrealistic. Realistically accommodating ourselves, we come to terms with ourselves where we are and as we are. We accept our situation. We do not merely play the part: we become the part . . . There is to be no wavering, no playing around.[4]

Kariel's critical view of our condition is not to be taken lightly. The social facts of our everyday world frustrate our needs and make us feel insecure. As rapid social change increases such insecurity, we reach out desperately for something firm, something concrete to hang on to. The norms of modern society proclaim that security and success come only to those who specialize themselves for a certain narrow professional role. Wavering between roles and playing around with them is discouraged as nonprofessional and decadent behavior. To succeed in maintenance society, you must help maintain its role-structure by fitting your needs and values into its boxes. This social intolerance for personal and professional ambiguity carries over to the thinking processes within roles themselves—including the role of political scientist.

Typical political scientists are very defensive about the early stage of development in their discipline. Understandably, many of them cannot stand the ambiguity that colors so much of politics. They look longingly to the "firmer," "more concrete," and "more systematic" fields of the natural sciences as more developed models to shoot for. They look for universal and stable rules, proven hypotheses, and concrete findings. Science comes to be viewed as a static, utopian state to be achieved, not as a never-ending creative process in which the scientist bobs around.

Yet the *true* scientific method entails getting to know a system of thought only in order to waver fruitfully in it, to play around creatively with it. After all, that's what scientific discovery means in the natural sciences.

> **Creative theorists play with systems; theoretical maintenance men become systematized. Or, learn to do in the system before it does you in.**

STRUCTURAL-FUNCTIONALISM: AN EVALUATION

This book is not called "Political *Science* for Human Beings," because that might reify science or the systems view. It is not called "Political *Art* for Human Beings," because that might imply the possibility of pathological idealism always inherent in the individualist view. Names become reifications that must be broken up to get at the thought that created them. Thus, even the name "politics" reifies one aspect of reality to the exclusion of other aspects equally relevant. Perhaps this is one reason why some of the most creative rethinking in politics in the twentieth century came about only through the influence of other disciplines such as anthropology, sociology, psychology, mathematics, and philosophy.

One area in which political theorists have borrowed ideas from biology, anthropology, and sociology is *structural-functionalism*. This paradigm or best-selling theory seduced many American political scientists in the 1960s and is still probably the dominant framework behind most recent textbooks in politics. Those taking the structural-functional approach spend most of their time asking, Which social structures fulfill which necessary functions in order to keep this society going? The structural-functionalists are basically a group of theoretical maintenance men—as demonstrated earlier in the two chapters on comparing politics.

The Hidden Bias

All structural-functional approaches to social science share one common element: they relate one part of a society or social system to another part or to some aspect of the whole.[5] This assumption exposes a basic difficulty with structural-functionalism. That is, by assuming the existence of a certain kind of social system or whole to be necessary, structural-functionalists begin with a hidden value bias or purpose or vision of that whole.

To have a secret purpose in using the scientific method is called the teleological fallacy. Structural-functionalism's purpose is system stability.

The word "teleological" derives from the Greek word *telos*, meaning end or purpose. Part of the scientific method is to make all basic value judgments or assumptions *explicit*. So to hide or fuzz over a purpose is a fallacy that loads the dice in analysis. Of course structural-functionalists have a right to be maintenance men. But if they make *scientific* claims based on their analysis, they are duty-bound to admit their hidden bias.

Structural-functionalists are maintenance men who often don't admit it.

Maintenance men often use the ideas of others to maintain existing reality or social systems. Structural-functionalists, for example, borrowed some basic ideas from organismic thinking in biology. The *organismic* approach assumes three things: (1) Certain *functional* requirements (such as oxygen, food, and water) must be satisfied to keep an organism alive and operating. (2) The *structures* and processes that satisfy these necessary functions in normal cases are concrete and can be described (structures in a human being, for example, include the source of oxygen and the nose). (3) If some of these typical structures are destroyed or are inadequate, compensating mechanisms or alternative structures must exist to keep the organism going (such as the mouth or artificial breathing devices if the nose cannot be used).[6]

Origins of Structural-Functionalism

Organismic thinking in biology, anthropology, and sociology inspired organismic thinking in politics. Beware of carrying the baggage of others without checking it first for hidden goods.

It was easy to leap from analyzing living organisms as structural-functional survival systems to analyzing societies and political systems *as if they were living organisms*, with necessary functions that had to be met by some structure or other.

But easy analogies should be questioned, since they often result in reification. For social systems are *not* comparable to biological systems on all levels. Biological breakdowns are not the same as social breakdowns. Indeed, the basic problem with structural-functionalism is that it cannot adequately explain the meaning of social change for human beings.

INVITATION

Imagine yourself back in the Inlandia of Chapter 1. The structural-functionalist would search for the necessary functions to be satisfied to keep the state of Alphonse and Balthazar going. What functions might they identify? What structures exist that are mentioned or not mentioned that might satisfy these functions? If hunger-satisfaction is a necessary function, and clam digging and cracking is an appropriate structure, how can the social scientist detect the breakdown of Inlandia *before* the full catastrophe occurs? How does the meaning of such potential decadence and crisis differ for Alphonse and Balthazar on the one hand and Raz Putin and Colombo on the other? Compare these differences in meaning with differences in perception between the maintenance men and the revolutionaries in your own society. What tools might you recommend for each, based on your reading so far?

(Recall the tools suggested in chapters on comparing politics.)

A Tool for Maintenance   Structural-functionalism was first explained in Chapter 6 and applied and evaluated in Chapter 7. As a best-selling theory or paradigm in our time of maintenance, structural-functionalism merits coverage and evaluation from different perspectives. Human beings must recognize it for what it is—a tempting tool for maintenance men that can be applied *to* or *by* everyday citizens to maintain the social system by keeping its functions in line. Of course, the Know-It-All elites and Know-Something middle classes are apt to try to keep the best functions for themselves, stabilizing themselves in structures upon the backs of the Know-Nothings of the lower classes, who cannot afford fancy ways of defense or offense. But as soon as Know-Nothings of all classes begin to become politically aware of the meaning of tools like structural-functionalism, they can ask: Whose structure? Whose functions? Whose needs are best satisfied by stabilizing existing social facts or structures? Whose needs are least satisfied? Which needs does the existing social system satisfy for everybody? For nobody? Who pays most and who gets least?

In thinking about or using structural-functionalism, recall its basic assumption: there are certain necessary functions in society that must be fulfilled by some structure to keep the social system stable. The "necessity" of such functions and the "desirability" of stability over all other values are the aspects of structural-functionalism that make it a tool for maintenance men (who are often out to maintain their interests and need-satisfaction before those of others). Such maintenance men can, of course, be professors of political science as well as governmental or corporate elites.

As pointed out in Chapter 7, structural-functionalism is useful for describing the variables or social facts that frustrate or satisfy human needs in an existing social system. In this sense, it often maps the *distance from* a politics for human beings by presenting static snapshots of existing reality. It provides a bird's-eye view of social functions and structures, rather than an insight into social processes through the human psyche. Structural-functionalism is a useful map for the foreigner to read before arriving in a strange culture. Once he has arrived, however, he will find he needs more precise and sensitive tools that allow him to explore the inner meanings of the culture and its people. He will want to go beneath the outer skin of social structure and the "normal" functioning that works to stabilize the social system.

A Tool for Human Beings

By using the rhetoric of "structures" and "functions" in "systems," structural-functionalists hoped to overcome the parochialism of particular political situations and to make the study of politics more "scientific." They did succeed in identifying universal elements that tend to appear in most political systems. But the basic principle behind their theories was taken from another, more comprehensive theory: *systems theory.* For the purpose of most structural-functional maintenance men was to *maintain stability in the existing political system* that they were studying. System stability or equilibrium legitimized their "necessary functions" and "alternate structures."

SYSTEMS THEORY

Systems theory was first developed as a tool in neurology by scientists studying brain behavior.[7] W. Ross Ashby and W. Gray Walter created systems theory to explore analogues for functions of the brain— described in Ashby's *Design for a Brain.* Gray designed a machine with a motor and headlights that could plug itself into a wall socket to recharge its battery when its headlights grew dim and could plug itself into a gas pump when it started to run out of gas. Ashby and Walter did not make the mistake of reifying these mechanical analogues by identifying them with the real brain system. But other theorists applying systems theory to politics sometimes did make this mistake.

Origins of Systems Theory

For in essence, general systems theory develops a kind of abstract mental machine—a transcending, self-stabilizing idea of coherence that is ideally capable of explaining all human interactions, from cell systems within an organism to large, complex social systems. Such theorists usually define a *system* as a set of elements or units, which interact in some way and are set off from their environment by some kind of boundaries. In this sense, a human cell, a cat, a car, a home, a movie, a couple, a philosophy, a chess game, and a war all qualify as systems. Political scientist K. W. Kim even went so far as to suggest, tongue in cheek, that such diverse elements as Napoleon, a star, and a bottle of brandy could be defined as a system (though "system-stability" in this case might be hard to come by!).

Criticisms of Systems Theory

Systems theorists argue that by developing abstract systems of interacting elements (*inputs, interaction, outputs,* and *feedback*) they can transcend the impressionistic, personal uniqueness of everyday life and develop universal principles that might explain everybody and everything everywhere.

In domestic politics, for example, how all of politics works is explained in terms of activities (inputs) people put into the conversion machinery of interest groups, parties, and government. This machinery treats *inputs* as *throughputs* and converts them into *outputs.* As one political scientist of German derivation observed, "By the time you get through, you're *kaput.*" Inputs are usually demands (I need help) or supports (here are my taxes). Outputs tend to consist of laws governing behavior and the distribution of goods. Outputs may be material—money for the poor (welfare), money for the rich (subsidy). Outputs may be symbolic—appearances of the president on television reassuring us he's not a crook, rituals swearing in a new president, raising the flag at half-staff in national mourning, and so on.

This systems approach amounts to neutralizing the uniqueness of the everyday human being to get him to fit a formula of the largest common denominator—the system. Clearly what this theory gains in scope it loses in depth. Indeed, this is one reason why political scientists working in the field of greatest scope—international politics—have found systems theory a particularly attractive approach. It gives them a good rationale for trying to explain everything in the world in general rather than much in particular. Perhaps it is no accident that, according to one source, none of the systems theory frameworks has been able to lay down intellectual policy for the field of international relations theory or to stimulate the empirical research necessary to validate it.[8]

Although systems theories avoid the parochialism of individual case studies, they fail to tap the meaningfulness of individual experience. One must begin any research in human behavior with the assumption of either an abstract, general system or of the meaning of a particular human being. And these two assumptions are incompatible as first premises. Either system first or self first, not both. This book clearly assumes that the self-first approach is the most meaningful one for a politics for human beings.

In summary, systems theorists define a *system* as a set of interacting elements or units that are set off from their environment by some kind of boundary. Conceiving of political life as an input-interaction-output-feedback system of equilibrium, such theorists maintain: (1) This approach avoids narrow parochialism and gives the theorist a comprehensive picture of the larger, interactive patterns of stability and change in and between social units. (2) The approach is interdisciplinary and stimulates comprehensive theories and general hypotheses of political interaction.[9] Perhaps the two best-known works on systems theory as applied to politics are David Easton's *The Political System* (1953) and Morton Kaplan's *System and Process in International Politics* (1957).

Critics of systems theory argue: (1) Its stress on equilibrium and systems maintenance gives such theorists a static and conservative bias that prevents them from adequately explaining social change or the importance of specific individual acts. (2) Its comprehensive level of generality gives only a superficial view of everything. (3) The concept of "system" is a dehumanizing reification that blinds the theorist to the trees for the sake of an imaginary forest.

In short, systems theory is a useful tool for maintenance men who wish to persuade the masses that their comprehensive view of stability can slow down decay and head off revolution. Creators and revolutionaries, on the other hand, might well call such claims repressive.

COMMUNICATIONS THEORY

Cybernetics extends systems theory into *the science of communication and control.* The inputs and outputs become *bits of information* in terms of which the processes of political decision making are traced. The citizen as human being interacting in politics with other human beings vanishes almost totally from the scene of analysis—all that is left of him is his "message." One problem is that mistakes are easily made when the message is mistaken for the individual and his intentions. The greater part of any communication is visual, not spoken. When communications theorists take the spoken word—or even just an abstract summary of many spoken words—as a "bit of information," they are getting less than half the message.

Failures of communication are especially likely when little is known about the background and environment of the individual who sends the message, for it is these that give the message meaning. For example, the Second World War dragged on in the Pacific for months because a surrender message from the Japanese was misunderstood. A Japanese word that meant "to take a stand" was taken as a signal of intransigence because its subtler meaning, "to consider," was not taken into account. Correct understanding would have let the United States know that the Japanese were ready "to consider" coming to terms to end the war.

All communications separated from the individual who communicates pose such dangers. Even in daily life, speaking to a person directly gives us more chances to get across nuances or to explain or backtrack—and thus avoid conflict—than a letter that leaves interpretation totally up to him.

The reason social scientists undertake to separate the individual from his words is that it is easier this way to quantify what is being said. Anything that can be reduced to numbers is easily handled in a closed scientific system of analysis. Ironically, such social scientists do not take into account that the very fact that they have to separate the individual from his words is itself proof that individuals, who after all are the living actors of politics, are not easily quantified. You can quantify the *words* of an individual, but what you may have left is a word game, not the study of living politics.

Information resulting from system outputs in communications theory *feeds back* into the system so that those in control of *steering* it can make adjustments to keep the system going and to stave off *entropy*—the tendency of a closed system to deteriorate. Hence, it is not surprising that the theory of cybernetics or communications emerged from World War II—a time in the political cycle when maintenance men were desperately searching for means to gain control of decay and to restore order in their national and international political systems.

Origins of Communications Theory

The first comprehensive communications theory was developed by Norbert Wiener in *Cybernetics: Control and Communication in the Animal and the Machine* (1948). Wiener's ideas grew out of his observation of wartime advances in electronic processes such as sonar, radar, radar-directed anti-aircraft fire, and the message-coding and communications networks that these developments required.[10] Karl Deutsch, the first political scientist to apply the ideas of cybernetics to a model of politics in *Nationalism and Social Communication* (1953) and *The Nerves of Government* (1963), interpreted communications to be literally "the nerves of government." His theory focuses on how decisions are made as seen through message flows between decision makers, message storage and retrieval, and the reactions of decision makers. He claims that such a cybernetic focus brings fruitful insights as to how political systems are controlled, how they survive, how they change.[11] Needless to say, such cybernetic models are handy tools for maintenance men in times of decay who want to recover political stability through communications control.

Communications Gone Wrong

The Watergate affair is the most notorious recent example of what happens when politicians take into account only those aspects of reality encompassed by communications theory. Top maintenance men in the Nixon Administration thought that system stability could be maintained by eliminating or destroying dysfunctional bits of information on the one hand, and by trying to bug or control all information affecting their future power on the other. They supported the use of microphones to get "instant feedback" on possible political opposition, regardless of private rights.

Even here the application of simple communications theory is a dubious enterprise—as most of the Watergate participants kept "explaining" at the hearings what they really meant by the words that the communications system had recorded. In doing so they endorsed a more human method of analysis, such as the sociology of knowledge or phenomenology, which gets into people's heads to find out what they mean, recognizing that where you stand in a system gives you different perspectives on what you and others do. But it was exactly such a human approach that many of the Watergaters earlier on had refused to make available to their victims, when they imposed their personal "objective" view onto a world populated by diverse others.

It is no accident, in our apolitical era of technological efficiency, that President Nixon relied heavily upon public relations men, telecommunications experts, and lawyers brought up more on theories of communications control than on philosophy, ethics, or the Bill of Rights. Ironically, communications theory can perhaps best explain how fast entropy set in on Nixon's White House system when Watergate leaks emerged—bits of information undermining one Nixon aide after another. The more White House officials tried to cover up Watergate information leaks, the more deeply the president's aides and the president himself became implicated in the scandal, as the cover-up failed and the press refused to be intimidated. But Nixon's men failed to learn from experience. Even after the Watergate affair was exposed, the United States Information Agency was directed by the Nixon Administration to carefully monitor the use of its equipment by foreign television networks in broadcasts concerning Watergate. This kind of political behavior is about as effective as deodorizing horseshit, after the horse has fled the barn, to hide the fact that such an animal has ever inhabited the place.

Uses of Communications Theory

Since communications theory carries much of the theoretical baggage of systems theory with it, it's a particularly handy tool for well-heeled maintenance men who seek to stabilize their position by controlling information that might undermine it. As such, communications theory remains systems-oriented rather than individual-oriented, and individual freedom may end up losing out to Know-It-Alls who seek to control it with cybernetic machines. But if used with this danger in mind, cybernetics does give the political thinker a paradigm that is open-ended to change (though with a stability bias) and that has the advantage of focusing on the information flow between individual decision makers.

MATHEMATICAL MODELS

One day not long ago, two ants—Felix and Phoenix—met on a path. They came to an abrupt halt to prevent a head-on collision. Who would step back for whom? That was the political problem to be solved.

Cause or Correlation

Fortunately, there was a political scientist nearby who just happened to be working on a thesis—"A Stochastic Mathematical Model of Political Conflict Among Ants"—for his Ph.D. degree. Simultaneously Felix and Phoenix sought his advice as to how to resolve their dispute. He answered by giving them a hypothesis.

> **A hypothesis is a tentative proposition that is derived from a theory and relates two or more variables. Meaningful scientific hypotheses can be tested in the real world.**

The political scientist, Short-Sighted Sherlock, had a cybernetic theory or paradigm to explain the political behavior of ants. He believed that somewhere Out There was a closed deductive mathematical system of interrelated hypotheses that would perfectly explain all possible conflicts arising between ants.

> **Thinkers using mathematical models hope to find closed deductive**

systems of hypotheses that will explain all possible behavior.

In a display of methodological overkill, Sherlock used a general theory of communication overload to explain this clash of individuals. According to Sherlock's "General Theory of Feeler Static," feeler friction in any ant community was bound to be great enough to make political conflict inevitable. Some ants would be forced to put up or shut up. The question was—which? The Short-Sighted hypothesis was, "*If* ant A had a shorter expected life span than ant B, *then* ant B would give in to ant A." The reason was simple: the older you get, the less you have to lose, and the more stubborn you become.

Well, at first this hypothesis made Felix, the male winged ant, feel very good. For everybody knows that male winged ants live shorter than any other kind of ant—female or neuter. Felix reasoned, "I am variable A—the *independent variable*—in the hypothesis, since my life span is clearly shorter than that of this wingless female (Phoenix). She is, therefore, variable B—the *dependent variable*. Hence, what she will do depends entirely upon what I do. I *cause her to behave* the way she does."

Alas, the feelings of Phoenix did not go along with this fine winged male-chauvinist ant. "Is he *really* a male?" she asked. "To me he looks more like a neuter disguised in wings. And everybody knows that neuter and female ants have about the same life span, especially in our community. Therefore, we both have an equal chance of becoming A, the independent causal variable, so why should *I* give in?"

Short-Sighted Sherlock became worried as he watched Felix and Phoenix get redder and redder with anger, their communicative feelers going crazy with static. "I've got it," he thought. "I must liberate them from this conflict by changing my rigid *causal* hypothesis to a *correlational* hypothesis."

Causal "If-then" hypotheses imply that every time independent variable A exists, the predicted relationship to B will NECESSARILY follow. Correlational "the more-the more (or less)" hypotheses claim less: the more times A exists, the more times B is LIKELY to follow.

Sherlock's less short-sighted hypothesis was, "The more ant A thinks ant B will die sooner and vice versa, the less conflict is *likely* to result and the happier the ants will *probably* be." Felix and Phoenix rejoiced at hearing this more flexible hypothesis. For now each could secretly pretend the other would probably die sooner, feel sorry and step aside accordingly. They both learned from the experience that a good male chauvinist is not necessarily a dead one . . .

The difference between claiming a *causal* relationship and a *correlation* in an hypothesis is critically important. To say "If President Noxin scratches his nose, then a bell will ring in FBI headquarters" implies that *every* scratch will *cause* (or be followed by) a ring. On the other hand, the claim "the more scratches, the more rings" merely implies a high probability of a ring following a scratch. "If-then" causal statements are more rigid and harder to prove than "the more-the more" correlational hypotheses. Furthermore, mathematics has provided deductive rules for correlational hypotheses that can be turned into equations and statistical formulas if the quantity of the variables or elements in the hypothesis can be determined.[12] Hubert Blalock shows how to do this concisely in *Theory Construction—From Verbal to Mathematical Formulations* (1969).

Advantages and Disadvantages of Math Models

The use of mathematical models usually implies that a closed deductive system could, in theory, explain all possible cases. Moreover, it assumes that variables (such as people) can be turned into numbers. Often such systems-thinking and quantification end up in reification and in de-emphasizing the human element in the equation. Thus, in Chapter VII it was shown that to use the zero-sum model in game theory as applied to politics, it is necessary to assume (1) a closed system or game exists, and (2) whatever player A wins in the game, player B *must lose exactly*.

Political theorists such as William Riker have argued that such zero-sum game situations are the essence of politics. But rarely is a political game situation *exact* enough in its payoffs to fit this model perfectly. Furthermore, closed zero-sum thinking usually becomes a negative self-fulfilling prophecy that kills the possibility of cooperation. A politics for human beings, defining politics as a social act that seeks to satisfy human needs, makes the opposite assumption—that all political situations are *potentially* open-ended, variable-sum games in which both political parties can gain *more* in the long run by cooperating. Needless to say, closed deductive mathematical models are not usually applicable to such open-ended variable-sum thinking.

Mathematical models are useful in the study of politics (1) to create hypothetical logical situations and thereby generate hypotheses and theories (such as simulations and game theory); (2) to order political information that is easily turned into numbers into hypotheses related to a general theory (such as voting statistics and behavior, economic and military statistics, or population growth trends); and (3) to work backwards from the outcomes of past political situations to see how "rational" the participants were according to a mathematical model that could have maximized their interests. An example of the last use is analyzing President Kennedy and Premier Khrushchev's eyeball-to-eyeball decision making in the 1962 Cuban missile crisis.

Drawbacks involved in using math models are (1) they tend to assume a closed, deductive system in order to explain human political behavior that is often open-ended, nonrational and unsystematic; (2) they often tempt the theorist to turn into numbers variables and values that are not easily quantifiable (such as "power," "lives," or "body-counts," or "status"); and (3) the systems and numbers reification resulting from the use of such models can dehumanize politics and implies a conservative bias.

The Irrational Basis of Rationality

The difficulty with mathematical models is that they begin with abstractions rather than with individual human beings—they are in the system-first camp. Furthermore, such models tend to assume that human beings will behave rationally, and that "rational" has a universal definition that crosses all cultures. Unfortunately, what is "rational" for a man living in a Latin country who "works to live" may not be perceived as rational by a person living in an Anglo-Saxon country who "lives to work," and vice versa. For rationality involves not only a means-end calculation, but a culturally conditioned way of thinking or calculating as well. Thus in describing the nature of Zen Buddhist thinking as compared with the linear, grasping nature of Western thought, philosopher Alan Watts writes:

> One must start by "getting the feel" of relativity, and by knowing that life is not a situation from which there is anything to be grasped or gained—as if it were something which one approaches from outside, like a pie or a barrel of beer. To succeed is always to fail—in the sense that the more one succeeds in anything, the greater is the need to go on succeeding. To eat is to survive to be hungry.[13]

Human beings can use mathematical models to create consistent hypotheses and theories once a basic value assumption or cultural context has been assumed. But without spelling out such individual human assumptions first, mathematical models become meaningless voids. Thus the mathematician Kurt Gödel has given us a rigorous proof of the fact that every logical system rests on at least one premise, or assumption, whose validity it cannot demonstrate.[14] In other words, there is no such thing as a totally self-contained, self-sufficient, logical system of rationality. Mathematical models without references to human assumptions outside themselves are just a form of nonsense.

INCONCLUSIONS

System-oriented theories of politics tend to be deductive and stability-oriented. That is, systems theorists tend to assume the existence of a system or set of hypotheses related to system-stability or equilibrium and then to look at specific political cases to find evidence to prove or disprove such theories. The imagined system becomes the camera or lens that determines the selection and colors of the still snapshots that it captures. Cybernetic systems theorists do the same thing, but with a movie camera. As such, systems-oriented theories are useful tools for maintenance men who seek to keep their political system going, regardless of what happens to any particular individual or minority of individuals in it—some trees must be cleared for the sake of the forest.

Systems theorists root out odd trees to save forests.

**Self-oriented theorists open
the boundaries of forests to
save odd trees.**

"System-first" approaches imply a totalitarianism of thought. For the primacy of the system means that any individual human being becomes secondary to the goals of system preservation and system stability. And since individual selves are not focused upon, their development as human beings, in terms of their universal needs, becomes secondary as well. The development of the existing system, as it is abstractly understood by governmental and academic elites, becomes the end as well as the beginning. In the process, systems theories dehumanize individual selves for the sake of greater theoretical scope and consistency within the theorist's view of existing reality.

But the meaning of "reality" depends upon who sees it and where he sits. The experience of meaning is made possible by the affect or feeling we attach to our actions and events. As Camus noted, man's thought is his nostalgia. And one's nostalgia depends upon how well he is fed, brought up, educated, and treated in existing reality *as he sees it.* Some experience existing reality as inconsistent, unjust, unreasonable, and humiliating. Most human beings are not privileged enough to sit in a quiet ivory tower or to have enough time to work out coherent theories of social reality. The politics of everyday life for the majority of men means catch as catch can in fulfilling their own personal needs. Whether this view is egoistic or not is realistically beside the point. What matters is that most human beings recognize politics as meaningful only to the extent that they can relate political events to their own personal needs.

REFERENCES

1. For a lucid discussion of this dispute, see W. G. Runciman's incisive *Social Science and Political Theory* (London: Cambridge University Press, 1963), Chapter 1.

2. Colin M. Turnbull, *The Mountain People* (New York: Simon and Schuster, 1972).

3. David Easton, "The Current Meaning of Behavioralism," in *The Limits of Behavioralism in Political Science* (Philadelphia: The American Academy of Political and Social Science, 1962), p. 8.

4. Henry S. Kariel, *Open Systems: Arenas for Political Action* (Itasca, Illinois: F. E. Peacock, 1968), p. 5.

5. Francesca M. Cancian, "Functional Analysis: Varieties of Functional Analysis," in *The International Encyclopedia of the Social Sciences*, vol. 6, ed. David Shils (New York: Macmillan, 1968), p. 29.

6. Robert Merton, "Manifest and Latent Functions," in *Social Theory and Social Structure* [Glencoe, Ill.: Free Press (orig. 1949) 1957]. Merton, a sociologist, provided a structural-functional paradigm for other social scientists in need of a theory.

7. Morton A. Kaplan, "Systems Theory and Political Science," *Social Research* 35, no. 1 (Spring 1968), p. 30.

8. Charles McClelland, cited in K. J. Holsti, "Retreat from Utopia: International Relations Theory, 1945–1950," paper presented at the Sixty-sixth Annual Meeting of the American Political Science Association, Los Angeles, California, September 8–12, 1970, p. 10.

9. See David Easton, *The Political System* (New York: Knopf, 1953) and Morton Kaplan, *System and Process in International Politics* (New York: Basic Books, 1957).

10. Norbert Wiener, *Cybernetics: Control and Communication in the Animal and the Machine* (Cambridge, Mass: MIT Press, 1948).

11. Karl Deutsch, *Nationalism and Social Communication* (Cambridge, Mass.: MIT Press, 1953), and *The Nerves of Government* (New York: The Free Press, Macmillan, 1963).

12. See Hubert Blalock, *Theory Construction—From Verbal to Mathematical Formulations* (Englewood, N.J.: Prentice-Hall, 1969).

13. Alan W. Watts, *The Way of Zen* (New York: Vintage Books, 1965), p. 116.

14. See E. Nagel and J. R. Newman, "Gödel's Proof," *Scientific American* 196, no. 6 (June 1956), pp. 71–86.

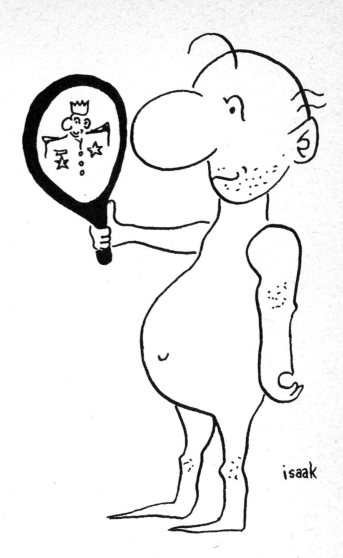

isaak

11 **Wherein the reader experiences the alternative to thinking politics through the system: thinking politics through the self. Moreover, he sees how different the self looks through behaviorism, behavioralism, and postbehavioralism, represented by B. F. Skinner, decision-making theory, and phenomenology respectively.**

11 Thinking Politics Through Your Self

In the late twentieth century, human beings have become cynical about large systems—of thought or of politics. For such systems were efficiently used for the most inhumane of purposes in World War II. The more politically aware people become of the tension between existing political systems and their own human needs, the more they tend to accept self-oriented as opposed to system-oriented views of reality. But collectively—especially among social scientists—political awareness of self-oriented theories came slowly. The classical emphasis upon the importance of the individual self and human needs had to be excavated from dead social facts and technological reifications that kept people down to keep states up.

In social and political science, the awareness of the importance of the political self developed in three stages: behaviorism, behavioralism, and postbehavioralism. Behaviorist thinkers tried to view the human self with cool objectivity—as they would rats or other animals. Behavior*alists* pried into the *human* self a bit more, asking not only what stimulates people to react in a certain way, but how their feelings and thoughts affected such actions. Finally, in the 1970s, social science has entered a postbehavioralist period in which the true position of the human self in society has begun to be exposed: postbehavioralists and others building a new political science ask, What is the relevance of this social situation or political event for the majority of human beings? Is it just? Does it help to frustrate or to satisfy human needs? Whose needs? This book is a postbehavioral, though not anti-behavioral, attempt to find a way to answer such questions.

Behaviorist theorists are those who believe that individual behavior can be sufficiently explained merely by analyzing what *stimulates* man *as animal* and observing how he *responds,* without any reference to the mental events or feelings or values that may be present inside the individual. Behaviorists are self-oriented, in that their focus is upon the behavior of particular individuals. But in their theory they treat individuals as black boxes, to be kept as closed as Pandora's box to prevent unpredictable subjective feelings and thoughts from popping out. Such theories date back at least to the second decade of this century—to John B. Watson's theories that an *objective* science of human psychology could only be developed through S-R (stimulus-response) psychology. This approach does not attempt to investigate what goes on inside the "black box" of the mind, but focuses upon *what individuals do under different conditions.*[1]

S-R behaviorists focus on what men do, not on what men are. They tend to see human beings as

**conditioned black boxes. And
human beings respond accordingly.**

Philosophically speaking, behaviorism grew out of empiricism and logical positivism. That is, validity or truth, according to this kind of thinking, is only what can be concretely sensed or measured. What you see, smell, or touch counts, and counts only insofar as a means exists to measure this phenomenon. Ideas such as love, hate, justice, or self-actualization are either empty concepts or scientifically meaningless subjective notions.

Behaviorism, based solely on the analytic approach, holds that all behavior phenomena are ultimately reducible to physical and chemical events. The human organism is viewed as a physical object governed by the same principles as other physical objects. Mind and purpose have no place in this theory. By eliminating the intuitions of the mind, behaviorists hoped to get rid of the mind-body problem and create a science of psychology as rigorously empirical as the natural sciences.

Clearly a politics for human beings, based on distinctly human needs and values, cannot accept the black-box assumptions of behaviorism. For although behaviorism is self-oriented to the extent that it focuses on individual human behavior, human beings lose all personality and distinction in a theory that reduces them to the same status as the atoms of physics or chemistry. The intentions and motivations of human beings—aspects of behavior so vital in politics—cannot be included in the framework of the behaviorists. Yet behavioristic thinking still dominates the psychological assumptions of many social scientists, particularly due to the great influence of the best-known behaviorist of our times, B. F. Skinner.

**B. F. Skinner:
An Example of
Behaviorism**

Burrhus Frederic Skinner has become the best-known American behaviorist in the late twentieth century through his controversial theories of social control. During his education Skinner became intrigued by animal behavior and learning and spent years studying rats and pigeons. Soon he transferred this stimulus-response behavior observed among other animals to human beings, arguing that "behavior is shaped and maintained by its consequences," and that "little or nothing remains for autonomous man to do and receive credit for doing."

For Skinner, a human being is merely the sum of his past behavior patterns, and his future behavior is merely a projected consequence of what he expects to follow from his past experiences. This assumption leads to Skinner's theory of operant conditioning. This theory holds that people can learn a new behavior—and love it—simply by being induced to carry out the behavioral operation over and over. Pleasurable or painful stimuli may be used but ultimately the behavior is its own reward. Enter, for a moment, Skinner's controversial utopia, *Walden II*—a novel about a community based on the principles of behavioral engineering and positive reinforcement of certain stimuli:

"But when a particular emotion is no longer a useful part of a behavioral repertoire, we proceed to eliminate it."

"Yes, but how?"

"It's simply a matter of behavioral engineering," said Frazier.

. . .

"Some of us learn control, more or less by accident. The rest of us go all our lives not even understanding how it is possible, and blaming our failure on being born the wrong way."

"How do you build up a tolerance to an annoying situation?" I said.

"Oh, for example, by having the children 'take' a more and more painful shock, or drink cocoa with less and less sugar in it until a bitter concoction can be savored without a bitter face."

"But jealousy or envy—you can't administer them in graded doses," I said.

"And why not? Remember, we control the social environment, too, at this age. That's why we get our ethical training in early. Take this case. A group of children arrive home after a long walk tired and hungry. They're expecting supper; they find, instead, that it's time for a lesson in self-control: they must stand for five minutes in front of steaming bowls of soup.

"The assignment is accepted like a problem in arithmetic. Any groaning or complaining is a wrong answer. Instead, the children begin at once to work upon themselves to avoid any unhappiness during the delay. One of them may make a joke of it. We encourage a sense of humor as a good way of not taking an annoyance seriously. . . .

"In a later stage we forbid all social devices. No songs, no jokes—merely silence."[2]

Later in *Walden II*, Skinner has Frazier argue that "democracy is the spawn of despotism"—the tyranny of the masses, and that the only ideal alternative is an elite board of behavioral managers or controllers. The goal of these managers—or maintenance men—is to interpret the genetic endowment with which we are born and then administer the appropriate positive or negative reinforcement or stimuli for the best interests of the evolution of all.

In a speech in December 1972, Skinner argued that the problem with American society is that institutional sanctions are breaking down and that most people are living for the present, for immediate short-term need gratification. Further, he continued, this selfish malaise is encouraged by the existentialists and phenomenologists, whose focus on the here and now prevents them from planning for the future and may help to undermine our very survival. Such decadent philosophies, he noted, are characteristic of times going from maintenance to decay.[3]

In questioning from the audience, it became clear that Skinner was not familiar with the future orientations so important in much of the literature of existentialism and phenomenology. Furthermore, one of the authors in that audience had the uncomfortable impression that Skinner has never lived in the present at all, that he is merely a behavioral link between past responses and future contingencies, forsaking the present for an imagined future. Likewise, he leaves out everyday human feelings in his theory for the sake of "necessary" evolutionary stimulus-response patterns that he would have behavioral engineers impose on us all.

In *Beyond Freedom and Dignity,* Skinner argues that the struggle of men for freedom is not due to a will to be free, but to behavioral processes in the human organism that seek to avoid adverse features of the environment. Skinner believes that men should spend less time worrying about illusions of the mind such as freedom and dignity and more time analyzing the kinds of control to which they are exposed. Or, in the terms of a politics for human beings, they should become research assistants for technological Know-It-Alls or maintenance men.

Note that the focus of Skinner as a behaviorist is not upon human needs or values, but upon the social facts of control. Our question is not whether human behavior should be studied or not, but what the researcher's first assumptions should be. Both social controls and human needs must be analyzed together to define political tensions. But political consciousness of such tensions begins in an individual's mind as perceived human needs. Politics begins with an idea.

Skinner's conclusion from his study of operant conditioning is that individuals are shaped by their environment—by stimuli outside of themselves. As a result, he concludes, they have neither freedom nor dignity. On the contrary, anti-behaviorists might argue that conditioning works exactly because human beings will create and attribute their own meanings and feelings for behaviors repeated long enough. For example, sociologists ranging from Durkheim, studying suicide, to Peter Berger, studying religion, have observed that human beings cannot live without imbuing their world with meaning. Their observation indicates that the picture of human learning is much more complex than Skinner suggests. While human beings may be conditioned to learn a behavior through negative or positive "rewards," the source of the inner meaning they attribute to that behavior is themselves.*

BEHAVIORALISM
The Black Box Opens

isaak

Social scientists interested in what men think and feel as well as in what they do were critical of behaviorism, although they respected its attempt to be scientific. Such thinkers transformed stimulus-response behaviorism into stimulus-organism-response (S-O-R) behavioralism by opening up the black box of the human mind.

> **S-R behaviorists became S-O-R behavioralists when they began to feel for the human organism.**

In political science, behavioralism soon came to stand for a movement away from historical or legal approaches to politics and towards the scientific method, towards studying how human beings

---

*The degree to which workers supposedly well conditioned into performing onerous tasks actually attribute private meanings to their conditioned behavior is demonstrated in over 130 interviews in Studs Terkel, *Working: People Talk About What They Do All Day and How They Feel About What They Do.* (New York: Pantheon, 1974).

actually behave. As a movement in political thinking, behavioralism rejected mere speculation, advocated the need for empirical evidence to support theories, and, most significantly, *focused on the individual as the basic unit of analysis* in the political system. This movement was stimulated by government support for social science research during and following World War II.

Techniques for analyzing propaganda soon were used to develop survey methods for measuring public opinion and individual attitudes. Values and ethics were momentarily suspended from the scientific analysis of facts, and scholars assumed it was possible to separate the *normative* (value judgments) from the *empirical* (fact judgments). Many were optimistic that a pure science of politics could be developed, much like physics—a systematized science with quantitative methods and empirical rigor. Furthermore, behavioralism encouraged political scientists to open their departments and to become interdisciplinary—to learn from biologists, sociologists, and psychologists. Structural-functionalism, systems theory, and communications theory were all offspring of this interdisciplinary behavioral movement.[4]

Decision-Making Theory: An Example of Behavioralism

One of the most fruitful developments of the behavioral movement was decision-making theory. Decision making is a useful focus for a politics for human beings, since it analyzes individual behavior within the context of the social environment and synthesizes the self and system views. Also, decision-making theory was one of the first approaches in American political science to draw fully upon the insights of neighboring disciplines, such as sociology and psychology. Decision-making theorists focus upon how human beings maximize values or utilities in different sociopolitical roles.

Decision-making theorists focus on maximizing values through roles according to the probabilities of who usually gets what in the political system.

One of the common assumptions of behavioralists is that facts or empirical matters can be separated from values or normative matters—at least during the period of investigation. This fact-value or is-ought split led to the development of two schools in decision theory: *decision analysis,* which analyzed the facts of past decisions, and *decision theory* proper, which created rational models of how human decisions ideally ought to be made. For example, some political decision analysts such as Richard C. Snyder, H. W. Bruck, and Burton Sapin examined past foreign policy decisions to derive a framework of social and psychological variables that would help them to analyze future decisions empirically.[5]

On the other hand, Herbert Simon, a public administration specialist, broke the ground for decision theory proper by constructing a theory of rational choice in order to explain the influences upon decision making in an organizational environment.[6] Eventually, of course, the "is" and "ought" theorists got together to create a synthesis—a model of decision making that separates values from facts but allows human beings to weigh both the "is" and "ought" in the decision process. This more sophisticated theory, which became very popular in schools of business administration (at Harvard in particular), is easily illustrated.

Take the case of Alphonse P. Cracker III. Cracker has just learned that a *role* is a specific pattern of social conduct that provides the basis for potential power or *potency*. This concept is useful, since as a budding decision theorist Alphonse has always believed that the only road to self-actualization for him is rationally manipulating others to maximize his own values in social problem-solving situations. After years of practicing at game theory and simulation—sophisticated offspring of decision theory—Alphonse has become more simple in his old age. He has developed three basic rules that are guaranteed to maximize the values of any Cracker who is not content to remain just an ordinary Cracker:

Decision Theory Made Simple

(1) List all the available acts or alternatives open to you.
(2) List all the possible states of the environment or decision contexts (actions assigned to you in your role in a system and other social facts).
(3) Calculate the cost of the consequences of each act in the event of each possible decision context, choosing that alternative that costs least and maximizes your most important value or utility.[7]

This decision-making approach assumes that the alternative acts and possible decision contexts are independent of one another and can be calculated separately. Furthermore, it assumes that man is basically rational and can maximize his values by calculating the *subjective* probabilities of the decision contexts with which he will be confronted.

Consider the case of Cracker's last chance to become more than an everyday Cracker. His role: that of an aging astronaut. His decision context: module commander of the last Apollo moon mission that the taxpayers will tolerate. Cracker steps into the rocket—Sisyphus XIII —bound for the moon. All the experts tell him that the objective reliability of his rocket is 99 percent (only one rocket in a hundred should fail).

But just as the rocket is about to take off, Alphonse signals Mission Control that he is dubious, that maybe the life of an everyday Cracker isn't so bad after all, and that he wants his supervisor to shoot off a few rockets just like his to give him courage. The first rocket is shot off, exploding in mid-air. The second rocket gets off the ground but then fizzles into the sea. The third rocket disintegrates on its pad.

At this point, Alphonse thinks the costs of the probable consequences of the moon-shot alternative are not worth the possible gains.

In his mind the so-called objective 99 percent probability of success fell to 70 percent with the first failure, then to 40 percent with the second, and to 20 percent with the third. Finally, he decided that the *subjective* probability of success was so low that he would not risk his life. As the decision theorist Ronald Howard points out: "We should consider probability as the reading of a kind of mental thermometer that measures uncertainty rather than temperature. The reading goes up as data accumulates that tends to increase the likelihood of the event under consideration."[8]

Although decision theory has the advantage of focusing on human choice in social problem-solving situations, it has some problems. A human being is not always rational, he does not always know what his value priorities are, and often he is not self-disciplined or educated enough to perceive the subjective probabilities of his situation accurately and thus maximize his values. People, as human beings, must first begin with a more basic approach that helps them analyze what they want and how they see their situations—a postbehavioralist approach such as phenomenology.

isaak

INVITATION

Prepare a skit with one or two other people, illustrating the application of one of the behaviorist or behavioralist theories above to a social problem that interests you. What values does your choice of this theory imply? Does it uncover the meaning of the problem to those involved? Can it help to solve the problem?

Postbehavioralism as a movement toward a new political science sprang up in the late 1960s out of the tension some political scientists felt between human needs and social facts. The social facts were a massive American war in Vietnam, injustice and alienation at home, and ghetto and youth riots (as well as police riots).

The political science profession either dealt with these problems not at all or studied aspects of them "objectively." Behind the banner of "objectivity," postbehavioralists argued, lurked an unwillingness and inability to criticize what was happening. Merely describing "objectively" what was going on had the social impact of endorsing the status quo. Furthermore, some political scientists engaged in so-called policy research, using their behavioral tools to help the army, the Central Intelligence Agency, the police, the president, Congress, and corporations—but never the North Vietnamese army, the poor, the black, the unorganized.

Higher human needs—like love, self-esteem, and self-actualization—were not on the agenda of American political scientists. Neither were basic human needs, like food and shelter for those who did not have them. Feeling the tension between what political science was

POSTBEHAVIORALISM AND THE NEW POLITICAL SCIENCE

doing and what they felt it ought to do, some political scientists first demanded that something be done and finally organized a counter-movement calling for "relevance."

Behavioralists and traditionalists counterattacked. "Relevance for what?" they asked, insisting that science must be neutral. On becoming president of the American Political Science Association and its 15,000 members, political scientist Heinz Eulau said:

> . . . we are not set up or organized for political action or the propagation of political points of view. . . . My objection to political action groups in the Association is not that they may have certain aims, some of which I probably share, but that they seek to use, and I think, misuse the Association as an instrument for the achievement of their political aims. . . .[9]

To this postbehavioralists replied that the association had already been politicized for nearly seventy years, in that its activities and the research of its members supported the existing political establishment, a system of social inequity at home, and aggression abroad.

Most postbehavioralists claim to be as scientific as their more orthodox colleagues. Many have even adopted behavioral tools. What they demand of their colleagues, however, is a recognition that *all* research is political. But most orthodox political scientists persist in drawing the line between "objective" research and politicized research.

The outcome of the battle is not evident. The postbehavioralists clearly have on their side some of the great theoreticians of science, including Immanuel Kant and Max Weber. But science is moved not simply by theory but also by financial and institutional support. Access to research-funding institutions, including governments and private foundations, is retained mainly by scholars espousing objectivity.

The development of postbehavioralism can be analyzed both in terms of ideas and in terms of politics.

The Ideas of Postbehavioral Political Science

In terms of ideas, the issue revolves around the meaning of "objectivity."

Objectivity implies studying things "as they really are," without fear or favor, bias or prejudice. It is the modus operandi of the detective who asks the victim of a crime for "just the facts, Ma'am!" To this the victim might reply: "But what facts? *All* the facts? My life story? Or just the facts relevant to the crime?" And the victim might add: "What are you going to *do* with the facts once you get them? Am I going to have to get involved?" For example, a girl who is raped by a fellow worker in an organization can sometimes lose her job by pressing charges and giving police "all the facts."

Questions—whether put by police or scholars—are always asked from a specific point of view. They are relevant to a problem that the investigator defines. As such they are *subjective,* as philosopher Immanuel Kant and sociologist Max Weber point out.

Kant's writings are difficult to present briefly. But one commentator put Kant's point this way: "Something of what Kant is after is plain enough. We can never attain knowledge without asking the right questions, and the rightness of the question depends as much on us as on the things."[10]

Recall that Max Weber later related Kant's point to research in the social sciences, writing: "There is no absolutely 'objective' scientific analysis of . . . 'social phenomena' independent of special and 'one-sided' viewpoints according to which . . . they are selected, analyzed and organized for expository purposes." And: "All knowledge of cultural reality . . . is always knowledge from *particular points of view*."[11]

Results of an investigation are similarly *subjective*. Since the investigation was originally designed to help specific individuals—the police or political scientists—solve their problem, the results are likely to help those individuals, not victims, criminals, or people quite unlike political scientists. A police investigation *may* be useful to the victims of crimes or even to criminals, but first they would have to translate results set to solve police problems into results designed to solve their own personal problems. Similarly, government and business professionals are more likely than the ordinary citizen to understand the research results of political science professionals, because they share professional languages and common interests and define political problems similarly.

The only thing objective about research is the investigation process itself, postbehavioralists argue. Once the problem is defined and once we are conscious of whom the solution is intended to help, we must proceed scientifically. That is, we must consistently follow the inner logic of the research process. If we do not, we produce results useless to ourselves or anyone else.

Postbehavioralists tend to ask themselves three questions about their research:

1. Why did I define the problem the way I did?
2. Am I scientific (logical) in my actual research?
3. Who can benefit from my research? To whom are my results relevant?

In contrast, they argue, behavioralists and others who claim "objectivity" in their research fail to ask the first and the last questions. The term "objectivity" veils the fact that research is always research *for* somebody. The concern for relevance *and* science is demonstrated in the following example of how a conscious postbehavioral political scientist sees research:

Suppose a man is attempting to escape from a burning house. He finds the door locked, several times over, and possibly jammed as well. *(Subjective point of departure.)* In a panic, he claws at the locks and wrenches on the knob, but, as suddenly, by an enormous effort of will, he calms himself, holds in suspense his awareness of the threat to his life and even the physical sensations of the heat on his back, and looks at the door coldly: that is, with impersonal objectivity. *(Beginning the cool inner logic of science.)* Moreover, he constitutes the locks, bolts, hinges, and the door itself as so many objects in a world governed by the laws of mechanics. On this basis he might then construct a series of quick experiments to determine when all the locks were thrown open and where, precisely, the door was jamming. And so forth, until he was able to burst out into a subjectively appreciated freedom. *(Final relevance of research.)*[12]

The Politics of Postbehavioral Political Science

Politically, criticism of the old political science found its most successful organization in the Caucus for a New Political Science, which defined itself as a "broad coalition of scholars of varied backgrounds, professional interests, and political preference, united in intellectual commitments vital to the profession."

The Caucus was not necessarily directed against the tools of behavioralism, but its members demanded consciousness of the reasons and purposes of research, as well as social conscience. In 1973 the Caucus came within 59 votes of electing its own candidate as president of the American Political Science Association. In a statement of purpose, the Caucus shows a commitment to diversity:

> The Caucus believes in free inquiry and opposes any orthodoxy. Scholars should respond to social as well as methodological concerns, studying peace as well as war, revolution as well as stability, corruption as well as institutionalization. The profession must leave room for normative theorists and 'value-free' empiricists, qualitatives and quantitativists, gadflies and technicians.[13]

In an interview for *Politics for Human Beings,* Professor H. Mark Roelofs of New York University, the first Caucus chairman, recounts how the Caucus got started:

PfHB:* Professor Roelofs, you were the first chairman of the Caucus for a New Political Science. We have suggested that politics can be understood as developing in five steps. Could we test this against your organization's history? For example, we suggest that politics arises out of a tension between human needs and social facts. . . .

Roelofs: The two graduate students who founded the Caucus at the 1967 Chicago convention of the APSA certainly exhibited that kind of tension. What created this tension was their feeling that American political science, the profession they were about to join, had become increasingly irrelevant to what was happening politically to the United States and in the United States.

PfHB: After defining what they want, people who engage in politics usually try to identify and mobilize others who want the same thing . . .

Roelofs: That, too, happened. The two graduate students and their friends called a meeting of people who were unhappy with the profession and the nature of the general program at the convention. A collection of people showed up, some actively interested and others coming along largely out of curiosity.

The first meeting was attended by a hundred people and prompted a discussion about a possible name for the group . . .

*Politics for Human Beings.

Names make social relationships more real.

. . . and the name "Caucus for a New Political Science" was adopted, in large part because at that point we were nearly unanimous that we wanted to be a group within the APSA and were not anxious to found a competing organization.

That night a second, broader meeting was held. It was attended by a large group of people.

Organizing and mobilizing others strengthens a political relationship.

The intent was to broaden support and hear the reports of those of us who had been asked to draft statements of principles and purpose.

Politics begins with an idea— it helps to spell it out.

What we had been talking about was the fact that the convention panels, and therefore the profession, had totally ignored the war in Vietnam and the riots that occurred that summer. We wanted that corrected not only at the next convention but in the profession's activities all year long.

At that meeting, one of the graduate students, Sanford Levinson, again took the chair, but as the meeting developed he announced that he and some friends had to leave—to hear the annual address by the president of the association. Quite a few of us decided not to leave—we didn't want to hear the president—and to push the formation of our own group.

PfHB: Entry into political activity often depends on motivation, even personality, in Harold Lasswell's sense that people with inner tensions often displace these onto public objects and in this way become political leaders. Was the fact that the actual founders of the Caucus temporarily withdrew at a crucial point and that you and others went on a matter of interest or personality?

Roelofs: More personality. And also age. And social circumstance. If you're a guy who is young, without the security of tenure, and come from an Ivy League school with a tradition of caution—as a lot of the original founders did—you're more likely to be uncertain, in a completely forgiveable way, on where and how far to go. I had tenure, I had made my bets long ago, and I knew what was important and unimportant to me—and apparently conveyed that to some of those who hung on. That's how I became chairman.

> **Personality makes a difference
> as to who becomes political
> and how far they'll go.**

The main point of that meeting, however, was the decision to keep the Caucus within the association.

PfHB: Doesn't that already indicate a commitment that you had figured out what the game was in the political environment of the association—and that you were willing to play the game?

Roelofs: Not so much a willingness to play the establishment's game. What motivated us was professional ideals. We wanted to remain political scientists and were unwilling to give up our identity. We believed the profession had an important and respectable role to play in society.

PfHB: What happened next in 1967?

Roelofs: The result of the second meeting was a third the next day. More than 300 people showed up.

At that time a lot of business was done toward trying to define ourselves on two fronts.

> **When doing politics,
> it helps to know who you are
> and what you want.**

I pushed very hard to try to get the group to put together some kind of structure: an executive committee, to be elected, with a defined number of people and officers. There was a considerable amount of opposition from people who were saying we were aping the establishment mode of doing things and who wanted a more free-flowing pattern. This was a position I thought amounted to patterns so free-flowing that there would be no responsibility and no authority for guiding the institution or doing anything outside the institution. Without that organizational structure we could not have been any kind of force inside the APSA.

> **Politics, reform, revolution
> are not likely to succeed
> without organization.**

The other point was to get an idea as to what we should do as a group. On this my memory is indistinct. There were a lot of things we could do. It seems we made no definite commitments at the time. We thought that if we could pull together an executive committee, largely based in and around New York City, we could work out some schemes over the year. That's pretty much what happened.

As that year went forward, we step by step stumbled into doing one thing or another. We organized a newsletter.

No communications, no politics.

We also decided to try to amend the association constitution in order to commit it to investigating controversial issues. And in time we decided to run a slate of candidates, including one for president-elect. But we mostly tried to define ourselves by organizing our own panels for the next convention to deal with controversial issues of the day. We even tried to do the APSA thing, only better, including meetings in Washington that really hurt our budget. . . . We overestimated our resources. But probably the most interesting thing that happened was how all of us came to a much broader understanding of the issue of relevance.

Defining yourself is a process that is never finished.

What we came to recognize was that the established pattern of behavior in the profession was far from irrelevant; on the contrary, it was all too relevant. We discovered the political character of the APSA. This was a revelation to a lot of us older members who had written off the APSA as a very stuffy institution. What we found was, as the saying goes, that we have met the enemy and he is us. A lot of younger people were far quicker to learn this lesson, and they were impatient and not sympathetic that older people, including myself, had to go through a long process to arrive at the same position.

Politics is getting others to share your ideas.

In the 1968 convention, we then presented a very exciting series of panels on issues of the day—Vietnam, city riots, the nature of the American ideology, the problems of the profession even though we were crowded off into doing them on Saturday, when everybody usually goes home after a week's conventioneering. We drew large crowds, and we shook up the establishment. They reported frankly to me that they were "amazed."

In the process of creation, the postbehavioral movement toward a new political science reveals at least five basic characteristics:

1. Research and thinking should be relevant to human needs and social justice.[14]
2. Researchers must exercise the moral responsibility of deciding who will use their research results—whether action based on their work creates or destroys a community that could satisfy human needs.[15]

3. Researchers have an active obligation to invest beneficial knowledge obtained from the community back into the community.[16]
4. Researchers must return to a creative scientific process that recognizes that all methods are not "objective" in themselves, a method or means always being relevant to a human intention or end.[17]
5. Social scientists must be open to new methods and new ways of seeing, describing, and living social events.[18]

Phenomenology: An Example of Postbehavioralism

Phenomenology begins and ends with the conscious experience of self. By intentionally breaking apart the appearances of everyday life to get at its roots, the phenomenological method allows the human being to question the stock responses and recipe knowledge he's been carefully taught by his society—routines that may well serve more to frustrate than to satisfy his needs. *Phenomenology is the science of getting beneath the appearances of everyday life.* In the late twentieth century, the term usually refers to the study of events *as phenomena* and is associated with a movement in German philosophy centered loosely around Edmund Husserl.[19]

Husserl's phenomenology is logically prior to all empirical science, focusing upon essences of individual experience rather than upon mere "matters of fact." The method is reductionist. The investigator "brackets out" the unnecessary to arrive at the essences or essential aspects of everyday life as experienced and reported by the people living it. The phenomenologist asks one question of the factual world of everyday life: "What are the fundamental assumptions of everyday life without which such life is not thinkable or doable?"

In asking this question, the phenomenologist does not focus upon behavior, like the behaviorist, but upon *experience*. He focuses not upon stimulus-response habits, but upon intentions acted out by particular human beings in everyday life. Existentialists, such as Albert Camus, were intellectual offspring of phenomenological thinking.

Camus describes the theme of "the Intention" made fashionable by Husserl and his followers:

> Originally Husserl's method negates the classical procedure of the reason . . . Thinking is not unifying or making the appearance familiar under the guise of a great principle. Thinking is learning all over again how to see, directing one's consciousness, making of every image a privileged place. In other words, phenomenology declines to explain the world, it wants to be merely a description of actual experience. It confirms absurd thought in its initial assertion that there is no truth, but merely truths. From the evening breeze to this hand on my shoulder, everything has its truth. Consciousness illuminates it by paying attention to it. Consciousness does not form the object of its understanding, it merely focuses, it is the act of attention, and, to borrow a Bergsonian image, it resembles the projector that suddenly focuses on an image. The difference is that there is no scenario, but a succes-

sive and incoherent illustration. In that magic lantern all the pictures are privileged. Consciousness suspends in its experience the objects of its attention. Through its miracle it isolates them. Henceforth they are beyond all judgments. This is the "intention" that characterizes consciousness. But the word does not imply any idea of finality; it is taken in its sense of "direction": its only value is topographical.[20]

To understand our world we must learn to penetrate to what others really see and want: their *intention*. Thus it is through the notion of *intention* that political *consciousness* reveals its meaning to human beings in everyday life. Human needs lead to particular value assumptions, which focus the spotlight of consciousness on intentions. I need to value to intend to become. And in becoming conscious of the tension between my initial need and perceived social facts in my everyday world, I am motivated to act politically with others to solve our mutual problems.

Of course, by focusing on subjective intention, phenomenology does not claim to have a handle on "the objective truth." For as Camus points out, from this perspective there is no one truth, only truths. In other words, to reify or freeze one aspect of reality and label it "the truth" is presumptuous and narrow-minded. Reality is so multifaceted and complex that human beings cannot hope to capture its entire "truth" in any one instant. Therefore it is necessary for human beings to look at reality from a value perspective, to experience life with intentions. But phenomenology goes further to give us a rigorous method with which to analyze everyday intentions more precisely. This method can be used to discover needs and interests that we share with others.

The phenomenological *method* developed by Husserl involves three basic steps:

First, *consciously attend to phenomena as they appear* in experience—see things freshly as you experience them in everyday life, suspending your old judgments about them for the moment. This data-first beginning makes rigorously applied phenomenology one of the most empirical of methods. For example, look at a political action involving two or more people—not from your old standpoint or through the concepts you've been taught in school, but freshly, as if it were the first political event that ever occurred and you were the first reporter to describe such an event.

Next, *reduce the phenomenon to the aspects essential in its particular presentation to you by bracketing out the unnecessary*. In other words, after looking at an object or action freshly, perform a strip-tease upon it, questioning its taken-for-granted aspects to cut down its meaning to its essential aspects. For instance, in looking at a political event as if for the first time, *bracket out* your unnecessary perceptions to get at the core. In Chapter 1, Alphonse and Balthazar are not just playing games on the beach, as they might first appear to be doing—they are satisfying their mutual hunger with clams by dividing the labor (the bracketed-out *essence* of the everyday appearance). In short, if you can perceive everyday life with clear eyesight and full intellectual consciousness, you can get at the most meaningful core of undistorted appearances.

Finally, *examine the essences you perceive to uncover the workings of consciousness that make them possible.* Or ask the question, Without which assumptions would this political phenomenon or experience in everyday life not have been possible? In the case of Alphonse and Balthazar, the phenomenological method was applied in Chapters 1 and 2 to uncover the following working of consciousness that made their political event possible. At least two people perceived and communicated a shared tension between human needs and social facts and mutually initiated a relationship to resolve that tension (hunger in this case). What we have derived here are the assumptions without which political consciousness would not be possible.

As you use the phenomenological *method* as a tool to explain everyday life over and over again, you begin to arrive at a *theory* of phenomenology general enough to explain most specific social events most of the time. Notice how the phenomenological method above leads naturally to the four aspects of the phenomenological theory of the social world. The meaning of any social world involves:

] *At least two* human beings [
] Each *with intentions* deriving from values or needs [
] Mutually acting out intentions in *interactions* —each in
    terms of the perceptions and anticipations of the
    other [
] And *the parts* of the world *at that moment* that are
    mutually perceived to constitute the *social world*
    for these two human beings. [

Although the method and theory of phenomenology are not difficult to understand, they take great discipline to use consistently and can have complicated implications. Perhaps the most important effect of using the phenomenological perspective is that the existing social world of everyday life is never taken for granted but is constantly being reconstructed. This effect has two vital humanistic consequences that prepare the way for a politics for human beings. First, phenomenology forces each person to constantly pay attention to the perceptions of the other, to put himself in the other's shoes. This way of thinking makes people more sensitive to each other's feelings, thoughts, ways of being.

Secondly, phenomenology stimulates human beings to transform the social facts of their everyday life, to humanize and reconstruct its most essential aspects. Human beings are encouraged to recreate all those aspects of social life that they can control, to turn as much of social life as possible into a period of creativity—rather than tacitly supporting taken-for-granted maintenance thinking or accepting fatalistic, cyclic decay thinking.

If you perceive America to be going from a period of maintenance to a period of decay, as the authors do, you will sense a personal need to make your own social reality as humanistic as possible, in contrast to the dead social facts surrounding you and taken for granted by so many. Phenomenology is a method of achieving political consciousness of the tension between your most essential needs and the most frustrating of social facts. It helps you to rethink and reconstruct your everyday life. Politics begins with an idea, and such an idea can easily come by thinking through phenomenology. Clams for breakfast, anyone?

INCONCLUSIONS

System first or self first, that is the question. To think through the system is necessary at times to understand those who maintain it *as social facts*. But it's easy to lose yourself in the abstractions of systems thinking. Some alternatives are three traditions of thinking that begin with the self: behaviorism, behavioralism, and postbehavioralism. The human self, according to behaviorism, becomes merely a matter of stimulus-response, of black-box conditioning. Values, emotions, ideas, and mental events are cut out as nonscientific garbage. Only the kick-me-kick-you world of the five senses remains. Man comes and goes in a ratlike way, his present flattened out into a link to the past that determines his future. More power to the maze—to the system.

Behavioralism takes the self of behaviorism and puts back values, attitudes, and feelings into the organism. The self is now stimulus-organism-response. Data is collected to explain, to predict, and to control human behavior. But to what end? Who benefits most from such research? Who least? These latter questions were raised by the postbehavioralists—people who want to benefit from the findings of behavioralism but believe that such social research should be aimed at satisfying human needs and creating conditions in which social justice becomes possible. These thinkers are suspicious of claims of "objective," "neutral" science when they see that the "hard-headed" scientific research most heavily funded by the government is for destructive offensive and defensive weapons systems. They want a hard-headed, warm-hearted science that aims toward human needs.

REFERENCES

1. John B. Watson, *Behavorism* (Chicago: University of Chicago Press, 1924).

2. B. F. Skinner, *Walden II* (New York: Macmillan, 1948), pp. 103 and 108 respectively. Also see Skinner, *Beyond Freedom and Dignity* (New York: Bantam/Vintage, 1972).

3. B. F. Skinner's speech on "Beyond Freedom and Dignity" at Fordham University, December 5, 1972.

4. For the history of the behavioral movement in political science, see Robert Dahl, "The Behavioral Approach in Political Science: Epitaph for a Monument to a Successful Protest," *The American Political Science Review* 55, 1961, pp. 763–772; David Easton, "The Current Meaning of Behavioralism," in *The Limits of Behavioralism in Political Science,* ed. J. C. Charlesworth (Philadelphia, Pa.: The American Academy of Political and Social Science, 1962); and Heinz Eulau, "Political Behavior," in *The International Encyclopedia of the Social Sciences,* ed. David Sills (New York: Macmillan, 1968).

5. See Richard C. Snyder, H. W. Bruck, and Burton Sapin, *Foreign Policy Decision-Making* (New York: The Free Press, 1962).

6. See Herbert A. Simon, *Administrative Behavior—A Study of Decision-Making Processes in Administrative Organization* (New York: Macmillan, 1957). Also see Simon's *Models of Man—Social and Rational* (New York: Wiley, 1957).

7. For a summary of political decision-making approaches in general and an example of how this three-stage decision approach can be applied to actual policy choices, see R. A. Isaak, "Political Decision-making Theory and Foreign Policy," *The Montclair Journal of Social Sciences and Humanities* 2, no. 1, Summer 1973 (Montclair State College, Upper Montclair, New Jersey), pp. 35–55.

8. Ronald Howard, "The Science of Decision-Making," mimeographed (Stanford, California: Institute in Engineering-Economic Systems, Stanford University, 1968), p. 4–5.

9. Heinz Eulau, in *P. S.* (American Political Science Association newsletter), Fall 1971, p. 547.

10. A. D. Lindsay, *Kant* (London: Oxford University Press, 1936), p. 48. A standard edition of Kant's relevant work is Immanuel Kant, *Critique of Pure Reason,* trans. Norman Kemp Smith (New York: St. Martin's Press, 1965); see specifically the section on "The Transcendental Analytic."

11. See his essay "'Objectivity' in Social Science and Social Policy," in Max Weber, *The Methodology of the Social Sciences,* trans. Edward A. Shils and Henry A. Finch (New York: The Free Press, 1949), pp. 72 and 81. Weber's italics.

12. H. Mark Roelofs, "Political Science and Political Commitment," paper presented at the 1972 annual meeting of the American Political Science Association at Washington, D. C.

13. "CNPS: Statement of Purpose," *A New Political Science* (newsletter of the Caucus for a New Political Science,) Winter 1974.

14. For a typical argument along these lines, see the essay by Christian Bay, "Thoughts on the Purposes of Political Science Education," in George J. Graham and George W. Carey, eds., *The Post-Behavioral Era: Perspectives on Political Science* (New York: McKay, 1972), pp. 88–99. Bay was the first opposition presidential candidate fielded by the Caucus for a New Political Science in the American Political Science Association's elections. Bay also suggests using Abraham Maslow's need hierarchy as the basis for a new politics of human needs: Christian Bay, "Politics and Pseudopolitics: A Critical Evaluation of Some Behavioral Literature," *American Political Science Review* 59, no. 1 (March 1965), pp. 39–51.

15. See Kalman Silvert, *Man's Power: A Biased Guide to Political Thought and Action* (New York: The Viking Press, 1970).

16. For an example of how social science can be turned to help human communities from which it derives knowledge, see Charles Hampden-Turner, *From Poverty to Dignity: A Strategy for Poor Americans* (Garden City, N.Y.: Doubleday, Anchor, 1974).

17. What has been called the "objectivist illusion" has been criticized by theorists of knowledge from Immanuel Kant to Max Weber. The "objectivist illusion" is the assumption that there is a social reality in itself, apart from the people who create it and continue to maintain it. This illusion "deludes the sciences with the image of a reality-in-itself consisting of facts structured in a lawlike manner; it conceals the constitution of these facts, and thereby prevents consciousness of the interlocking of knowledge with interests from the lifeworld." A most recent criticism of this illusion, from which the above comment is cited, is Juergen Habermas's essay "Knowledge and Human

Interests: A General Perspective" in his *Knowledge and Human Interests* (Boston: Beacon Press, 1972), pp. 301–317.

18. See Henry Kariel, *Saving Appearances: The Reestablishment of Political Science* (North Scituate, Mass.: Duxbury Press, 1972).

19. For a good English introduction to Husserl, see Marion Farber, *The Foundation of Phenomenology: Edmund Husserl and the Quest for a Rigorous Science of Philosophy* (Cambridge, Mass.: Harvard University Press, 1943). For a useful phenomenological tool for beginning social scientists, see Peter Berger and Thomas Luckman, *The Social Construction of Reality* (Garden City, N. Y.: Anchor Books, 1967).

20. Albert Camus, *The Myth of Sisyphus* (New York: Vintage, 1955), p. 32.

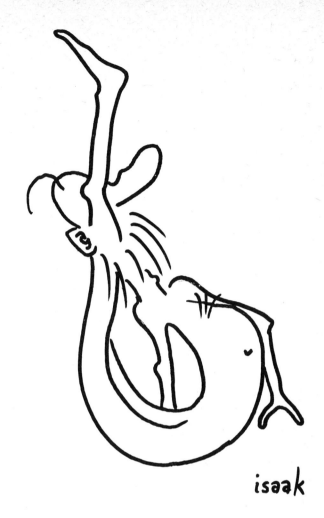

isaak

12 Wherein the reader perceives the difference between everyday thinking and political thinking, and sees how classical and future political thinking relate. He also sees how such thinking can be used for criticizing societies that frustrate human needs and for constructing alternative societies that might satisfy human needs.

12 Classical and Future Political Thinking

Once there was a flock of geese. They were kept in a wire cage by a farmer. One day, one of the geese looked up and saw that there was no top to the cage. Excitedly, he told the other geese:

"Look, look: There is no top. We may leave here. We may become free."

Few listened, and none would turn his head to the sky.

So, one day, he simply spread his wings and flew away—alone.

—Soren Kierkegaard

Everyman is born into some Inlandia or other. There he grows accustomed to the social facts he finds—so much so that he often comes to view them as inevitable. If he suffers and sees that his political system cannot possibly satisfy his needs, he often comes to believe that life *is* suffering, that there is nothing to be done. If he hears of enchanting places elsewhere where his needs might be met, he often closes his ears to keep his comfortable belief that such alternatives are utopian poppycock. The human being is often a creature of habit who accepts his lot without question, who believes that political thinking is too much trouble. He often slowly gives up the struggle for his full humanity, believing that how things are is how things will be.

In our time of mass technology, many voluntarily give up the political will to become themselves to apolitics. Apolitics is the ideology that asserts the superiority of technical problem solving over the common-sense solution of human needs. The era of apolitics is a product of technological society and man's devotion to technique. The world has become too complex, social change moves too fast, many believe that life is beyond their control. They refuse to think politically, either through the system or through themselves. For slowly they have come to believe they *are* the system. National patriotism for their technological society has consumed their self-respect. Battered by Vietnam and mocked by Watergate, they have become numb and passive. They don't care anymore. They'll take what they can get and exit when their time comes. If they have become a silent majority, they have chosen to become silent, they have chosen to know nothing.

But there are others. Some refuse to give up so easily. Some struggle despite all odds to change the social facts that frustrate their needs. Some reject the lies and seek to oust the liars. Some believe, with Jean-Paul Sartre, "We only become what we are by the radical deep-seated refusal of that which others have made of us." This chapter deals with the difference between Know-Nothings and political human beings in our apolitical era. It is the end and the beginning of an attempt to sketch a politics for human beings.

How can we do political thinking? When does it become necessary to think politically to resolve tensions between human needs and social facts? And how does such thinking differ from everyday thought? This chapter seeks to answer these questions by linking classical political thought with future political thinking and by showing how political thought can be used for social criticism and the positive construction of alternatives.[1]

Political thought is different from everyday thought, just as politics is different from social life. *Everyday thought* involves the knowledge of routines established long ago to solve someone else's problems —the Founding Fathers', for instance. If we stick to such stock responses in a time of rapid change, our thoughts will lose themselves in circles like rats in a maze. Since routine political systems are mazes created to solve old problems, mere everyday thinking is unlikely to provide an exit from new political problems.

Political thinking, on the other hand, can provide an escape from a maze of unworkable social facts. It begins with the intention to resolve the tension between human needs and social facts—no matter what the consequences are for the maintenance of present social facts. From the viewpoint of social facts and of those interested in maintaining them, political thinking is always subversive thinking, for it questions the unquestionable and unstabilizes the rules of the game. From the viewpoint of reformers and revolutionaries, on the other hand, maintenance men think politically to define social facts as inevitable when they aren't, and to keep the status quo up when it keeps many human beings down. Lewis Carroll's March Hare was the ultimate maintenance man:

> "Take some more tea," the March Hare said to Alice, very earnestly.
> "I've had nothing yet," Alice replied in an offended tone: "So I can't take more."

Here Alice is clearly conscious of the tension between her desire and the social facts on the one hand and the lie or mistaken view of the March Hare on the other. Know-Nothings who become politically conscious soon become wary of elites who promise them more when they have yet to receive the first serving. Others take what doesn't come and suffer accordingly.

Everyday Thinking Man's brain mediates between the challenges of nature and the needs of his existence. By sensing human needs, perceiving environmental challenges, and calculating suitable responses to bridge the gap, the brain continually enables man to adapt to his natural and social surroundings.

Everyday thinking is old, routinized political thinking that has aged into habit. As such, all social routines of everyday life are mainly the result of the brain's adaptation to existing social facts. They were constructed out of political thinking some time ago to solve the tensions between needs and facts.

A camper lost in the woods might recall the social routine of sending up smoke signals to signify to others his need for help. Or a man being mistreated in his job might skip above his immediate superior to complain to the president of the organization, obeying the habits of the traditional hierarchy of authority.

Such thinking always involves knowledge of accepted routines. Its success may well depend on the inventiveness the actor uses in applying his knowledge to a specific situation.

A member of the United States Senate avails himself of everyday thought when he remembers to call a quorum in the absence of enough members so he can stop a debate that isn't going his way. Such a quorum call may signify many things: "I don't like what's going on, and I know the routine to stop it," or "I know how to stop the everyday political routines of the Senate, and somebody better negotiate with me if he wants them to continue." But this is not creative politics.

Procedural inventiveness may create shock or surprise, reveal alternatives that opponents had not anticipated, or even temporarily block normal procedure. But no matter how inventive or successful, the application of such knowledge stays within the fundamental routines of the game being played. Other players may be momentarily resentful, but ultimately they accept such thought as being within the rules of the game.

Everyday thinking is calculating how to apply familiar social routines to problem solving.

But when does political thinking evolve in everyday life?

Political Thinking

Human beings move toward thinking politically when their maps for getting along with familiar social routines no longer seem to work. Political thinking usually emerges with crisis in everyday life—with exposed tensions between needs and social facts that cannot be relieved using habitual, everyday solutions.

The lost camper sending up smoke signals may give up when he realizes that what he has read about Indian lore may no longer be read by anyone else.

The employee complaining to the company president may suddenly realize that it is to the president and company's advantage if he continues to be exploited by his immediate superior—the president won't help him out.

The poor litigant in a democratic country's courts, faced with a corporation's battery of well-paid lawyers, may soon abandon his routine problem-solving thinking that tells him that "all men are equal before the law."

The citizen who has given a dollar to the presidential candidate of his choice and sees business and industry giving millions of dollars to the opposition candidate, who eventually wins, may be on his way to taking up nonroutine political thinking.

The working man who sees his savings destroyed by inflation and his money buying less food the more he makes may be ready to think outside of the official "political" routines of the everyday.

Alternatives to Thinking

Unfortunately, political thinking is not the only response to crisis.

The stress of crisis diverts us from unworkable routines, but we know—from physiological psychologists—that under too much stress we may respond emotionally rather than through rational thought. Alternative responses to rational cognitive functioning of the brain are emotional fight and flight, and, under extreme stress, the paralysis of terror which disables us from responding at all.[2]

The ultimate form of flight—suicide—has been discovered to be often a response to intolerably swift changes in social routines. Sociologist Emile Durkheim observed that people committed suicide when there were rapid changes in economic conditions—whether for the better or for worse.[3]

Under other conditions, rapid social change can bring about aggression, as in the Nazi reaction to Germany's social crisis. Political scientist James C. Davies has noted that violent lashing out at society may take place when individuals see their expectations disappointed, specifically when there is a sudden downward turn in a longer trend to satisfy expectations.[4]

But there are also people who are sensitive to the stresses around them yet are capable of cooly studying them and thinking of a way out. More than 2,500 years ago, two men—Plato and Aristotle—reacted to the decay of their own society with analyses and designs for new systems that have affected us ever since. Karl Marx, thrown out of Germany, France, and Belgium for helping make the bourgeois revolution of 1848, calmly set about doing a socio-economic critique of the political routines of his day and created a method of analysis that turned half the world away from such routines.

In a small but symbolically important way, individuals of the counter-cultures have recently used reason to determine that there must be a better way for resolving the tension between their human needs and social facts. Their reasoning resulted in their creation of thousands of little worlds in which they tried to construct a politics for human beings.

Interest: The Focus for Thinking

If thinking is the human brain's attempt to adapt man to his environment, it makes sense to assume that such thinking usually takes place in reference to specific problems we have in the environment. In other words, we think acutely about those parts of our environment that have become problematical for us.

All thinking is focused by human interests.

The camper who realizes he has become lost focuses his thinking on the fact of greatest momentary interest to him—finding his way back.

The father who cannot feed his children with wages paid in inflated money focuses his interest on food and how to beat inflation. Yet, at the same time, those who make money through inflation—for example, merchants who jack up prices and then convert their profits into goods that resist inflation (perhaps gold)—focus their interest on how to keep inflation going.

The same problem, then, can be and will be thought about in terms of the personal interests that people differently affected have in solving the problem.

Whether political thinking is engaged in ultimately depends on whether people have an interest in the maintenance, decay, or creation of an existing society. Those who still have something to expect of older patterns or routines for problem solving may insist that new political re-thinking is illegitimate—perhaps even that it should be prohibited. Prohibitions against teaching communism are of this nature. So was the Catholic Church's prohibition against the teaching of Protestantism, or against Galileo's contention that the earth was not the center of the universe.

Similarly, in a bolshevik communist country, those in power may forbid thinking Maoist or Castroist communism. Even on the simpler family level, the father may forbid his son to talk of new ways of problem solving if such notions threaten his own security in his older ways. The son who tells his fifty-year-old father he is stupid for working all his life, only so he can retire at sixty-five and "enjoy life," may be attacking the life-time ideology of his father.

**Political thinking exposes
personal interests in creation,
maintenance, and decay
in a society.**

In any kind of thinking, what we consider relevant depends on our interest. The light of our interest throws a cone of brightness onto reality that shows up relevant data while plunging into darkness all data not seen as relevant to our interests.

Interest: Defining Relevant Facts

The lost camper considers relevant only those parts of reality that can help him become found: matches, wood, a blanket to send up smoke signals. The worker is interested only in those aspects of reality that might change conditions that exploit him.

What is striking about both these examples is that the individual determines which data are relevant to his problem solving by identifying his problem as a type of problem solvable under old stand-by recipes. The camper identifies his specific problem under the *type* of problem, "Being Lost." The worker identifies his as one of the type of problem, "Worker Exploitation." They find the relevant pieces of reality useful to them through the recipe answers for "Being Lost" and "Exploitation," which prescribe certain routines for the solution of each problem.

Little original thinking is involved in such typical problem situations. I simply put myself through the following stages and the typical answer to the typical problem seems to automatically pop out:

1. I perceive I can go no further unless I manipulate my environment. (Being lost and being exploited both threaten an end to a trail.)

2. I ask myself, How is this problem similar to problems experienced in the past?

3. I try to match up data from my present problem experience with pigeonholes in a variety of model problems stored in my memory.

4. If I succeed in the matching process, I will eventually pigeonhole the experience "I don't know where to go from here" in the typical model problem "Being Lost." Similarly the worker, perceiving that he is stuck in exploitation, will say to himself: "Aha! This is a problem of the type 'Worker Exploitation.' I have overcome such abuse in the past by complaining, and I can do it again."

5. Identifying a specific problem under a model program type already suggests the relevant pieces of reality that must be manipulated to solve the problem.

But what if reality has radically changed since I last used my model problem to identify a solution? What if other campers have switched from smoke signals to two-way radios—and I am lost without one? What if, while I am trying to complain to improve my job situation as usual, other workers have stopped doing politics of work?

Similarly, in the case of American politics, a politician's colleagues in the U.S. Senate may cease doing politics as usual. What if they switch from a politics of give and take to a politics of ideology bent on taking but never giving when principle is at stake?

Suddenly the focus of my interest widens. Old recipes no longer provide standard solutions. The cone of light they shed on reality now seems too narrow. Formerly relevant facts are no longer relevant alone; other facts must be searched out to explain that which cannot be explained by references to model problem-solving routines. Suddenly I desperately try to cast my light of interest onto elements of reality that I have previously been content to leave in darkness.

Political Thinking As Widening Interest

It is at this point that movement toward political thinking in the true sense may begin—if we can keep reason dominant over our emotions.

The everyday thinker concerns himself with what *is* and with long-used routines for getting along in that reality. His knowledge is knowledge *about* the world.

The political thinker, born when everyday life breaks down, concerns himself with *why* something is (he needs to explain the breakdown of routine to reorient himself) or with how the world *could* be (repelled by the confusion of breakdown, he may want to create his own world). His knowledge is not merely knowledge about surface realities, but knowledge of the facts, reasons, and purposes hidden behind those routines.

Political Thought in the Cycle of History

Political thinking is always two-pronged thought. The individual who thinks politically concerns himself with what human life *could* be if human needs alone were considered. At the same time, the political thinker takes into account how close he *can* realistically get to that ideal, given the limits of social facts. To paraphrase the historian of philosophy Werner Jaeger, the political thinker lives in the tension between the ideal and the real.

The mixture of these two orientations varies with where the political thinker stands in the historical cycle, whether in a time of maintenance, decay, or creation.

In a time of maintenance, the best that political thinking can do is explore the question, What human needs can we begin to satisfy, given the resistance of social structure in a time of maintenance?

In a time of decay, it becomes possible to shift political thinking to ask, Which social facts of maintenance are most likely to give way when attacked for the purpose of achieving human needs?

In a time of creation, when social facts have crumbled as much as they ever will, it becomes possible to move closest to the ideal of human needs. In such times, the political thinker asks, What is the ideal society for our time, given what we know about human needs, and how can it be put into effect?

Full political thinking is possible only in a time of creation, when all the human needs can be taken into account—survival needs, safety needs, esteem needs, love needs, and self-actualization needs. But it would be a mistake to argue that someone is not engaged in political thinking merely because he struggles over the tension between human needs and social facts in a time of maintenance. There are more political thinkers of that type than all great political philosophers put together—simply because times of maintenance persist longer than times of decay and creation.

Most of us who try to think about the politics of human needs in our time are political thinkers of this less glorious maintenance type. Nevertheless the fact of our political consciousness distinguishes us sharply from those who think in mere everyday routine—those whose consciousness is confined by the thoughtlessness of times of maintenance. Such individuals are not lesser beings, but they are imprisoned in habitual social thinking.

But true politics begins exactly when the routines of everyday life no longer work. Political thinking is the response to the breakdown of routines. The great political systems of Plato, Aristotle, Hobbes, Rousseau, and Marx are all responses to such crises.

When voters don't vote, when presidents don't preside but run wild with power, when Congresses fail to pass laws solving problems—such conditions can trigger the beginning of political thinking.

Political thinking begins with the crisis of routines.

The reason why human beings like ourselves had better begin to do some political thinking is that many routines no longer work for us.

There is a handy way for determining whether the time is ripe to engage in political thinking.

Spotting A Time for Political Thought

The sociologist Alfred Schutz analyzed the conditions under which routine social thinking is abandoned and replaced by what we call political thinking. He concluded that what he called "thinking-as-usual" ceases when any one of the following basic assumptions ceases to be taken for granted. It is interesting to note the extent to which these assumptions no longer apply in America:

1. The assumption that social life will continue to be the same as it has been so far, that the same problems requiring the same solutions will recur and that, therefore, our former experiences will suffice for mastering future situations.

> **In America, social change has passed by the recipes of political problem solving designed in the eighteenth century.**

2. The assumption that we may rely on the knowledge handed down to us by parents, teachers, governments, traditions, habits, and so on, even if we do not understand its origin and real meaning.

> **In an era of rapid social change, disillusionment with traditional knowledge has set in.**

3. The assumption that in the ordinary course of affairs it is sufficient to know something *about* the general type or style of events we may encounter in order to manage or control them.

> **Even American politicians of maintenance have discovered that knowing why manipulation of voters works gives more power than merely knowing how.**

4. The assumption that neither systems of recipes of getting along in the social world nor the underlying basic assumptions just mentioned are our private affair, but that they are likewise accepted and applied by our fellow human beings.

> **Watergate is the most recent demonstration that the recipes for engaging in old political routines are no longer accepted by all. Similarly, corporations are imposing private solutions on public problems.**

As these assumptions break down around us, we experience, in Schutz's words, that "the cultural pattern no longer functions as a system of tested recipes at hand; it reveals that its applicability is restricted to a specific historical situation.[5]

What is the quality of the everyday thinking that we must abandon and replace? And how do we recognize political thought?

In answer to the first question, Alfred Schutz suggests the following characteristics of everyday knowledge:

> In his daily life, the healthy, adult, and wide-awake human being (we are not speaking of others) has this knowledge, so to speak, automatically at hand. From heritage and education, from the manifold influences of tradition, habits and his own previous reflection, his store of experiences is built up. It embraces the most heterogenous kinds of knowledge in a very incoherent and confused state. Clear and distinct experiences are intermingled with vague conjectures; suppositions and prejudices cross well-proven evidences; motives, means and ends, as well as causes and effects, are strung together without clear understanding of their real connections. . . . This kind of knowledge and its organization I should like to call "cookbook knowledge."[6]

In contrast, we suggest that political thought and political knowledge require a form of mental operation and quality of knowledge relatively superior to everyday knowledge and thought. The following points characterize the *political thinker:*

He recognizes that the human world in its social and political complexity is a man-made world; he rejects the world as given.

He recognizes that there is a tendency in the development of societies for social facts to move out of tune with human needs.

He recognizes that political thinking must be a permanent ongoing activity if the tension between human needs and social facts is to be kept at a minimum.

He recognizes that no matter how strong his personal prejudices or biases, the social facts constructed and maintained by his fellow human beings have an existence of their own that the distortions of his mind cannot affect.

He recognizes the need to make value choices at some point in his design of a political solution to a problem, but he does not let his bias distort the logical construction of means to achieve his values. He knows that an act of will is required in making ultimate values choices, but that only acts of logic based on empirical testing can assure the efficient achievement of his goals.

In sum, the political thinker keeps the distinction between empirical reality, values choices, and logic clear in his mind. *He accepts the reality of the people and social facts around him for the purposes of manipulating that reality to achieve his values in the least costly (most logical) way.*

Political knowledge and political thought combine the goals of philosophy with the means sought by science to reach such ends. In times of decay like our own, such thinking can serve two purposes: criticism and construction.

To illustrate these purposes, first we apply the work of three major political thinkers to the criticism of our condition. Second, we try to show how we used political thinking to construct the new theory proposed in this book.

POLITICAL THINKING AS CRITICISM

Human beings have been thinking politically for ages to solve tensions between needs and realities. They may have created more problems than they solved, but their latest creation—technology—poses man's terminal problem: the abolition of thought. Thinking is replaced by conditioning, mind by brain, ends by means. Man in tension creates technology to ease his conditions, aiming toward an ideal in which man does not have to exert effort or think at all. But as efficiency becomes the highest value, human needs become secondary to the needs of the technological system. As people cease to think, the distance between the original technological programming and their human needs increases. Irritating as it may seem in the pseudocomfort of technological convenience, those vaguely sensing the threatened termination of man as human being will have to begin thinking again.

But who can teach technological people to think again as human beings?

Surely not the products of a technological society. If the problem is to think again as human beings, the first task is to find the people who last did. The great philosophers must be studied, because knowing them may enable us to think our way into becoming human again. After all, many classical philosophers assumed that man is the center of the universe.

Not all philosophers are relevant to all experiences. Three philosophers are especially relevant to the American political experience: Thomas Hobbes, the philosopher who best described human nature as it is taught to Americans; Aristotle, the philosopher most basic to the construction of the political cage in which Americans are kept; and Herbert Marcuse, the philosopher who has come closest to unmasking the social-psychological conditions that keep Americans repressed in the technological dimension. Understanding these three philosophers enables human beings to know how philosophy, first truncated into science, has since been flattened into technology. Without such understanding, the individual loses the awareness that technology is merely a means to needs and values—and risks becoming merely an extension of technique.

Thomas Hobbes: Are We Really Nasty, Brutish, and Short?

Thomas Hobbes tried to be a human being in the sixteenth century but did not get beyond adolescence. When the century came to a close, Hobbes was twelve years old. But like Americans today, he extended his adolescence and later summarized his life as follows: "In 1588, the year of the Spanish Armada," wrote Hobbes, "my mother gave birth to twins: myself and Fear." Historical conditions in England were rugged. Social facts were hard. Life for most people, as Hobbes put it, *was* nasty, brutish, and short. No wonder Hobbes claimed that a science of human nature must be based on concrete, sensual facts.

Philosophy was squeezed out between mathematical deduction and empirical observation. For philosophy is the study of wisdom, but Hobbes's science, which we have inherited, is merely knowledge of techniques to ward off death.

That is why in America philosophers are hard to come by, and scientists are preoccupied with nuclear abstractions to ward off death—from nuclear biology to nuclear physics. America is rampant with Hobbesian fear for physiological needs and collective security.

To Hobbes, all people in a state of nature are beasts in a war of all against all. To control this war, not to abolish it, Hobbes sees people driven to create a mechanical monster—the State. He called this monster the Leviathan after an awe-inspiring mythical beast of the Bible. Hobbes's theory was that the Leviathan, being more powerful than men alone, would keep all men in awe, preventing them from taking each other's property and lives in ways other than those con-

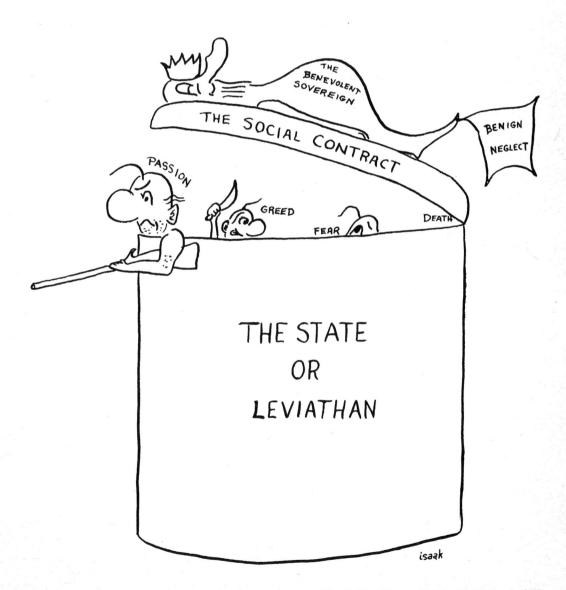

doned by the State. To understand how these ideas worked their way into the American political system, one must first understand how Hobbes's psychology explains political acts.

Hobbes's atomistic psychology assumed that the world was made up of particles of matter, all permanently in motion. Human perception resulted from the banging of particles against the senses. When a particle banged hard enough against the eye, seeing began. Even thinking was stimulated by material particles banging into the brain. Likewise, in the social world Hobbes saw people as atomistic particles banging into one another until the heavier ones displaced the lighter ones.

This war of atomistic individuals was solved by the idea of the social contract. Initially, each person had two kinds of rights: to get as much of what there is to get as he could, and the right to use any means possible. In order to secure what he had against war and death, he had to give up the right to use any means to the sovereign. In Hobbes's time the sovereign, possibly a king in parliament, was to act as umpire to enforce the rules regulating the conflict of individual interests.

INVITATION

Imagine you are in a large American city at three o'clock in the morning. Would you fear like Hobbes? What if anonymous bodies come banging up against you in the darkness? Would you feel alive, alone, and afraid? Would you react aggressively? If so, Hobbes is alive and well in America. And so are your physiological and security needs.

Aristotle: From Golden Mean to Mediocrity

If Aristotle lived in America today instead of the fourth century B.C., he would be astonished at how he has been used to keep the Hobbesian concept of human nature in check. Like Hobbes, Aristotle lived in a time of tension, when Greek city-states had entered the cycle of decay. But where Hobbes stressed the tension between fear and matter, Aristotle thought to resolve the tension between the ideal and the real. Unlike Hobbes, Aristotle was a philosopher of the whole human being who tried to design a way to live that would satisfy all levels of needs—not just the physiological and security needs. In his *Nichomachean Ethics,* Artistotle tries to teach men how to do their best with existing social facts, and later how to use social facts to achieve their highest potential purpose (contemplation of the good).

His *Politics*—a jumble of his students' lecture notes—provided a tool for the American Founding Fathers that captured this tension in the nature of human beings. He begins with the classical Greek cycle of government: three forms of government, each of two varieties —good and bad. The good kind of government by one is a benevolent monarch; the bad, a tyrant. Good monarchs are inevitably corrupted by power into tyrants. Tyrants are eventually overthrown by a government of the few, which is also of two kinds: the good, aristocracy; the bad, oligarchy. The corruption of the few by power brings on a takeover by the many. The bad kind of government of this sort is democracy (mob-rule). The good kind is *politea*—a *mixed government* of the few and the many. Artistotle believed that the most stable government is a *politea* with a large middle class. *Politea* constitutes a golden mean between the corruption of the few and the passion of the many.

INVITATION

Imagine that the president of a university calls upon you to design an admissions policy based upon Aristotle's politics. Note that in ordering the three values of stability, equality, and quality into priorities, if quality is chosen, only the best get in, and stability and equality lose. Some say quality education is not democratic, and even that the social mobility permitted by "open admissions" is more important than educational quality. How you stand on this issue depends on your needs, what you have got, and who pays. To what extent does the short-term mixing of your techniques in manipulating admissions policy allow you to avoid value choices?

If you ever wondered how the psychologist Sigmund Freud and the sociologist Karl Marx would explain twentieth-century America, you might want to talk to the expatriate German philosopher Herbert Marcuse.

Herbert Marcuse: Technique vs. Eros in a Flat World

In his *One-Dimensional Man,* Marcuse describes the tension between America's psychological *self* and its social *system.* Through the profound reification that he calls one-dimensional society, in which all human beings are homogenously flattened out, Marcuse sensed the coming of apolitics. He writes, "Domination is transfigured into administration. The capitalist bosses and owners are losing their identity as responsible agents: they are assuming the function of bureaucrats in a corporate machine . . . the tangible source of exploitation disappears behind the facade of objective reality."

Perhaps the most important tool Marcuse gives human beings for unmasking the tension between self and social system is the concept of *repressive desublimation.* To understand concepts or tools like this it helps to take them apart, to dereify them. Dereifying this concept is illustrated by Figure 12–1.

After playing the game, notice the social implications of your behavior, according to Marcuse:

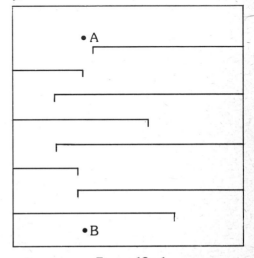

Figure 12–1

Getting There in America
To Play: Connect Points A and B

SOLUTION 1: Most human beings respond as in Figure 12−2 in the box of technological society, obeying society's commands without question. He who totally obeys the rules of the maze is Marcuse's "normal" repressed, sublimated individual in America.

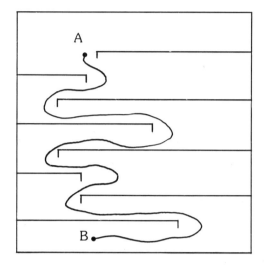

Figure 12−2

Getting There in America
Solution 1

SOLUTION 2: He who falsely thinks he is free by deviating *within* the box of technological society (Figure 12−3) is Marcuse's "liberated" *repressed, de*sublimated individual in America.

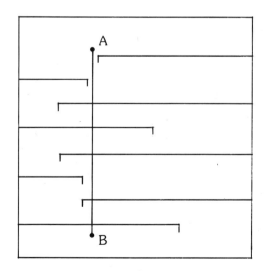

Figure 12−3

Getting There in America
Solution 2

SOLUTION 3: He who perceives a way to totally escape the maze of one-dimensional society (Figure 12−4) is Marcuse's "free" unrepressed, desublimated individual—very rare in America.*

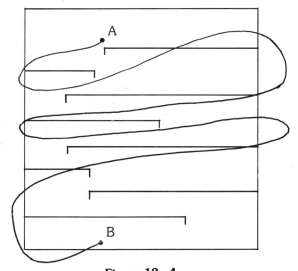

Figure 12−4

Getting There in America
Solution 3

Solution 1 represents the majority of the citizens in a technological society such as America—"normal" human beings repressed by social facts and their supposed inevitability, human beings who sublimate their real desires for the sake of the social system and its rules of the game. Here Marcuse adapts Freud's idea of the sublimation of human drives—acting out a more basic drive in substitute, "acceptable" ways. For example, instinctual sex drives are sublimated into socially approved love behavior. From Marx, Marcuse takes the idea of social repression. To repress, in Marx's view, is to keep down human consciousness by use of social facts such as class.

Combining Freud and Marx together, we arrive at Solution 2 of the maze. This represents *repressive desublimation,* the socially enforced substitution of alternate behaviors for the acting out of actual human drives or potential. Marcuse realized that a one-dimensional technological society can give the illusion of meeting true human needs by providing outlets for the desublimation or liberation of man's substitute behaviors. A good example of such repressive desublimation is the United States' liberal laws on the distribution of pornography that divert the deeper sexual drives into socially acceptable channels. Historian Theodore Roszak describes this phenomenon:

> Let us take the time to consider one significant example of such "repressive desublimation" (as Marcuse calls it). The problem is

*We are indebted to Michael O'Rourke, a former undergraduate at Fordham University, for the origins of this idea for presenting Marcuse.

sexuality, traditionally one of the most potent sources of civilized man's discontent. To liberate sexuality would be to create a society in which technocratic discipline would be impossible. But to thwart sexuality outright would create a widespread, explosive resentment that required constant policing; and besides, this would associate the technocracy with various puritanical traditions that enlightened men cannot but regard as superstitious. The strategy chosen, therefore, is not harsh repression, but rather the *Playboy* version of total permissiveness which now imposes its image upon us in every slick movie and posh magazine that comes along. In the affluent society, we have sex and sex galore—or so we are to believe. But when we look more closely we see that this sybaritic promiscuity wears a special social coloring. It has been assimilated to an income level and social status available only to our well-heeled junior executives and the jet set. After all, what does it cost to rent these yachts full of nymphomaniacal young things in which our playboys sail off for orgiastic swimming parties in the Bahamas? *Real* sex, we are led to believe, is something that goes with the best scotch, twenty-seven-dollar sunglasses, and platinum-tipped shoelaces. Anything else is a shabby substitute. Yes, there is permissiveness in the technocratic society; but it is only for the swingers and the big spenders. It is the reward that goes to reliable, politically safe henchmen of the status quo. Before our would-be playboy can be an assembly-line seducer, he must be a loyal employee.[8]

Although Roszak's illustration of the repressive desublimation of sexual drives in the 1960s might have to be updated somewhat to include braless fashions and other innovations of the 1970s, his point is well taken. Through the subtle process of repressive desublimation, eros or love is easily flattened out into technique, art into harmless social expression, and science into technology. We are so well socialized to believe we are free *en masse* that few of us bother to step outside of the rules of the game to really see if we are free individually to satisfy our human needs as we choose. We think politically through the system, not through ourselves.

And this means that we have a false or repressed political consciousness, that we are not truly political thinkers at all, but mere routine everyday thinkers with political airs and conventional ideological colorings. By becoming the system, we have lost ourselves in an individual political sense. We imagine ourselves to be political conservatives in the suburbs or political liberals in the communes, when in fact we have become apolitical, allowing technological elites to decide the most important political issues of the day. By our selfish consumption of everyday life, we have given up our political freedom to the maintenance men of apolitics, the experts in the know—the Know-it-Alls. We become political Know-Nothings by enthusiastic choice!

INVITATION

Imagine that you live in Marcuse's one-dimensional society in which human beings are just things. Technology has so flattened out your personality and eros that only your tech-

niques are left. Does Marcuse's viewpoint provide you with a way out? If you are a thing conditioned by other things, where does the dead-end end? Marcuse suggests becoming a hippie, artist, or member of a counterculture. With these in the vanguard of the revolution, who do you think will win?

The three political thinkers or philosophers just discussed can all be used for taking societies apart, for political *criticism*. Thomas Hobbes' theory of politics, for example, is useful for the pathological realist—the man who believes that men without a society and sovereign ruler to keep them in line will fall naturally into conflict or war, making off with each other's wives, lives, and property. Hobbes is a very useful model for the law-and-order maintenance men to keep in mind.

Applying Philosophy for Criticism

Aristotle is also useful as a critical tool for maintenance men—though his political thought is broad enough in scope to be useful to those operating in periods of creation and decay as well, with other than mere maintenance goals. Reading Aristotle can help the political actor to realize the need to balance conflicting groups and classes in a formal, legal system. For example, the American Founding Fathers learned from Aristotle that a large middle class makes for a stable political system, so they attempted to balance the lower and upper classes in a constitutional system that would be open for the initiative of citizens in the middle class.

Marcuse's concept of repressive desublimation becomes useful as a critical tool at this point, revealing that officially "open" middle-class politics may actually repress basic human needs and be psychologically closed. That is, Marcuse might argue that in America, Alphonse and Balthazar will become middle class and have middle-class values—or else! There is no escaping the technological, capitalistic rules of the game in America today unless people develop a critical political consciousness, according to Marcuse. All human beings become one-dimensional, giving up self to the system.

However, by reifying technological society, Marcuse is not sufficiently aware of the dynamics of apolitics. He realizes that technology provides techniques, philosophy, values. His social criticisms are often accurate and scathing. But can he explain the full range of human needs? He lacks a post-Freudian psychology—like Maslow's—based on contemporary empirical research. Is man merely the prisoner of oppressive systems? What is the positive alternative to present society, and how can it be constructed?

In this final section of the chapter, we summarize our own perspective for constructing a politics for human beings. In a small way, the kind of thinking engaged in here can be used by anyone interested in escaping the tensions of an existing system and in constructing a new paradigm for understanding and conducting political life.

POLITICAL THINKING FOR CONSTRUCTION

The Problem:
A Philosophy for
Human Beings

What do two political scientists do who find the world rotten and most of science contributing to making it worse?

They do what all individuals stirred to political thinking do: define the problem and try to find a method to solve it.

The problem as we saw it was twofold.

First, the problem was the political world. Recall political scientist Bernard Crick's observation, "No state has the capacity to ensure that men are happy; but all states have the capacity to ensure that men are unhappy."[9] In our daily lives, and in our analysis of politics at the domestic and international levels, we found that everywhere human life was so conducted as to frustrate the satisfaction of our human needs and those of others. Everywhere man was at war with every other man over who was to get a share of what the psychologist Abraham Maslow called physiological needs (food, water, rest) and safety needs (physical and psychological security). Remember psychiatrist R. D. Laing's perception that normal men have killed a hundred million of their fellow normal men within the last fifty years to achieve such needs.

When it came to the needs for self-esteem, love, and self-actualization (developing each human's capacities to their fullness), the picture looked worse. Leaders and classes fulfilled their self-esteem needs by dehumanizing and demeaning others, often by murdering them by the millions, as the Nazis did to the Jews. Was there any political system that could claim to be set up to fulfill the human need for love? Some systems claimed to aim at the self-actualization of their citizens, only to kill millions of them in purges and wars.

What made such a world gone mad possible?

The worlds that people create derive their meaning from their knowledge of themselves. Most modern people get their knowledge of themselves through science and its techniques. This world was clearly dehumanizing because science had been developed into a dehumanizing technique. The early social scientist Auguste Comte had demanded a social science that would enable us "to know in order to predict in order to control."* Social science, while still not too successful at predicting, had come a long way toward controlling. And the controls, of course, were being exercised on behalf of those who held power—those who specialized in keeping the world rotten—against those who were powerless. Until quite recently it was almost impossible to find a social scientist who would engage in research for the *powerless*—after all, the powerful paid.

The problem with the use of science, including social science, we realized, was not simply a matter of evil people using neutral knowledge. It was a matter of the development of a system of knowledge that was perfectly suited to reach the values of political and social life as perceived by modern man: dehumanization, alienation, fragmentation, reification. Indeed, to become "modern" has come to mean that one adopts the ideology of scientism as taken-for-granted routine. As philosopher Jürgen Habermas has noted, "modernization" means

*"Savoir pour prevoir pour pouvoir."

that traditional community norms are overwhelmed by technologically exploitable knowledge—applied science that dominates the social world to the point of being uncontrollable by human beings using democratic process.[10] As scientism replaces humanism, apolitics replaces politics. Man becomes modern and technologically effective at the expense of losing his most human traits if he accepts scientism as an ideology of social life.

What system of knowledge could be developed that would lead naturally toward a humane set of goals and the politics to reach them?

The first step toward developing a politics for human beings is the definition of goals.

Defining Normative Goals

Critical of many goals of existing systems, we adopted the list of human needs suggested by Abraham Maslow. Recall that these are:

Physiological needs (food, water, rest).

Safety needs (physiological and psychic security).

Love needs (warmth, affection, inclusion).

Esteem needs (positive evaluation of the self by the self and others).

Self-actualization needs (the creative expression of the self, based on fulfilling the first four needs and on the fulfillment of each individual's capacities).

Think for a moment about how these needs might be satisfied.

Even a cursory analysis shows that of all the five needs, only the first two, physiological and safety needs, might be accomplished by going into isolation from other people. I can gather my own food, if there is enough in nature, and perhaps find safety to consume it, while I am away from all other humans. But even with these needs, human beings have found that several people together can provide better protection against nature and other human beings. Even satisfying these basic needs tends to be a cooperative enterprise.

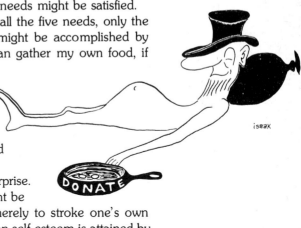

Similarly, although esteem needs might be fulfilled individually by activity designed merely to stroke one's own ego to maximize selfish gains, greater human self-esteem is attained by working with and through others so that each self supports the creative potential of other selves in cooperative solutions to human needs. And it is clear that love needs cannot be fulfilled at all by your lonesome self. A person who wants to love needs a lover, that much seems obvious.

Once you think about it, it will also be obvious that the powers of self-actualization are heightened in the company of others. Thus, for example, the authors were able to write this book as it exists only because when the mind of one of us started going in circles, the mind of the other helped him out of the maze. Moreover, the goal was to try to do something for others—the readers. Self-actualization is a mutual enterprise, based on the maxim that two selves are better than one when it comes to developing human capacities. So it became clear that all human needs could be satisfied best with other human beings. The next task was to gain some idea of what it was in daily life that prevented us from satisfying these needs.

Defining the Obstacles of Social Reality

In social reality we found a society in operation that was designed to frustrate Maslow's five needs from the cradle to the grave:

In childhood, we are socialized into competitive games of how to "beat" the other kid.

In school, we learn to compete for grades, never sharing our notes or our knowledge; in other words, we do everything possible to reduce actual learning, which is a process of communicating with others.

On the job, we learn to sell the other guy before he sells you—doing "better" than he, outdoing him, beating him.

In the family, we play dehumanizing roles. A man who expects his wife to go to the dishpan while the "men" talk about grave matters of the day is treating her as less than human. A wife who expects her husband to be a travelling salesman or a guy on overtime in order to support her and the children economically, while being virtually divorced from sharing life with them, is treating him as less than human. And of course anyone who accepts a dehumanizing role is an accomplice during the fact.

In domestic politics, you are supposed to get what there is to get for you and your constituents first—and to hell with the other guy. If this means getting a license to make profit while polluting the breath away from the lungs of the other guy (including the breath of your kids, wife, and friends), go ahead and do it. Forget that we're all on this world together. Remember, politics is conflict.

In international politics, we learn to "get" any other guy who is or might become a threat. Wipe him out. Firebomb him. Set his homes afire. Maim him. Throw him out of airplanes to teach others a lesson. Murder. Rape. Plunder. If you don't, he might do it to you.

Out of this system emerges not a human being, but a beast who in Thomas Hobbes's sense is truly alone, alive, and afraid. In this system we live estranged from one another, deprived of the opportunity to become ourselves with others, longing for love never found, doubtful of our self-esteem and the esteem of others, and often starving for the basic necessities of food, rest, shelter. For such a person there can be no security in heaven or on earth.*

Defining the Alternative

If men and women cannot satisfy their human needs in a politics of all against all, it follows that they might try peace.

How could such a peace be achieved?

Obviously *cooperation* rather than *conflict* suggests itself as a possible method. But the good will to cooperate is not enough. The

---

*We noted that this system of politics as conflict tended to reify or freeze five kinds of existing social facts which frustrate human needs: values, personalities, social and political institutions, and rules of the game.

obvious short-run advantages in being brutal and competitive are difficult to defer for qualitative gains in the long run. It seems almost hopeless to teach men so oriented that there is any other alternative.

Yet our behavior as irrational people is often the result of what "rational" people have taught us about the nature of man. Hobbes's concept of man as vicious beast that had to be kept in a zoo under the control of a warden—the Leviathan—has influenced our Constitution, our institutions, and our assumptions about daily life.* The assumptions of science about man as a being that can be analyzed apart from daily life in the bright isolation cubicles of psychologists similarly filter down into our daily lives. Industrial psychology and sociology design our environment at work, and psychoanalysis and psychiatry emphasize the separateness of individual identities (as if one could ever actualize himself apart from others) and design the standards of our daily private lives.

Knowledge is always a blueprint for understanding ourselves in the world and for acting in it. The knowledge of science filters down to us through the powerful conditions of technology and social and economic institutions that treat men and women as things. Naturally following that blueprint of scientism, we treat each other as things.

How can an understanding of the world be developed that has less debilitating and more humanizing consequences?

The Alternative: Phenomenology   Science today is roughly split into two camps: those who tell us there is only one social reality and they almost have the key to it, and those who argue that social reality becomes whatever human beings make it.

Most social science, including political science, is the science of society. The *science of society* increasingly affirms the overriding reality of the system within which we live as against ourselves. It tells us that we are obligated to keep the system going. Such a science, of which systems analysis and structural-functionalism are examples, sees men and women as mere cogs and wheels performing roles and functions within institutional structures of the system. This view tends to freeze social facts into inevitable conditions.

The alternate social and political science must be a science for human beings. A *science for human beings* concerns itself with making life human. The logic of fulfilling our five human needs commands that such a science must show us how it is to our advantage to interact as human beings in order to fulfill our needs as human beings.

Fortunately, such a science is already available in phenomenology and merely needs extension into the realm of politics.

The isolated, dehumanized individual is the unit of analysis or focus in traditional science. Phenomenology's unit of analysis is a group of at least two human beings linked through their interaction and mutual understanding. To remove an individual from this group is to destroy

The Phenomenological Model of Man

*See the section on Hobbes in this chapter, pages 274 to 276.

†Phenomenology = literally, knowledge (-ology) of appearances (phenomena). See Chapter 11, pp. 256 to 259.

the reality that existed when he was in the group, interacting and sharing meanings. This is why traditional science, which isolates individuals, begins to destroy what is human in people as soon as it begins to study them. Men and women lose their essential humanity when isolated from other men and women.

The unit of analysis recommended by phenomenology consists of:

] At least two individuals [
] each with intentions (goals) [
] engaging in interaction to make real these intentions [
] and deriving meaning from understanding each other's intentions. [
] This mutual understanding becomes the social reality of these two individuals. [

A number of important new insights come out of this view of human beings. These can be used both for doing and studying politics. And, as we have argued, to *truly* think politics is to *do* it.

Intentions   If I want to do politics with another individual, I must first try to understand the subjective intentions with which he approaches me. I cannot treat him as a mere object. If I don't recognize him as a willful subject, I can never know whether his perceived needs are the same as mine—that is, I can never engage him in politics. I must try to reduce the tension between my partner as social fact and myself before attempting to reach my goals with and through him.

Interaction   All human needs are better achieved through politics as social acts involving others, and some—love, esteem, and actualization—can be achieved *only* that way. Therefore, doing politics involves a commitment to action—specifically, interaction. Those of us who desire to satisfy all our human needs are condemned, pleasantly or unpleasantly, to a continuing process of acting out our intentions in full view of others, of hoping they will understand and share our intentions and reciprocate, of talking and explaining when they don't. *Action* flows from isolated individuals.

Interaction is sets of actions mutually directed at one another and understood as such. It becomes possible only when we orient our own subjective world toward the likely subjective perceptions of an other and when he or she does the same toward us. This does not bar the possibility of conflict. But even conflict is meaningful only when we understand our mutual intentions, and to the extent that we engage in conflict, such understanding is less likely.

Meaning   Intended political acts can become meaningful only as others understand them. Such acts can become reality only as such understanding leads to reciprocal counter-acts that, together with our acts, are interaction. To the extent that we deal with satisfying human needs, *meaning in social and political life can be gotten only in the company of others* who also seek to satisfy human needs. The meaning of an interaction is the mutual understanding of each other's goals, purposes, and methods.

Anyone who has ever been in love knows that the experience of being with the beloved represents a level and quality of meaning that cannot be achieved alone.

Anyone who has tried to develop self-esteem knows that interacting with others and thus obtaining their appreciation beats telling yourself that you have identity and worth.

Anyone who has faced a problem and reached the limits of his capacities to solve it knows that having another individual join him with *his* capacities to solve the problem is an infinitely more satisfying experience than muddling along alone. This is true whether the problem is writing a book, teaching a sonnet, starting a farm, or raising a child. The possibilities of different ways to self-actualize through and with others are infinite.

Reality　Under this view of human beings, the nature of reality itself is exposed. What is real to you and me about this book is only that which we have mutually understood. The book becomes real for you not only because I intended to make it meaningful for you but also because you did not treat me and my product as a mere object but tried to get into my head for what I meant. Because we did not stand face to face when you tried to comprehend my meaning, you did not have the advantage of direct interaction. If you and I did stand face to face, our chances of understanding each other would be infinitely greater. Nevertheless, this filtered communication is a typical *example* of what becomes real between people.

What becomes real between people is a set of interactions, accompanied by meanings originating in each of them, *as these interactions are mutually understood.* The only social or political reality we can know is that which we ourselves have built by devoting to it our intentions, committing our actions, trying to understand each others' actions, and transforming them into interactions. To the extent that these interactions are mutually understood, we have created between us our personal reality. To the extent that others mutually understand their interaction in terms of their own meanings, our problem as political and social scientists is to see these interactions from the perspectives of the actors involved. But neither participant nor observer can ever *impose* reality. *Reality is always constructed by human beings involved in interaction.*

Analysis　Finally, while it is possible analytically to take apart the reality-creating relationship, each of these terms—*intentions, interaction, meaning, reality*—must be understood in the context of each other. It is *not* possible to experimentally take an individual out of his interactional context and ask him what his intentions *"really"* were. The result of such isolating questioning is that the individual will tell you what his intentions really are *in the interaction he is now involved in with you.*

As the political philosopher Eric Voegelin said:

> Human society is not merely a fact, or an event, in the external world to be studied by an observer like a natural phenomenon. . . . it is a whole little world . . . illuminated with meaning from within by the human beings who continuously create and bear it as the mode and condition of their self-realization.[11]

Especially when studying the world-creating problems of trying to satisfy human needs through a politics for human beings, the scientist must become very aware (1) of his own intentions, (2) of the intentions of others, (3) of the process by which interaction with his subjects produces a new reality, with new meanings, that is distinguishable from the intentions of any single participant.

On these grounds, how does the political scientist apply the phenomenological method?

The Phenomenologist's Method

The phenomenologist approaches any political situation with the assumption that it involves (a) at least two individuals; (b) needs of individuals expressed through intentions; (c) actions of each individual, oriented both toward accomplishing his intentions and toward the intentions of the other individual; (d) the mutual translation by these individuals of their intentions into a relationship; (e) their recognition of this relationship or interaction as constituting their social reality.

We are now ready to translate the standard analysis of politics with its limitations into the limitless analysis leading to a politics for human beings.

First, our assumptions. If these are correct, then the tendency toward a politics for human beings is irrepressible, because all human beings interact out of intentions. Ultimately these intentions can be traced to human needs, no matter how much existing social reality or social facts distort them. The problem of politics we must face is one of trying to resolve the tension between human needs and social facts. Such tension is unavoidable in any age because, as man and his created environment both change, human needs or social facts undergo development, bringing ever new tensions. Despite the motivating force of human needs, success in constructing a politics for human beings is not guaranteed. We can tie ourselves in knots in our tangle with social facts (for perfect examples, see the poems of psychiatrist R. D. Laing, appropriately called *Knots*[13]), or we can design a strategy in which human needs win out.

Here is one such strategy. It suggests that we use the insights drawn from phenomenology to melt the all-too-solid flesh of social facts down to their bare bones.

To apply this strategy:

Recognize politics for what it is. Politics is not just process. It is made up of both process and purpose. Human goals come out of human *needs*—for example, Abraham Maslow's listing: physiological, security, love, self-esteem, self-actualization. (See Chapter 2 and Chapter 6.) Any process that calls itself politics and does not deal directly with human needs is likely to be not politics but *pseudopolitics.*

Recognize that politics and political systems have no life of their own. They are man-made. (See the creative activities of Alphonse and Balthazar in Chapter 1.)

Recognize that social facts are not insuperable. They are the intentions of others—whether conscious or not, whether human or inhumane.

Recognize that to do politics for human beings means to bring the intentions of yourselves and others closer to human needs.

Proceed to prepare a politics for human beings by first freeing people's minds to recognize human needs. Such mental liberation involves teaching ourselves how to overcome our own minds' disabling tricks: *one-dimensionality, alienation, reification, pathological ideology,* and *stasis.* For examples of attempts to free people's minds, see our own attempt (Chapter 3, pages 39 to 46), the attempts of everyday and not-so-everyday Americans (Chapter 4, pages 59 to 73), the tools of analysis for comparing politics (Chapter 6, and Herbert Marcuse's effort (this chapter, pages 277 to 281).

Give yourself a chance for concrete political success by figuring out where you stand in political time and space. Different times and different power positions give you different chances and opportunities. *Time:* Know whether you live in a time of maintenance, decay, or creation. *Space:* Know your access to sources of power—*class, status, institutions.* Learn the steps for doing politics in the face of social facts that won't relent (Chapter 3, pages 48 to 52), and learn how to avoid mistakes in taking the steps (Chapter 4). See how well international figures oriented themselves in Chapter 8.

Remember that concepts are only tools—not your master. When you use the standard variables for the analysis of politics—*rules, values, socio-economic status, institutions,* and *personality*—Remember that behind these variables are human beings who need only to recognize the idea that *they* can design their own rules and values, use class and status and institutions for their own purposes, and shape and reshape their personality. And, in a time of rapid change, they are likely to!

Phenomenological political scientists do not discard traditional or behavioral tools of social science. We use them.[12]

But we are deliberately conscious of the bias they carry. All frameworks carry their own biases, but we insist on opening such baggage.

As Max Weber has pointed out, it's perfectly appropriate (even necessary) to have a bias in our social science. The question is, are you biased consciously or unconsciously. And, are you biased for or against human beings in the theories you use to grasp the world.

All theories become attitudes. As an attitude, phenomenology focuses the political scientist upon needs and social conditions of everyday life. Within this attitude, he selects tools that give him solutions affirming human needs as the goals of politics and human interaction as its condition.

In America today, what is called politics presents itself superficially as conflict—as struggle between people over whatever goods there are to get. Consequently, much of political science has treated politics as a subject to be understood through conflict models.

The logical extreme of a conflict approach is that each of us lives in his own private world, that each reaches out of that world occasionally to snatch something he wants out of someone else's world, that each builds his private world by grabbing goods from others.

This view ignores such questions as, How does it become at all possible for each of us to recognize there are other private worlds beyond our own from which to grab goods? If each lives in his own little nation, how does he manage to communicate enough to engage in the *inter*-national relations *between* individuals to haggle over the goods? How do we even know that the *others* in their private worlds are human like ourselves, and potentially capable not only of understanding us but of valuing goods we want? And besides, is there never a case when we cooperate with any of these others to get goods, rather than just grasp and grapple and scuttle off with our loot?

The fact is that "we do not, each one of us, experience the life-world as a private world; on the contrary, we take it for a public world, common to all of us, that is, for an intersubjective world. Not only do we encounter our fellowmen within the life-world as this world is given to us, but we also take it for granted that they are confronted with the same world and the same mundane existence as we are."[14]

In traditional political terms, this means that even when two senators, or two political groups, are engaging in conflict to grab what there is to grab, they do so within a mutual understanding of *rules of the game.* These rules of the game constitute the mutually shared meanings of their social relationship. Most importantly, these rules contain warning signs about how far each can go in conflict without endangering the existence of the relationship altogether.

In America, for example, conflict over the goods is resolved by threatening and bludgeoning and finally negotiating and compromising—but no one is supposed to *ever* ask for so much as to put the opposition out of the game permanently. In other words, those in Nixon's White House who burglarized, bugged, lied, and sabotaged, using the institutions of government and the millions of corporation money, were subverting the American rules of the game. In fact, they almost walked off with the game. The pathology of thinking of politics only as conflict, in this case, almost cost an entire nation its existence as Americans had known it.

The largest example of all of the pathology of the conflict approach is the present threat to the existence of the world. By thinking about international relations in terms of conflict, we have reaped nothing but violence, war, and the doom that lies in our atomic missile silos.

Nevertheless, many political scientists still ignore those fundamental aspects of human interaction that make any kind of life—whether conflict or cooperation—possible at all.

As the political scientist Hwa Yol Jung writes:

Unfortunately, in contemporary American political theory there is a pervasive tendency that polarizes conflict and cooperation in order to place a one-sided premium on conflict and competition as the essence of politics. For too many the political system is synonymous with a system of conflict.[15]

For example, political scientist Robert A. Dahl sees politics and conflict to be "inseparable twins."[16] And E. E. Schattschneider, another political scientist, saw the language of conflict to be at the heart of all politics. Schattschneider did go so far as to recognize that individuals, especially the relatively powerless, needed to cooperate in order to achieve their goals against others. But this cooperation, he said, would be achieved by widening the scope of existing conflict and thereby attracting more troops into the battle—some of whom might come over to your side. Ultimately he saw democratic government as the greatest single instrument for the spread and nationalization of conflict.[17]

Ironically, some of the early founders of political science were quite conscious of the cooperative foundation of all politics. Their students simply defected from that consciousness. For example, the dean of American political science, Harold D. Lasswell, even while arguing that "the science of power (in the narrowest sense) is political science,"[18] approvingly cites the definition of power by another founder of the discipline, Charles E. Merriam:

> It cannot be concluded, as many have, that the essence of the power situation is force, in the sense of violence and physical brutality. Altruism as well as egoism has a place in human relations and organization, and cooperation has as genuine a position as coercion.[19]

Further, unlike some of his students, Lasswell understood quite well that a relationship of political power presupposed agreement and understanding over values; that is, mutual sharing of meanings and intentions. "The power relation presupposes specified valuations: we speak of power as a control over value practices and patterns. Values are presupposed, moreover, by sanctions, which are without effectiveness unless their application does in fact constitute a deprivation."[20]

In other words, the struggle for power that many political scientists see as the central machinery of politics is anchored in a shared world, the precondition of the development of meaningful conflict—or cooperation. Only within the context of these shared meanings and the structure of relationships they represent is it possible to study conflict or power struggle.

Especially in times of decay and creation of political systems, it follows that the emphasis of a science of politics must be on the process of interaction by which human beings seek to construct means and structures to reach their major objectives, rather than on conflict. For unless conflict is mere blind unfocused rage, it is not possible until after agreement over values, meanings, and interactions has been reached. And until conflict is recognized as a pathological deviation from the norm, political science will remain a biased tool not towards recognizing and actualizing human possibilities, but towards building around humanity a barbed-wire fence of our limitations, within which we are encouraged to exterminate ourselves.

Practical Applications II: Comparative Politics

Other nations, like our own, are mankind's laboratories in which people in different international and natural environments use different techniques to translate similar sets of needs into goals.

A science for human beings is of particular use for making the results of these experiments mutually comprehensible. This can be done in two ways. First, if we accept a standard set of human needs—for example, physiological, safety, esteem, love, and actualization needs—then the performance of different nations in the satisfaction of these needs can be evaluated. Nations can be ranked as to the degree to which they fulfill human needs. Thus those of us critical of our own nation's performance can at least roughly know from which country *not* to borrow.

Secondly, a phenomenology of comparative politics is absolutely necessary if we are to understand the meanings that others in other countries attribute to their behaviors. This is always a difficult task, because as goals differ elsewhere, the meanings of behavior differ. It would be impossible to borrow techniques from other countries for reaching our goals if we had no way of understanding the meaning of the behavior in which others engage to reach their goals. Such understanding cannot be had if we impose our understanding of ourselves on the behavior of another people. (See Chapter 6 for a detailed discussion of these problems.)

Practical Applications III: International Relations

The largest opportunity and challenge for both a science and a politics for human beings exist today in the field of international relations. A quick glance at the opportunities shows the absolute necessity for an approach to living together for the purpose of satisfying universal human needs.

First, only in international relations has it become totally clear that what we need is not more theories, technologies, or examples of doing conflict. The world is saturated with both the knowledge and the capacity of how to make conflict more efficient, total, and final.

No, what is needed here is not more knowledge about how to manipulate the engines of power, competition, and violence. The human species and its survival cannot be treated by political scientists or anyone else as a "game" in which you win some and lose some (that is, in which some amass millions of dollars, while many others pay the price in infant mortality, starvation, illness, and debilitating work). Such games may be just barely bearable in domestic politics, but if you want to be that kind of politician or political scientist on the international level, we must say a final "No" to you before you nullify all of us.

Unfortunately, such international politicians still exist. President John F. Kennedy and the Soviet leader Nikita S. Khrushchev played such a game with the life of the globe when they teetered on the brink of nuclear war over the 1962 Cuban missile crisis. The president's brother Robert later admitted to the depth of U.S. commitment by commenting that what he and his brother were worried about most in the crisis were all the children who might die if we ended up in a nuclear war.

Second, whereas individual nations are usually characterized by one set of rules of the game from which it is difficult to escape, there never has been a single institutional pattern of behavior on the global scale. There is no one way of thinking about how international relations should be handled. Since World War II, there have emerged at least two major ways of thought regarding *international law:* the traditional system espoused by the West, and the system of socialist legality espoused by some Communist countries, especially the Soviet Union.

In the traditional system, *procedural* safeguards are put before substantive issues to *maintain* an existing distribution of goods. In the newer socialist system, procedural safeguards play a secondary role to the achievement of *substantive* values, like the development of a not-yet-reached socialist-communist ideal society.

In international law, old-timers among nations have a vested interest in preserving procedures that maintain their dominance. Newcomers among nations have an interest in becoming dominant and are likely to have to undermine existing rules of behavior to get their way. This is why socialist countries, especially the Soviet Union, have been accused, correctly but without real understanding, of breaking so many treaties. While the danger exists that adherents of either the traditional or socialist system may become so convinced of the rightness of their approach as to reify it, at least there is no universal reification of how to solve the problems of international relations through international law. Yet, as long as that absence continues, there is still hope for thinking about the problem; reification, of course, ends thought.

Third, political international organizations are weak. This might be considered a bad thing if international politicians were sane—that is, if they understood universal human needs and were willing to build organizations for the purpose of doing an international politics for human beings. The situation being what it is, the lack of an all-powerful international organization may be a good thing. As a result of this vacuum, for example, it has been possible to develop cooperative economic organizations, such as the European Common Market, much more concerned with basic human needs than traditionally political ones. Also, those who would build international political organizations for human beings do not find their way blocked by already existing global institutions. Of course, the hundreds of reifications called nations competing in the world are a formidable obstacle of another kind.

As always, the challenges of reification and mutual alienation face us in the international sphere also—except that there such problems are on the largest possible scale. Yet those determined to do an international politics backing away from conflict and mutual destruction—Henry Kissinger, for example—are able to find opportunities (see Chapter 8, pages 177 to 184). And there are some political scientists who are beginning to work on the problem of defining standards of human needs against which to measure national policies, standards that could be expanded to a global scale.[21]

Practical Applications IV: An Ethics for Human Beings

The most difficult thing to teach or learn is the idea that—for whatever reason—we as human beings ought to behave in this or that way. An ethics for human beings always seems to bring obvious advantages to the other guy while leaving our benefits in doubt.

But we have seen that achieving and securing the five basic human needs is dependent on the type of interaction exposed by phenomenology. Therefore, we are now put in the position of either engaging in a politics for human beings or not getting anywhere close to satisfying those needs.

If you don't want love, which can be gotten only through the give and take of interaction, then reject the idea of treating others like yourself, don't try to understand their intentions, don't interact with them, don't share meanings with them, don't construct reality with them.

Do similarly if you don't want self-esteem, if you don't want to self-actualize, and if you want to live at lower levels of satisfaction of physiological and safety needs than you could reach with and through others.

Understanding the process of human interaction and involving ourselves in it stands thus unveiled as an instrumental ethic—a categorical imperative stating what we must do if we want to satisfy human needs—that is, if we want to be human.

He who rejects this ethic cheats mainly himself. You *can* reject this ethic, but you have to be willing to take the consequences of becoming or remaining less than human.

The only values assumption involved in this ethic is the assumption that any living being, including human beings, strives to optimize its chances for using all its potentials and capacities. Because human beings are not given a world to live in, but must construct their own, the development of creative interaction is a human necessity that we can perceive as our obligation if we want to be human.

Suddenly other ethical imperatives are exposed as mere necessities. For example, Immanuel Kant's categorical imperative that we treat other human beings as we would like to be treated ourselves emerges as one of the operative conditions that makes interaction possible. If I do not treat you as a human being essentially deserving of the respect and dignity that I deserve, it will be impossible for me ever to try to understand your intentions in my terms or to begin interaction with you. Only if I assume that each other person contains an essential bit of my self does communication and interaction become possible at all.

Without intending to create an ethic, the phenomenological sociologist Alfred Schutz uncovered the basic assumptions that we all take for granted in conducting everyday life.[22]

Schutz's assumptions are as important to the understanding of the social world as Kant's concepts are to the understanding of the natural world. Kant points out in his *Critique of Pure Reason* that the idea of space is absolutely necessary to the idea of matter or objects. Objects can be distinguished only if there is space to separate them.

Object space in the natural world becomes people space in the social world. Take, for example, Schutz's distinction between self and other. The idea of the other is necessary to separate human subjects, to distinguish between realms of my sphere of social action and the others' sphere of social action. Although many people may take this distinction for granted, its importance is shown by the disasters that befall us when the distinction is not made. There are three kinds of such disasters: either I think my ego extends through the totality of the world (megalomania), or I think I am the other (schizophrenia), or my ego, crushed by a hostile and all-powerful world, dissolves (alienation).

Positively speaking, only if we differentiate between ourselves and others do we see that our individual integrity depends on the distinction from others. And only if we make this distinction can we understand others' will to be, anticipate the conflict of wills, and see the need to communicate to resolve conflict.

The problem of communicating arising from Schutz's first assumption, the distinction between self and other, leads to his second assumption: similarity between self and others. Only if we assume that each other contains a bit of our self—similarity—does communication become thinkable. Inter-subjectively meaningful language is possible only with such similarity.

If we accent differences in our intersubjective communication, we arrive at a we-they politics of differences (politics as who gets what when how, interest group politics, ethnic politics, racism). If we accent similarities, we work towards a universalistic politics of cooperation that enables all human beings to self-actualize.

As we have said, the assumption of similarity makes communication possible. It enables each of us to see that it is possible to step into another's shoes without losing ourselves. And in turn, stepping into another's shoes enables me to take his perspective on the world. Problems become common only when we slip in and out of each other's perspectives. Or, to paraphrase Ronald Laing, self-actualization becomes possible only when I step out of my mind.

Of course, Kant realized this a long time ago when he advised us to treat each other as we would treat ourselves. As we pointed out, self-actualization takes a long time. But using Kant's categorical imperative as an end and Schutz's similarity assumption as a means, we now know how to slip into each other's shoes and make a beginning.

Further support for this ethic comes from scientific findings that some people say they are interested in the moral self-actualization implied by Kant's imperative. On a six-level scale of moral judgment developed by Lawrence Kohlberg, and derived from the empirical studies of Jean Piaget, the highest stage of self-actualization is described as follows:

Stage 6: Individual Principles—Conscience or principle orientation. Orientation not only to actually ordained social rules but to principles of choice involving appeal to logical universality and consistency. Orientation to conscience as a directing agent and to mutual respect and trust.[23]

Given the choice between alternatives in a number of stories illustrating different moral dilemmas, a significant number of people placed themselves in Kohlberg's highest moral stage.

Second, it was found that fully 75 percent of people with a Stage 6 capacity for moral judgment refused to torture a bound victim, in an experiment testing obedience done by Stanley Milgram. On the other hand, only 13 percent of those at lower stages of moral judgment refused to execute the victim in the experiment. (Of course the torture and execution weren't really applied, but none of the torturers and executioners were aware of this.)[24]

Knowing how to step into an other's shoes not only keeps you from killing and maiming people, but may help you actualize yourself. Of course, to achieve this highest level of moral development you may have to rebel against lower-developed others like Adolf Hitler and Adolf Eichmann, who treated human beings as things and executed millions of them. To see others as human *subjects* of a social world *like* yourself deters you from treating them violently as alien *objects* totally unlike yourself. You must rebel against people treating others as objects so that we may all one day be treated as subjects in the human commonwealth.

INCONCLUSIONS We have tried briefly to give our approach through political thinking to the major problems we perceived in the world.

The central problem we saw was the misuse of traditional science, including political science, which had led inevitably to man's present dehumanizing condition.

The science we suggested as a substitute was a science for human beings that would recognize universal human needs and provide a method for satisfying those needs humanely. The study of human interaction through phenomenology seemed to provide such a method.

Some practical consequences of this approach were discussed in the case of politics in the United States, in other countries, and between countries. Finally, we concluded that in a very practical way our approach led logically to an ethic of always respecting others' dignity, their intentions, their understanding of us. Our suggested ethic for mankind is that each of us try to determine what needs are essential and universal and commit himself to humane interaction as the only method through which human needs can be satisfied.

We expect that scientific investigation of human needs and normative evaluation of their consequences will still further clarify the human condition. We do not mean to impose Abraham Maslow's synthesis of needs as the final answer. Further, phenomenology as an approach needs much more refinement. What we propose here is, however, a program of thought and political action based on those goals and methods currently available that seem to have the greatest chance of achieving a politics for human beings. We conceive such a politics, like a science for human beings, as a never-ending process to which we must dedicate our search for knowledge and our judicious commitment to interaction.

1. Much of this chapter was inspired by the investigations of the sociologist Alfred Schutz of the differences between everyday and scientific thought. See his *Collected Papers,* vol. 1 (The Hague: Martinus Nijhoff, 1964), Part I, Section I; and ibid., vol. II, "The Well-Informed Citizen" and "The Stranger."

2. D. O. Hebb, *A Textbook of Physiological Psychology* (Philadelphia: W. B. Saunders, 1966).

3. Emile Durkheim, *Suicide* (New York: The Free Press, 1951).

4. James C. Davies, "Toward a Theory of Revolution," in *When Men Revolt and Why,* ed. James C. Davies (New York: The Free Press, 1971).

5. On thinking as usual, see Alfred Schutz, *Collected Papers,* vol. II (The Hague: Martinus Nijhoff, 1964), p. 96. For the immediately preceding citation see loc. cit.

6. Schutz, *Collected Words,* vol. II, pp. 72–73.

7. Herbert Marcuse, *One-Dimensional Man* (Boston: Beacon Press, 1964), p. 32.

8. Theodor Roszak, *The Making of a Counter-Culture* (Garden City, New York: Doubleday, Anchor, 1969), pp. 14–5.

9. Bernard Crick, *In Defense of Politics* (Baltimore: Penguin Books, 1964), p. 151.

10. Juergen Habermas, "Technology and Science as 'Ideology,'" *Toward a Rational Society: Student Protest, Science and Politics* (Boston, Beacon Paperback, 1971), pp. 81–122.

11. Eric Voegelin, *The New Science of Politics: An Introduction* (Chicago: University of Chicago Press, 1952), p. 27.

12. On the inclusion of phenomenology within the scientific method, see Arnold Brecht, *Political Theory; The Foundations of Twentieth-Century Political Thought* (Princeton, N.J.: Princeton University Press, 1970), p. 53.

13. R. D. Laing, *Knots* (N.Y.: Random House-Pantheon Books, 1970).

14. Aron Gurwitch, "Introduction" to Alfred Schutz, *Collected Papers,* vol. III (The Hague: Martinus Nijhoff, 1966), p. xiii.

15. Hwa Yol Jung, "The Political Relevance of Existential Phenomenology," in *Existential Phenomenology and Political Theory: A Reader* (Chicago: Henry Regnery, 1972), p. xiii. For more advanced students, this reader serves as an excellent companion volume to this book. Jung's article first appeared in *The Review of Politics* 33, no. 4 (October 1971), pp. 538–63.

16. Robert A. Dahl, *Modern Political Analysis* (Englewood Cliffs, N.J.: Prentice-Hall, 1963), p. 105.

17. E. E. Schattschneider, *The Semi-Sovereign People* (New York: Holt, Rinehart & Winston, 1960).

18. Harold D. Lasswell and Abraham Kaplan, *Power and Society: A Framework for Political Inquiry* (New Haven: Yale University Press, 1968), p. 82.

19. Charles E. Merriam, *Political Power* (New York:MMcGraw-Hill, 1934), p. 20. Cited in Lasswell and Kaplan, *Power and Society,* pp. 76.

20. Lasswell and Kaplan, *Power and Society,* pp. 76–77.

21. See, for an example of an approach taking into account the total needs of man in his total environment, Peter A. Corning, "The Problem of Applying Darwinian Evolution to Political Science," paper delivered at the Eighth World

Congress of the International Political Science Association, Munich, Germany, August 31–September 5, 1970. This paper contains a proposed set of indicators against which to measure public policies' contribution to species survival. See also Peter A. Corning, "The Biological Bases of Behavior and Some Implications for Political Science," *World Politics* 23 (April 1971), pp. 321–370, for a general exposition of the problem of thinking of mankind as in a long-range global environment of shared time and space.

22. See especially Alfred Schutz, *Collected Papers,* 3 vols. (The Hague: Martinus Nijhoff, 1964), Vol. 1, Part 1, "On the Methodology of the Social Sciences," and Part 2, "Phenomenology and the Social Sciences," and Vol. II, the essay "Some Structures of the Life World."

23. See "Stage and Sequence: The Cognitive-Developmental Approach to Socialization," by Lawrence Kohlberg in *Handbook of Socialization Theory and Research,* ed. David A. Goslin (New York: Rand McNally, 1969), p. 376. For Kohlberg's inspiration, see Jean Piaget, *The Moral Judgment of the Child* (New York: The Free Press, 1965). Charles Hampden-Turner was the first, to our knowledge, to relate Kohlberg's moral judgment scale to Maslow's need hierarchy and both to social science models of thought. His summary of Kohlberg's scale, beginning with the most primitive stage: "(1): obedience and punishment orientation. Egocentric deference to superior power . . . or a trouble-avoiding set; (2): Instrumental Relativists—Naively egoistic orientation. Right Action is that instrumentally satisfying the self's needs and occasionally others'; (3): Personal Concordance—Good Boy orientation. Orientation to approval and to pleasing and helping others; (4): Law and Order: . . . Orientation to doing duty and showing respect for authority for its own sake; (5): Social Contract Orientation; (6): Individual Principles . . . " [see pp. 295—296 this volume]. See also Hampden-Turner's *Radical Man: The Process of Psycho-Social Development* (New York: Doubleday, Anchor, 1971). pp. 135—136.

24. Lawrence Kohlberg, "Education for Justice . . .," Ernest Burton Lecture on Moral Education, delivered at Harvard University, April 23, 1968 (Harvard School of Education, mimeographed). See also Lawrence Kohlberg, *Stages in the Development of Moral Thought and Action* (New York: Holt, Rinehart & Winston, 1974).

Epilogue:
The Politics of Politics
for Human Beings

All definitions of politics are political acts.

Isaak and Hummel are not exempted from this truth. In attempting to create a new paradigm, we acted, like all human beings in crisis, out of tension between human needs and social facts. Indeed, the reader who arrives at this point experiences his own tension between what he expected to find in the book, as defined by his needs, and the social fact of what he found. There is only one way for a reader to judge whether any paradigm fits his needs before trying it out, and that is to see if the authors had experiences similar to his crises. This involves the sociology of knowledge—which asks, "Says who?" It assumes that anyone's knowing about the world depends on where and how he stands in society.

Even the awareness about apolitics and our escape from it through a new paradigm had to come out of experience with it. This experience began in the middle-class Eighth Street Drugstore, shortly after a class in American social and political thought with political philosopher H. Mark Roelofs at New York University. At that time, Isaak was still trying to overcome a typical Californian's alienation from New York, and Hummel, working eight hours a night on a newspaper and studying full time during the day, was trying to overcome alienation from himself. Roelofs had just finished giving the class a history of the homogeneous alienation of all Americans from their needs, and had delivered his Doom lecture. Isaak ordered three cups of very black coffee; Hummel, ten aspirin, and a fellow Roelofsian, Howard Smuckler, a chicken-soup sandwich. (Howard since then finished his M.A. on the history of the dialectic and decided to become an electrician's helper, his only present burden being a toolbox that he defines as too heavy. Such intuitive escapes are not easily come by.)

Roelofs had just pointed out that the reason we were alone, alive, and afraid in mass society was that Americans had become stuck on the only political idea they ever had: Thomas Hobbes's concept of man as rugged individualist trying to ward off death at the hands of others by the endless acquisition of things. The result: institutionalization of the war by all against all in federalism and checks and balances, making it in the interest of no one to have a concept of society, obligation, or general welfare.

This observation later enabled us to develop the idea of pathological realism—a conflict approach that becomes self-fulfilling prophecy and threatens survival itself by ignoring cooperative aspects of politics.

The three of us concluded that the only way out of American isolation was to do what we were doing—to establish a social relationship. In later contact with sociologist Peter Berger, who led us to Max

Weber and Alfred Schutz, this insight received its theoretical justification. Weber gave us the answer to the major problem of social scientists, later applied to our approach to comparative politics: If you want to understand events in other cultures, ask the inhabitants for the meanings they ascribe to these events.

Schutz, joining sociology with phenomenology, extended Weber's insight to everyday life, noting that each individual lives within his own subjective world, and that the problem of human beings is to create an intersubjective world of meanings that make social life possible. This idea influenced our approach to international politics, along with the insight of political scientist Kyung-Won Kim, who noted that in the French Revolution ideological rigidity caused both conservatives and revolutionaries to misperceive each others' social worlds, leading to revolutionary violence and repressive reaction.* This example led us to recognize the pathological elements in all ideologies, particularly in the extremes of ideological realism and ideological idealism.

Kim also first introduced one of us to the idea of the humanistic psychologist Rollo May that crazy people can be understood in terms of their needs only if you enter their mad world and learn their mad language. Later the psychiatrist Ronald Laing noted that it is important to study crazy people in a world in which normal men kill 100 million of their fellow normal men in a period of fifty years. In personal conversation with Rollo May, the inspiration struck us that no human being has a right to keep his madness to himself, that powerlessness is the ultimate corruption of man's will to be human, and that healthy aggression is the way out of apolitics and into the creation of self with others.

Rollo May also helped divert us from the temptation of pathological idealism at least implicit in Alfred Schutz, Ronald Laing, and Immanuel Kant. Pathological idealism results from the reification of personal subjective experience—in Kant, the experience of time and space; in Schutz, the experience of the meaning of action; in Laing, the experience of emotion. We recognized in ourselves a common human failing: the tendency to believe that one's own experience can be valid for the world. We then saw the other side of Kant, Schutz, and Laing—that time and space also are objective realities against which an idealist can break his head, that one's own meanings, once shared with others, become a powerful social reality, and that one cannot experience another's emotion as his own experience, but must nevertheless deal with it.

At this point we realized that there are such things as social facts. Politics could not be conceived as merely a social relationship in which idealists create themselves through others, but would have to be defined to take into account the hindering or helpful presence of social and political institutions in various stages of development. Playful and purposeless earlier readings in the philosophy of history now fell into conscious coherence: the cycles of civilization conceived by Oswald Spengler, Pitirim Sorokin, and Arnold Toynbee.

*Kyung-Won Kim, *Revolution and International System* (New York: New York University Press, 1970), p. 131 ff.

Inspired by these macro-cycles in which history is the actor and the social micro-cycles of Karl Marx and Peter Berger in which man creates his world and is created by it, we invented a social macro-cycle within which an individual can locate himself as an actor in a changing world of social facts: creation, maintenance, and decay. For at this point it became obvious to us that an individual trying to actualize his ideas might be well-advised to locate himself in social time and space. Creation is difficult in times of maintenance but easier in times of decay. The immediate pay-off of this approach was that we recognized that at least two cycles were going on in America at the same time—grinding people between them. The traditional American political game is going from maintenance to decay, from enthusiastic support for political institutions to doubt about the system and self-doubt. Simultaneously, the average American does not hesitate to perceive his job as his first need, nor to accept apolitics—the ideology of corporation monopoly over the basic decisions of his life.

Through acquiescence and unconscious acceptance, people have allowed corporations to create the era of apolitics, which has gone from creation to maintenance. In this sense the behavioristic psychologist B. F. Skinner is more right than he knows—corporations have already taken us beyond freedom and dignity. Where in the corporation is there consideration of values such as love and hate, freedom and justice, of socialization as the patient teaching of values to be willingly accepted in behavior, of the whole human being in the Renaissance sense? Values are replaced by stimulus-response, socialization by conditioning, personality by roles, class by skills, love by sex.

How much further can we get away from humanity? Ground between these two cycles—traditional politics and apolitics—how can Terminated Man even dream of a politics for human beings? The answer is to be found in universal human needs. We scented this when we discovered that our graduate school experience failed to meet our human needs. We felt like the Pavlovian rats and dogs that turned off psychologist Abraham Maslow when he was in graduate school. In reaction to his experience with the paradigms of conditioning, Maslow wrote his first paper, "Psychoanalysis as a Status-Quo Social Philosophy." Similarly, we found that the prevailing paradigms of political science masked a static society in which an apolitical standard of normality conditions the individual into a passive role, rather than cutting to the core of the tension between social facts and human needs. Our response was *Politics for Human Beings*.

Actually such a politics has yet to be constructed. Moreover, the task will never be finished. But to begin, human beings must first recognize their needs. In the future these may turn out to be as manifold and ever-changing as evolving man himself. However, for our present stage of development, Maslow has suggested this hierarchy of needs: physiological needs, security needs, love needs, self-esteem needs, and self-actualization needs. If we are not to fall into the trap of conditioned value-relativism, in which any human being's values are valid as long as he has the power to enforce them, we must begin with what we have. Beginning with these needs, we offer no panacea, merely a temporary tool to help human beings discover creative power: the definition of politics as a social act to resolve the tension between human needs and social facts.

To Explore Further

Although the footnotes and the suggestions in the Invitations provide the reader with ways to go deeper into some of the topics covered in this book, the following is a short additional list of lucid or provocative readings on central themes.

For a literary introduction to the nature of politics, read William Golding's novel *Lord of the Flies*, Eugene Ionesco's play *Rhinoceros*, or Philip Green and Michael Walzer's reader *The Political Imagination in Literature* (New York: The Free Press, 1969). For a philosophical introduction, read Ernst Cassirer's *The Myth of the State* (New Haven, Conn.: Yale University Press, 1946), Plato's *Republic,* or Albert Camus's *The Rebel* (New York: Alfred Knopf, 1956). Lucid socio-psychological treatments include Kenneth Boulding's *The Image* (University of Michigan Press, 1956), Henry Kariel's *Open Systems: Arenas for Political Action* (Itasca, Illinois: F. E. Peacock, 1968) and Elliot Aronson's *The Social Animal* (San Francisco: W. H. Freeman, 1972). For an economic view, see Morton Mintz and Jerry Cohen, *America Incorporated* (New York: Dell, 1972).

On "Understanding Politics," Chapter One

Two standard works that "define" politics include Harold Lasswell's *Politics: Who Gets What When How Why* (New York: McGraw-Hill, 1936) and David Easton's *The Political System* (New York: Alfred Knopf, 1953). The need to move beyond these standard views of politics is expressed in Henry Kariel's *Saving Appearances: The Reestablishment of Political Science* (North Scituate, Massachusetts: Duxbury Press, 1972); Charles McCoy and John Playford, eds, *Apolitical Politics* (New York: Thomas Y. Crowell, 1967); and George Graham and George Carey, eds., *The Post-behavioral Era: Perspectives on Political Science* (New York: David McKay, 1972). To understand why politics can be fruitfully defined as a social act that seeks to solve the tension between human needs and social facts, see Peter Berger and Thomas Luckmann, *The Social Construction of Reality* (Garden City, New York: Doubleday, Anchor, 1967); Alfred Schutz's *Collected Papers,* Volume I (The Hague: Martinus Nijhoff, 1964); Kalman Silvert's *Man's Power* (New York: The Viking Press, 1970); and Colin Wilson's *New Pathways in Psychology—Maslow and the Post-Freudian Revolution* (New York: Taplinger, 1972). After *Politics for Human Beings* was written, we discovered two books that serve to empirically ground its definition of politics with Abraham Maslow's need scale: Jeanne N. Knutson's *The Human Basis of the Polity* (Chicago: Aldine-Atherton, 1972); and Joel Aronoff, *Psychological Needs and Cultural Systems* (Princeton: Van Nostrand, 1967). This definition is also supported in the sociological community by Amitai Etzioni in "Basic Human Needs, Alienation and Inauthenticity," *American Sociological Review* 33 (1968), pp. 870–885.

On "Defining Politics," Chapter Two

On "Doing Politics," For a handbook on how to create student action and research groups
Chapter Three and put them to work effectively, see Ralph Nader and Donald Ross,
*Action for a Change—A Student's Manual for Public Interest
Organizing* (New York: Viking, 1973). To create research designs to
help analyze and resolve urban crises through actual case studies, see
Robert A. Isaak and Elizabeth Kraus, eds., *Free Cities: A Primer for
Urban Liberation*, (Palo Alto, California: Page-Ficklin Publications,
1975). For the politics of setting up a free school, see Jonathan
Kozol, *Free Schools* (New York: Houghton Mifflin, 1972). To change
your university, see Harold Taylor, *How to Change Colleges—Notes
on Radical Reform* (New York: Holt, Rinehart and Winston, 1971).
To know how it feels to be in the midst of the national American
political process, see Hunter S. Thompson, *Fear and Loathing: On
the Campaign Trail* (Straight Arrow Books, 1973). To understand
how apolitics is done in multinational corporations, see Anthony
Sampson, *The Sovereign State of ITT* (New York: Stein and Day,
1973).

On "Executing Politics," A number of official records on the Watergate investigation are already
Chapter Four available; others are still forthcoming.

Aside from materials bearing directly on the scandal, some background material may shed perspective on the events within the general context of American politics. Outstanding among background
materials is "The Watergate File" issued by Warner Modular Publications of Andover, Mass. Of special interest in this set are the following:
Daniel R. Fusfeld, "The Rise of the Corporate State in America";
William J. Chambliss, "Vice, Corruption, and Power"; Bertram Gross,
"Friendly Fascism: A Model for America"; and Fred I. Greenstein,
"The Best-Known American."

Among government publications, raw data are provided by the
proceedings of various court hearings and trying cases involving
Watergate suspects. A most important document should be U. S.
Government, Senate, Senate Select Committee on Presidential Campaign Activities, *Watergate Hearings before the Senate Select Committee on Presidential Campaign Activities,* vols I-VIII (Washington, D. C.:
U.S. Government Printing Office, 1973) and the reports of the committee and of the House Judiciary Committee.

For a history of events, see Congressional Quarterly Service,
Watergate: Chronology of a Crisis (Washington, D. C.: Congressional
Quarterly Inc., 1973), which also provides detailed accounts of the
hearings and struggles over information and biographies of major participants.

Two articles of opinion on Watergate are published in the
magazine *Current:* "The Role of the President," *Current,* no. 153,
July/August 1973, on what should be done after Watergate, and
"Meaning of Watergate: Symposium," *Current,* nos. 154 and 155,
October/November 1973.

For further perspective on Nixon and McGovern, see William A.
Dobrovir et al., *The Offenses of Richard M. Nixon: A Guide for the
People of the United States* (New York: Quadrangle Books, 1974) and

James David Barber, "The Presidency after Watergate," *World*, July 31, 1973, as well as Richard Dougherty, *Goodbye, Mr. Christian: A Personal Account of McGovern's Rise and Fall* (Garden City, N.Y.: Doubleday, 1973). A standard reference on the campaign is Theodore H. White's *The Making of the President 1972* (New York: Atheneum, 1973), which had to be updated at the last minute after the Watergate affair was exposed in *The Washington Post.* The Post's prize-winning exposé still makes good reading.

An insider's viewpoint of McGovern is Gary Warren Hart, *Right from the Start* (New York: Quadrangle Books, 1973), in which McGovern's national campaign director gives his day-by-day journal of McGovern's campaign from the primaries to the election. An outsider's account of the entire Watergate affair is given in Linda Jenness and Andrew Pulley, *Watergate: The View from the Left* (New York, Pathfinder Press, 1973).

For a deeper understanding of *political culture*—the ideas according to which Americans play the traditional game of politics—see Louis Hartz, *The Liberal Tradition in America* (New York: Harcourt, Brace & World, 1955); and H. Mark Roelofs, *The Language of Modern Politics* (Homewood, Ill.: Dorsey, 1967). For empirical support that Americans are still guided by their traditional political ideas: William Watts and Lloyd A. Free, *State of the Nation* (New York: Universe Books, 1973). For the record of operative ideals left by the Constitution-makers: *The Federalist Papers,* in various editions.

On "Playing the American Game," Chapter Five

On national political institutions and processes: For *Congress:* Stephen K. Bailey, *Congress Makes a Law* (Random House, Vintage Books, 1950); by the same author, *Congress in the 70's* (New York: St. Martin's Press, 1970). On the *presidency:* Louis W. Koenig, *The Chief Executive,* revised edition (Harcourt, Brace & World, 1968); and Richard E. Neustadt, *Presidential Power* (New American Library, Signet Books, 1964). On the *Supreme Court:* Henry Abraham, *The Judiciary,* 2nd ed. (Boston: Allyn and Bacon, 1969); Theodore L. Becker and Vernon G. Murray, eds., *Government Lawlessness in America* (New York: Oxford University Press, 1971); and William O. Douglas, *Points of Rebellion* (New York: Random House, Vintage Books, 1970).

On interest group politics, the standard theoretical text is David B. Truman, *The Governmental Process—Political Interests and Public Opinion;* 2nd ed. (New York: Knopf, Borzoi Books, 1971). For recent *interest groups in action,* showing that some are more equal than others, see Morton Mintz and Jerry S. Cohen, *America, Inc.* (New York, Dell, 1972). For *recent party politics:* Richard M. Scammon and Ben J. Wattenberg, *The Real Majority* (New York: Coward, McCann & Geoghegan, Capricorn Edition, 1971). On how politicians see the voters, and whom they pay attention to: John W. Kingdon, *Candidates for Office: Beliefs and Strategies* (New York: Random House, 1968). On how Americans feel about politics and their government: Watts and Free, *State of the Nation,* already cited in this section, and John P. Robinson et al., *Measures of Political Attitudes* (Ann Arbor, Mich.: Survey Research Center—Institute for Social Research [University of Michigan], 1968).

For alternatives to public politics and attempts to create a private politics of everyday life, see Theodore Roszak, *The Making of a Counter Culture—Reflections on the Technocratic Society and Its Youthful Opposition* (Garden City, N.Y.: Doubleday, Anchor Books, 1969); Richard Poirier, *The Performing Self* (New York: Oxford University Press, 1971); Mary White Harder, James T. Richardson, and Robert B. Simmonds, "Jesus People," *Psychology Today* 6, no. 7 (December 1972).

On the development of a new apolitics, pioneering work dates back as far as A. A. Berle and Gardiner Means, *The Modern Corporation and Private Property* (New York: Macmillan, 1933).

The best recent book on the degree to which political decisions affecting the public are made privately by corporations is a collection of essays edited by Andrew Hacker, *The Corporation Take-Over* (Garden City, N.Y.: Doubleday, Anchor Books, 1965). See also A. A. Berle, *Economic Power and the Free Society* (The Fund for the Republic, 1957), and his *Power Without Property* (New York: Harcourt, Brace, 1959). Significant bases for a Marxian argument along the same line are Herbert Marcuse, *One-Dimensional Man: Studies in the Ideology of Advanced Industrial Society* (Boston: Beacon Press, 1966) and the critique of Marcuse by Juergen Habermas, "Technology and Science as 'Ideology,'" in Habermas, *Toward a Rational Society: Student Protest, Science and Politics* (Boston: Beacon Press, 1970).

On the agony of everyday life in the technological world, see the testimony of working people in Studs Terkel, *Working: People Talk About What They Do all Day and How They Feel About What They Do* (New York: Random House, Pantheon Books, 1974).

On how to use a creative and committed social science to help solve the agony of human needs, see Charles Hampden-Turner, *From Poverty to Dignity: A Strategy for America's Poor* (Garden City, N. Y.: Doubleday, Anchor, 1974).

On making a beginning toward rethinking politics in the apolitical era, see Ralph P. Hummel, "Technology and World Politics: The Need for a Conceptual Revolution," paper presented to the annual meeting of the New York State Political Science Association, March 30, 1974, Syracuse, N.Y.

On "Comparing Politics for Outsiders," Chapter Six

Two excellent books on comparative politics: Harry Eckstein and David Apter, eds., *Comparative Politics* (New York: The Free Press, 1968); and Lucian W. Pye, *Aspects of Political Development* (Boston: Little, Brown, 1966). Another worthy book is *Ideology and Discontent*, edited by David Apter (New York: The Free Press, 1964), particularly the outstanding article by Philip Converse, "The Nature of Belief Systems in Mass Publics," which deals with the attitudes of elite versus "mass" Americans.

To learn how to define and relate variables in correlations and meaningful hypotheses in comparing politics, see Hans Zetterberg, *On*

Theory and Verification in Sociology (Totowa: Bedminster Press, 1964); Bernard Berelson and Gary Steiner, Human Behavior, shorter edition, ed. Bernard Berelson, (New York: Harcourt, Brace & World, 1967); and Hubert Blalock, An Introduction to Social Research (Englewood Cliffs, New Jersey: Prentice-Hall, 1970).

To go deeper into the meaning of comparing politics in terms of the perceptions of human beings and their everyday experience, see Helmut Wagner's edited collection, Alfred Schutz on Phenomenology and Social Relations (Chicago: University of Chicago Press, 1970); Gregory Bateson's Steps to an Ecology of Mind (New York: Ballantine, 1972); H. P. Dreitzel, ed., Recent Sociology #2 (New York: Macmillan, 1970) on "ethnomethodology;" and The Hidden Dimension by Edward Hall (Garden City, New York: Doubleday, Anchor, 1969) on the anthropology of space in different cultures. To sample psycho-history, read Erik Erikson's Gandhi's Truth (New York: Norton, 1969.) on the leadership level; and Robert Jay Lifton's Death in Life; Survivors of Hiroshima (New York: Random House, 1967) on the level of mass psychological experiences of political acts. An important essay to consider before attempting a phenomenological approach is Max Weber's "Objectivity in Social Science" in The Methodology of the Social Sciences, the Shils-Finch translation (Glencoe, Ill.: The Free Press, 1949).

On "Comparing Politics Through Insiders," Chapter Seven

To understand how human beings become involved in the abstract immensities of international politics, see Otto Klineberg's The Human Dimension in International Relations (New York: Holt, Rinehart and Winston, 1964); Herbert Kelman's reader International Behavior: A Social-Psychological Analysis (New York: Holt, Rinehart and Winston, 1965); and Robert Isaak's Individuals and World Politics (North Scituate, Mass.: Duxbury Press, 1975). The relationship between international politics from the individual's viewpoint and international politics from the nation-state's or international system's viewpoints is incisively exposed in Kyung-Won Kim, Revolution and International System (New York: NYU Press, 1970); Anatol Rapoport's Fights, Games and Debates (Ann Arbor, Mich.: University of Michigan Press, 1960); and Kenneth Waltz, Man, the State and War (New York: Columbia University Press, 1959). For a short satire on the necessity of the war system to keep America going, read Leonard Lewin's Report from Iron Mountain—on the Possibility and Desirability of Peace (New York: Dell, 1967).

On "Internationalizing Politics," Chapter Eight

Suggestions as to the cause of rebellion and revolution in politics can be found in William Lutz and Harry Brent, eds., On Revolution (Cambridge Mass.: Winthrop, 1971); Kyung-Won Kim, Revolution and International System (New York: New York University Press, 1970); Albert Camus, The Rebel (New York: Knopf, 1956); and Rollo May, Power and Innocence (New York: Norton, 1972). The relationship between scientific and political revolutions in ideas is lucidly explained in Thomas Kuhn, The Structure of Scientific Revolutions

On "Revolutionizing World Politics," Chapter Nine

(Chicago: University of Chicago Press, 1962). That such revolutions often begin in the reflections of language is clarified in Alfred Korzybski's "On the Semantics of the Einstein Theory" in *Science and Sanity: An Introduction to Non-Aristotelian Systems and General Semantics* (Lakeville, Conn.: The International Non-Aristotelian Library, 1958). The socio-psychology of such revolutionary behavior is brilliantly explained in Charles Hampden-Turner's *Radical Man—The Process of Psycho-Social Development* (Garden City, New York: Doubleday, Anchor, 1970).

On "Thinking Politics Through the System," Chapter Ten

One of the best books relating old political thinking to modern political thinking is William T. Bluhm's *Theories of the Political System* (Englewood Cliffs, N. J.: Prentice-Hall, 1965). A lucid book on the rethinking of politics in the twentieth century by borrowing paradigms from other natural and social sciences: W. G. Runciman, *Social Science and Political Theory* (Cambridge: Cambridge University Press, 1963). Also see *Conduct of Inquiry* by Abraham Kaplan, a philosopher of science (San Francisco: Chandler, 1963); and Peter Winch, *The Idea of a Social Science and Its Relation to Philosophy* (New York: Humanities Press, 1958). A useful reader on the strengths and weakness of recent social science paradigms is May Brodbeck, ed., *Readings in the Philosophy of the Social Sciences* (New York: Macmillan, 1968).

On "Thinking Politics Through Yourself," Chapter Eleven

For sources of postbehavioral political thinking, see George Graham and George Carey, eds., *The Post-behavioral Era: Perspectives on Political Science* (New York: McKay, 1972); Henry Kariel, *Saving Appearances: The Reestablishment of Political Science* (North Scituate, Mass.: Duxbury Press, 1972); Juergen Habermas, *Toward A Rational Society—Student Protest, Science and Politics* (Boston: Beacon Press, 1970); and Hwa Yol Jung, ed., *Existential Phenomenology and Political Theory: A Reader* (Chicago: Henry Regnery, 1972).

On "Classical and Future Political Thinking," Chapter Twelve

For classical political thinking, begin with Plato's *Republic,* Aristotle's *Politics,* and the summaries of the old thinkers in George Sabine's *A History of Political Theory* (New York: Holt, Rinehart and Winston, 1961). For classical political thought in America, see Vernon Louis Parrington's *Main Currents in American Thought* (New York: Harcourt, Brace, 1927); Louis Hartz, *The Liberal Tradition in America* (New York: Harcourt, Brace and World, 1955); and H. Mark Roelofs, *The Language of Modern Politics* (Homewood, Illinois: Dorsey, 1967), Chapter 6.

For future political thinking, those philosophically inclined might enjoy Juergen Habermas's *Knowledge and Human Interests* (Boston: Beacon Press, 1972). Readers interested in the sociology of human relations with political implications should read Erving Goffman's *Interaction Ritual* (Garden City, New York: Doubleday, 1967). Similar, but more psychological and phenomenological, is Ronald Laing's *The Politics of Experience* (New York: Ballantine, 1967).

Those economically inclined might taste *Corporations and the Cold War*, edited by David Horowitz (New York: Monthly Review Press, 1969); and Morton Mintz and Jerry Cohen, *America Inc.* (New York: Dell, 1972). For the politicalization of aesthetics and language, see Richard Poirer's *The Performing Self—Compositions and Decompositions in the Languages of Contemporary Life* (New York: Oxford Univ. Press, 1971). For the politics of mental illness and "normality," see Ken Kesey's novel *One Flew Over the Cuckoo's Nest* and the psychologist Thomas Szasz's *Ideology and Insanity—Essays on the Psychic Dehumanization of Man* (Garden City, New York: Doubleday, Anchor, 1970).

To construct your own social-psychology of the politics of everyday life, read Peter Berger and Thomas Luckman, *The Social Construction of Reality* (Garden City, N. Y.: Doubleday, Anchor, 1967); Alfred Schutz, *Collected Papers*, vols. I-III (The Hague: Martinus Nijhoff, 1964); Charles Hampden-Turner, *Radical Man: The Process of Psycho-social Development* (Garden City, N. Y.: Doubleday, Anchor, 1971); and Robert White, *The Study of Lives* (Chicago: Aldine-Atherton, 1963) and *Lives in Progress: A Study of Natural Growth of Personality* (New York: Holt, Rinehart and Winston, 1966).

A reader that goes well with *Politics for Human Beings* is Edward S. Greenberg and Richard Young, eds, *American Politics Reconsidered: Power and Inequity in America* (North Scituate, Massachusetts: Duxbury Press, 1973). To understand why it is necessary to be political to be human in our era, see Albert Camus's *The Myth of Sisyphus* (New York: Vintage Books, 1955). Or, as George Orwell put it, "If you want a picture of the future, imagine a boot stamping on a human face."

Index